Intermediate Price Theory

Intermediate
Price Theory

Sidney Weintraub

Professor of Economics, University of Pennsylvania

Illustrated

CHILTON BOOKS
Publishers

A Division of Chilton Company
Philadelphia and New York

To Sheila
who recalls when it first began

Preface

Reviewers were generally kind to my first book on *Price Theory* and it has encouraged me to think that a new and different edition would have its uses in the intermediate courses devoted to this subject. While other interests have caused me to put aside the task of revision for over a dozen years I have continued teaching the subject and hope that the present volume will serve a wider audience. To this end I have sought to simplify the exposition and to make the basic points more readily accessible to the student.

There is, if anything, less need now than previously to affirm the thought-clearing that price theory provides in approaching concrete problems. Despite the advances by way of econometrics, statistics, and empirical studies, the concepts developed in the intermediate price theory course remain basic; unless a student masters them, progress in economic study becomes hopelessly obstructed. As it is possible to offer too much in a chapter, I have split up some sections with exercises to offer the student some respite for reflection as he endeavors to absorb the ideas immediately developed. I hope that this device will be acceptable to those who feel that the theoretical pace can prove to be too fast to be sustained by most students who take such a course.

In my own classes I generally select a few of the major ideas of each chapter rather than discuss each point at length; I think the textual discussion is generally ample to enable the student to fill in the gaps. My own experience also leads to the view that it is easier to interest students in the subject matter if the development of market demand and cost ideas comes very early in the term; this explains the shift of the theory of consumer behavior to chapters 5 through 7 even though this material constitutes a logical, if formidable, beginning. If the student's attention is quickly aroused to the reality of the theoretical framework, it is easier to retain his concern with the more abstract materials.

Beyond these changes, the book still contains a reasonably comprehensive analysis of the diverse market situations and price phenomena elaborated in the theoretical literature. Relatively few advances in these areas have occurred in recent years; the excitement of the 1930's has waned though one can hope that this is only a temporary pause, for the problems of an optimal pricing, selling, and product structure still remain. Awareness that monopolistic and oligopolistic forms may have something to contribute by way of product progress and commodity innovation deserves wider exploration. A textbook writer is always optimistic enough to think that some students may want to pursue such ideas and their ramifications toward original work on these themes.

My own course on Price and Distribution Theory supplements these pages with my book on *An Approach to the Theory of Income Distribution*. As I attempted to explain there, it seems to me that distribution theory must draw from both micro- and macro-theory in order to be meaningful. Others may wish to consider these ideas anew.

Professors Paul Davidson and Almarin Phillips did me a service in reading some of these pages. Mrs. Eve McCall was left with most of the typing, assisted by other members of the fine departmental secretarial staff. Mrs. Gladys Decker supervised the preparation of the work and performed the numerous tasks of coordination during the period when I was on leave from the University. I am grateful for this assistance.

Contents

Preface vii

Part I. Some Basic Concepts of Demand and Supply

  1. On the Study of Price Theory 1

  2. Demand and Elasticity Concepts 9
      The Demand Curve; Revenue Concepts; The Point Elasticity of Demand; Arc Elasticity; The Cross-Elasticity of Demand

  3. Production and Costs 25
      Factors of Production; Fixed and Variable Factors; Constant-Product Curves; The Minimum-Cost Condition; The Expansion Path; Nonminimum Cost Analysis; Factor Substitutes and Complements

  4. Costs and Factor Productivity 43
      Total, Average, and Marginal Cost; Law of Variable Proportions; Returns to Scale; Factor Productivity and Costs; Planning Curves; The Elasticity of Costs and Supply

  5. Consumer Behavior 67
      Utility Theory; Indifference Analysis; The Marginal Rate of Substitution; The Price Line and the Equilibrium-Purchase Combination; Income and Price Variations; Negative Income Effects

  6. Consumer Behavior—(*Continued*) 85
      Substitutes and Complements; The Elasticity of Substitution; Commodity Dimensions; Summary; The Theory of Revealed Preferences; Numerical Utility for Choices Involving Uncertain Prospects

  7. The Pure Theory of Exchange and Optimal Resource Use . 101
      The Pure Theory of Exchange; Optimal Resource Use; Social and Private Products; Measures of Consumer Well-Being

Part II. Market Behavior of the Firm

    8. Pure Competition 127
        Fixed Stocks of Goods; Varying Supplies of Goods; Vary-
        ing Amounts of Equipment; Stable and Multiple Equi-
        libria; Pure Competition and Optimal Resource Use;
        Some Neglected Points

    9. Equations of General Equilibrium: Input-Output Analysis and
        Linear Programming   155
        Input-Output Analysis; Linear Programming

    10. Monopoly   172
        Monopoly Equilibrium; Output Restriction; Price and
        Output Interrelations; Measures of Monopoly Power;
        Special Equilibrium Cases; Nonpecuniary Motives; Mo-
        nopoly and Optimal Resource Use

    11. Duopoly and Oligopoly   198
        Output Followers; Output Leaders; Joint Maximization
        Analyses; Market-Price Assumptions; Economic War-
        fare; Market Agreements; Duopoly Instability; A Con-
        cluding Remark

    12. Monopolistic Competition 225
        Market Interdependence; Selling Costs; Space and Mo-
        nopolistic Competition

    13. Product Variation and Entry Under Monopolistic Competition 253
        Commodity Diversification and Sealed Entry; Monopoly
        Pricing and Innovation; Innovations and Price Repercus-
        sions; Product Variation; Nonprice Competition; Mo-
        nopoly and Progress; Entry Impediments and Heterogene-
        ous Competition

    14. Buyer's Domination and Bilateral Monopoly 271
        Monopsony Equilibrium; Monopsony in Consumer Mar-
        kets; Monopsony and the Cost Curves; Monempory;
        Duopsony Problems; Bilateral Monopoly

Part III. Extensions of Price Theory: Multiple-Product Firms and an
        Introduction to Dynamics

    15. Cost Interdependence 289
        Joint Production; Cost Interdependence; Vertical Inte-
        gration; Monopoly and Integration; Monopsony and
        Integration; Cost Interdependence in Time

16. Interrelated Demand 308
Discriminatory Pricing; Substitute Goods; Complementary Goods; Monopsony Discrimination; Demand Interdependence Over Time; Inventory and Profit Expectations

17. Path Analysis and Imperfect Adaptations 336
The Cobweb Theorem; Change and Equilibrium Processes;
Monopoly Price Movements; Rigid Prices

18. Time and Uncertainty 353
Uncertainty and Optimal Output; Uncertainty and Plant
Layout; Uncertainty and Economic Development; Pricing
and Economic Welfare

Index 375

Intermediate Price Theory

Abbreviations and Symbols

AC	Average cost
AP_x	Average product of factor X
AR	Average revenue
D	Demand
E_c	Elasticity of total costs
E_d	Elasticity of demand
E_p	Elasticity of productivity
E_s	Elasticity of supply
E_{ss}	Elasticity of substitution
$_IE_x$	Income elasticity of demand for X
$_{px}E_y$	Cross-elasticity of demand
$I\text{-}C$	Income-consumption curve
MC	Marginal cost
M_L	Index of monopoly power
MP_x	Marginal product of factor X
MR	Marginal revenue
MRS	Marginal rate of substitution
$P\text{-}C$	Price-consumption curve
P_m	Monopoly price
P_x, P_y, P_z	Price of commodity X, Y, Z
S	Supply
TC	Total cost
TP_x	Total production, with factor X variable and other factors constant
TR	Total revenue
ΔX	Increase in X (say, from 19 to 20)

PART I
Some Basic Concepts of Demand and Supply

Chapter 1

≈≈

On the Study of Price Theory

There is the story, undoubtedly often duplicated and recounted even more frequently, of the professor who began employing the Socratic method by asking his class what they expected to derive from their study of Price Theory. Needless to say, he was a trifle nonplused by the unhesitant reply of the student whom he addressed: "A grade, sir."

In due time, this will be forthcoming—at the end of the course. But in between there are more solid and substantial reasons for the study, for it is through the price system that some basic problems of our economic and social system are resolved. It will be our concern to develop some of these issues as our work progresses.

Economic Activity in Free Economies

Economic activity in free economies is organized through the price system. It is not uncommon in economic analysis nowadays to derogate the study of price making and to stress, instead, the forces determining the volume of income, output, and employment. Despite the intrinsic importance of these topics, their study lacks cohesion and relevance unless the forces responsible for the particular price and output magnitudes, which comprise the national income aggregate, are understood. Major questions concerning the kinds of goods produced, their individual quantities, and the productive factors engaged in their production can be answered only by a study of price formation. This book deals with this array of subjects, the older sphere of value theory.

In confining ourselves to the study of the theory of price making, we are consciously cutting ourselves off from other important and major areas of economic study. But this is essential for progress in understanding; the course upon which we are embarking involves specialized study —it is a field that has to be cultivated intensively. Experience indicates that, at the end of this immediate path, the road opens wider, thus permitting movement at faster speed, with greater facility and without constant detour and digression, into the vast and detailed subjects of economics, including the theory of aggregate (national) income; the theory of employment, of international economics, and regional relationships; the intricacies of the theory of growth, and the subtleties of the related studies in the theory of development. The latter are of vital concern in the world today, where the embarrassment of income disparities and the compulsion of material progress dominate public policy. Studies in income distribution, in the business cycle, in monetary and fiscal policy— all emanate from the same head, sometimes in small, sometimes in greater, measure. All of them invoke the concepts of price theory and its implications for the theory of the firm and consumer behavior.

Thus, while it is easy to demonstrate impatience with a study that professes to be theoretical, arid, mostly divorced from current topical events, the best justification for its disciplined thought-clearing is to be found in the frequent recourse to its abstractions in the various areas of economic study. Despite differences in viewpoint, in teaching emphasis, in preconceptions on the order of topics, or in the space allotment, there are few economists who would advocate its abandonment; more than ever, there is a return to these fundamentals in the training of economists. The proof of the pudding here is in the eating; while it is possible to know a good deal about economic phenomena without proficiency in this subject, it is less disputable that familiarity with its concepts conveys insights and eliminates some grosser absurdities and more palpable fallacies from arguments. In this respect, it is like an electronic brain: it speeds thinking on a wide array of important subjects, more often indirectly rather than directly. Trivia can be by-passed, analyses that have been encountered and resolved many times before can be dispensed with, and concentration on the more complex and substantive issues can be facilitated.

The Plan of Subsequent Chapters

Logically, it would seem best to begin with the theory of the consumer, for, ultimately, all productive activity is destined for his ends. Pedagogically, it seems more rewarding initially to examine market-demand phenomena; this will be our procedure in Chapter 1, where demand and elasticity concepts encountered in earlier economics courses are developed, perhaps a bit more rigorously and elaborately. Temporarily, this ends our preoccupation with the theory of demand; there is a return to some deeper facets of the subject, at the level of the consumer and the household, in Chapters 5–7, after a stronger grasp of the concepts of price theory has been achieved.

Certain aspects of the theory of production (especially those associated with the selection of productive factors at each level of output when firms are guided by the principle of minimizing total production

costs) occupy Chapter 2. The elucidation of the condition of cost minimization will facilitate the analysis of a broad range of problems. The
significance of the insight imparted by this principle becomes apparent
when we introduce the additional assumption that price making is directed, ordinarily, to profit making. But it has even deeper implications:
unless the principle of minimum-cost output is grasped, the idea of economical production and resource management eludes us. In the welfare
propositions drawn from modern economic analysis, this relationship has
a profound and persuasive bearing.

Chapter 3 is a further extension of the study of production; major
cost concepts are sketched and the laws of returns are elaborated: these
constitute the contemporary version of the older principle of diminishing
returns. A careful attempt is made to weld the ideas on physical returns
with movements in production costs. After having reached this stage,
we are ready for market analyses, to investigate the determination of
prices and output quantities in various concrete circumstances.

Thus Part I is concerned with the preparation of vital concepts that
will stand us in good stead in all of economic study and also become
peculiarly indispensable as we delve into the essence of price theory, en-
compassing the theory of price determination in markets subject to
various degrees of competition and monopoly. The exact extent of output, the height of individual prices, the pattern of resources used, the
dimensions of advertising, and the speed of product innovation and the
extent of commodity variation depend on the combination of competitive
and monopoly forces.

We conclude the study of price theory by sketching some of the ideas
in a more realistic setting, incorporating the arguments into multiple-
product firms, importing some recognition of the special difficulties occasioned by the passage of time and the uncertainties engendered for
human conduct. Some brief remarks on the welfare consequences, and
the partial answers afforded by price theory alone, round out the work—
at the intermediate level sought. It is idle to pretend that the answers
to important issues are simple or definitive, or that price theory alone
illuminates them. But it is an essential component of the full set of ideas
that must be brought to bear on these matters.

The Economic Principle

Because we shall be dealing with the problems of the consumer and
the firm (and their concerted actions which culminate in prices, outputs,
and resource-use), there is some danger that, in our more concentrated
study, we might underplay the basic purpose of economic study or the
reason for economizing in economic organization. The overriding principle governing our entire subject, whose comprehension enables the

economist to dismiss certain proposals as uneconomic and thereby unworthy, is embraced in the fundamental idea of *opportunity cost;* this is also designated as the theory of alternative-use value, or of displacement cost: all of these terms are viewed as synonymous.

In the elementary textbooks, this principle is at the bottom of the concrete "guns *versus* butter" illustrations, to emphasize that a society always has to choose between alternatives. So far as the consumer goes, one expenditure of income is always alternative to another; for a factor, one choice of occupation involves the sacrifice of another; in production generally, producing more of one commodity and diverting more resources to its output means that some factors must be deflected from other uses. This concept gives vitality and weight to the entire study of economics: without alternative uses there would be no need to economize in the use of resources or in the allocation of income. Barring substitute productions—or if more of the same product could not be produced by the firm or industry with a less wasteful amount of resources—then there would be little purpose in cutting costs, in doing the job efficiently. Thus, this principle gives substance and character to all of economic study; those appreciative of its enormity and universality are able to give sharper, clearer, more incisive answers to pressing economic issues.

Undeniably, this principle enjoys its full fruition only under full employment: with unemployment there can be more of both, *more* guns and *more* butter, more houses and more roads, more schools and more TV sets. But our goal is full employment: we want to understand how the economy operates in these circumstances. Even with underemployment, a choice still remains between objectives, between more military outlays or more welfare projects, between more government activities or more private operations, etc.

Even on recognition of the modern *Affluent Society,* the theory retains its force. Actually, most of the world has not reached the fortunate status of freedom from worry over the provision of moderate standards of comfort for practically all of its inhabitants. Secondly, even in those places more providentially endowed and more cognizant of the powers of modern technology, there is still the need to select between the expansion of goods and services in the public as against the private sector of the economy. Within each compartment there is the need to decide on whichever alternative promises the fuller life: even the student, ordinarily relatively well supported in his educational endeavors by parental assistance, must make choices. The ubiquity of choice is indisputable. And this signifies the operation of the economic principle of opportunity-cost. There is a displaced alternative in all we do: *the real cost* of a study of price theory, of business cycles, of organic chemistry, or of Shakespearean literature, *consists of the alternatives that must be sacrificed,* signifying the courses we do not take, the fictional reading we have no time to do, the part-time job that has to be rejected. School attendance consistently involves the immediate sacrifice of income and work opportunities during the educational process. Affluent societies which devote more resources to education are, thus, under the same sovereign master, controlled by the operation of the fundamental economic principle.

The Nature of Theory

The word *theory* has been stressed in these initial remarks; we shall use the word synonymously and interchangeably with *analysis*. Only the obstinate would contend that theory and analysis have a meaning which is the antithesis of fact. All that is meant to be conveyed by either term is that we are in studious pursuit of *relationships*. Facts are independent entities, *individual events limitless in number*. To bring some order among them, to detect their causal sequence or mere interdependence, so that we may interpret real world occurrences, is the task of analytic study and the aim of serious study in all fields. But, it is to be observed, we seek to ascertain *important* relationships—those that are revealed in a wide range of phenomena. It is the latter uniformities which aspire to the status of a law or scientific principle.

Economics as a Science

Inherently, it is frivolous and academic to dispute or attempt to arbitrate the issue of whether or not economics "really" is a science. Whether physics is or is not a science is unimportant—the vital point is that the study of physics illuminates a range of matters that are inscrutable without its devices. Similarly, the light that economic analysis can throw, however dim and obscure it is in certain sectors, is such that no one who has acquired a working knowledge of its perceptions will readily sacrifice it. Its deficiencies invite repair.

For those who prefer a further word on this controversy, over and above the agnostic attitude that it really matters little what we choose to call our subject, these comments might be warranted. What do we mean by *a science?* At least four facets seem to open up. In the first place, science demands a systematic study and an honest point of view, a desire for understanding, for knowledge in a special area. Economics surely can qualify on this count—along with musical and literary criticism! Secondly, a science must use the principles of logic, either verbal or mathematical and symbolical. Again, there is little to trouble us on this score: if mathematics constitutes the key, current economics can fly through the door! More important, the physical sciences are able to experiment, to test their hypotheses; they are able to devise laboratory designs, *and under controlled conditions,* to see whether or not the structure of ideas is correct: each rocket on a launching pad constitutes a practical experiment.

In this respect, economics suffers compared to the physical sciences: it is ordinarily unable to set up such controlled tests. Yet, because we are "unable to double every one's money income" to test, say, the Quantity Theory of Money, or to verify other relationships that have been presented as typical economic principles, special tools of statistical theory and of economic history have been devised. Largely, the latter consists of an endeavor to uncover how the relations worked out in the past, in the greatest uncontrolled laboratory of all—namely, the actual economic system. Clear and comprehensive conclusions can seldom be drawn: they command unanimity only when the forces were of such overpowering strength that additional complexities and cross-currents tended to be overcome. Statistical economic time series constitute a similar tool for grappling with the historical processes in which economic forces operate; this type of data collection and processing involves concentration on types of historical phenomena which lend themselves to quantitative tabulation. But the fact that it is a particular way of studying history must be stressed; neither apparatus, the more formal quantitative and statistical or the more casual qualitative and descriptive, would be necessary if suitable laboratory techniques existed.

It is in the lack of a laboratory that economics suffers in comparison with the physical sciences. But this blockage has fostered the development of the counter-tools mentioned: surely it is not unscientific to create new tools to tackle problems whose understanding is stymied by the inapplicability of conventional laboratory methods.

In the last analysis, the ultimate test and triumph of all science consists in its ability to make accurate predictions of ensuing phenomena: every time the physicists and the engineers ready their missile for firing, they are making just such a prediction. When the test fizzles, someone guessed wrong—someone goofed on the prediction!

It is hard to give convincing proof that predictions by trained economists over a wide range of economic phenomena are superior to predictions of less tutored and less sophisticated forecasters. Suffice to say, economists are reluctant to abandon their methods, attesting at once (on a charitable interpretation) to a belief in their usefulness, rather than reflecting an inherent stubbornness or vested interest. Undoubtedly, advice for public policy requires the mental discipline which economic theory imparts. Analyses which reject its structure are generally more foolish—meaning more contradictory—than arguments grounded in its substance.

Policy debates in the political arena undoubtedly entail predictions of the consequences of a particular policy. It can be vouchsafed that the discussion and implementation of public policy would be improved, and would be less scrambled and confused, with a greater apprehension of the concepts of economic theory.

The Degree of Mathematical Sophistication

We shall find that most of the significant relationships extracted by economic theory can be described verbally. Many parts of economic theory—maybe all of it—admit of treatment by mathematical methods. But there is little reason to believe that this method must be employed or that it is superior in all contexts[1]; the account that follows is innocent of any high mathematical pretensions. Geometrical devices are introduced where these are suitable and enlightening. Abbreviations, which border on mathematical symbolism, have been incorporated to avoid tedious repetition of familiar concepts. The book's one main debt to mathematics consists in extensive usage of the incremental idea, or Greek symbol *delta*, written Δ. Curiously, we recognize it for what it is— a bit of harmless symbolism—when it appears on the doorplate of a fraternity house, and we impute to it a simple and comprehensible meaning. Yet, when we meet it in mathematics, we are prone to become alarmed and ascribe to it all sorts of dreadful connotations. Once this initial fright vanishes, we discover it to be an expedient means of communication, for it is intended merely to signify a difference, usually a small difference. Thus,

$$X_2 - X_1 = \Delta X$$

Hence, if the value of X_2 is 20 and X_1 is 19, then ΔX is, of course, 1. Or, when we regard $X_1 + \Delta X = X_2$, then ΔX is described as an *increment*. With a minus sign before it, it would denote a *decrement*, as it would if in the preceding equation $X_1 > X_2$.

Exercises and Extensions

To render the subsequent text reasonably concise while sufficiently comprehensive so that a rather full exposure to price theory is experienced, the following pages contain various exercises alongside the theoretical analysis. These should be construed as a form of quiz, to test the student's comprehension of the ideas developed and to permit him to extend the basic principles. Some of the questions open up fascinating problems that could be explored with profit—but at the expense of

---

[1] Mathematics is an *incomplete* language; when we say "let Y stand for the income level and K for the stock of capital," we scarcely know what either signifies, what to include in each, without recourse to ordinary language.

other ideas in the time usually allotted to a course in Price Theory. Of course, this is the principle of opportunity-cost at work; it has been thought desirable to abandon these alternatives in order to probe the indispensable fundamentals for a reasonable mastery of the subject. The student is advised at least to ponder mentally the answers to the questions raised.

Chapter 2

೧೨

Demand and Elasticity Concepts

In Chapter 2, we propose to review some familiar demand ideas such as the demand curve, the elasticity of demand, and total, average, and marginal revenue. Much use will be made later of these common tools of the economist's workbench.

THE DEMAND CURVE

Technically, the individual demand curve is a geometrical picture relating market prices and the quantities wanted of a commodity by an individual at each possible price. If we measure prices vertically and quantities wanted horizontally, a sample demand curve, lettered D_1D_1', embodying the relationship, is provided in Figure 2.1(A). Rather than refer to the demand curve, we may on occasion wish to specify the demand schedule. This is a tabular statement of the quantities wanted at the various possible prices. Table 2.1 contains part of a demand schedule for neckties. At a price of \$5.00, 3 ties will be bought; at \$4.00, 5 ties;

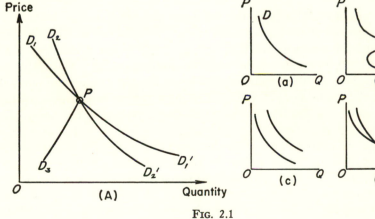

Fig. 2.1

9

at $3.00, 7 ties, etc. For simplicity, the intermediate price and demand quantities have been omitted.

TABLE 2.1—DEMAND SCHEDULE FOR NECKTIES

Price	Quantity Wanted
$5.00	3
4.00	5
3.00	7
2.00	12
1.00	20
0.50	35

If all the points of this demand schedule are plotted on a graph, the familiar demand curve emerges. Since our demand schedule pertains to but one individual, the demand curve is likewise an individual phenomenon. By constructing demand schedules for each prospective purchaser *and then adding the quantities wanted by the full market group at each price*, we can derive the market-demand curve.

There is this fact to note about the demand curve or schedule: each point on it represents an *alternate* market possibility for the period of time in which we are interested; each point on the curve reveals the quantities that will be bought if the corresponding price is announced in the market. The curve (or schedule) is not to be interpreted to mean that, if a price of $4.00 is named, 5 ties will be bought by our individual, and that, if immediately thereafter the price falls to $3.00, he will buy 7 additional units. Each point is to be understood as signifying only the quantities that will be bought if that price is named to prevail for the period of time we are investigating.

Premises of the Demand Curve

In our grade-school arithmetic, we could not solve the problem until we were apprised of the "given conditions." This is true in all reasoning. For example, if you are told that Johnny went to the store with $1.00 and spent $.20, you can answer that he returned with $.80 in change. If he went with $5.00, the answer will be $4.80, etc. If we were not told of the given conditions yet were asked how much change he returned with, we could not answer the question—there would be too many possible answers!

Likewise, we cannot know what the demand curve will look like unless we have some initial information. In short, the demand curve must rest on at least the following premises: (1) given tastes; (2) given money income; (3) given other prices, or their mode of variation with each price of the commodity under discussion. A change in the data, which also involves implicitly the number of consumers in the market and the relative distribution of income, can shift the entire course of the demand curve.

Consequently, when we say that demand *increases,* we have in mind a complete rightward shift in the demand curve, as shown in Figure 2.1(c), so that, at the same prices as formerly, individuals will buy greater amounts or they will be willing to pay higher prices for the same amounts as they formerly purchased. A decrease in demand signifies a leftward shift in the entire schedule. While the demand quantity has reference to a point on a particular curve, a change in demand connotes a movement from one curve to another. Sometimes the shift in demand will be erratic, as in Figure 2.1(d), so that there is an increase in demand above the intersection of the old and the new curves, and a decrease below the intersection.

Changes in the rate at which consumers desire to make purchases in the market, when market price is constant, are thus ascribable to a change in *tastes,* in *income,* or in movements in *other prices.*

Variations in Other Prices

Suppose that P_y (where Y is a widely recognized substitute good for X) is constant, while P_x rises, say, from the level denoted at point P in Figure 2.1(A). The portion of the market-demand curve that ensues for commodity X will follow the course, say, of D_1P, with sales falling off rapidly as P_x mounts because of the shift of consumers from X to Y at the constant P_y. Conversely, if P_y holds firm as P_x falls, the diversion of purchases will be from Y to X; the PD_1' portion of the curve represents this situation.

Alternately, we can envisage that, as P_x rises, the diversion of demand to Y causes a rise in P_y. The demand curve for X, then, will follow the course D_2P in the upper regions; as P_y is higher, the quantities wanted of X will be greater than before. Similarly, P_y may follow P_x downward, perhaps because of the fall-off in the sales of Y as P_x is lowered. The new curve section for commodity X is thus PD_2', compared to PD_1'.

In brief, D_1D_1' is a demand curve for X drawn on the hypothesis of other prices being constant (P_y being representative of other goods), while D_2D_2' assumes variations in other prices as P_2 alters. Undoubtedly, the slope of the curve drawn on the constancy hypothesis is gentler than that of the curve drawn on the assumption of other prices moving in the same direction as P_x.

Conceivably, as P_x falls from the height indicated at P, and if other firms take active measures to counter the price fall (lowering their price, say, by 10 per cent for each 1 per cent fall in P_x), then the quantities wanted of X may slump precipitately despite the reduction in P_x. The lower bend of the demand curve for X may turn backward, as does PD_3. If the rival firms respond to a price rise in X by raising their own prices, while reacting sharply to a price fall, then the demand curve for X will take the form D_2PD_3, with the kinked corner at P. If the rivals' prices are constant for a rise in P_x, but decline disproportionately to a fall in P_x, the demand curve for X may resemble D_1PD_3.

Short- and Long-Run Demand

Sometimes a distinction is drawn between *short-* and *long-run* demand curves. Whatever the assumption regarding other prices, a demand curve such as D_2D_2' can be interpreted as listing the immediate demand quantities of X if P_x changes to any of the possible levels to which it might go. However, if the new P_x rises above P, as time passes and consumers become more aware of alternate purchase opportunities, the sales of X may recede as compared to the immediate response. If the new P_x lies below P, and as consumers acquire this knowledge only slowly, fitting X into their purchase scheme gradually, sales may be continually enlarged at the lower P_x levels. The demand curve for the "short-run" thus resembles D_2D_2', but for the "long-run," if each P_x held firm for a longer time duration, the demand curve would be D_1D_1'. The pivot at P indicates that this is the immediately ruling price.

Demand Curve = Sales Curve = Average-Revenue Curve

Other names are often given to the demand curve. Looked at from the point of view of the seller, this curve can be described as a *sales curve*, for each point on it denotes the sales that can be made at each price. Some writers are fond of terming it an *average-revenue curve*, since each vertical price point represents the average revenue received by the seller for the corresponding quantity of market sales. Some writers draw a distinction between the demand curve of an industry and that for a firm, reserving the older term (demand curve) for the former and calling the price-quantity relationship a "sales curve" when the reference is to the firm. We, however, shall use the three names synonymously, for there is little to be gained by terming inherently like phenomena differently.

A more fundamental issue is (1) whether the demand curve is a subjective fact (a mental image in the mind of the entrepreneur), or (2) whether it is a market fact (an objective phenomenon which painstaking empirical investigation can reveal), or (3) whether the dual phenomena exist. As we shall consider the possible divergence of subjective and objective sales curves later, for the moment we can assume the coincidence of the two.

Questions

1. By demand, do you mean a point on the curve or the full curve? What do you mean by an increase in demand?
2. Do you have a demand for only 2 suits of clothes, 3 neckties, and 2 pairs of shoes per annum—and 1 automobile? Discuss.
3. Why must we be careful in specifying the premises of the demand curve?
4. Explain why the long-run demand curve will slope more gently than the short-run curve.
5. How long a time period is the demand curve designed to cover?

REVENUE CONCEPTS

The demand curve has already been denoted as an average-revenue curve. The concepts of total revenue (TR), average revenue (AR), and marginal revenue (MR) ought to be developed more systematically and the corresponding curves drawn. Although the revenue sums refer to demand phenomena, they are looked at from the standpoint of the seller or business firm, the recipient of the consumer outlays.

In brief, writing P to symbolize price and Q to symbolize sales quantities, with the subscript n indicating that the sums change with changes in the sales volume, the revenue concepts can be defined algebraically as:

$$TR_n = P_nQ_n \tag{2.1}$$

$$AR_n = \frac{TR_n}{Q_n} = \frac{P_nQ_n}{Q_n} = P_n \tag{2.2}$$

$$MR_n = \frac{\Delta TR_n}{\Delta Q_n} = TR_n - TR_{n-1} \tag{2.3}$$

Total revenue refers to the total expenditure of consumers, or price multiplied by the corresponding demand quantity. Measuring total revenue on the vertical axis, in Figure 2.2(A) the abscissae points represent the quantities bought for each TR, and thus implicitly at each P.[1] Normally, the curve is bell-shaped—for, at a very high price, sales are zero—so that the curve originates at O, rises and reaches a maximum, and ultimately (because price approaches zero when very large quantities are sold) turns back again to the horizontal axis.

Average revenue (or the demand price) is equal to the total consumer outlay on a given number of units, divided by the self-same quantity. Thus, the AR and the demand curve are one and the same. Marginal revenue refers to the change in total revenue resulting from a 1-unit

---

[1] With price discrimination, AR or price is not unique per unit of sales.

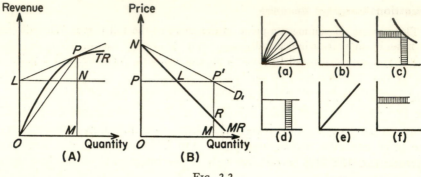

FIG. 2.2

increment in sales volume; the MR curve thus depicts the change in TR resulting from further sales.

A typical curve set is shown in Figure 2.2. Although all three curves can be drawn on the same chart field (since money sums are measured in all cases on the vertical axis), to avoid encumbering the diagram the TR curve is placed in Figure 2.2(A) and the AR and MR curves in Figure 2.2(B). If the firm sells in a purely competitive market, in which the price remains constant whatever quantity it sells, the TR curve becomes a straight line starting at the O-origin (for perfectly divisible goods) and rising at a constant rate equal to the price for each further unit of sales. (See Figure 2.2[e].) For this case, AR and MR are equal to one another, and thus both are equal to the price.

If the seller could dispose of further units of output only at a lower price per unit, the total-revenue curve would resemble the TR of Figure 2.2(A). To derive the unit price of average revenue geometrically from the TR curve, we can extend a vector from O to the point on TR for the sales quantity in which we are interested and note its slope; for example, the demand price for the quantity OM would be indicated by the ratio PM/OM, which is also the slope of the vector from O. As we move rightward, out to greater sales quantities, the slope of the vectors will generally fall, as in Figure 2.2(a), denoting a lower price for greater sales volumes.

MR can be deduced from the TR curve by drawing a tangent to the TR curve and extending it to the ordinate axis; the slope of the tangent will indicate the additions to total revenue made by a further increment in sales. Its value is given by the ratio PN/LN in the figure. When TR reaches a maximum, $MR = O$; a tangent to the TR curve will become horizontal, indicating no change in TR as sales increase. Aside from the case of pure competition, MR will be less than AR. Let us investigate this last relationship more thoroughly.

Price and Marginal Revenue

The normal downward-sloping demand curve reveals that, to sell an additional unit of output, price must fall. Marginal revenue, the change in total revenue consequent upon a further unit of sales, is thus a resultant of the two forces: (1) the income derived from the additional unit sold, which is equal to the new price, and (2) the loss of income due to the fact that all those units salable at a higher price must be marked down to the new price because, aside from discriminatory pricing, only one price can rule in the market for the full sales quantity. TR will increase and MR will be positive only if the magnitude of the first sum exceeds the latter sum.

Schematically, if P refers to the new, *lower* price required to expand sales by 1 unit, and Q refers to the sales that could be made at the previous higher price (involving a sales quantity 1 unit less than that actually sold at P), and ΔP signifies the necessary price reduction to expand sales by 1 unit, we can write[2]:

$$MR = P - Q\Delta P \qquad (2.4)$$

If, as under competitive market conditions, the firm can dispose of additional units at the market price, ΔP reduces to zero and $MR = P$; price and marginal revenue become one and the same. Otherwise, so long as price falls as sales expand, $Q\Delta P$ is of definite magnitude and, hence, $P > MR$. At each sales volume, each point on the normal demand curve will thus lie above the MR curve. Clearly, MR may be positive or negative; it will be negative when $Q\Delta P > P$, implying that the price sacrifice on the previous volume of sales overshadows the extra receipts from extending sales.

MR can also be related to the area under the demand curve. If, from any point on the demand curve, we extend perpendiculars to both the X and the Y axes, so as to enclose a rectangle (as in Figure 2.2[b]), and do the same at the neighboring demand point, then if the area of the new rectangle exceeds that of the old, MR is positive. This requires that the area added to the portion of the rectangle common to both prices exceed the area lost. Thus, in Figure 2.2(c), the cross-checked horizontal segment indicates the revenue lost as price falls (the $Q\Delta P$ magnitude of the formula), while the cross-checked vertical segment is the equivalent of the new price P. When the latter exceeds the former, MR is posi-

---

[2] For a more precise formulation, see footnote 8, p. 18. For a continuous demand curve, writing the demand equation as $P = f(Q)$, then $TR = Pf(Q)$ and $MR = dPQ/dQ = P + Q(dP/dQ)$, where dP/dQ is negative.

tive; when the two are equal, $MR = O$. In the limiting case of a horizontal demand curve, as in Figure 2.2(d), which we will shortly describe as a perfectly elastic demand curve, $P = MR$. Otherwise, invariably, $P > MR$.[3]

Average- and Marginal-Revenue Curves

There is a simple geometrical relation between AR and MR curves for linear demand curves, as D_1 in Figure 2.2(B); it can be proved that the descent of the marginal curve is twice that of the average-revenue curve. Thus, MR will cut the horizontal axis—or any line parallel to OX—only one half as far along as does the D_1 curve. Merely by drawing tangents from the OY axis to any point *on any demand curve whatever,* we can ascertain the marginal revenue for the sales volume indicated at the tangency point; this can be done by directing another straight line from the OY intercept of the tangent to the demand curve and running this new line to only one half the OX abscissae intercepted by the tangent itself. The MR can be read off the new correspondent line at the ordinate height (above the sales volume) of original tangency.[4] Hence, whatever the shape of the AR curve, the MR points can be discovered geometrically.[5]

If the demand curve is convex to the origin, it can be proved that the MR curve will intersect a line parallel to the horizontal axis at a point which is less than one half the intersection of the demand curve and the horizontal line. If the demand curve is concave, the MR curve will cross the horizontal line at a distance of more than one half the abscissae length cut off by the demand curve D. These relations are illustrated in Figure 2.3(A) and (B). In each figure ON amounts to one half OR.[6]

[3] This relationship will be reversed when the demand curve is abnormal and upward-rising to the right. Then $MR = P + Q\Delta P$, with the minus sign turning to a positive magnitude.

[4] Thus, in Figure 2.2(B), at price P the total revenue is equal to $OM \cdot OP$, which is also equal to the full area under the MR curve, $ONLRM$. By similar triangles, $NPL = LP'R$, so that RM is the marginal revenue when price is $OP(= MP')$ for the sales quantity OM.

[5] To prove that the slope of MR is twice that of the demand curve for linear curves, let the equation of D_1 be $P = A - MQ$; then

$$TR = AQ - MQ^2$$

and

$$MR = d(TR)/dQ = A - 2MQ$$

The slope of the MR curve is thus $2M$, while that of the demand curve is M.

[6] See Mrs. Robinson, *Economics of Imperfect Competition,* pp. 30 and 40, for the original statement of these geometrical relations.

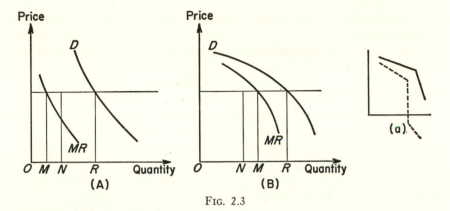

Fig. 2.3

Backward-Falling Demand Curves

If the AR curve has a sharp corner even though it never turns back, then the MR curve will be discontinuous, containing two identifiable branches (see Figure 2.3[a]). At the sharp turning point, MR is likely to be negative, for, in enlarging sales by ΔQ, the price drop ΔP is likely to be precipitous. Likewise, if the demand curve curls back, as D_1PD_3 in Figure 2.1(A), the MR curve will have two distinct branches. Over the upper portion of the demand curve D_1P, the MR curve will be of normal form, while, for the segment PD_3, the MR curve will lie *above* the PD curve.

Questions

1. Construct some simple demand schedules. Compute the marginal revenue by multiplying price times quantity and by means of equation (2.4). Which procedure is simpler?
2. Could the TR curve originate at any point other than the O-origin? on the OY axis? on OX? Must the TR curve ultimately turn down toward the OX axis? Explain.
3. Draw some demand curves with kinks or sharp corners. Trace in the accompanying MR values.

THE POINT ELASTICITY OF DEMAND

The concept of the *point elasticity* of demand (E_d) needs to be developed, for henceforth we shall use the idea frequently. The elasticity of demand is defined as the ratio of the proportionate increase in the quantity wanted to a slight relative decrease in price. Thus,

$$E_d = \frac{\dfrac{\Delta Q}{Q}}{\dfrac{\Delta P}{P}} = \frac{P\Delta Q}{Q\Delta P} \gtreqless 1 \tag{2.5}$$

Disregarding the implicit negative sign, the ratio can range from zero to infinite values.[7]

When E_d is zero, demand would be described as perfectly *inelastic* at that price; a tangent to the relevant point on the demand curve would run parallel to OY. When the E_d is greater than unity, demand is described as *elastic*; when a tangent to the demand curve is parallel to OX, so that E_d tends toward infinite values, demand is regarded as perfectly elastic. When $E_d = 1$, demand is described as of *unit* elasticity. To repeat: the elasticity concept refers rigorously only to an incremental movement along a demand curve.

Elasticity and Total Revenue

Another way of expressing the elasticity relationship is in terms of movements in total expenditure as price falls. If, after a small price fall, consumers spend the same amount on the commodity as formerly, so that TR is unchanged, it can be proved that $E_d = 1$. If expenditure increases, then $E_d > 1$ and demand is declared to be elastic. If $E_d < 1$, a smaller sum than formerly will be spent on the good after the slight price fall.

To prove these relations between the elasticity of demand and total expenditure, we note that, if $E_d > 1$, the numerator of the elasticity formula exceeds the denominator, thus: $P\Delta Q > Q\Delta P$. But $P\Delta Q$, the numerator, corresponds exactly to the first part of the marginal-revenue formula, while the denominator, $Q\Delta P$, is the other component of the MR expression. Total consumer outlay, we know, increases when MR is positive, and thus when $P\Delta Q > Q\Delta P$, or when $E_d > 1$.[8] When demand is inelastic, then $P\Delta Q < Q\Delta P$; MR would then be negative and the TR curve would turn down, implying that total consumer outlay would decrease as price falls. If the demand curve is a rectangular hyperbola, or of the form $PQ = k$, then its elasticity is unity throughout and marginal revenue is always zero.

[7] For the abnormal backward-bending demand curves, as D_1PD_3 in Figure 2.1(A), the ratio, normally negative (though conventionally construed as positive), would be positive.

[8] A minor discrepancy, however, is that, in the MR formula, P is the "new" (lower) price while Q is the "old" sales quantity. The proof can then be approached in this way: $MR = (P - \Delta P)(Q + \Delta Q) - PQ$. Multiplying, canceling, and dropping $\Delta P\Delta Q$ as being of an extremely small order, $MR = P\Delta Q - Q\Delta P$. Thus, MR depends, as before, on whether

$$\frac{P\Delta Q}{Q\Delta P} \gtreqless 1$$

But this last relationship is, of course, E_d.

Elasticity and Marginal Revenue

Algebraically, the following relations of P, MR, and E_d can be established. Knowing any two, we can immediately deduce the third.[9]

$$E_d = \frac{P\Delta Q}{P\Delta Q - MR} = \frac{P}{P - MR} \tag{2.6a}$$

$$MR = P\left(1 - \frac{1}{E_d}\right) = P\left(\frac{E_d - 1}{E_d}\right) \tag{2.6b}$$

In these formulae, E_d is construed as positive for normal demand curves. According to (2.6a), above, $P - MR = P/E_d$. Hence, diagrammatically, the distance $P'R$ in Figure 2.2(B) is equal to P/E_d.

A Geometrical Measure of Elasticity

Occasionally, we might find Marshall's geometrical measure of demand elasticity useful. Drawing the tangent to a demand curve at a point P, and extending it to cut OY at t and OX at T, the ratio of the lengths PT/Pt will yield E_d. When both lengths are equal, demand is of unity elasticity; when PT exceeds Pt, demand is elastic or of greater than unity elasticity.[10]

A Geometrical Comparison of Demand Elasticity

For comparing the respective elasticities of points on *different* demand curves, a modified version of the Marshallian measure has been proposed.[11]

To compare the elasticity at points P and R on demand curves D_1 and D_2, respectively, draw the usual Marshallian tangents to each point, extending them to cut the axes in Figure 2.4(B). Connect the alternate extremities, t and T, to form the line Tt. Then draw PW horizontally and RV vertically, to cut Tt at W and V.

The elasticity at R is

$$RT/Rt' = VT/Vt \tag{2.7}$$

[9] See Mrs. Robinson, p. 36. All of the relations follow from the fact that

$$E_d = \frac{P\Delta Q}{Q\Delta P} \quad \text{and} \quad MR = P\Delta Q - Q\Delta P$$

[10] For the proof, see Alfred Marshall, *Principles of Economics*, ed. 8, pp. 102, 103, 839.

[11] A. P. Lerner, "Geometrical Comparison of Elasticities," *American Economic Review* (March 1947), p. 191. For an approach in terms of angles, see John S. Henderson, "Geometrical Note on Elasticity of Demand," *American Economic Review* (September 1946), pp. 662–663.

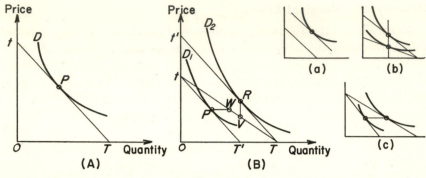

FIG. 2.4

This last result follows from the laws for similar triangles. Similarly, the elasticity at P is

$$PT'/Pt = WT/Wt \tag{2.8}$$

Hence, the relative elasticities can be elaborated with reference to the division of the one line, Tt. If $W = V$, then the elasticities are the same: R will lie directly above W. If WT exceeds VT, as in the figure, then the point elasticity at P is necessarily greater than at R.

Questions

1. Prove that the slope of the demand curve is not the same as the point elasticity. When will they be equal?
2. Given a total revenue curve of the form $PQ = 35$, draw TR. Draw AR and MR. What is E_d?
3. Prove that the geometrical measure of E_d is equal to PT/Pt.
4. Prove:
   a. A vector from the origin will intersect a family of parallel linear demand curves at points of equal elasticity. If tangents to nonlinear curves fall along the vector, the E_d will be the same at each point.
   b. For a linear family, a perpendicular to OX will intersect the upper curve at a greater E_d than the lower curve. The reverse would be true for a perpendicular to OY.
   c. If E_d is the same at a given output, the tangents will meet on OX. They will meet on OY if E_d is the same at a given price.
5. Draw a demand curve. Draw a tangent to a point on the curve. From OY, at the price involved at the point of tangency, draw a diagonal to OX, at the output involved at the tangency point. What is the relation between the slope of the tangent, the slope of the diagonal, and the point elasticity of demand?

ARC ELASTICITY

In the real world, changes in price are generally finite. Properly interpreted, the E_d concept refers to incremental movements from point to point along the demand curve. Often the best we can do in practice is to learn whether total expenditure increases or decreases, and then state in broad terms whether demand is or is not elastic over the range of variation. If we desire to measure the change more precisely, there are a number of formulae that we might use to measure the *arc* elasticity; none of them provides the same answer as the true point elasticity. The smaller the price difference $P_1 - P_2$, where $P_1 > P_2$, the better will be the approximation.

If P_1, Q_1 is the original set of price and quantity coordinates, and P_2, Q_2 is the new set after the finite price change, the ratio $(Q_2 - Q_1)/(P_2 - P_1)$ must figure as part of any measure of arc elasticity, for this is the $\Delta Q/\Delta P$ component of the point E_d. To measure the proportional changes, we need to multiply the numerator by P and the denominator by Q.

But this is precisely the area of arbitrariness. If we were contemplating a price fall, we could multiply by P_1/Q_1, while, for a price rise, we could multiply by P_2/X_2. But both measures would be defective in that they involve a different value for the downward movement as compared to the upward price movement. Even worse, neither of the measures would equal unity, as would the point elasticity, when total expenditure in the two price situations is the same. Slight arithmetical tests would prove this. For example, take $P_1 = \$2$, $Q_1 = 300$, $P_2 = \$1$, $Q_2 = 600$; then

$$\frac{P_1(X_2 - X_1)}{X_1(P_1 - P_2)} = \frac{\$2(300)}{300(\$1)} = \frac{\$600}{\$300} = 2 \qquad (2.9)$$

while

$$\frac{\$1(300)}{600(\$1)} = \frac{\$300}{\$600} = \frac{1}{2} \qquad (2.10)$$

It is desirable that a measure of arc elasticity equal unity when total consumer outlay is constant, as in the illustration. If we used P_1/Q_2 or P_2/Q_1 as our multiplier, this condition of unity elasticity for a fixed outlay would be satisfied. But each of these measures would exhibit some asymmetry, revealing a different value as we move up the arc for a price rise from P_2 to P_1 as compared to a price fall from P_1 to P_2.[12] Logically, the elasticity should be the same in either direction.

The Measure Recommended

To meet these difficulties, it has been suggested that an average of P_1 and P_2, and Q_1 and Q_2, be used as a multiplier. The most suitable arc elasticity thus becomes

[12] In all but the unity case.

$$E_d = \frac{\dfrac{(P_1 + P_2)(X_2 - X_1)}{2}}{\dfrac{(X_2 + X_1)(P_1 - P_2)}{2}} \tag{2.11}$$

$$= \frac{(P_1 + P_2)(X_2 - X_1)}{(X_2 + X_1)(P_1 - P_2)} \tag{2.12}$$

In our simple illustration, this will yield a value of 1.

With the measure suggested, geometrically we could still use the Marshallian ratio PT/Pt; but P this time would be located midway between P_1 and P_2. The demand curve, therefore, is implicitly assumed to be linear between the two points P_1 and P_2.

Questions

1. If you were working in a drugstore and contemplated changing the price of toothpaste, cosmetics, etc., which elasticity concept would you use in estimating the effects on sales and on receipts?
2. In the light of your notion of marginal revenue, is it or is it not reasonable to expect important annual reductions in automobile, television, or appliance prices generally? Make some realistic estimates of demand elasticities.
3. Discuss some of the main problems in attempting to ascertain actual demand curves. Do you suppose that business firms make efforts to understand demand phenomena for their wares? Do you think they can make informed guesses? Explain why or why not.

THE CROSS-ELASTICITY OF DEMAND

The concept of the (point) cross-elasticity of demand is another useful demand idea. This refers to the ratio of the relative change in the quantity demanded of commodity Y, given a relative (incremental) change in the price of good X. Hence, this serves as a measure of demand interdependence between goods. Thus,

$$E_y^{P_x} = P_x \Delta Q_y / Q_y \Delta P_x \tag{2.13}$$

The cross-elasticity can assume positive, negative, or zero values—in contrast to the direct elasticity which is (usually) negative.

Normally, if X and Y are substitutes, then $E_y^{P_x} > O$. That is, a rise in P_x (with P_y constant) will increase Y's sales. For complements, Y's sales will slump, given a rise in P_x. To illustrate, if automobile prices were to rise tremendously, gasoline sales would fall off. Or, if the price of electricity were to rise substantially, appliance sales might be reduced. For independent or unrelated goods, $E_y^{P_x} = O$; e.g., newspapers and Cadillac automobiles.

An illustrative set of cross-demand curves appears in Figure 2.5. The *S* curve denotes the case of substitute goods, *C* reflects complementary interdependence, and *I*, rather complete demand independence of the two goods.

Measures of arc cross-elasticities can also be formulated for practical calculations.

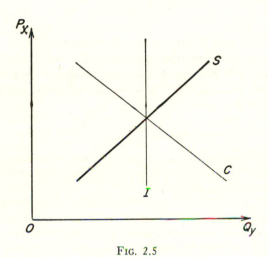

FIG. 2.5

The Coefficient of Price Interdependence

Instead of linking relative changes in the sales of commodity *Y* to proportionate price movements in *X*, we may sometimes want to measure the degree of price interdependence, for, in some problems where the markets are interrelated, a change in one price, as ΔP_x, will induce a movement in another price. Thus, assuming the initial change ΔP_x,

$$E_{P_y}{}^{P_x} = \frac{\dfrac{\Delta P_y}{P_y}}{\dfrac{\Delta P_x}{P_x}} = \frac{P_x \Delta P_y}{P_y \Delta P_x}$$

Normally, the value of this coefficient ought to range between positive and negative values of unity. For substitutes, a price rise of commodity *X* on the order of 1 per cent ought, at most, to elevate P_y by the same proportion. For complements, the price interdependence will be negative unless both complementary items are subject to a simultaneous increase (or decrease) in demand (or cost).

Questions

1. Cite 10 brand-name goods for which you think the cross-elasticities of demand are positive; negative; zero. Which list did you complete most quickly? Can you explain why? Are you puzzled as to the best classification for some of the items? Explain why or why not.
2. Do you think the concept of cross-elasticity, or something akin to it, influences the pricing decisions of business firms? Why or why not?
3. Make some simple estimates of cross-elasticities in the case of the cigarettes you smoke, the meals you eat, or the entertainment you indulge in; e.g., movies as against bowling. How large a relative price change is required for a significant change in your purchase pattern in each case?
4. How significant would you judge the cross-elasticity to be: (a) in the automobile market; (b) in the cigarette market; (c) in your choice of a restaurant for lunch or other meals?
5. Measure the cross-elasticity of demand geometrically. When do you get positive values? When are they negative?

Chapter 3

Production and Costs

After the foregoing survey of demand ideas, our attention turns to the theory of production.

Two aspects of this study are developed in this chapter: first, there is the purely technical side consisting of the input-output relations, for generally a product can be produced in manifold ways—the technological forces are seldom such as to impose a unique factor combination. Secondly, because there are manifold technical possibilities, factor costs will prove to be the decisive element in determining the precise combination of resources selected for production. An entrepreneur bent on maximizing income will choose the least-cost combination for each quantity of output; this introduces an economic aspect to the production problem.

The technological alternatives and the optimal economic factor assortment will thus be elaborated in the following pages. Borrowing a simple mathematical idea, the technical possibilities relating factor use to output of a particular commodity are expressed in a production function such as $Q = f(A, B, C, \ldots)$, where Q refers to the quantity of output and $A, B, C, \ldots$ are the factors used in its production. The production function pertains to a given state of knowledge, for, with new achievements in the technological arts, the possible input combinations to obtain a definite output are invariably enlarged.

Before we begin the particular studies of this chapter, certain terms must be defined.

FACTORS OF PRODUCTION

Using as synonyms the terms resources, factors, and agents, all human and nonhuman *tangible* sources whose presence (or absence) makes a difference to output are defined as *potential* agents of production. It is the productive factors that provide the inputs responsible for the output. It is of the essence that the use of these factors be subject to human control, or that their results be subject to human appropriation and prediction, for then rational valuation and utilization become possible. Still, factors so defined are only potential agents of production; whether or not they will actually be employed will depend on the market demands for their services and on the income-leisure valuations of factor owners.

Our definition, it should be observed, places its stress on the output effect of a tangible factor. Yet, firms will pay for the services rendered by intangible sources, such as advertising, patents, insurance, and "good will," and, occasionally, may pay to influence legislation and social attitudes. Although these outlays are not directed toward the use of productive factors, they are, nonetheless, outlays that are productive of income. Hence, it is useful to distinguish between *output* factors and *income* factors; the former contribute to output and income while the latter are significant solely because they augment income, even though a definite physical quantum of output cannot be ascribed to their presence.[1]

Literally, there are a myriad potential productive agents. The classical trinity of land, labor, and capital (goods) is defective from a realistic standpoint except as a shorthand classification that magnifies similarities and minimizes differences. A more precise definition would suggest that, insofar as agents are imperfect technical substitutes one for the other, they belong to separate factor classes. Complete substitutability of one agent for another in each of the diverse uses would thus be characteristic of all resources comprising a factor class.[2] Being perfectly substitutable, the members of a factor class can also be described as *homogeneous* factors.[3] While we shall not wholly abandon the traditional classification of productive factors, actually the main separation we require in the theory of production and price is that between *fixed* and *variable* factors. In general, whatever vitality the older classification possesses is due to its fairly high correlation with the categories necessary in price and income theory, with land being generally a fixed factor, labor a variable one, and equipment sometimes one and sometimes the other.

In a nonintegrated output structure, firms will generally purchase unfinished materials from other firms. Certain products are thus *interme-*

[1] Judicious legislation may likewise facilitate production and thereby be subject to some social valuation, as compared to unwise legislation. But, to the valuing subjects, legal institutions are data around which production is organized; they affect the content of economic life though they generally leave the formal nature of the underlying relationships unaffected. They may well be excluded at the present stage, although they can be regarded as intangible *institutional* factors of production that contribute to the social output and income.

[2] Factor classes are thus regarded from the standpoint of the entrepreneur. To make sure that owners of the homogeneous factors will view all employment in the same way, and thus will accept identical incomes for each output of which they are capable, we must posit that they are identically natured.

[3] In terms of the indifference curves, the *MRS* among them would always be constant although not necessarily unity. See the definition of a commodity on p. 90.

diate factors that, to the using firm, are factors of production indistinguishable in principle from other productive factors. Intermediate factors vanish, however, being embodied in other products, when we view output as a whole or visualize a fully integrated output structure in which a firm completes all the materials and the processes incident to final production.

Versatile and Specific Factors

Among the categories of imperfectly substitutable factors, *versatile* factors can be separated from *specific* factors.[4] Versatile factors can be consigned to more than one output use; specific agents are adapted solely to a unique output. Although versatility and specificity are, in practice, a matter of degree, the sharp classificatory demarcation is useful and significant; for a purely specific good, the economic problem of its use is the simple one of deciding whether the one product that it can produce does have a positive value. Versatile factors pose a more complex problem; the significant economic issue involves an appraisal of the most valuable of their diverse uses.

Although we speak of a firm hiring or purchasing productive factors, it is only the *services* provided by the factor that are sought: it is the services that comprise the productive inputs. A firm, for example, pays wages not for the laborer as an individual but rather for his productive services, values not the land as such but for the services it renders, etc. Even in a slave economy, the outlay for the slave is intended to acquire control of his services.

Questions

1. Suppose that you are contemplating producing automobiles, men's shirts, or a child's toy. What are the technological aspects of the problem? If advice is sought, what professions are likely to provide it?
2. If you knew the price at which the product *must* sell because of competition, how would you proceed to select the productive factors?
3. Write an essay on the concept of a productive factor, in your own words and not relying on the definition given above. What do you see as the main problems in defining a productive factor?
4. Enumerate 5 illustrations each of a versatile and of a specific factor. Which illustrations come most readily?
5. How valid do you regard the distinction between "income" and "output" factors? Are they equally basic ideas? Explain.
6. It is said that a system of law and order makes a tremendous contribution to production. How can the contribution be estimated? Should statutory laws and customs be regarded as productive factors or not?

[4] See F. von Hayek, *The Pure Theory of Capital*, p. 251. The term *specific goods* is attributed to F. von Wieser, *Social Economics*, pp. 81–85, A. F. Hinrichs, trans.

FIXED AND VARIABLE FACTORS

The division between fixed and variable factors, which is the fundamental classification for the theory of production, deserves further elaboration.

Fixed Factors

Fixed factors are those factors whose total cost is constant over some range of output. For example, assuming zero depreciation through use, the total cost of using machinery (consisting of interest charges on the sum invested and depreciation charges as a result of the passage of time) remains constant whether output is at zero or rises to 10,000 units; greater output, however, might entail the introduction of, and expenditure upon, additional equipment. The services of some factors will be fixed for greater ranges of output than for others. The machinery in the foregoing illustration may be contrasted with an inspection foreman who can supervise, say, 1 to 500 units of output.

Variable Factors

Variable factors are those whose quantity and cost alter with movements in output. The precise line for distinguishing them from fixed factors is in the increased total cost of using them with continuously increased output. Sometimes a factor is technically fixed although the payment for its services is variable—for example, machinery installed as a unit but paid for according to use. Or it may be the other way around, as in the case of flat monthly charges for telephones in homes regardless of the number of calls made. From the standpoint of the entrepreneur, the essential feature is not the technical nature of the factor, whether fixed or variable, but the terms of hire. Analytically, however, the technical nature is of the utmost importance in devising the most economic method of hire.

Divisible and Indivisible Factors

As a further distinction among fixed factors, some are divisible while others are not. Divisible fixed factors are those whose total cost is constant, although technically the factor consists of separable units which may be utilized independently. Fundamentally, they are variable factors, though the exigencies of construction or the mode of hire may compel that they be purchased as a unit. For example, if 1,000 acres of land are rented, the full acreage need not be cultivated when only one man is used to farm it; it may be more sensible for him to till part of it more intensively. Or a plant may be purchased as a unit although it may contain a dozen identical wings or units of independent, identical machines.

Indivisible factors, on the other hand, are constructed as a single mass: the irreducible unit must serve over a wide range of outputs. Divisibility or indivisibility thus refers to the mode of use, and not to the terms of payment for fixed factors. We shall find that the degree of technical divisibility of the factor is of crucial importance in shaping the course of the marginal-cost curve.

CONSTANT-PRODUCT CURVES

After this definitional array, we can now make more rapid progress in our study of the theory of production. In Figure 3.1, let us suppose that quantities of productive factors are measured along OX and OY. Furthermore, let each curve connect factor combinations capable of producing the same volume of output, while positing that the ascent up the curve system involves higher output levels. What are called the indifference curves in the theory of consumption are termed, in the theory of production, *isoquants* or *constant-product curves*. Curve 100, denoting 100 units of output, shows all the possible alternate ways of producing this amount of goods: more of factor Y and less of X, and vice versa, can be chosen in the production plan of the firm. Curve 200 lends itself to the same interpretation. Obviously, the entire diagram can be filled up with a *family* of isoquant curves, one for each output level. (Only 3 curves are drawn in Figure 3.1 so as not to clutter the field unduly.)

The major restriction on the field is that the isoquants may not intersect one another. Also, the isoquant field reveals that factors X and Y are substitutable at each output level. Normally, there will also be some other factors employed—resources other than quantities of X and Y. In drawing our chart these must be assumed as constant, for, otherwise, a particular combination of X and Y will not always culminate in the same output.

Exploring some further aspects of the constant-product curves, we can

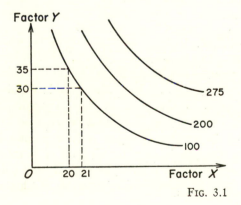
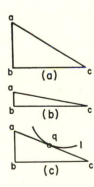

Fig. 3.1

compute the *marginal rate of substitution* (*MRS*) between the factors. For two factors this is *the ratio of the decrement in Y required to compensate for a unit increment in X while leaving output unchanged*. Thus,

$$MRS = -\Delta Y / \Delta X \qquad (3.1)$$

That is, suppose that 100 units of output are produced with 35 units of factor Y (unskilled labor, say), and 20 units of factor X (skilled labor). It may be possible for the same 100 units to be produced with $30Y$ and $21X$. Thus, the *MRS* would be 5/1, for $-\Delta Y = 5$ and $\Delta X = 1$.

Marginal Product and Marginal Rate of Substitution

The notion of the marginal product of a factor may be introduced at this point: it refers to the change in total output made by a further unit of a factor ($\Delta Q / \Delta X$ or $\Delta Q / \Delta Y$, say), when the amount used of other factors is held constant. Thus, one more skilled man added to the work force may increase output by 10 units while one more unskilled man might advance output by only 2 units.

Hence, if we define the marginal product of a factor as the addition to total output made by a further unit of that factor, the *MRS* can also be referred to as the ratio of the marginal products of X and Y; thus, if the *MRS* is $2Y$ for $1X$, the marginal product of X (or MP_x) must be twice that of Y (or MP_y). If a unit of X adds 10 units to total output, a unit of factor Y adds only 5 units to total output. Thus,

$$MP_x / MP_y = MRS = -\Delta Y / \Delta X \qquad (3.2)$$

Isoquants Represent Input-Output Relations

Each isoquant, clearly, represents the relations between a particular volume of output and alternative combinations of inputs. Each isoquant contour thus denotes the alternative technological opportunities for factor-use in producing a certain output quantity. As we move up the isoquant field and use increasing amounts of *both* factors (or at least more of one while the other is unchanged), total production is enlarged.

A truncated list of combinations of factors X and Y for producing 100 and 200 units of a hypothetical commodity is presented in Table 3.1. Illustrative marginal rates of substitution are also listed.

Thus, the Y factor may refer to unskilled labor and X to skilled labor; or one may be male, the other female; or Y may refer to man-hours of labor and X to acres of land, etc. In any event, 50 units of Y plus 18 units of X can produce 100 units of output; 26 units of Y and 22 of X can do the same. Similarly, when output is Q_2 or 200, $110Y$ and $37X$ can produce this volume; the 200 can also be produced by $80Y$ and $41X$, or by the intervening factor combinations.

TABLE 3.1—INPUT-OUTPUT AND *MRS* RELATIONS

$Q_1 = 100$			$Q_2 = 200$		
Factor Combinations		*MRS Ratios*	*Factor Combinations*		*MRS Ratios*
Y	*X*	$\Delta Y/\Delta X$	*Y*	*X*	$\Delta Y/\Delta X$
. . .	. . .		. . .	. . .	
50,	18	. . .	110,	37	. . .
42,	19	8/1	101,	38	9/1
35,	20	7/1	93,	39	8/1
30,	21	5/1	86,	40	7/1
26,	22	4/1	80,	41	6/1
. . .	. . .	. . .	. . .	. . .	. . .

As remarked earlier, the *MRS* ratios can also be interpreted as ratios of marginal products. To illustrate, if the *MRS* is 8/1, then 1 unit of *X* adds to output as much as 8 of *Y*, or the marginal product of the former is 8 times greater than each unit of the latter.

A Proposition on Slopes and the MRS

To those with even a dim recollection of their previous mathematics course, it has already been apparent that the *MRS*, in geometrical terms, refers simply to the slope of the isoquant at each point. Slopes of curves, for the mathematician, are measured by the tangent to the curve. The value of the tangent depends on the ratio $\Delta Y/\Delta X$, or the change in the *Y*-height for a unit change in the *X*-distance. Of course, this relation *is* the *MRS*—when *Y* refers to amounts of one productive factor and *X* refers to amounts of the other productive agent.

Figure 3.1(a) and (b) is drawn to emphasize these ideas. What is the slope of the line *ac* in each case? Mathematically, this would be measured by the ratio *ab/bc*. Where this ratio is rather high, as in Figure 3.1(a), then the slope is steep; where the ratio is lower, as in Figure 3.1(b), the slope is gentler. In effect, the steepness or gradient of the hill is measured by conceiving an individual, say, who wanted to traverse the path from *a* to *c* as first burrowing down to *b* from *a*, and then tunneling out from *b* to *c*.

In Figure 3.1(c), the slope *ac* is tangent to curve 1 at point *q*. Thus, the slope at point *q* is equal to *ab/bc*, and will be negative. If we blew up this diagram to the size of Figure 3.1, the slope of the tangent at *q* would, of course, measure the MRS at point *q*.

The slope of a straight line, as *OX* or a flat plane, is zero (for

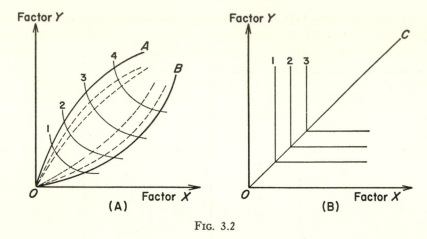

Fig. 3.2

$\Delta Y = O$). The slope of a vertical line, as OY or a wall, is infinite, for $\Delta X = O$.

Ridge Lines and Isoclines

While, in theory, the MRS, or $\Delta Y/\Delta X$, may be either positive or negative, it is the good sense of the entrepreneur in production that rules out the excess quantities of factors implicit in a positive substitution ratio; a positive MRS would entail that adding more X *and* more Y would merely keep output intact. The isoquant would thus tend to run in a northeasterly direction. Manifestly, it would be unprofitable for an entrepreneur to employ more factors than the minimum quantity necessary for the output volume.[5]

Ridge lines OA and OB are consequently drawn in Figure 3.2(A) to rope off the area of rational factor use, containing within their bounds the curve sections in which the MRS is negative and where the isoquant slopes are convex to the origin. *Factor combinations outside these confines are uneconomic.*

At each point on the ridge line, beyond which factor combinations are excluded, tangents to each particular constant-product curve are

---

[5] The possibility, in practice, is not to be ruled out entirely. A large firm located in a small community might "over-employ" factors merely to retain local good will. Analogously, labor unions often insist on antiquated hiring practices; two electricians might be ordered for work when one man's services might suffice, with one electrician standing idly by, watching the other labor. In military service, a battalion commander might often use a company to do the work that could be accomplished by a platoon; that this happens is accountable for by the fact that the commander does not have to pay for the hire of labor, as would a private business firm. Small wonder, then, that wasteful practices may be countenanced.

parallel to either the OX or the OY axis. This denotes an infinite or zero MRS and implies that the marginal product of one of the factors is zero at the particular output level. When the tangent to a constant-product curve is vertical, the MRS is infinite (written ∞); when it is horizontal, the MRS is zero. In the former case, $MP_y = O$; in the latter, $MP_x = O$.

If we draw the segments of the isoquant curve that lie outside OA and OB, they assume an elliptical shape, as the dashed lines in Figure 3.3(a), evidencing that the same output can be produced with multiple quantities of X (or Y) and a constant quantity of Y (or X). But, in

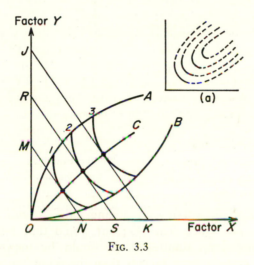

FIG. 3.3

these areas outside the ridge lines, the MRS is positive, implying that if X, say, is increased, Y also must be increased if output is merely to be held constant. If X has a positive marginal product, that of Y must be negative, and vice versa. The ridge lines exclude, therefore, the areas of excess quantities of factors or negative marginal products of one or the other factor. Within the ridge lines, the condition of a decreasing MRS prevails along each constant-product curve, so that, in this area, each isoquant is convex to the origin. Convexity will mean that the curves are of the general shape drawn in Figure 3.1.

Ridge lines OA and OB connect points of equal (infinite or zero) marginal rates of substitution or ratios of marginal products. Within the ridge lines, other points of equal MRS, or relative marginal products, can also be isolated and then connected. Doing so, we derive the dashed lines in Figure 3.2(A) which correspond in shape, nature, and direction to the ridge lines; these are termed *isoclines*. Along each isocline the MRS (or the ratio MP_x/MP_y) from isoquant to isoquant is therefore constant. Ridge lines are, thus, a special type of isocline, at which one

MP is zero and the other relatively infinite. Writing K to symbolize some constant value along each isocline, we obtain, as the defining characteristic of an isocline,

$$MRS = -\Delta Y/\Delta X = K$$

On ridge line OA the value of K is infinite; on OB, $K = 0$.

Unique Factor Combinations

Products that can be expanded only by a unique simultaneous increase in both factors imply an isoquant field such as that shown in Figure 3.2(B). Increases in one factor unaccompanied by increments in the other would be futile. The usually divergent ridge lines OA and OB coincide in this case, and the result is the straight line OC in the figure. In contrast, when factor X is perfectly substitutable for Y, the isoquants would be straight lines running, say, from $1X$ to $1Y$, $2X$ to $2Y$, etc. Axes OX and OV would then constitute the ridge lines and the isoclines would be straight lines emanating from the O origin.

Questions

1. In typical production problems, which factors would be variable and which fixed? Distinguish, in concrete illustrations, between divisible fixed and indivisible fixed factors.
2. What is the key idea in the definition of a constant-product curve? In the marginal rate of substitution?
3. Explain why the MRS and the ratio of marginal products are one and the same.
4. Given the production function:

$$Q = \frac{x^2 + y^2}{x + y}$$

   draw a part of the production function when $Q = 30$. Compute the MRS when $X = 10$; 11; 12. Which values of Y lead to redundancy?
5. Given the production function: $Q = 15x_y - bx^2 - 8y^2$. Also, $P_x = \$2$, $P_y = \$6$. How much of X and of Y are used when $Q = 50$? when $Q = 100$? What is the total cost of production in each case?

THE MINIMUM-COST CONDITION

The isoquant study has disclosed the various input-output relations. As there are many ways of producing the same output, the factor combination actually selected will depend on factor prices; rationally, the entrepreneur will choose the least-cost combination for each output.

The Factor-Cost Line

An isoquant provides a way of representing the factor combinations that can yield a given output volume. Let us now find a graphic picture of factor costs.

Suppose that the price of factor Y—unskilled labor, say—costs $1 an hour, while factor X, skilled labor, is priced at $2 an hour. If the firm were to spend $100 on the hire of these agents, it could thus hire $100Y$ and zero X, or $98Y + 1X$, $96Y + 2X$, ..., down to zero Y and $50X$. If it were to spend $200 as a total cost outlay, all the possible purchase combinations could be doubled.

In sum, then, because of the market prices of the factors (which are assumed to be constant and beyond the influence of the firm), 1 unit of factor X can be acquired if the firm uses 2 units less of factor Y. This is the *market-substitution ratio* implicit in the respective $2 and $1 prices. On this basis, a graphic representation of factor-cost phenomena can be constructed.

Diagrammatically, a price line, or a *factor-cost line* (or an *isocost curve*), can be drawn from the vertical to the horizontal axis on the assumption of a given total-cost outlay and a given set of factor prices. Thus, MN in Figure 3.3 can be interpreted as containing on its path all the combinations of factors that can be hired at a total cost outlay of $100. The line RS can be regarded as entailing a total outlay of $150; JK can then represent $200, etc. The slope of the factor-cost line in each case is equal to 2, for $-\Delta Y = 2$ and $\Delta X = 1$. Thus,

$$\text{Slope of Isocost Line} = \frac{-\Delta Y}{\Delta X} = \frac{P_x}{P_y} \qquad (3.3)$$

The factor-cost curve thus indicates the maximum factor combinations that can be hired under the given hypothesis. As each factor-cost line embodies the maximum combinations that can be hired for a given total cost, lesser combinations of the factors can also be hired, for their total cost would be less than that for the combinations included on the line.

The Condition of Minimum Cost

Since the market substitution rate at which the X factor can be hired to replace the Y factor depends on the ratio of factor prices (P_x/P_y), the slope of the factor-cost line $(\Delta Y/\Delta X)$ is equal to this ratio. In seeking to minimize the total cost of producing a given output volume, an entrepreneur will substitute one factor for another at each total-outlay level until the MRS is equal to the ratio of factor prices; this involves the tangency between isocost and isoquant, as shown in Figure 3.3. Unless these factor quantities are chosen, the entrepreneur is not maximizing output for his cost outlays on factors. We shall elaborate on this in a moment.

Alternately, the total-cost outlay for the particular output is not being minimized unless the $MRS = P_x/P_y$. In the older formulation, the equilibrium condition of minimum cost at each level of output was described in terms of the equality between the ratios of marginal products and factor prices. All these formulations are equivalent.

To elaborate: at the tangency position, the slope of the isoquant (which is the MRS and is measured by $\Delta Y/\Delta X$) equals the slope of the isocost, which is also measured by $\Delta Y/\Delta X$ and is equal to the ratio of factor prices. Thus,

$$MRS = P_x/P_y \qquad (3.4)$$

Alternately,

$$MP_x/MP_y = P_x/P_y \qquad (3.5)$$

or,

$$MP_x/P_x = MP_y/P_y \qquad (3.6)$$

If several factors are hired,

$$MP_x/P_x = MP_y/P_y = MP_z/P_z = J$$

where J is some constant typical of all these ratios.

A numerical illustration can be considered as a tentative proof of this proposition. To the left of the tangency position, the slope of the factor-cost line would intersect several isoquants, implying that, at each intersection, the ratio of the $MRS > P_x/P_y$. Suppose that

$$MRS = -\Delta Y/\Delta X = 4/1$$

or

$$MP_x/MP_y = 4/1$$

while the factor-price ratios are

$$P_x/P_y = \$2/\$1$$

Refraining from the hire of $2Y$, the firm can acquire $1X$; in productivity, however, $1X = 4Y$. Consequently, output can be augmented by the switch in factor hire or, alternately, the given output can be produced at lower cost, for $4Y$ can be released on the addition of $1X$, involving a total cost saving of \$2.

If $MRS < P_x/P_y$, the results would be similar except that now the hire of factor X would be reduced while that of Y would be increased: this inequality would appear to the right of the tangency position where the factor-cost line intersected isoquants of lesser output. The incentive to alter factor-use disappears only when $MRS = P_x/P_y$.

When this condition prevails, the factors hired represent the equilibrium combination—that is, the minimum-cost combination for the particular output—or the factor combination of maximum output for the given total cost, given the factor price as well as factor-productivity circumstances. The point of the geometry thus can be summarized as meaning that, when isocost and isoquant intersect, the output volume can be increased for the same total cost or the particular output involved can be produced at a lower total cost.

Questions

1. Write the general equation for an isocost when factor prices are constant. When total outlay is $50, and $P_x = \$2$, $P_y = \$1$, what information does the isocost equation reveal?
2. For discontinuous cases in which factor-use cannot be varied by incremental amounts, how would you express the condition for minimum cost?
3. In question (1), how many combinations of factors can be hired? Suppose that variations can take place only by 1 unit of a factor, how many combinations can be hired? What, then, is the *economic* nature of the production problem?

THE EXPANSION PATH

Superimposing a number of isocosts on our figure (as MN, RS, and JK in Figure 3.3), each parallel to one another to indicate the constancy of factor prices, and noting their points of tangency to the isoquants, we can extract the factor combinations that will be selected as output expands and factor outlays are increased while factor prices are constant. Linking up the various equilibrium combinations traces the *expansion path* of the firm. This path is the locus OC in Figure 3.3, representing the minimum-cost factor combinations for the successive levels of output.

When factor prices are constant, the expansion path follows the course of an isocline, since the latter is defined as connecting points of constant MRS, while the expansion path connects points at which $P_x/P_y = MRS$. Hence, when the ratio P_x/P_y is constant, the MRS along the expansion path is always the same, and thus isocline and expansion path coincide.

The expansion path departs from a given isocline only when factor prices vary with changes in the output level.[6] If the relative factor prices confronting the firm were to change independently of the firm's own output and factor demand, a new series of isocosts would have to be drawn and a new expansion path would emerge, coinciding with another isocline. As would be expected, if P_x fell relatively to P_y, more of X would be utilized and X substituted for Y at each output level. Producers are envisaged as able, through borrowing (or lending excess sums), to command the outlays necessary for expansion to any output point that they choose along the appropriate path.

Moving upward along the expansion path, as the factor combinations

[6] See below, pp. 277–278.

are being successively enlarged, and on the assumption that factor prices are constant, the relationship that will be satisfied is

$$MP_x/MP_y = P_x/P_y = K \qquad (3.7)$$

NONMINIMUM COST ANALYSIS

If the expansion path is a straight line, with a slope of $\Delta Y/\Delta X = \overline{K}$, the increase in the hire of factor Y relative to that of X is never altered; the marginal products of X and Y can be described as falling (or rising) in a constant proportion as output advances along the path of minimum cost. If the expansion path is linear and also passes through the O origin, the ratio of factor-use is never altered. The expansion path may, instead, wind around toward the OY axis, implying an ever-rising slope and enabling us to infer that, as output advances, the marginal product of the X factor falls faster than that of Y, with the latter better suited to the higher levels of output. Conversely, if the expansion path flattens out, becoming almost parallel with the horizontal axis, it will be the X factor that is most effective at the higher output levels. If the expansion path has a slope greater than unity, the marginal product of X falls faster than (or fails to increase as fast as) that of Y as output grows. Although these remarks apply to the expansion path when factor prices are constant, they are always relevant in describing the shape of the isoclines whose course is independent of factor prices.

Production Efficiency and Nonminimum Costs

The equality of marginal rates of substitution of factors and relative factor prices is required for cost minimization when factor amounts can be continuously varied in use. This is the condition for efficiency in production. *Practically all the remarks on wasteful resource use by firms can be reduced to a statement of a failure to equate ratios of marginal products to factor prices.*

There is another matter qualifying this principle which has been ignored so far. In outlining the condition of minimum cost are the tacit suggestions (1) that firms consciously strive to produce at minimum cost and (2) that they are competent to secure this objective. If ignorance in calculation prevents them from producing as economically as possible, then the subject can be disposed of abruptly; resources valued at, say, $100 by the community will be devoted to producing 70 units of output when the same output can be turned out at, perhaps, $40. This will imply economic waste and inefficiency, pure and simple. Invariably, excess factor-use will be due to an inadequate conception of the production function—that is, of all the points on the isoquant curves in the two-factor model.

The more interesting case, however, is that in which the firm does apprehend the condition of minimum cost yet *prefers* to lavish a greater outlay sum on an output rather than to undertake the entrepreneurial efforts associated with cost reduction. All along we have been writing as if minimum-cost equilibria emerged automatically, without entrepreneurial evaluations and judgments of factor productivity, without efforts in the way of hiring some factors while releasing others. Realistically, these elements must be introduced.

In general, costs will be minimized if the entrepreneur's effort is regarded as valueless or if he prizes further pecuniary income to any personal exertion entailed in cost minimization. Where further effort to minimize cost is irksome to him, or where the added income is less valued than the comfort of lesser effort, costs will not be fully minimized. A precise analysis of this situation would be facilitated by the use of indifference curves, which will be developed later.

Considerations of this sort throw a cloud over the concept of cost minimization and shake our confidence in the fidelity of concrete instances to our sharp mental images. The degree of error occasioned by the stronger presentation of the theory will be less serious whenever businessmen are largely driven by income incentives, while appraising lightly the arduousness of their own efforts.

Questions

1. Distinguish between the expansion path and the isocline. How many defining characteristics are there for the former? for the latter?
2. What would the expansion path be like if the firm were *not* interested in minimizing costs?

FACTOR SUBSTITUTES AND COMPLEMENTS

When only two factors of production are used and output is at a given level, each factor will be a substitute for the other. That is, carpenters can be a substitute for bricklayers, lumber for bricks, skilled labor for unskilled labor, equipment for labor, etc. On the other hand, when output expands, almost all of the productive agents will be used in greater amount. A commonsense approach thus suggests that factors generally will be substitutes at a constant output and will be complements at a changing output.

Analytically, writing ΔQ for the increase in output and ΔX (or ΔY) for the change in the use of factor X (or Y), the marginal product of each factor for a small increase in its use is given by $\Delta Q / \Delta X$. Within the ridge lines, this ratio will be positive; thus, $\Delta Q / \Delta X > 0$.

Suppose we have three factors, as carpenters (X), bricklayers (Y), and lumber (Z). Suppose, too, that there is an increased amount of lumber on hand to a builder—perhaps because its price has fallen. Our question is: what happens to the marginal productivity of another carpenter? of another bricklayer?

We might suspect, in this case, that

$$\frac{\Delta}{\Delta Z}\left(\frac{\Delta Q}{\Delta X}\right) > 0 \qquad (3.8)$$

$$\frac{\Delta}{\Delta Z}\left(\frac{\Delta Q}{\Delta Y}\right) < 0 \qquad (3.9)$$

That is to say, the marginal productivity of bricklayers will fall, for they are now less important in the scheme of things. Carpenters will be more useful, with their marginal productivity rising, as in (3.8). Case (3.8) thus involves complementary agents, while (3.9) is the mark of substitutes where the marginal product of one factor falls when there is an increase in the use of another.[7]

The redundancy relation has a resemblance to complementarity in that it portends a joint increase in the two factors even at the constant-output level. But this is a rather spurious view of complementarity in that one factor is so negatively productive, tending by itself to decrease output, that the other factor has to be augmented in order to recover the output level. Complementary relations, instead, belong to a world of three or more factors. Factors X and Y are substitutes if the unit increase in factor X, and the consequent decrement in Z, to keep output unchanged, decreases the *MRS* of Y for Z. Y is complementary to X if the *MRS* of Y for Z rises as X is increased and Z is diminished at the constant-output level.[8]

Although, at a given output level, factors are likely to be substitutes, as output expands the output effect is likely to lead to an increased use of all factors, especially if the ridge lines form a fairly narrow band. In a very real sense, therefore, factors may be regarded as "complementary" as output advances.

Limitational Factors

A further type of factor relationship may be unearthed. Conceivably, a given volume of output may not be possible without a very definite

---

[7] More precisely, these definitions reduce to:

$$\frac{\partial^2 Q}{\partial z \partial x} > 0 \quad \text{and} \quad \frac{\partial^2 Q}{\partial z \partial y} < 0$$

[8] Professor Hicks defines factor relations at varying output levels in his *Value and Capital*, pp. 93–98. The regressive relationship of a factor and product which he adduces has a certain counterpart in the redundant factor.

and irreducible quantity of factor X, while further increases of X for the same amount of output may be unavailing so far as replacing other factors is concerned. Perhaps, for every *additional* unit of output, factor X will have to be increased by 1 unit, otherwise output will be frozen; X can then be termed a *limitational* factor. In food processing, for example, more of a particular ingredient may be an indispensable prerequisite for a further unit of output, although labor and equipment may be substitutable in combining the ingredient and producing the final product.

Substitution, then, is not possible for the limitational factor at each output level, while, with varying output, the marginal product of all

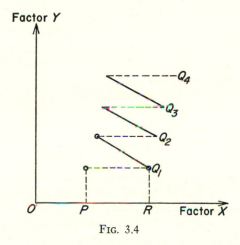

FIG. 3.4

other factors will be zero unless the appropriate elemental quantity of the limitational factor is also added. Thus, at each level of output, a limitational factor is rigidly independent of all other factors; the constant-product curves composed out of the limitational factor and every other factor will thus be rectangular projections of the axes (see Figure 3.2[B]).

Indivisible Factors

Besides the limitational factors for which substitution is impossible at any output level, there may be indivisible factors that permit only very limited substitution. Machinery, for example, is often erected only in discrete standardized "lumps." Technological considerations, let us say, require output to be produced only with this equipment, although within limits labor is substitutable. Factor Y in Figure 3.4, where the OY scale contains only the real integers and is blank at other than constant additive amounts of Y, is the indivisible factor; only the discontinuous 1, 2, 3, ... units of Y can be engaged while factor X is regarded as perfectly continuous. Using $1Y$, output can be expanded by using more of X; OP of X is perhaps essential at a minimum. When output goes to Q_1, however, it may be produced either with $2Y$ and just over OP of X, or with $1Y$ and OR of X. Some substitution thus remains; a type of constant-product curve can be derived by connecting these two points. Similar isoquants can be traced, connecting other points of constant output with diverse factor combinations. It can be seen by drawing in the isocosts that, as the total outlay increases, the tendency will be for more equipment to be ordered.

Fixed Factors and Heterogeneous Factors

As we look back over this chapter, we must stress the fact that, if the volume of fixed factors changes, in all likelihood the entire isoquant field (and hence the expansion path) will have to be redrawn. For relevance, therefore, the analysis must postulate either that fixed factors are missing from the production process or that, whatever their quantity, their total is constant over the range of output likely to be chosen by the firm.

The factors that comprise the isoquant field, among which the firm can choose, are variable factors. These factors are individually part of a homogeneous group, or factor class. If all factors were heterogeneous, completely dissimilar in respect of productivity, it would generally not be possible to depict the minimum-cost combination schematically. To maximize output for any given outlay, the firm would have to be envisaged as selecting first those factors whose marginal physical product, relative to their price, was a maximum. Any other mode of expansion would fail to minimize output costs. Sometimes, as more heterogeneous factors are added and the total factor combination is enlarged, the marginal physical product of factors already hired may decline. If so, and if the ratio of its marginal product to its price is below that of another factor, opportunities for profitable substitution will arise.

Questions

1. Illustrate several instances of factor substitutes and complements. Do your illustrations refer to unchanged or changing output levels?
2. Can you think of concrete examples of limitational factors? What would the isoquants look like if one factor were limitational?
3. Are factors largely heterogeneous or homogeneous, in your view? Would or would not this argument be equally valid from the entrepreneur's standpoint?

Chapter 4

Costs and Factor Productivity

The cost curves which are so prominent in economic thinking will now be described, for they will be required later in the studies of price behavior. Following the cost concept, the law of diminishing returns (redefined as a law of variable-factor proportions) will be derived from further analysis of the production function. The separate discussions will be locked together by a demonstration of the relationship between factor productivity and costs: the vitality of the study of the laws of return in a price economy is ascribable almost entirely to its implications for costs.

To round out the treatment of cost curves, planning curves will also be examined, as well as the measures of cost and supply elasticity.

TOTAL, AVERAGE, AND MARGINAL COST

The cost curves of economics relate factor-cost outlays and output; curves of total, average, and marginal costs have their analogy with the revenue curves elucidated earlier. Using the symbol Q = output, we require the following abbreviations:

$$TC = \text{total costs}$$

$$TVC = \text{total variable costs}$$

$$TFC = \text{total fixed costs}$$

$$MC = \text{marginal costs}$$

$$AC = \text{average total costs}$$

$$AFC = \text{average fixed costs}$$

$$AVC = \text{average variable costs}$$

Recognizing that the various cost magnitudes fluctuate with output, we must attach a subscript n to each symbol to denote the output quantity, as TC_n, AVC_n, MC_n. The definitions follow:

43

$$TC_n = TVC_n + TFC$$

$$AC_n = TC_n/Q_n$$

$$AVC_n = TVC_n/Q_n$$

$$AFC_n = TFC/Q_n$$

$$MC_n = TC_n - TC_{n-1} = \Delta TC/\Delta Q$$

Viewing this array of cost ideas, we cannot hereafter conscionably speak of costs without specifying what cost concept and what output level we are considering. Further, as a greater quantity of output always involves some additional costs—some more labor or materials, for example—we can posit, as the "law of costs," that *total costs always increase with a rise in output.* Average costs or marginal costs may fall, but total costs must rise.

Relating this discussion with the isoquant and expansion-path analysis of the preceding chapter, we see that the minimum total cost for each quantity of production (or the maximum output associated with each level of total cost) can be read off the expansion path, from the total factor cost responsible for the output indicated by the isocost that is tangent to the particular isoquant along the expansion path.

The Cost Table

A hypothetical illustration of the relations between the various cost categories and output is provided in Table 4.1. Total costs, it will be observed, always rise as output increases. The same is true of total variable costs. Total fixed costs, however, are rigid despite the movements in output. Average fixed costs invariably fall with greater production. Marginal costs may be derived as the difference between the total costs of two successive output levels or the spread between successive total variable costs. Generally, average total and average variable costs first fall and then rise; at their minimum values they are equal to marginal costs. The *AVC* minimum is reached before the *AC* minimum.

Cost Diagrams

In Figure 4.1(A), costs are measured along the vertical axis and output along the horizontal axis. If total fixed costs are equal to *OR*, total costs will start at *R* and run the gamut *TC*; the *TC* curve of Figure 4.1(A) is regarded as a typical total-cost curve. *Each point on TC,* tied as it is to the expansion path, *discloses the minimum total cost of producing the particular quantity* of output. The *TVC* curve originates at *O* and runs parallel to *TC*, but always at a distance *OR* below it; for, as

TABLE 4.1—COSTS AND OUTPUT

Output (Q_n)	Total Costs (TC)	Total Fixed Costs (TFC)	Total Variable Costs (TVC)	Average Costs (AC)	Average Variable Costs (AVC)	Average Fixed Costs (AFC)	Marginal Costs (MC)
1	$130	$100	$ 30	$130.0	$30.0	$100.0	$30
2	154	100	54	77.0	27.0	50.0	24
3	169	100	69	56.3	23.0	33.3	15
4	180	100	80	45.0	20.0	25.0	11
5	200	100	100	40.0	20.0	20.0	20
6	226	100	126	37.6	21.0	16.6	26
7	254	100	154	36.3	22.0	14.3	28
8	285	100	185	35.6	23.1	12.5	31
9	317	100	217	35.2	24.1	11.1	32
10	351	100	251	35.1	25.1	10.0	34
11	386	100	286	35.0	26.0	9.1	35
12	422	100	322	35.1	26.8	8.3	36

the definitions disclose, this sum (OR) always separates the curves. The TFC curve is always horizontal, at a height equal to the total sum of fixed costs.

The AC of any output can be discovered diagrammatically by drawing a vector, such as OL in Figure 4.1(A), from O to any point on TC; the slope of this line, which is measured by LM/OM, yields AC. If the slope of the vector falls as output increases, it signifies a falling AC. Likewise, starting from OR (the height of TFC), the slope indicated by ST/RT always indicates the AVC.

A vector from O to TFC would denote the movement in AFC; since the vertical component is always constant while the horizontal segment always increases, AFC must fall with advancing output.

Marginal Costs

Marginal costs (MC) are the additions to total cost accompanying an increment in output. In Table 4.1 they were obtained by deducting the total cost of producing $n - 1$ units from the total cost of n units.

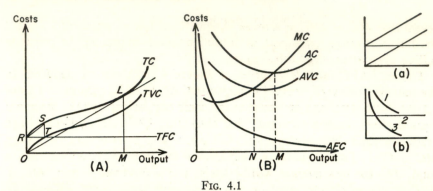

Fig. 4.1

Diagrammatically, the marginal costs can be ascertained by drawing a tangent to TC at each output, because the tangent would measure $\Delta Y / \Delta X$, or the increase in total costs (ΔTC) as output expanded (ΔQ). In following the movements of the tangent to TC, we observe that it tends to fall as output moves on from low levels, diminishing in slope until it reaches a minimum gradient, and then gradually increasing. Hence, MC falls, reaches a minimum, perhaps remaining constant over a slight range of output, and then rises.

The paths of the AC, AVC, AFC, and MC curves accompanying the total curves of Figure 4.1(A) are sketched in Figure 4.1(B); they could all be superimposed, of course, on the chart field of Figure 4.1(A), although we have drawn them separately to avoid encumbering the figure.[1]

AC = MC at Minimum AC

For the case depicted in our diagrams, there will be one output at which $MC = AVC$ and another at which $MC = AC$. At the output at which the tangent to TC coincides with the AC vector from O, $MC = AC$. Further, at this output the slope of the vector from O to TC will be at a minimum; this implies that $MC = AC$ at the lowest level of AC.

The coincidence of a tangent to TVC and a vector from R to TVC will

---

[1] It might be asked why there is but one marginal-cost curve whereas there are three average-cost curves. Literally, our MC is one of marginal *total* costs. If we chose, instead, to speak of marginal variable costs, using TVC_n and TVC_{n-1} in our formula, the results would of course always be the same as when the TC values were used, for the TFC, which separates TC and TVC, will not affect the difference in the totals that comprise marginal costs. Marginal fixed costs, on the other hand, are always zero, for there is no change in TFC as output advances. Hence, there is but one marginal-cost concept and it reflects the changes in total variable costs.

For those with mathematical training, of course $MC = d(TC)/dQ$.

reveal that $MC = AVC$ at a lesser output than that at which $MC = AC$; the fall in average fixed costs as output increases allows AC to continue falling even after AVC turns up.

The AC, AVC, and MC curves of Figure 4.1(B) can be deduced, in the manner indicated, from the movements in the total curves of Figure 4.1(A). Both AVC and MC start at the same cost height on OY. Marginal costs decline, reach a minimum, and then rise. AVC falls and rises more gradually than MC, since it will fall when $MC < AVC$ and rise when $MC > AVC$; for, whenever a value below the average is added onto a total, then the new average will be lower, and vice versa. Finally, $MC = AVC$ at the minimum point on the AVC curve.[2] $MC = AC$ also at the latter's lowest point for the same reason; as AFC is now added to AVC, this intersection is to the right of the previous one: even though $MC > AVC$ (thus tending to push AC upward), the continued fall in AFC delays the rise in AC a while longer.

AVC approaches AC asymptotically, for AFC plays an ever smaller part in determining AC as output grows.

Other Cost-Curve Configurations

Although the TC and TVC curves of Figure 4.1(A) are regarded as typical total-cost curves—for they generate the U-shaped AC and AVC curves of Figure 4.1(B)—some other important curve sets ought to be considered.

Suppose that MC was always constant so that the MC curve was a horizontal line. Inasmuch as the addition to total costs would then always be the same, AVC would also be constant and the AVC curve would coincide fully with MC. The AC curve, however, would fall and approach AVC asymptotically. Both TC and TVC, in this event, would be linear and rising.

[2] To prove this analytically, write T for TVC and X for output. Then, at the minimum AVC value,

$$\frac{d(T/X)}{dX} = O \qquad (4.1)$$

Differentiating (4.1),

$$\frac{X(dT/dX) - T}{X^2} = O \qquad (4.2)$$

Therefore,

$$\frac{dT}{dX} = \frac{T}{X}$$

Hence, marginal costs equal average variable costs. To prove that this is at a minimum rather than a maximum AVC, would require that we show the second derivative to be positive. A similar proof holds for the derivation of $MC = AC$ at the latter's minimum point.

TFC is, of course, always horizontal. As AFC_n (the Y value) multiplied by the number of units (the X value) is always constant and equal to TFC, the AFC curve is always a rectangular hyperbola and is always independent of the shape of the variable-cost curves, TVC, AVC, or MC. The relevant total curves are drawn in Figure 4.1(a) and the average curves in Figure 4.1(b). In Figure 4.1(b), the curve labeled "1" is AC, "2" represents MC ($= AVC$), and "3" represents AFC.

Since the cost curves are derived implicitly from the expansion path, which discloses the *minimum-cost factor combinations,* at each point on the total (average or marginal) curves the variable factors are presumed to be hired in such proportions that the ratios of marginal physical products to factor prices, for all factors used at each output level, will be equal: this ratio will not, of course, be constant as output advances. If the firm does not endeavor to minimize total costs for each output level, the TC curve will be given a lift. The TC points will then not represent the minimum total cost of producing the corresponding output.

Questions

1. Prove conclusively that $AC_n = AVC_n + AFC$. Also, that MC equals marginal variable plus marginal fixed costs.
2. Can you think of exceptions to the "law of costs"? What assumptions are implicit on factor prices and factor productivity? Can one also speak instead of a "law of variable costs"?
3. How important are average fixed costs when output is very large? output small? Can one argue, therefore, that unit fixed costs are decisive in price making in mass-production industries? Explain.
4. Prove that average costs do not always rise when marginal costs rise. What is the correct statement of the relation between a rise (or fall) in one and in the other? Give some simple illustrations (in terms of batting averages, football yardage-gained statistics, average personal income of a club taking in new members, for example) to show your grasp of the difference between average and marginal values.
5. With a total cost curve such as $\diagup$, draw the total, average, and marginal cost-curve set.
6. a. Prove that AVC reaches a minimum at a lesser output than AC.
   b. What is a rectangular hyperbola? Why does AFC *always* have this shape? What is the geometric property of this curve?

LAW OF VARIABLE PROPORTIONS

We abandon temporarily the further study of the cost curves and return to the isoquant field; later we shall tie the two together even more tightly than before.

Assuming that there are but two factors of production, let us probe the output consequences of holding one factor constant while altering the amount of the other. This is the method of the familiar law of dimin-

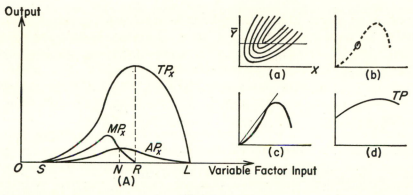

FIG. 4.2

ishing returns which is, more accurately, a law of *variable proportions* in factor-use, for one factor is constant while the other is increased relative to it. In our isoquant field we can visualize that, at some height on OY, representing a fixed amount of factor Y, we draw a horizontal line parallel to OX which would cut across the field, beginning at factor combinations outside the pale of economic rationality—to the left of the ridge line OA. As it moved to the right, denoting an expanding X and a still-constant Y, it would intersect curves of ever higher output, reaching a maximum at the ridge line OB; beyond OB, total output would decline.[3]

Total-Product Curves

Let us develop these ideas more schematically. Suppose that, in Figure 4.2(a), we inserted some pins into a horizontal line drawn to traverse the isoquant field at a height equal to the fixed amount of factor Y; in length the pins ought to be proportionate to output so that we would have a model, drawn to correct scale, of the relative size of output as more of factor X was added to the constant amount of factor Y. Concentrating our attention on the pins inserted into this cross-cut of the isoquant field, we observe that the figure that would evolve when the pins were folded back to lie flat on the plane would resemble curve TP_x in Figure 4.2(A), where we measure total output (Q) vertically and quantities of factor X horizontally. The height of the total-product curve (TP_x) would be zero until at least some minimum amount of X (say, OS), was combined with the fixed Y; no isoquants—not even the portions outside the ridge

---

[3] Another concept of "diminishing returns" assumes that factor Y decreases as X increases, or vice versa. Essentially, it amounts to taking a cross-cut of the production function along a path such as that normally traced by the factor-cost lines.

lines—would cross this segment of the chart field. TP_x would rise and reach its maximum at that quantity of X located at the ridge line OB for the constant amount of factor Y; it would thereafter taper off as further amounts of factor X (amounts of X outside the ridge line B), were employed.

On the same field we can draw an MP_x curve showing the marginal physical product of X (the additions to total output made by a further unit of X) while Y was constant. Symbolically,

$$MP_n = TP_n - TP_{n-1} = \Delta Q/\Delta X \tag{4.3}$$

where $_n$ now refers to the amount used of factor X.

Likewise, an AP_x or average physical-product curve can be sketched, where

$$AP_n = (TP_n/X_n) \tag{4.4}$$

with $_n$ being the number of units of factor X employed.

A Tabular Statement

To ascertain the MP_x and AP_x values, we would thus have to know, as our basic data, the relations between the amount of the variable factor hired and total output.[4] Given this information, MP_x and AP_x follow immediately. The first four columns of Table 4.2 contain an arithmetical statement of these relations.

TABLE 4.2—OUTPUT FROM 10 ACRES OF LAND WITH VARYING AMOUNTS OF LABOR

Number of Men (X)	Total Product (TP_x)	Average Product (AP_x)	Marginal Product (MP_x)	Acres Culti-vated per Man	Total Acre-age in Excess of or Below 1 Acre Tilled per Man	Total Product with 1 Acre Tilled per Man	Marginal Product of Total Excess or Deficient Acreage (MP_y)
7	66	9.4	...	$1\frac{3}{7}$	$7 \cdot \frac{3}{7} = 3$	70	-4
8	79	9.8	13	$1\frac{1}{4}$	$8 \cdot \frac{1}{4} = 2$	80	-1
9	90	10.0	11	$1\frac{1}{9}$	$9 \cdot \frac{1}{9} = 1$	90	0
10	100	10.0	10	1	$1 \cdot 0 = 0$	100	0
11	109	9.9	9	$1\frac{0}{11}$	$11 \cdot \frac{1}{11} = 1$	110	$+1$
12	116	9.6	7	$1\frac{0}{12}$	$12 \cdot \frac{2}{12} = 2$	120	$+4$

Geometrical Aspects

Geometrically, each MP_x value can be found by drawing a tangent to the TP_x curve at the particular amount of factor X in which we are

[4] For the production function $Q = Q(X, Y, Z \ldots)$, the marginal product of X is given by $\partial Q/\partial X$ and average product, Q/X.

interested; the slope of the tangent would denote the MP_x, since in this case the tangent measures the rise in output with an increment in the use of factor X. When the tangents are rising, the MP_x will be rising. At the amount of factor-use at which the gradient of the tangent is steepest, MP_x will be a maximum. In terms of the isoquants, when MP_x is rising and the tangents to TP_x are increasing, as illustrated in Figure 4.2(b), the isoquants will be closely bunched, because a smaller ΔX is required to expand output by 1 unit. As MP_x falls, the isoquants of successive outputs become farther apart.

AP_x can also be deduced geometrically by directing a vector from O to any point on TP_x in which we are interested; by thus dropping a perpendicular from TP_x to OX, and dividing the vertical TP_x amount by the horizontal OX quantity, we obtain AP_x. Merely by noting whether the gradient of the vector is rising or falling at successive TP_x points, we can determine whether AP_x is rising or falling as the amount of variable-factor use increases. When the vector from O is just tangent to TP_x, as in Figure 4.2(c), then $AP_x = MP_x$. At this point, AP_x is a maximum, for AP_x will rise only when $MP_x > AP_x$ and will fall when $MP_x < AP_x$. When the two are equal, AP_x is neither rising nor falling, suggesting that we must be at the peak of the AP_x curve.

Relations Between Total, Average, and Marginal Products

All three curves, appropriately lettered, are shown in Figure 4.2(A). At ON of X, when AP_x is at a maximum and equal to MP_x, it can be proved that we are at the OA ridge line in terms of the isoquant field: here the marginal product of the fixed factor Y is zero, operating neither to increase nor to decrease output. As AP_x is rising to the left of $AP_x = MP_x$, and assuming that factor Y (though fixed) is divisible, the marginal product of the fixed factor, MP_y, must be negative when less than ON of X is used with the fixed Y.

To indicate the proof by means of an illustration, let us examine Table 4.2, which contains some of the relations in the neighborhood of the maximum value of AP_x. Suppose that AP_x is at a maximum of 10 units of output when 10 men are used to farm the fixed acreage of 10 acres; each man thus farms 1 acre. Suppose, also, that when only 9 men are used, $AP_x = 10$, just as before; *thus, when each man farms 1⅑ acres, the total output is the same as it would be if each of the 9 men concentrated on working 1 acre each, allowing 1 acre to lie fallow. MP_y*, or the additional ⅑ acre of land beyond 1 acre per man—or a total of 1 acre of the 10 acres in our table—would have a zero marginal product.

If more than 1⅑ acres of land were cultivated per person, as 1¼ acres in our table, the excess land over 1⅑ acres used by each individual would *decrease* output by 1 unit: the marginal product of land at this stage would thus be *negative*.

On the other hand, when 11 men work the land, AP_x falls off again to 9.9—this is the other side of the AP_x maximum on the bell-shaped curve. Here, with each man tilling less than 1 acre each, average output is reduced: apparently MP_y is positive and total output could be expanded if each man had a little more land to cultivate. A rising AP_x, therefore, denotes a negative MP_y, while a falling AP_x implies a positive MP_y. When AP_x is at a maximum so that $AP_x = MP_x$, and MP_x is falling so that subsequently it lies below AP_x, MP_y is zero, neither positive nor negative. This, we know, is at the OA ridge line.

It follows that, if factor X were not available in an amount sufficient to render AP_x a maximum, it would be most sensible to utilize, with each unit of X, that amount of Y which would accompany X when AP_x is a maximum—1 acre, in our illustration. Allowing the rest of factor Y to remain idle would eliminate the negative marginal productivity of factor Y and augment total output.[5]

Ultimately, MP_x will fall to zero and TP_x will reach its peak; since MP_x is zero, TP_x fails to rise or fall, which implies that we are at the top of TP_x. At this point, AP_y (the average product of the fixed factor) will be at a maximum, because AP_y, just as AP_x, is equivalent to TP_x/Y_n, where Y represents the amount of the fixed factor Y. AP_y will thus reach its maximum when TP_x is a maximum, so long as Y is fixed. MP_y must thus equal AP_y here, and thereafter MP_y must fall. This implies, then, that as we are to the right of the lower ridge line in the constant-product field, the marginal product of Y is also falling while MP_x is negative.

In Figure 4.2(A), TP_x is at a maximum for OR of factor X. In terms of the isoquant field, this must be at the OB ridge line, for there $MP_x = O$. Thereafter, X is a redundant factor: additional X without additional Y would *diminish* total output.

Productivity Phases

Analytically, the TP_x curve could be divided into three regions: (1) A FIRST PHASE, ranging leftward to ON of factor X. From OS onward, MP_x is positive, MP_y is negative, and TP_x, AP_x, and AP_y are rising. (2) A SECOND PHASE, ranging from ON to OR of factor X. Both MP_x and MP_y are positive in this region, but AP_x is falling from its maximum and AP_y is rising to its maximum, with TP_x reaching its peak at OR. (3) A FINAL

---

[5] This presumes, of course, that factor Y, though fixed, is divisible. If Y is not divisible, then all of it must be used. Nevertheless, as long as AP_x is less than a maximum, we may infer that the same forces are at work affecting productivity as when Y is indivisible. It is to be noted that this entire statement of the change in output runs in terms of changing factor proportions and is limited to a production function which is homogeneous of the first degree. Emphasis on the scale of operations is reserved for the following section.

PHASE, beginning at OR where MP_x is zero and thereafter passing through negative values. TP_x starts its descent at this stage and AP_x continues its fall, becoming zero when TP_x is zero. AP_y also reaches its maximum at OR but thereafter falls.

The only area, therefore, in which both factors have a positive marginal product is in the second phase, between ON and OR of factor X, given the fixed amount of factor Y. Neither AP_x nor AP_y is a maximum within these bounds of X use.

Areas of Factor Utilization

We might ponder over Figure 4.2(A) for its intimations on the ultimate selection and hire of factors, even though for the final answer to this query we shall need information not only on the marginal productivity of factors but also on factor prices and product prices.

Consider, first, a simple case in which P_x, the price of factor X, is zero. Manifestly, with the fixed amount of Y, not more than OR of X will be employed. Analogously, given the market-factor prices, so long as Y is hired in definite amount, not less than ON of X will be engaged to work alongside the given amount of Y. For, with less than ON of X, MP_y is negative, becoming zero at ON; hiring less Y would be more prudent. On these considerations, the only area of rational-factor utilization must be in the second phase of Figure 4.2(A), where MP_x and MP_y (where Y is also envisaged as a variable factor on the assumption that X this time is held constant) are both positive and decreasing. Both must then be used to a stage of "diminishing returns," for otherwise there is a negative MP for some factor. It is to be observed that, in this region of rational-factor hire, $AP_x > MP_x$ and $AP_y > MP_y$. Factor choice is thus restricted to the area between the ridge lines. The exact selection will hinge, as stated, not only on factor productivity but also on factor prices and product prices.

A General Observation on Diminishing Returns

Leaving this examination of a production function for the output of a particular firm, let us consider why for a widely produced agricultural commodity—wheat, say—diminishing marginal and average products must prevail.

Suppose, say, that wheat—and all agricultural produce—could be produced under conditions of increasing average products. In general, this would suggest that, to raise standards of living and per capita output, population should be increased: the more labor, the more output per capita! Immigration on a vast scale, thus, would always raise living standards. Each country would cry: "Send us more people!"

At another plane of discussion it would also portend—if average products were rising—that land would be superabundant. Instead of seeking more land, each farmer would be better advised to get rid of acreage. By a *reductio ad absurdum* it could be demonstrated that all the wheat of the world could then be produced efficiently in a flower pot—or in a grain of earth!

A Nonhomogeneous Production Function

The production function hitherto examined, as in Figure 4.2(A), was homogeneous: output would be zero unless factor X, the variable factor, was at least OS in amount.

Suppose that output was positive even if X was zero. The TP_x curve would then originate on OY, as in Figure 4.2(d). Average product (of X) would fall continuously, with MP_x descending at a faster pace.

Questions

1. "Rather than speak of a law of diminishing, constant, and increasing returns, we speak of a law of variable proportions." On what semantic grounds would you prefer the latter terminology?
2. Draw some total-product curves that rise continuously, at both increasing and decreasing paces, as factor X is increased, rather than one which turns down, as in Figure 4.2(A). What happens to the marginal- and average-product curves? What would be the economic meaning of these cases? Justify—or criticize—the general shape of the curve used in the text.
3. Can you detect a slight difference in the sense in which marginal and average products are used for factor Y as against X in the discussion surrounding Table 4.2? Anything "wrong" in this usage?
4. Show why factor use must settle in the NR range on Figure 4.2(A) by continually eliminating greater amounts of factor X.
5. Through the world, and over much of its economic activity, would you argue that diminishing returns does or does not prevail? Elaborate.
6. Given:

$$Q = \frac{x^2 + y^2}{x + y}$$

draw the general shape of the production function, with Y constant at 10. Draw the AP and the general shape of MP. How does this TP curve differ from Figure 4.2(A)? What is your reaction to the portion of TP to the left of $X = 10$? How about the function $Q = 3X + 4Y$? (For illustrations of linear and homogeneous production functions, see R. G. D. Allen, *Mathematical Analysis for Economists,* pp. 284–289 and 315–322.)

RETURNS TO SCALE

Rather than vary one factor and hold others rigid in amount, as in the law of variable proportions, we can consider the changes in the physical productivity of factors as their combined use is expanded and output increased. This study is generally catalogued under the heading of the laws of "returns to scale."

Constant Returns to Scale

Suppose that output can be changed only by varying all factor quantities in exactly the same proportion—that is, increasing all of them by 50 per cent or doubling or trebling them, etc. Under these conditions, with a fixed proportionate variation in all factors, the proportionate increment in total output ought always to be the same as that of factor-use.[6] That is, a 10 per cent increase in all factors ought to increase output by precisely 10 per cent.

With fixed and indivisible factors present, however, constant physical returns to scale in this sense are generally unobtainable. Holding the amount of certain factors constant, by increasing the variable agents by, say, 10 per cent, will not ensure an equivalent relative increase in output; the movement may, instead, be in greater or less proportion than the alteration in the amount of the variable factors.

The Elasticity of Productivity

The ratio of the proportionate change in output to a proportionate change in variable factors can be measured by the *elasticity of productivity*. Symbolically,

$$E_p = \frac{\Delta Q/Q}{\Delta X/X} = \frac{X\Delta Q}{Q\Delta X} \gtreqless 1 \tag{4.5}$$

where Q represents output and X the initial amounts of variable factors. ΔQ is the increase in output and ΔX is the absolute amount of equiproportionate increase in variable factors.[7] When a 1 per cent change in output accompanies a 1 per cent change in variable factors, so that constant returns to scale are indicated (implying normally the unimportance of fixed factors), the measure equals unity. With $E_p < 1$, there are decreasing returns to scale; returns to scale are increasing when $E_p > 1$. If E_p always exceeded unity, production would be depicted as always taking place in a stage of rising marginal products.

Aligning the concept to the isoquant field, straight lines emanating from O would denote that the variable factors X and Y are always added in a fixed ratio; thus, if $10X$ and $10Y$ were initially employed, $1X$ would be added for each $1Y$ as output expanded. In Figure 4.3, line OG assumes that the factors are varied in a $1/1$ ratio; according to the figure, the

[6] This implies a linear and homogeneous production function.
[7] Writing $E_p = (\Delta Q/\Delta X)/(Q/X)$, note that, in the one factor case E_p depends on the ratio of marginal to average product.

doubling of factors, from $5X$ and $5Y$ to $10X$ and $10Y$, results in a 100 per cent rise in output, from 30 to 60. Along OB, however, factors are employed in a $10Y/4X$ ratio; doubling factors from the initial amount raises output from 30 to 70. On OH, the ratio is $3Y/10X$; doubling factors raises output to only 40 units from the previous 30.

The value of E_p is thus different in each case. Apparently, when the expansion path follows a line of equiproportional factor variation for some length, the elasticity of productivity can measure the composite factor productivity over this range of output. Whatever the production

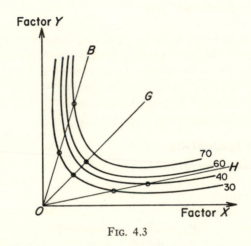

FIG. 4.3

function, variations in E_p reflect the changing proximity of the constant-product curves; when $E_p > 1$, the constant-product curves are bunched closely together, while, as E_p approaches zero, the constant-product curves tend to be widely separated in the chart field.

We recall that factor-use follows the expansion path (which is generally curved) as output increases. If factor prices are constant, the ratio of relative marginal products of the different factors will also be constant; this is the condition of minimum cost. If we are in a sector of the isoquant field in which $E_p > 1$, all marginal products will be rising: the fact that expansion occurs by a disproportionate increase in some factors merely attests to a rise in their marginal products at a faster pace than that of other factors.

If $E_p < 1$, all marginal products are likely to be falling, with the substitution favoring those factors whose marginal products fall more gradually. The point that we shall need to comprehend shortly is that, even though the ratio of marginal products to factor prices is the same for all factors at a *given* output level, this ratio, written as J, will alter with the output volume. If it rises, increasing marginal products are the rule; if it falls, decreasing marginal products are the rule. Thus, at each output level,

$$\frac{MP_x}{P_x} = \frac{MP_y}{P_y} = \frac{MP_z}{P_z} = J \tag{4.6}$$

At 100 units of output these ratios are, say,

$$\frac{10}{\$1.00} = \frac{30}{\$3.00} = \frac{75}{\$7.50} = J = \frac{10}{1} \tag{4.7}$$

At 130 units of output they may be

$$\frac{8}{\$1.00} = \frac{24}{\$3.00} = \frac{60}{\$7.50} = J = \frac{8}{1} \tag{4.8}$$

The marginal productivity ratio J has thus fallen from 10/1 to 8/1 as output has risen. Movements in E_p shed some light on changes in J.

Proportionality and Size in Returns to Scale

Returns to scale, it was averred, would always be constant if *all* factors were varied proportionately; the E_p was greater or less than unity only if some fixed factors were present that could not be augmented in enlarging output. Diminishing and increasing returns to scale have thus been ascribed *to a lack of proportionality among factors as output varies.*

This view of productivity phenomena has been contested on the ground that, if all factors were diminished to one tenth of their totals, output would be likely to fall off by more than 90 per cent because of the diminished opportunities for specialization and division of labor that are open to the reduced-factor group. Essentially, then, even if factors were fully divisible, the methods of production, the activities of entrepreneurial and supervisory personnel, and the arrangement of the work flow are not divisible. Operating alongside the influence of factor proportionality on output, there are thus laws of *size*. As factor-use grows, even though all factors are expanded proportionately, there will be a more than proportionate output expansion as the more numerous opportunities for the division of labor are exploited. Ultimately, since tasks can be subdivided too finely so that time is lost in waiting for the completion of other processes and tasks, the efficiencies of size will be reversed, with operating economies yielding to diseconomies. A "law of size" is thus alleged to be on a parity with the "law of factor proportions" in determining the changes in E_p.

Questions

1. How useful is the E_p measure likely to be in explaining resource use by the firm in expanding output by 10 per cent or more?

2. Draw a constant-product map and give numerical values to the successive curves when $E_p > 1$. Supposing that $E_p = 3$, draw the appropriate contours; if $E_p = 5$; if it equals ½.
3. Argue the definitional problems and the *a priori* validity of a law of size as distinct from that of proportionality. How do you interpret the remark of a famous economist—that you can duplicate any factory in Paris, but there is only one Paris—as an argument against the proportionality thesis and $E_p = 1$?

FACTOR PRODUCTIVITY AND COSTS

The cost curves related output quantities to cost outlays. The productivity studies of the law of variable proportions and the returns to scale stressed changes in the productivity of factors as output grew. It is imperative that these separate analyses of factor productivity and cost movements be bridged and their interdependence underscored. Actually, if we can extract the forces that determine MC, we have effectively explained the course of TC, TVC, AC, and AVC—for movements in marginal costs will account for their changes.

Marginal Cost with One Variable Factor

Starting with the simplest case in which several factors are fixed and one is variable, suppose that, to increase output, only extra labor is required. Writing W for the wage rate per laborer, ΔL for the amount of labor necessary to increase output by 1 unit, and MP_L for the marginal product of a given quantity of labor, then marginal costs are

$$MC = W\Delta L \tag{4.9}$$

But

$$MP_L \cdot \Delta L = 1 \tag{4.10}$$

and therefore

$$MC = \frac{W}{MP_L} \tag{4.11}$$

Thus, if the wage rate is constant, marginal costs will decline whenever marginal products rise and will rise whenever marginal products fall. If the marginal product of an additional laborer is 7 units of output, so that one man has to work one seventh of the ordinary work week to add 1 unit to total output, and the weekly wage is $70, then the marginal cost is $10. If the marginal product falls to 5, the MC will go up to $14. Cost movements thus reflect the variations in marginal products.

A similar relation can be elicited for AVC. Writing L for the total amount of the variable factor hired, with W the wage rate and AP_L the average product of labor, with Q_n denoting the amount of output, we have

$$AVC_n = \frac{TVC_n}{Q_n} = \frac{W \cdot L}{Q_n} \tag{4.12}$$

But

$$Q_n = AP_L \cdot L \tag{4.13}$$

therefore

$$AVC_n = \frac{W}{AP_L} \tag{4.14}$$

When the average product of labor falls because of diminishing (average and marginal) productivity, AVC will rise.[8] It is a simple matter to deduce (from [4.11] and [4.14]) that, at the output at which $MP_L = AP_L$, at ON amount of factor hire in Figure 4.2(A), $AVC = MC$.

Marginal Costs with Several Variable Factors

When there are n variable factors, the proof that diminishing productivity means higher marginal costs is slightly more intricate. By simple manipulations it is shown in the footnote that[9]:

$$MC = \frac{1}{J} = \frac{P}{MP} \tag{4.19}$$

P/MP in (4.19) refers to the common ratio of factor prices to marginal products. Hence, as factor productivity falls, or the ratio of marginal

[8] Implicit in this innocuous equation is a complete theory of the price level. See my *A General Theory of the Price Level* (1959).

[9] Assuming three variable factors—X, Y, Z—with their increase being ΔX, ΔY, and ΔZ, and their prices P_x, P_y, P_z, then

$$MC = P_x \Delta X + P_y \Delta Y + P_z \Delta Z \tag{4.15}$$

But

$$\Delta X = \frac{n}{MP_x}, \quad \Delta Y = \frac{r}{MP_y}, \quad \text{and} \quad \Delta Z = \frac{s}{MP_z} \tag{4.16}$$

where n, r, and s are the fractions of the unit of output for which the respective increments in each productive factor are responsible.

Therefore,

$$MC = \frac{nP_x}{MP_x} + \frac{rP_y}{MP_y} + \frac{sP_z}{MP_z} \tag{4.17}$$

But all the elements on the right contain the reciprocal of J, the condition of minimum cost for factor hire and output advances along the expansion path. Thus,

$$MC = \frac{n}{J} + \frac{r}{J} + \frac{s}{J} = \frac{n+r+s}{J} \tag{4.18}$$

Taking $n + r + s = 1$, as in the marginal-cost concept, then (4.19) follows directly.

products to factor prices decreases along the expansion path, marginal costs will rise. This formula is the generalization of the one variable-factor analysis, developed previously.

Factor Heterogeneity and Rising Factor Prices

If productive factors are all heterogeneous, so that we are debarred from drawing isoquants, isocosts, and the derived expansion path, then cost curves can still be used. If the firm is intent on producing each output at minimum cost, it would hire first those factors for which the J ratio was greatest. However, if several individuals of unequal skill are hired by the firm at the identical wage rate, with the most skilled persons employed first, the MC curve can be depicted as rising for what can also, in truth, be described as "diminishing returns." This cause of rising costs must be distinguished from rising costs under the assumptions of homogeneity among vast numbers of factors.

Finally, in all of our discussion, factor prices were presumed to be constant. If these should rise while marginal products are falling, we have dual causes of rising MC. If they rise while the MP's are growing, there is a neutralizing of the forces to some extent. If MP values rise while factor prices are falling, there are two strong elements leading to decreasing unit and marginal costs.

Questions

1. Do "diminishing-returns" phenomena refer only to some atypical agricultural illustrations or do they have meaning for manufacturing, or business firms generally?
2. Prove that a rise in productivity can lower unit costs. Also, that a rise in factor prices tends to raise unit costs and total costs.
3. When productive factors are heterogeneous from the entrepreneur's standpoint, but their price to him is the same, in what sense can "diminishing returns" be said to prevail?
4. Prove that, when AP is a maximum, then AVC is a minimum.

PLANNING CURVES

The cost curves of Figure 4.1 shown in this chapter were compounded from the phenomenon of the expansion path. All along, however, we assumed that the firm already had a stock of fixed factors and that the important questions were those concerning the amount of variable factors to be hired at each output level. There is still another problem to be explored: when the entrepreneurial group of the firm contemplates entry into a commodity field and plans to erect a plant and to equip it, it is faced with a choice in selecting not only the variable factors but also the fixed factors: at the planning stage all factors are variable. Analytically, it would be possible to describe the production function for each possible "layout"—as we may describe the fixed plant and its equipment. We can cut through some of the details, however, by examining merely the average and the marginal cost curves associated with each plant. Of course, in the final decision on the layout to be ordered, we would have to know not only the costs of production with each plant but also the nature of market demand and price phenomena.

Alternate Layouts

Suppose that there is but one type of plant that can be constructed—other plant varieties are unknown to architects and engineers. In Figure 4.4(A), the average cost of producing with this layout is shown by the curve AC_1, which falls to a minimum at 500 units of output. If, after appraising the profit potentialities and its access to funds, the firm planned to grow to a size large enough to accommodate an output of 2,000 units per annum, it would move to install four discrete replicas of the original operating plant. Hence, AC_2 is a twofold projection of AC_1

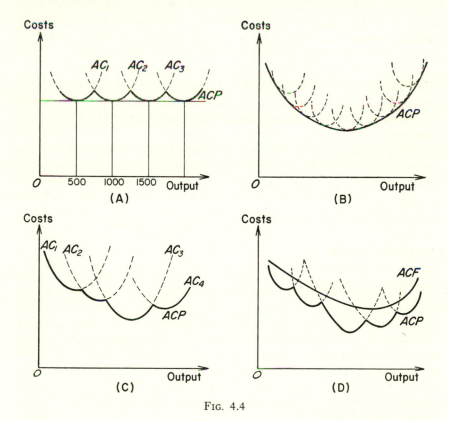

FIG. 4.4

and AC_3 is a threefold extension, etc., with each minimum at a multiple of 500 units of output.

In contrast, in Figure 4.4(B) each U-shaped AC curve denotes a different layout. In principle, we can surmise that there is an infinite variety of plants, each with minute technical gradations, so that *at each level of output* there is one particular plant and array of equipment which, if used, will minimize production costs. Although we have drawn only those curves that are associated with plants which minimize costs at some output level, innumerable other cost curves could be drawn higher in the chart field and assigned to plants that could be erected but that fail to obey this rule of minimizing costs at some output.

The Planning Curve

While each of the AC curves in Figure 4.4 is anchored to a particular layout or mass of equipment, by connecting the minimum AC points at each level of output, whatever their special cost-curve origin and the implied plant, we derive what is termed a *planning* curve (the heavy-lined ACP in Figure 4.4). The ACP curve, which is an envelope curve composed of minimal cost points, discloses the average costs of producing each level of output when the plant is still in the *blueprint* stage. If there are infinite varieties and gradations of plant, each point on the envelope curve can be abstracted from a different AC curve.[10]

When there are but few alternate types of layout, the envelope curve will merge with an AC curve for some range of output before gliding onto a subsequent AC curve; the transition will occur at the point of intersection of the more "capitalistic" structure (an AC curve farther to the right) with a less lavish capital plant. Thus, wherever $AC_1 < AC_2$, the envelope curve follows the former path; commencing at the output at which $AC_2 = AC_1$, the planning curve follows the locus of the latter. Drawing ACP in this way, it is possible to derive a curve which is *marginal* to ACP. If the planning curve is discontinuous, following sev-

---

[10] It is to be observed that the planning curve does not gather the minimum points from each AC curve, but only the minimum AC points for each output; there is a difference, for, by the time a minimum is reached on each particular AC, another layout may be less costly. The one minimum AC point definitely included on ACP is located on the AC curve whose lowest point lies closest to OX. As a tentative proof of the fact that the minimum point on each individual AC curve does not lie on ACP, we can consider that at each minimum AC point a tangent to AC would be horizontal. But if ACP were falling, the tangent to ACP at the same output would be falling; thus, the points of horizontal tangents would not lie on ACP. For an amusing anecdote on this point, see the footnote reference (p. 36) of Professor Jacob Viner on the controversy between himself and his draftsman on the drawing of ACP, in "Cost Curves and Supply Curves," *Zeitschrift für Nationalökonomie* (1932).

eral of the particular *AC* curves, the *MCP* curve will also be discontinuous, coinciding with the individual *MC* curves until the *ACP* curve itself switches onto a new *AC*. While the individual *MC* curves and the planning *MCP* curve compounded from them are not drawn in Figure 4.4, the principle of the *MCP* construction ought to be clear from previous analyses.

The planning curve *ACP*, to be sure, has a vitality only while the layout is still in the embryonic, conjectural, and planning stages. Once a particular layout has been constructed, the planning curve has only historical interest, a curiosity that is descriptive of the original cost potentialities facing the firm when it was pondering the several alternate production techniques. In Figure 4.4(C), if the firm decides to install the plant responsible for AC_2, then, after this plant is ready for operation, AC_2 alone will be the relevant cost path.

Economic Change and Output Flexibility

If market phenomena, in the sense of demand and price, were always constant so that the same output level always guaranteed maximum profits, then the firm would select that block of equipment which promised to minimize the unit costs for the particular amount of output. In view of market phenomena, however, it may be that output will fluctuate. In an unstable market, a firm may thus prefer a layout which is flexible enough so that, over any range of possible output, its average costs are below those experienced with any other mass of equipment. For example, in Figure 4.4(D), *ACP* is the planning curve molded from the U-shaped *AC* curves, several of which are drawn in the figure. *ACF*, however, is also an average-cost curve, attributable to a single plant which, although more costly for any particular quantum of output than any of the layouts embodied in *ACP*, is still so adaptable that, over a wide range of output, its *AC* is less costly than with any of the plants comprising *ACP*. If output is expected to be volatile, the plant implicit in *ACF* will prove best for maximizing profits.

The Bases of Output Flexibility

The causes of the output flexibility inherent in *ACF* are worth pondering. If the firm expected to produce only one output volume in successive periods of time, there would be one layout which would be more economical than any other. The plant would be so designed that it would be most efficient at this output level; and it would be relatively uneconomic for abrupt variations in production. Plant flexibility is largely the product of greater divisibility in the plant, achieved ordinarily by constructing numerous smaller but identical capital components, as smaller furnaces or duplicate wings of a factory, rather than a huge blast furnace or a gigantic conveyor-belt system that must be used as a unit or not at all. When equipment is divisible, a substantial fluctuation in output may be handled without a sharp change in marginal or average variable costs.

Output flexibility can also be secured by curtailing the volume of capital equipment employed per unit of output and substituting more variable factors for the fixed factors. Usually, by limiting the installation of equipment and favoring the use of variable factors, AC should become more nearly constant as output recedes or advances.

Questions

1. Would you regard the ACP curve of Figure 4.4(B) as most typical at the planning stage? Why or why not?
2. If you told an engineering firm that you contemplated producing men's shoes, how many blueprints for plants might they submit? In practice, how many might be proffered you if you gave them no further information? Why?
3. Prove that the ACP in Figure 4.4(B) is *not* tangent to the minimum AC points of any AC curve except that at the base of ACP.
4. Why might you prefer a flexible plant? How can you achieve flexibility? What does this suggest as to the possible economies if demand never altered? Would you use this as an argument *against* changes in tastes, or for laws to limit such shifts? Why?

THE ELASTICITY OF COSTS AND SUPPLY

Measures of the flexibility of output—that is, its responsiveness to cost and price phenomena—can be introduced at this point. Consider, first, the concept of the elasticity of total costs, written E_c.

The Elasticity of Costs

The elasticity of total costs is defined as the ratio of the relative change in total cost to a relative increase in output. Writing Q and ΔQ for the level of output and the increase in output, respectively, and C and ΔC for corresponding total cost (TC) ideas, then [11]

$$E_c = \frac{\dfrac{\Delta C}{C}}{\dfrac{\Delta Q}{Q}} = \frac{MC}{AC} \gtreqless 1 \qquad (4.20)$$

E_c is thus defined as the ratio of marginal costs to average costs. When $MC = AC$, $E_c = 1$. When $MC > AC$ and $E_c > 1$, we are to the right of the minimum AC point on our U-shaped AC curve.

[11] For $(\Delta C/\Delta Q) = MC$ and $(C/Q) = AC$. See Allen, *Mathematical Analysis for Economists*, pp. 260–262.

The Elasticity of Supply

As a companion measure to that of the elasticity of total costs, there is the older and more familiar notion of the elasticity of supply (E_o). If we define a supply curve as showing the quantities offered for sale at the different prices, and (in the normal case) as sloping upward to the right so that greater quantities are offered for sale at higher prices, then the elasticity of supply relates the proportionate increase in output to a relative change in price. The measure may exceed or be less than unity. Thus,

$$E_s = \frac{\Delta Q/Q}{\Delta P_x/P_x} = \frac{P_x \Delta Q}{Q \Delta P_x} \gtreqless 1 \qquad (4.21)$$

where Q denotes the quantity of output and P_x the market price, while the Δ's refer to increments of each. Whereas the elasticity of total costs relates the ratio of the proportionate increase in the total costs of the firm to the proportionate increase in output, the elasticity of supply relates the relative output change to a slight proportionate price change. Later, the supply curve will be linked to marginal-cost ideas.

When $E_s > 1$, the supply point is regarded as elastic; $E_s < 1$ supply is termed inelastic, denoting that only a slight increase in output takes place in response to the price change. When the market-supply curve becomes horizontal, because the MC curves of each firm are horizontal, supply will be perfectly elastic, with E_s assuming infinite values. If output is completely inflexible, so that the supply curve is perfectly vertical, the measure becomes zero.

For a simple diagrammatic test of the elasticity of supply, draw a tangent to the point in question, extending the tangent until it intersects an axis. If the tangent were to intersect the horizontal axis, supply would be inelasic, for this would imply that the tangent would intersect the vertical axis at a negative ordinate, as in Figure 4.5(B). If the tangent cuts a positive ordinate value, supply is elastic, as in Figure 4.5(A); if the tangent were to pass through O, supply would be of unit elasticity: a relative change in price would expand output in the same proportion.[12]

---

[12] The proof comes from:

$$E_s = \frac{MN}{OM} \div \frac{KS}{MR} = \frac{RK}{KS} \cdot \frac{MR}{OM} = \frac{PJ}{JR} \cdot \frac{MR}{PJ} = \frac{MR}{JR} \qquad (4.22)$$

for, by similar triangles,

$$\frac{RK}{KS} = \frac{PJ}{JR}$$

See R. F. Fowler, "The Diagrammatical Representations of Elasticity of Supply," *Economica* (1938).

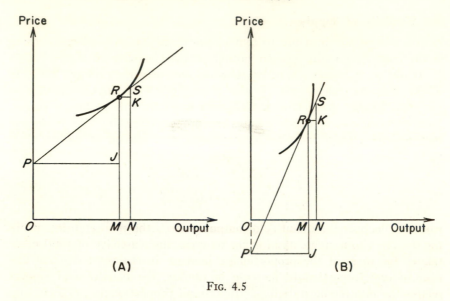

FIG. 4.5

When the measure takes a negative value, because of a supply curve that falls to the right, supply price is decreasing; supply is overwhelmingly elastic.

Questions

1. If $E_c = 1$ at every Q, draw *MC*, *AC*, *TC*, and *TFC*. At what E_c values is output expansion easiest? Would it be possible for business men, and accountants, to estimate the (arc) E_c?

2. Prove geometrically (a) that E_s differs at each point even for linear supply curves; (b) that in the upper reaches the E_s of linear curves originating on *OY* diminishes; (c) that for linear curves originating on *OX*, the E_s increases.

3. Using the simple linear supply curve $P = a + bQ$, prove the propositions in (2) analytically.

4. Draw a pencil of linear supply curves from a given *OY* point, as
   a. How would you describe the different curves in terms of an equation, such as in (3)?
   b. What is true of the supply elasticity of each curve at any given output?

5. Suppose that tangents to different supply curves are parallel. Which tangent would represent a higher supply elasticity? Draw a diagram.

Chapter 5

Consumer Behavior

This chapter is devoted to a study of certain aspects of the theory of consumer behavior. Actually, this analysis provides a logical beginning, for it is in response to demand forces that economic activity is undertaken; pedagogically, however, it has seemed wise to postpone the discussion until some familiarity with the method of economic analysis was secured so that minor stumbling blocks could be removed.

The critical problem is to demonstrate the properties of the equilibrium position on the assumption that a consumer of definite tastes and income, faced with externally determined prices, makes his purchase selection on the principle of maximizing his satisfaction. This is the maximizing problem of the household, the first of several maximizing problems that we shall meet.

Unfortunately, the theory of consumer behavior is not in a wholly settled state; there are several approaches vying for the center of the stage. As each has something to contribute, and as each illuminates the other, we shall outline the general content of the respective ideas. We commence (1) with utility and marginal-utility theory and then (2) focus on the indifference analysis at more length. Finally, we consider (3) the theory of revealed preference, and lastly (4) a numerical utility formulation.

UTILITY THEORY

The utility approach was developed during the great revolution in economic thought in the 1870's, in which demand ideas displaced cost ideas in the theory of value: the great creative minds involved in the movement were Jevons, Walras, and Menger, a cosmopolitan array of trailblazers from England, France, and Austria.[1]

[1] Later figures of note were Marshall, Clark, and Fisher.

The Basic Ideas

Basic building blocks in this utility approach are the concepts of total utility (U) and marginal utility (MU). Total utility refers to the total satisfaction derived from consuming a given quantity of a particular commodity. Total satisfaction will increase, at least to a point of satiety, as the amount possessed increases. Marginal utility refers to the *change* in total utility made by a further unit of the good. Diminishing marginal utility refers to the belief that the additions to total satisfaction must, after a minor interval at best, decrease.[2] The ideas, and the cardinal dimensions of utility theory, are revealed by the simple numerical illustration presented in Table 5.1.

TABLE 5.1—TOTAL AND MARGINAL UTILITY

No. of Units	Total Utility	Marginal Utility
0	0	0
1	35	35
2	65	30
3	90	25
4	105	15
5	115	10

Table 5.1 conforms to the principle of diminishing utility, for the marginal-utility column always falls. Presumably, with further units, total utility might even decrease and MU would be negative. As market conduct would never extend to this area, we can ignore this segment of the utility function. Finally, it should be underscored that **utility is conceived as being of a definite, quantitative (or cardinal) magnitude.**

Principle of Equimarginal Utilities

How does this approach explain the allocation of consumer outlay on the various goods available to the purchaser? For the case of n different commodities, the theory argues that consumers will want to arrange their consumption and purchase pattern until the following condition is satisfied:

$$\frac{MU_a}{P_a} = \frac{MU_b}{P_b} = \cdots \frac{MU_n}{P_n} \tag{5.1}$$

[2] Thus, $U = U(Q_x)$, where Q_x refers to the amount of the commodity. Also, $dU/dQ = MU$ and, for diminishing MU, $d^2U/dQ^2 < 0$.

That is to say, if, with 10 units of good A, the $MU_a = 45$ and its price is \$3, while for good B the $MU_b = 65$ when 8 units are bought at a price of \$5, so that $(MU_a/P_a) > (MU_b/P_b)$, total satisfaction will increase if more A and less B is bought. When the principle is satisfied the total utility is being maximized for the given outlay, under the stipulated prices and marginal-utility relations.

Another way of expressing principle (5.1) is to say that consumers will try to arrange their expenditure and purchase pattern in such a way that the marginal utility of each dollar (penny?) spent is exactly the same. If this condition is not satisfied, it is obviously possible to allocate outlay to better advantage.

The Derivation of the Demand Curve

Next, we proceed to the derivation of the demand curve.

Suppose we take one of the n-commodities—commodity m, say—as a *numeraire* or standard of value. Its unit price, therefore, is equal to unity: $P_m = 1$.[3] Further, suppose that its marginal utility is always constant; that is to say, if we drew up a schedule like Table 5.1, the marginal-utility values would always be the same: $MU_m = \overline{m}$. For simplicity, let us take $MU_m = 5$. Thus,

$$\overline{m} = \frac{MU_m}{P_m} = \frac{5}{1} = 5 \qquad (5.2)$$

We could then write (5.1) as

$$\frac{MU_a}{P_a} = \frac{MU_b}{P_b} = \cdots \frac{MU_{n-1}}{P_{n-1}} = \overline{m} \qquad (5.3)$$

With this relation, we are prepared to derive the demand curve for commodity A, say, whose utility values are given by Table 5.1. As $\overline{m} = 5$, then the following purchases of A will be made at the respective prices:

TABLE 5.2—DEMAND SCHEDULE FOR
COMMODITY A

P_a	Q_a
\$7	1
6	2
5	3
3	4
2	5

[3] For 1 unit of it exchanges for 1 unit of it by definition.

Thus, from equation (5.3) and the utility schedule shown in Table 5.1, we have been able to derive the demand curve for commodity A. What is required, then, are: (a) the utility function; (b) other prices; and (c) the constancy of the marginal utility of money.[4]

Substitutes and Complements

If MU_m were truly constant, an increase in income would be deflected solely to commodity M: the consumer would not devote any more of it to goods A, B, C, ..., etc. Marshall, however, assumed that, if income increased, MU_m would decrease—invoking the principle of diminishing marginal utility. On this basis, he was able to show that the quantity demanded of *all* goods would rise as MU_m fell in equation (5.2), involving the reduction in MU_a, MU_b, ..., etc., which could be accomplished by buying more of these goods.

So far, we have assumed that the utility from consuming good A is independent of that from goods B, C, ..., so that changes in the intake of A did not modify any of the other marginal utilities. If goods are substitutes, however, having more of one will *lower* the importance of the other: with more A the MU_b, MU_c, ..., will fall. For complements, having more of one will *increase* the MU of the other. Illustrations of substitutes are different kinds of cigarettes, cars, breads, shoes, radios, etc. Complements: an auto and gasoline, ham and eggs, bread and butter, etc.; briefly, those things that "go together."

Analytically, the increase in MU_b with a change in the amount of A can be positive or negative: that is, $(\Delta MU_b/\Delta Q_a) \lesseqqgtr O$.[5] If this relation is positive, the goods are complements; if negative, substitutes; if zero, the goods are independent. Manifestly, if the tastes are interrelated, as they will be in fact, then a change in the price of one can have demand effects extending beyond the particular commodity.

This is as far as we need go, for the moment, in developing the utility approach to demand theory.

Questions

1. Does utility refer to actual or estimated and anticipated satisfaction? Discuss. Suppose that there is some uncertainty about the utility to be attached to each quantity. How would this affect the theory?
2. Would or would not $U = 200Q - 3Q^2$ be an appropriate total-utility curve? What would MU look like? Plot the curves in rough fashion. Can *average* utility be calculated? (*Note: AU* is not introduced, for, in most applications, it is not regarded as relevant to conduct.)

[4] The constancy of MU_m is not absolutely necessary, but it simplifies the task. The assumption is due largely to Alfred Marshall.

[5] More precisely,

$$\frac{\partial^2 U}{\partial A \partial B} \gtreqless O$$

3. Do you regard the principles of equimarginal utility ratios as meaningful in terms of your own expenditure decisions? Explain.

INDIFFERENCE ANALYSIS

The indifference approach to consumer behavior, and demand theory, occupies us now.

The basic supposition of this approach is that an individual will be able to declare the goods he prefers if he is placed in a position to choose among them. Actually, his choice in the marketplace will be colored not only by his tastes but also by his income and by the market prices confronting him. These relations can be clarified by means of an indifference map.

The Individual's Indifference System

Imagine an individual, possessing definite quantities of several goods (denoted as A, B, C, ...), to be confronted with two other goods, X and Y. These may be specific commodities or broad classes of goods, as food and clothing. If he selects at random any one combination of the goods, there will be other combinations of the goods that will be regarded as neither better nor worse; they will be combinations of indifference or combinations of equal preference. Indifference curves illustrating these ideas are drawn in Figure 5.1(A).

Focusing our attention on the curves 1, 2, 3, ..., combinations of equal preference are found along each separate curve; thus, the individual will feel equally content with any of the quantities of X and Y depicted along the curve with index 1. Likewise, curve 2 represents other indifference combinations. On curve 2, each combination is preferred to any combination on curve 1; at P as compared to Q, for example, there is at least the same amount of Y plus more of X. And so it goes. Moving from curves of lower index to curves of higher index, we ascend to more highly preferred positions, because there is at least one commodity that is increased in amount while the other commodity is unchanged.

Tastes are thus defined independently of either income or prices. If income were large enough, the individual would select a combination of maximum gratification; more goods would then diminish well-being.[6] It should be observed that the separate indifference curves do not inter-

---

[6] This is at the summit of Pareto's "colline de plaisir," *Manuel d'Économie Politique*, ed. 2, p. 171, A. Bonnet, trans. If utility were measurable, we could employ a three-dimensional figure with heights above each indifference curve representing an actual quantity of satisfaction, rising according to some definite rate as we mounted the preference hill. If we are unable to measure utility, but can describe combinations of goods as embodying greater or lesser satisfaction, the three-dimensional representation fails. In the first view, utility is a cardinal quantity; in the second, it is an ordinal amount.

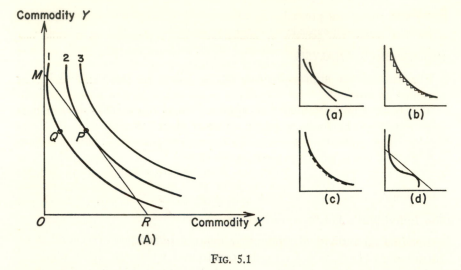

FIG. 5.1

sect; if they did, as in Figure 5.1(a), it would imply that certain combinations of the goods are equal simultaneously to combinations of both higher and lower preference: this is either nonsense or evidence of consumer irrationality.

Manifestly, the indifference system will have to be redrawn whenever tastes change. Likewise, the indifference curves pertain to two goods; they therefore presume the individual's stock of other goods to be constant. Changes in the quantities of consumer commodity holdings will entail a redrawing of the curve system.

The Major Characteristic of the Indifference System

A presumed scientific advantage of the indifference system is that the sole allusion to utility and satisfaction is in a relative sense; all that it is necessary to suppose is that an individual has preferences. The curve system crystallizes the onerousness of living on a human plane—the continual necessity of choosing, of selecting, of making decisions.[7] Rather than being two-dimensional, choice in the real world is n-dimensional, immune to any simple graphic representation. Normally, an individual will not know his preferences at consumption levels differing markedly from those to which he is accustomed. This unawareness would preclude the drawing of the full indifference map beyond the range of small changes, perhaps the usual changes in income; thereafter, the system of indifference curves will be either discontinuous or blank.[8]

[7] F. H. Knight, *The Ethics of Competition*, p. 88.

[8] Pareto mentions the absurdity of questioning a peasant on her preferences for diamonds if she becomes a millionaire. *Manuel d'Économie Politique*, p. 260.

Questions

1. Do you regard the concept of indifference—not preference—as a valid one, descriptive of real world phenomena? What evidence can you offer, one way or the other, in support or denial of the idea?
2. If indifference curves intersect, does this or does it not mean that people are "crazy" or "foolish"? What phenomena would you expect to observe if indifference curves were descriptive of behavior? Would this simplify or complicate the problem of producing to satisfy consumer desires? Explain.
3. If utility is assumed measurable, draw the three-dimensional utility surface. What restrictions would you place on the figure?
4. If individuals are able to choose only those combinations with which they are familiar, how does this restrict the indifference map? What implications does this have for the notion of habit as a dominant behavior factor? Would you accept this limitation on the indifference scheme or not?

THE MARGINAL RATE OF SUBSTITUTION

Let us see how the concept of marginal utility and the principle of diminishing (marginal) utility fit into the indifference analysis which eschews the older version of utility as an absolute quantity. Marginal utility referred to the increment in total utility made by the $(n + 1)$th unit to a stock of n units of a good. That is, if 10 units of a good afforded 250 units of satisfaction, and 11 units of the good afforded 260 units of satisfaction, the marginal utility of an eleventh unit was 10 units of satisfaction. All units being perfectly substitutable for one another, the loss of any one unit would lead to the same diminution in total utility.

The Relativity of Subjective Valuation

The objection to the notion of marginal utility is its suggestion of the measurability of utility. Confessing that we have no idea of the size or dimensions of a unit of utility and accepting preferences as the fundamental fact, it is thought best to drop utility terminology, for, unless extreme care is taken, absolutistic ideas and inferences on the measurability of utility will seep in.[9] As the propositions of analytical economics seldom, if ever, depend on the measurability of utility, it is wise to dispense with terminology that seems to imply it.[10] Only the relativity of subjective valuation needs to be stressed.

Marginal utility, in the older theory, was but a first step in the formulation of the principle of diminishing utility, according to which continuing increments to an individual's stock of goods yielded decreasing

---

[9] See J. R. Hicks and R. G. D. Allen, "A Reconsideration of the Theory of Value," *Economica* (1934), p. 56.

[10] See a path-breaking article by W. E. Johnson, "The Pure Theory of Utility Curves," *Economic Journal* (1913), p. 490.

additional amounts of satisfaction. Obviously, this "law" has no content if absolutistic ideas on utility are abandoned. The loss appears less disastrous when we recall that exceptions to it were always recognized: it was always qualified to exclude the "initial units" consumed over which rising marginal utility might be experienced. More significant is the fact that the principle itself was quite irrelevant, if not wrong, as a description of typical market phenomena. Individuals seldom cease their purchases of "a piece of pie," or of a radio, or of a suit of clothes, because of some patently diminished marginal satisfaction; instead, it is the reduced income available for other expenditures as a result of any particular purchase which constitutes the decisive factor. For most commodities, most people would hardly get beyond the rising portion of a marginal-utility curve; the illustration of consumers eating apples until they are sick is a crude explanation of the facts of market behavior. A person's income might have to be spent many times for such a surfeit to occur in his commodity purchases.

The MRS and Relative Marginal Utility

Rather than the consumption of a commodity until satiety, it is the pull of competing demands that limits the purchase of any particular good. However, for the analytical purposes which it served in explaining the equilibrium position, the principle of diminishing utility is replaced by that of a diminishing marginal rate of substitution among commodities.[11] The marginal rate of substitution (*MRS*) is defined as *the decrement in* Y *which will just compensate for an increment in* X, *leaving the individual in neither a better nor a worse position.* Thus, it refers to a movement along an indifference curve. The decreasing rate reflects the fact that, as X continues to be substituted for Y, the *MRS* ratio will be lowered: the unit increment in X will command an ever-smaller decrement in Y if the level of well-being is held constant.

Table 5.3 illustrates these relations. In column 1, combinations of equal preference are listed; each of the combinations of X and Y is located on an indifference curve similar to curve 1 in Figure 5.1. Commodity Y, say, represents neckties, and commodity X, shirts. Column 2 shows the individual's evaluations of the ability of a further quantity of X to replace an amount of Y without any diminution in well-being. Thus, when $27Y$ and $6X$ are at hand, the individual will be willing to release $5Y$ for $1X$. When $10Y$ and $16X$ are held, he will want $4X$ before surrendering only $1Y$. In column 3, we have the marginal rate of substitution: this is

[11] See J. R. Hicks, *Value and Capital*, ed. 1, p. 20. It is to be observed that, in his later work, Professor Hicks tends to revert to older ideas on cardinal utility. See his small book on *A Revision of Demand Theory*.

TABLE 5.3—INDIFFERENCE COMBINATIONS AND THE MARGINAL
RATE OF SUBSTITUTION

Indifference Combinations	Subjective Valuation of ΔX and ΔY	Marginal Rate of Substitution of X for $Y = (\Delta Y/\Delta X)$
$27Y, 6X$	$5Y = 1X$	5/1
$22Y, 7X$	$4Y = 1X$	4/1
$18Y, 8X$	$3Y = 1X$	3/1
$15Y, 9X$	$2Y = 1X$	2/1
$13Y, 10X$	$1Y = 1X$	1/1
$12Y, 11X$	$1Y = 2X$	1/2
$11Y, 13X$	$1Y = 3X$	1/3
$10Y, 16X$	$1Y = 4X$	1/4
$9Y, 20X$	. . .	. . .

the ratio derived by placing in the numerator the quantity of Y that would be sacrificed for a further increment of X, which becomes the denominator.

The MRS can thus be computed at each point along the indifference curve; as we move down the curve to the right, with the stock of Y becoming relatively depleted and X augmented, the MRS must fall. Drawing an indifference curve convex to the origin, as we have done, implies this very fact; namely, a decreasing capacity of X to replace Y.

Writing $-\Delta Y$ to represent the amount of Y that will be released for a further unit of X, symbolically ΔX, the MRS can be denoted by the ratio $-\Delta Y/\Delta X$. In Table 5.3 this ratio fell from 5/1 to 4/1, and ultimately, to 1/4. In the form $-\Delta Y/\Delta X$, the MRS can be discerned for what it is; namely, a rate of change along an indifference curve, measuring the descent downward on OY for an outward movement of 1 unit on OX. A "staircase" to exhibit this change is drawn in Figure 5.1(b). Mathematically, the movement in the MRS can be traced by drawing a tangent to each point on the indifference curve, for the value of the tangent is the measure of the slope or rate of change of the curve, and is equal exactly to $-\Delta Y/\Delta X$. The slope of the tangents, as shown in Figure 5.1(c), will vary from point to point on the indifference curve, or, more concretely, with changes in the relative quantities of X and Y on hand. The tangents will flatten out and lose their steepness as the stock of X increases and that of Y diminishes, signifying a lower $-\Delta Y/\Delta X$ ratio, and, thus, a decreasing MRS.

Basically, the notion of a decreasing MRS has its roots in the idea of diminishing marginal utility; the latter also fell as the quantities consumed increased, or rose as the quantities decreased. Thus, suppose that, when $27Y$ and $6X$ were possessed, the marginal utility of $1X$ (MU_x) amounted to 50 and of $1Y$ (MU_y) to 10 units of satisfaction. The ratio of marginal utilities would be

$$MU_x/MU_y = 50/10 \qquad (5.4)$$

so that our individual would be willing to surrender $5Y$ for $1X$. But this is simply an alternate statement of the MRS of X for Y: hence, we can write

$$MU_x/MU_y = MRS = -\Delta Y/\Delta X \qquad (5.5)$$

If the $5Y$ were actually traded for the $1X$, leaving $22Y$ and $7X$, the MU_x would fall, say to 44, in the light of the increase in X, and the MU_y would rise because of the decrease in Y, say to 11; the new ratio of marginal utilities would be 44/11. This is tantamount to an MRS of 4/1; the decline in the ratio of relative marginal utilities is thus equivalent to a decreasing MRS. If we always remembered to speak of *relative* marginal utility and always compared the utility of one good to another while maintaining our level of well-being constant, the central thought of the decreasing MRS could be conveyed just as pointedly and as precisely.

Questions

1. Prove:
   a. That marginal utility and marginal rate of substitution are not equivalent ideas.
   b. That diminishing utility and diminishing marginal rates of substitution are not equivalent ideas.
   c. From your own experience, which ideas do you regard as the more acceptable ones? Cite some illustrations from your own behavior.
2. What is the connection between the MRS and the slope of the indifference curve? On continuous curves, how many MRS relations can you find? Can you find the same MRS relations on all indifference curves? Explain.

THE PRICE LINE AND THE EQUILIBRIUM-PURCHASE COMBINATION

Let us suppose that an individual having a definite amount of money income (I) comes to the market to purchase commodities X and Y at market prices P_x and P_y. The problem is to determine the quantities of each commodity that he will purchase, on the principle that the consumer so allocates his income expenditure as to maximize his well-being.

The Price Line

We have already learned how to depict the tastes of the individual; these tastes are *subjective* facts. Purchases, however, will depend not only on his tastes, as reflected in the indifference curves, but also on his income and on the ruling prices. Let us represent schematically the *objective* facts of prices and income. Thereafter, we ought to be able to combine the subjective and objective phenomena and describe the forces determining the equilibrium-purchase intake of our individual.

Suppose that our consumer spent his full income I (equal, say, to $100) on commodity Y (selling, say, at a price of $1). To compute the maximum quantity of commodity Y that could be bought, we divide $I/P_y = (\$100/\$1) = 100$. On the indifference map of Figure 5.1, this Y quantity is represented by the distance OM. Similarly, when the consumer is directing all of his income to the purchase of X, the maximum purchase intake would be I/P_x, or amount OR, equal to 50 units if $P_x = \$2$. Since $P_x = 2P_y$, if the same distance represents 1 unit of a commodity along both OY and OX, then $OM/OR = 2$.

In view of the price relations, by foregoing the purchase of $2Y$ our individual can, in real terms, always acquire $1X$, signifying a value relationship or market rate of exchange of $2Y = 1X$. Thus, $P_x/P_y = -\Delta Y/\Delta X = 2/1$ where the latter ratio now signifies the constant-market rate of exchange between the two goods. Concretely, by withdrawing $2 from expenditure on Y, our consumer sacrifices $2Y$ and accumulates a sum of money with which to purchase $1X$. A diagonal such as RM in Figure 5.1, which contains all the *maximum* purchase combinations of X and Y open to the consumer, is termed a *price* line.[12]

The price line is also called a *budget* or *opportunity* line. The budget equation may be written: $P_xX + P_yY = I$. If prices are given, the consumer problem of choice and decision making is to select the quantities of X and Y which maximize well-being. For n-goods, where n-separate X's must be chosen, the budget equation is of the form:

$$P_1X_1 + P_2X_2 + P_3X_3 + \cdots + P_nX_n = I \qquad (5.6)$$

With income and prices constant, if less is spent on Y, in amount $P_y\Delta Y$, more can be expended on X, in sum $P_x\Delta X$. Thus,

$$P_x\Delta X = -P_y\Delta Y \qquad (5.7)$$

and

$$P_x/P_y = -\Delta Y/\Delta X \qquad (5.8)$$

The latter ratio is the rate of exchange of the two goods and denotes the slope of the price line which, in view of the constant prices, is constant.

---

[12] As with the MRS, the slope of the line RM can be measured at each point by the ratio of the vertical descent ΔY with the unit outward movement ΔX. As the ratio $-\Delta Y/\Delta X$ is constant in our illustration at $2/1$, the slope of the price line is invariant.

For the n-commodity case, with prices constant, the consumer problem is to choose the quantities of goods that yield maximum satisfaction. In contrast to the indifference curve which mirrors the subjective-taste phenomena, the price line portrays the external objective facts of prices and income and thus the alternative purchase possibilities. All combinations on and below the price line can be bought in the given income and price circumstances. The price line will be linear only when the ratio of market prices is constant.

The Equilibrium Position

After displaying the quantities of X and Y that *can* be purchased, the next step is to elicit the equilibrium position, consisting of the quantities that *will* be purchased. Generally, there will be one combination of the goods X and Y that can be bought which will be preferred to all other combinations.

In Figure 5.1, although the individual can buy any of the quantities located along the price line, the position of maximum well-being is at point P, where the price line RM is tangent to the indifference curve 2. At the point of tangency, the slope of the indifference curve equals the slope of the price line.[13] Hence, at the tangency position and for the full-income expenditure, $MRS = P_x/P_y$. In words, the rate at which individuals are willing to substitute goods in their purchase scheme in view of their tastes is brought into harmony with the market-price ratios or rates of exchange. This equilibrium property thus evolves out of a balancing by the individual of the subjective and objective facts of tastes, income, and prices.

To prove that the point of tangency between the price line and the indifference curve represents the most preferred purchase opportunity, we can imagine the consumer contemplating the expenditure of all his income on commodity Y. Thereafter, we visualize him as pondering whether it is desirable, in view of the prices, to forgo $2Y$ for the purchase of $1X$. Whenever the price line intersects the indifference curves, $P_x/P_y \gtreqless MRS$, signifying that the market-exchange rate differs from the preference ratio. When the $MRS > P_x/P_y$, the actual or tacit surrender of some Y (by a failure to buy it) will lift the individual onto a higher indifference level. If the MRS is 4/1, and if the exchange ratio is

---

[13] The slopes of the indifference curve and of the price line are both measured by $-\Delta Y/\Delta X$. But we must not make the mistake of assuming that their values are always the same; $\Delta Y/\Delta X$ is a mathematical measure used to evaluate all slopes. Referred to the price line, $\Delta Y/\Delta X = P_x/P_y$; referred to the indifference curve, it equals MRS. MRS equals P_x/P_y only when $\Delta Y/\Delta X$ is the same for each as at the point of tangency between an indifference curve and the price line. See p. 35, above.

but 2/1, the sacrifice of but $2Y$ will enable $1X$ to be bought, thus enabling well-being to be augmented by the mental equivalent of $2Y$; the individual will therefore hasten to purchase $1X$ and, implicitly, to divest himself of $2Y$.

Similarly, when $MRS < P_x/P_y$, as $1/1 < \$2/\$1$, the individual will observe that, by mentally forgoing the purchase of $1X$, he can be equally satisfied by acquiring $1Y$. But the market facts enable him to purchase $2Y$ when he cuts his X intake by 1 unit. Obviously, there is an incentive to buy more Y and elevate his level of well-being.

To conclude: when $MRS > P_x/P_y$, more X will be bought and less Y; when $MRS < P_x/P_y$, more Y will be acquired and less X. When $MRS = P_x/P_y$, the incentive to alter the purchase combination vanishes; here the subjective attitudes are consistent with the external price and income data. This is the equilibrium position; it represents the purchase combination of maximum satisfaction in the particular taste, price, and income circumstances. Until this position is realized, there will be a reshuffle in the expenditure plan.

Questions

1. a. Write the equation for the budget line. From it, prove that in the two commodity cases (a) its slope is negative and (b) it is equal to the ratio of prices.
   b. Write a budget equation for n-commodities. If, in the individual's purchase plan, some of the n-commodities were negative, how would you interpret these quantities?
   c. If market prices varied with purchases, with P_x rising (or falling), draw the budget line that conforms to these facts. Which of the respective lines best fits the facts, in your experience?
2. "The equilibrium position represents a balancing of subjective phenomena and objective facts." Explain.
3. What is meant by the "equilibrium position" in the analysis just concluded? Does equilibrium mean an absence of purchases or transactions? Explain.

INCOME AND PRICE VARIATIONS

After this exposition of the equilibrium position, we can relax some of our previous hypotheses. Continuing the assumption of constant tastes, and thus a rigid indifference map, let us suppose that income moves from I_1, to I_2, to I_3, $\ldots$, I_n. Prices are assumed to be constant while income varies.

The Income-Consumption Line

To represent constant tastes and prices with rising income, we need only to elevate the price-line parallel upward, as from RM to $R'M'$ in Figure 5.2. Another point of tangency ensues between the new price line and a higher indifference curve, as at L; for a further rise in income, point T would be the equilibrium point. Connecting the equilibrium points at each income level, as QLT in Figure 5.2, we describe an *income-consumption* (*I-C*) line. As the market prices are constant, and as in equilibrium at each income level the price ratio $P_x/P_y = MRS$, the income-consumption line relates points of identical MRS.

Normally, the income-consumption line will reveal that, as I rises with prices unchanged, the consumption of both (all) commodities will increase. The effect of the income change, from I to $(I + \Delta I)$ on the purchases of X and Y at the given prices, is termed the *income effect*.

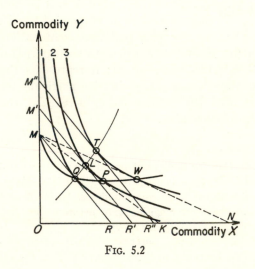

FIG. 5.2

The Price-Consumption Line and the Demand Curve

As another sample of the insight afforded by the indifference map in probing and elucidating certain problems in the theory of demand, assume that there is a change in P_x while I and P_y remain constant. This can be represented by a nonparallel shift in RM to KM, indicating a fall in P_x, since, at the constant level of I, more units of X and the same amount of Y can be purchased; the tapered slope of the price line indicates also that fewer Y need be offered in exchange for 1 unit of X, which signifies a lower P_x. Just as with income, the full plane can be covered with price lines emanating from M, showing the new price relations consequent upon the variation in P_x, with I and P_y constant. Connecting the points of tangency of each price line with the indifference curves, a *price-consumption* (*P-C*) path can be constructed, as $MQPW$ in Figure 5.2.

This opens up another important insight: *the price-consumption curve leads directly to the individual-demand curve,* for the quantities wanted of commodity X at each successive P_x can be read off the tangency points of the *P-C* curve. The premises of the demand curve, as remarked earlier, thus involved: (1) given tastes—the indifference map; (2) given income; (3) given prices of other goods, for which commodity Y is, in this case, representative.

Income and Substitution Effects

There is this to notice with respect to the price-consumption curve: a movement in P_x generates two effects—namely (1) an *income (I) effect*

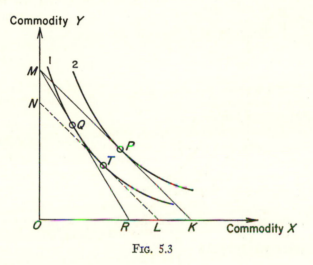

FIG. 5.3

corresponding to the change in the level of real income, and (2) *substitution (S) effect* through which the relatively high-priced commodity (Y, in this case) is replaced at the initial (or any) income level by the commodity that has fallen in price—commodity X in our illustration. Starting from a particular price line, as *RM* in Figure 5.2, the price-consumption line based on hypothetical decreases in P_x with P_y constant will, because of the S effect, lie below and to the right of an income-consumption line which presumes that the initial prices are constant and that only I varies.

Figure 5.3 demonstrates these relations. A fall in P_x is indicated by the movement in the price line *MR* to *MK*. The new equilibrium adjustment is at P, compared to the old position at Q. The movement from Q to P can be thought of as occurring in two stages: *first*, an S movement from Q to point T, which assumes that the new price relations *OM/OK* (equal to *ON/OL*) have been established but that the original real-income level is maintained, and *second*, an I effect, a movement from T on curve 1 to P on indifference curve 2, as a consequence of the rise in real income; the magnitude of the *I* effect is equivalent to an increase in money income, in amount $P_y \cdot MN$.[14]

At first sight, the purpose of separating the effects of a price fall in this way is perplexing and obscure. But we shall see that the two effects need not work in the same direction, and hence that their analytic separation is imperative. This will be elaborated shortly.

The *I-C* curve assumed prices constant and an income rise: the same results would follow for a proportionate price *fall,* money income unchanged. Similarly, *P-C* occurred with one price constant, the other varying, and money income constant. An intermediate pattern thus would ensue from disproportionate price changes, with money income fixed. All such variations can be worked out from the basic cases.

Questions

1. a. What *I-C* curves would you draw for an income elasticity $(E_I) \gtreqless 0$?
   b. Draw an *I-C* curve and show exactly the quantities involved in deriving the income elasticity of demand.
   c. What assumptions are involved in the E_I concept?
2. Draw a *P-C* curve and show exactly how you would derive an individual demand curve. What premises are involved for deriving the demand curve?
   a. What *P-C* curve would lead to an elastic arc elasticity of demand? inelastic? unity? How about perfect elasticity or inelasticity?
3. What alternative ways can you see of measuring *S*—and *I*—effects? What purpose can you see, at the present stage, in separating the two effects?

NEGATIVE INCOME EFFECTS

Usually, an increase in income with prices and tastes unchanged will increase the quantities purchased of both *X* and *Y*. To list all the possibilities: (1) the quantities purchased of both *X* and *Y* may increase; (2) the quantity of *X* (or *Y*) may increase with *Y* (or *X*) unchanged; (3) purchase of *X* may increase while the quantity demanded of *Y* decreases, or vice versa.

Inferior Goods

The third case admits the possibility that *Y* (or *X*) may be an *inferior* good, so that the *I* effect will be negative. An inferior good is one consumed at lower income levels which drops out of the purchase plan as

---

[14] Hicks usually measures the substitution effect along the new rather than the old indifference level (*Value and Capital,* p. 31). The sum of the effects, under either method of measuring them, must be the same: the new equilibrium position must culminate at *P*. But the income component and the substitutionary component will have slightly different values under each procedure. See J. Mosak, "On the Interpretation of the Fundamental Equation of the Theory of Value," *Studies in Mathematical Economics and Econometrics in Memory of Henry Schultz,* p. 70.

income rises and a shift to *superior* goods sets in. Bread, oleomargarine, cheap clothing, etc., can be cited as illustrations of inferior goods. The possibility of a negative I effect is important from a theoretical standpoint because it explains an interesting and abnormal demand situation in which the sales quantity *falls* despite a lower price for a good.

The various I effects can be shown graphically by following the course of diverse income-consumption curves. On a backward-bending income-consumption curve that curls up to the Y axis, X is the inferior good, less of it being bought as income rises.[15] On a fairly horizontal (vertical) curve, the demand for X alone (or Y alone) is increased with a rise in income; purchases of the other commodity are unaffected. With a normal I effect, the demand for both X and Y will be increased simultaneously.[16]

As the consumption of X is decreased when it is an inferior good, the implications in utility terms are that the marginal utilities are interdependent to the extent that an increment in Y so reduces MU_x that the former stock of X must be *reduced* to equate the MU_x/MU_y ratio to the price ratio after the income improvement.[17]

Negative Income Effects and a Price Fall

To appraise the importance of the income effect released by a price fall, let us develop the possibilities of a fall in P_x, with P_y unchanged,

[15] The appropriate indifference field can be superimposed by remembering that each point on the income-consumption line represents a point of tangency between an indifference curve and a price line for higher income at unchanged prices.

[16] The income elasticity of demand for X, measuring the proportionate increase in the purchase of X with a relative rise in income, can be written as

$$_IE_x = (\Delta X/X)(\Delta I/I) = I\Delta X/X\Delta I \gtreqless 0$$

being <0 if X is an inferior good. A similar measure can be formulated for Y.

[17] The interpretation of a negative I effect can be facilitated by considering it in relation to the MRS. Given the ruling prices, say $P_x/P_y = \$3/\$1$, for equilibrium the MRS must be equated to P_x/P_y at each income level. Normally, after a rise in I (equal to ΔI), the preservation of the equality will involve the purchase of more of both X and Y. But if X is the inferior good, less X will be bought despite ΔI. Implicitly, this suggests that, if there were a vertical upward movement on the indifference map, with more Y and an unchanged amount of X bought, or a horizontal rightward displacement with more X and the same Y purchased, the MRS at either of these positions would be less than 3/1—for it is only 3/1 with fewer units of X bought, and the law of decreasing MRS must hold at the new indifference level.

The marginal utilities cannot be *independent;* if they were, the restoration of the equilibrium-utility ratio would involve more of X and Y. But this would preclude the possibility of an inferior good. Thus, the law of a decreasing MRS involves more than merely the retention of the law of diminishing utility.

on the quantities wanted of X. Since a fall in P_x occasions an S effect, rotating a price line from M in Figure 5.3 will invariably increase the quantity wanted of X at the original indifference level. This much is certain: the increase in quantity is a consequence of drawing indifference curves convex to the origin.[18] But the I effect is not so definite; normally, it will be positive and will also work to expand the sales of X. If the income effect is abnormal and negative, with X an inferior good, there are the three possibilities—namely, that $S \lesseqgtr I$. Only when the I effect overshadows the S effect will the X purchases fall off. An illustration is provided in Figure 2.1(b) in Chapter 2.

As a practical matter, a negative I effect is unlikely to exceed the S effect except when the individual is spending a large part of his income on the commodity.[19] Then the savings on the price fall are so substantial and the prospect of consuming other superior substitutes is so bright that the individual's purchases of the particular good may decrease. But, usually, we can expect that the quantities wanted will increase as prices fall. For the complete market this is the more likely, because the decreased purchases by some consumers will be counterbalanced by the increased quantities wanted by others who are now able to include the good in their consumption plan as its price moves down. The "law of demand" will apply to all except strongly inferior goods.

Questions

1. a. Is the "inferior-good" category important or unimportant, in your view? (How about second-hand markets, for clothing, cars, furniture, etc.?)
   b. How would such goods be handled in a marginal-utility approach?
2. Prove conclusively that diminishing marginal utility would preclude the inferior-good concept. If so, is a diminishing MU the equivalent of a diminishing MRS? Explain.
3. If the negative-income effect is small, how important would the inferior-good concept be? What is your guess, then, on the magnitude of negative I effects compared to S effects?

[18] See the odd curves drawn in the lucid work by Ruby Turner Norris, *The Theory of Consumer's Demand*, Chapter II especially.
[19] As in Marshall's famous "Giffen case." *Principles of Economics*, ed. 8, p. 132.

Chapter 6

◊◊

Consumer Behavior—(Continued)

This chapter continues the analysis of consumer behavior, beginning with some further aspects of the indifference approach.

SUBSTITUTES AND COMPLEMENTS

At a constant level of real income in a two-commodity world, goods can only be substitutes for one another; an increase in the consumption of one commodity, with the indifference level unchanged, requires a decrease in the intake of the other. But when we introduce three or more commodities, it is possible for two of the goods to be *complementary* at the assumed income level and for their consumption to increase at the expense of other commodities.

Substitutes and Complements

Rather than symbolize the third commodity Z as merely a simple commodity, we might regard it as a sum of money representing a composite of all commodities; they may be lumped together so long as the relative prices of the commodities included are constant.[1] Viewing Z in this way, we can define Y as a substitute for X if the *MRS* of Z for 1 unit of Y decreases when X is increased by 1 unit and Z is decreased by the amount necessary to keep the level of well-being unchanged. Y can be declared complementary with X if the *MRS* of Z for 1 unit of Y increases as 1 unit of X is substituted for Z at the constant-indifference level.[2] Y, a substitute for X, may itself have other substitutes or complements. Commodities will thus be related to one another, either faintly or firmly, as substitutes or complements, or competing or completing goods in the full-preference system.

To elaborate, assume that X is substituted for Z at a constant indiffer-

---

[1] This device for handling commodity interrelations has been termed the "law of composition of goods." See O. Lange, *Price Flexibility and Employment*, p. 106.

[2] See Hicks, p. 44.

ence level when, say, $100X$, $100Y$, and $100Z$ are possessed, and when the MRS ratios, neglecting the negative signs, are: $\Delta Z/\Delta X = 6/1$ and $\Delta Z/\Delta Y = 4/1$. As X rises to $101X$ and Z falls to $94Z$, a fall in the MRS of Z to X from 6/1 to, say, 5/1 must occur. If $\Delta Z/\Delta Y$ also diminishes, from 4/1 to 3/1 despite the constancy in Y holdings, then X and Y are substitutes: additional Y, because of the additional X, becomes less important in the individual's desire schema.

In the contrary instance, when X is increased and the individual is prepared to sacrifice more Z than formerly to acquire a unit of Y—for example, to sacrifice Z for Y at the rate of 5/1 rather than 4/1—then X and Y are complements. Literally, Y is more essential after the expansion in X.

The definitions of commodity interrelations assume a given indifference level. Undoubtedly, the degree of substitution and complementarity is likely to alter with the income level. As an example, at low levels of income bread and cake are likely to be substitutes and, as income rises, they are more likely to be viewed as complementary items.

Price Interrelations

Substitutionary and complementary taste relations are likely to lead to the interdependence of prices. If there is a price fall for X, say, then the increased purchase of it will lower the relative importance of its various substitutes, decreasing their demand and tending to reduce their price. Complements will tend to be affected in opposite fashion: more automobiles on the road because of lower car prices will tend to raise gasoline prices. This is not to overlook the possibility, however, of a simultaneous increase in the demand for *all* complementary items, thus raising their individual prices. For those individuals whose tastes (or income) have not altered, however, price pressures for complementary items will tend to be neutralized with a price rise in the one setting up downward price reactions in the other.[3]

The Instability of the System

The availability of a substitute good tends to restrain a price rise, originating, say, in P_x, by causing a diversion in demand to substitutes and diffusing the rising-price forces in P_x over a wider area. The effect of numerous substitutes, therefore, is to render a particular market more stable than otherwise. But, for the economic system as a whole, a preponderance of substitute relations contains an omen of instability, since a price movement in one market will have ramifications, identical in

[3] As the definitions apply to a *given* indifference level, income effects of price changes are omitted. With the exception of inferior goods, these always tend to increase all demands and raise all prices, given a fall in the price of one good.

direction, in all the other markets comprising the price chain. Their calm will be destroyed and the entire system disrupted, however small the initial force. These disruptions can be limited, and checked perhaps, by highly elastic supply phenomena which can act as an effective shock absorber.

Questions

1. a. What practical difficulties can you find in applying the definitions of substitutes and complements? Are the categories "unreal" or "unimportant" ones?
   b. What is the connection between the definitions and the cross-elasticity of demand? What objection would you make to using the latter as a defining instrument?
   c. Cite about a dozen pairs of items that might move from a substitute to a complementary relation as income changes for the better.
2. As the number of individuals in the market alters, or relative costs of production change, what may happen to the price interrelations of substitutes or complements? How do these facts affect or limit the basic analysis?
3. How does the respective preponderance of substitutes or complements affect the stability of the price system?

THE ELASTICITY OF SUBSTITUTION

We consider now an elasticity measure of the substitution relations disclosed by indifference analysis.

The crucial importance of the *MRS* among factors, or among commodities for consumers, in determining the hire or purchase combination has been underscored. So far, we have not provided any measure of the *degree* of substitution between X and Y which is independent of units and uninfluenced by whether one commodity is stated in terms of tons and the other in ounces, or whether one factor is stated in terms of acres and the other in numbers of men.

If we write X and Y to represent the initial quantities of commodities or factors on hand, and $\Delta(X/Y)$ for the ratio of the changes in their amounts, with ΔMRS reflecting the change in the marginal rate of substitution as the quantities possessed varies, E_{ss} is formulated as follows:

$$E_{ss} = \frac{\Delta(X/Y)/(X/Y)}{\dfrac{\Delta MRS}{MRS}} \qquad (6.1)$$

In words, E_{ss} is equal to the relative change in the ratio of factors (or commodities) used, divided by the relative change in the marginal rate of substitution. The changes are measured along an indifference curve or isoquant. Let us examine the meaning of E_{ss} diagrammatically.

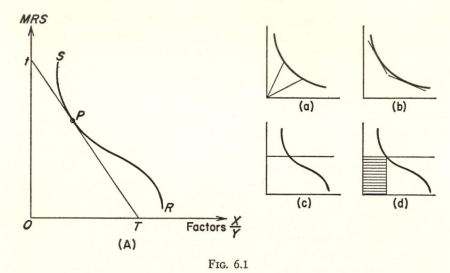

FIG. 6.1

Graphic Representation of E_{ss}

In Figure 6.1(A) we measure the *MRS* vertically; the *MRS* starts at zero and rises to infinite values. Along the *OX* axis, the ratio (X/Y) of factor (or commodity) *X* to factor *Y* can be plotted. This ratio also will begin at zero, for at the origin zero *X* will be associated with a large amount of *Y*. Choosing either an indifference curve or an isoquant as the source of our data, we can locate points in the chart field of Figure 6.1 by associating the *MRS* ratios to the respective X/Y ratios. In this way, a marginal rate of substitution curve, such as *SPR*, can be traced. The *SPR* curve will be extremely steep when a small variation in the ratio of goods or factors used causes a severe change in the *MRS*; it will be flat when the *MRS* scarcely changes despite a substantial dislodgement of the relative quantities of *X* and *Y*. In the former case, the indifference curve will tend to be parallel to either axis, whereas, when *SPR* is horizontal, the indifference curve will approximate the straight line typical of perfect substitutes.

The slope of a tangent drawn to any point on *SPR* is equal to

$$\Delta MRS/\Delta(X/Y) \tag{6.2}$$

Relating this change to the former values of *MRS* and X/Y at the point of tangency, we have the E_{ss}. Recalling the geometrical measure of the elasticity of demand, if we draw a tangent to any point of *SPR*, as at *P*, and extend it to cut the axes, then $E_{ss} = PT/Pt$.

When E_{ss} tends toward infinite values, *X* and *Y* are perfect substitutes. Conversely, when E_{ss} is zero, there is an utter lack of substitutability. These are the limits that E_{ss} can take. Thus, when ΔMRS is zero (as with perfect substitutes), we find that E_{ss} becomes very large; when ΔMRS is extremely large, then E_{ss} approaches zero.

Demand Elasticity and the Elasticity of Substitution

It is possible to associate E_d with both E_{ss} and the income effect elaborated earlier. If we write E_x for the elasticity of demand for X with respect to a change in income, and E_{ss} for the elasticity of substitution, with K_y the proportion of income spent on Y, for two commodities the elasticity of demand for X is

$$E_d = K_x E_x + K_y E_{ss}\text{[4]} \tag{6.3}$$

In terms of Figure 6.1, we measure the movement down one MRS curve and then allow for the rise in income.

Thus, where E_{ss} is zero, E_d will be greater, depending on the proportion of income spent on X and the magnitude of the income elasticity E_x. When E_{ss} is large, even if $K_x E_x$ is zero E_d will still be substantial. Although these separable components of E_d are hopelessly tangled in the final purchase decision, the equation does elucidate the underlying taste and income components that shape E_d.

One particularly interesting case drawn from the production sphere is that in which the production function is a linear and homogeneous one, such as $Q = AX^\alpha Y^\beta$, with $\alpha + \beta = 1$. In this, the $E_{ss} = 1$ at all points so that equation (6.3) is simplified: an SPR curve, as in Figure 6.1, will appear as a rectangular hyperbola. Such Cobb-Douglas functions, as they are called, have evoked much attention from economists in the past because they seem applicable to much of the evidence drawn from real-world facts.[5]

Questions

1. Draw two separate indifference curves, and from them, show how you would proceed to derive corresponding points for measuring the elasticity of substitution.
   a. Do the same for a vertical, a horizontal, and a right-angled indifference curve. What are the respective E_{ss} values? Why?
2. Draw a curve relevant for measuring the E_{ss} (as in Figure 6.1). At any point on it, what is the magnitude disclosed by the rectangular area under the curve?

---

[4] For three or more commodities, the formula is more complex; we can still employ the dodge of lumping all other commodities together as one good. See "A Reconsideration of the Theory of Value," *Economica* (1934), p. 202, and Allen, *Mathematical Analysis for Economists*, pp. 340–345.

[5] See Paul H. Douglas, "Are There Laws of Production?", *American Economic Review* (March 1948).

(That is, by $MRS \times X/Y$.) If the ratio of factor prices is equal to MRS, what, then, is the significance of this area?

   a. Under what assumptions, then, is this device useful to measure relative-factor incomes?

3. "The elasticity of demand is a compound result which combines outlay, income, and substitution effects in varying proportions." Elaborate.

COMMODITY DIMENSIONS

As a final topic under the indifference approach, we might consider the definition of a commodity, a term we have been using frequently. Its casual meaning is clear: items which in all external manifestations exhibit the same bundle of physical characteristics are identical commodities. Immediately, we are thrown against the venerable query of whether technical substitutes located in different places are, after all, perfect substitutes. Most of us would agree that they are not; that wheat in Chicago is not the equivalent of identical wheat in New York— an appeal to the market would dispel any doubts on this score. As consumers in the one place usually pay a price differing from that in the other market, apparently the items purchased are not identical. Since each purchase consists of a bundle of form and time-and-place utility, it has been customary to state that goods must, at a minimum, be defined with respect to these indices. Actually, what is ordinarily bought as a single product is instead a complex joint product, not only composed of elemental stuff available at a certain time and place, but also packaged in a definite way, associated with a particular type and volume of advertising, and sold on specific credit terms in a certain "toned" shop with some proviso as to delivery. Normally, a commodity contains at least these many facets.

If items of a commodity class had to be identical in all these dimensions, by definition we would probably preclude any prospect of perfect competition. Each seller would be offering a different product and each would be a "monopolist."[6] However intense the competition in any more fundamental sense, the world would be described as one of ubiquitous monopoly. This definition is thus too stringent; red tennis balls would be different commodities than white tennis balls even though consumers might be completely indifferent between the two.

This last remark furnishes a clue to a sounder basis of classification than an appeal to technical and institutional dissimilarities. Ultimately, consumers judge whether commodities are identical or not. Fully substitutable in all uses, from the standpoint of consumers, the goods are the same. After all, this is the reason why goods with the same technical attributes are commonly regarded as identical, and why, when separated

---

[6] As Mrs. Robinson has described it.

in space, they are viewed as different goods. Perfect substitutability is thus the criterion. In terms of $\dot{M}RS$ ratios, these would always be constant and, generally, equal to unity. The indifference curves would degenerate into straight lines, normally running, say, from $1X$ to $1Y$, $2X$ to $2Y$, etc. Price discrepancies between the goods would not be tolerated; as the elasticity of demand for any one seller, at the price charged by his competitors, would be infinite, a higher-priced seller would either have to meet the lower price of the competitor turning out the same good or else watch his sales fall to zero.[7]

Consumer Determination

Consumers, on this view, adjudge the degree of identity of goods and the interdependence of markets. Practically everything that is of interest to the economist in distinguishing among commodities resides in their valuations. When consumer valuations indicate less than full substitutability, we are dealing with different commodities. A major complication of this approach is that all consumers will seldom evaluate commodities identically; their indifference maps will rarely be exact replicas of one another. But, if MRS ratios between two (or several) goods are constant, and roughly the same for a goodly number of purchasers, there will be a high degree of demand elasticity among the separate commodities; when price ratios departed from the substitutionary ratios, a precipitate replacement of one good by the other would set in. In practice, a high degree of price sensitivity of a substantial body of users will denote the presence of an alternate, almost identical, product.

Questions

1. a. Cite some illustrations in which physically identical goods will not be perfect substitutes.
   b. Do the same for perfect substitutes despite physical nonidentity.
   c. Are business men buying raw materials, such as tomatoes for catsup or soup, interested in physical identity or not? How about consumers, in this respect?
2. Would or would not possible price discrepancies for physically identical goods ever be large? Discuss. How is the E_d related to this question?
3. Are goods likely to be viewed as perfect substitutes by some people and not by others, or are they not? How important would you think this class of phenomena to be? Give concrete illustrations, as far as possible.

[7] This holds true unless sales quantities are rationed by the lower-priced seller. The case of linear indifference curves running, say, from $2Y$ to $1X$, $4Y$ to $2X$, etc., would also yield perfectly elastic demand curves and would imply identical commodities; as an illustration, different-sized coals might provide heat in the constant ratio, say, 2/1. If the indifference curves indicate perfect substitutability in their central regions, but become perpendicular near the axes, the derivative-demand curves would be elastic over a good part of their range.

SUMMARY

The indifference-curve approach undoubtedly has illuminated certain facets of the theory of consumer demand. In concluding this survey, we might assess some of its key assumptions and ponder the stumbling blocks in the way of any theory of rational demand.

The indifference-curve technique assumes that the individual knows his preferences and that they are consistent, in the sense that if A is preferred to B, and B to C, then A is valued more highly than C. Ruled out, therefore, are cases of impulsive behavior that do not involve an estimate of preferences, and irrational (inconsistent) behavior. It would be vain to deny their occurrence, but little can be said of them on a general plane. Either we must grant that they are the less important manifestations or else forego the prospect of developing a theory of economic behavior to describe the market facts.

The stipulation of a decreasing MRS must be invoked for the same reason; an increasing MRS would imply that the consumer was willing to offer ever greater amounts of Y for X as his stock of the former decreased and the stock of the latter increased, with well-being unchanged; ultimately, consumers would be pictured as allocating their full outlay to but one commodity. This would constitute an evasion of the market facts, although it might 'have some bearing in the actions, say, of the drunkard. But we do class (and dismiss) such action as irrational. Likewise, if the indifference curves contained a concave kink, as in Figure 6.1(d), it could be shown that the tangency of the concave portion of the curve to the price line denoted a *minimum* rather than a maximum position of well-being. So long as we are prepared, on introspection or empirical investigation, to grant that, when consumers buy commodities selling for $2 and $1, they expect to derive twice the satisfaction from the former, then our concepts and the equilibrium solution hold firm.

More vulnerable to the structure is the posulate that tastes are unchanged. The entire indifference map is drawn on this basis and remains valid only if the preference relations are rigid. The definitions of substitutes and complements were themselves expressed as properties of a given taste structure. If tastes are ephemeral and volatile, subject to chronic and unpredictable flux, then the entire superstructure of the indifference analysis rests on shaky foundations. Systematic methods for dealing with the interrelations among tastes (and thus among markets) would have to be abandoned. Considering that the impact of knowledge and education in our world is very gradual, and acknowledging the weight of habit, perhaps the hypothesis of a given taste structure is close enough to the facts.

A technical disadvantage of the indifference curve lies in its inability to deal diagrammatically with more than two, or at most more than three, goods. Throughout the discourse the stock of other goods must be held constant, otherwise the preference ratios for the two goods under consideration will be upset. In effect, it must be assumed that there are but two goods available for purchase or that expenditure equilibrium has been established in other markets, between all pairs of goods and between goods and savings, and that the individual has ready for expenditure on the remaining two commodities an income sum that will, after allocation between the two commodities, assure him of maximum satisfaction. The importance of the stocks of goods on hand cannot be exaggerated in evaluating market behavior with respect to durable goods. For perishables its significance diminishes.

In the same vein, preference ratios will also be contingent on stocks held by other consumers. There are the two cases of taste interdependence: some goods are more highly desired when there is a widespread consumption of them. The "keeping up with the Joneses" phenomenon of goods in "emulation demand" would, to some extent, comprise one category. A less invidious instance is represented by those goods bought in conjunction with purchases by friends: the purchase of golf clubs becomes more important when friends take up the game, for example. The second case consists of goods that appeal to the snob as a vehicle for "conspicuous consumption," as Veblen called it, only when the price goes sufficiently high to prevent these items from being widely bought. In either event, indifference systems change with the possession of the goods by others; in the one case presumably because price has fallen and purchases have become more universal, and in the other case because prices have risen. Both situations are inimical to ordinary analysis; rather than taste phenomena being, along with cost phenomena, the ultimate explanation of *price* phenomena, it is the price phenomena that are causal in the formation of tastes. Our methods are unsatisfactory here. But their shortcomings are not a serious drawback if these situations do not comprise the major cases of the consumer market.[8]

Questions

1. Estimate the importance of (a) impulsive and (b) habitual behavior in economic life. Do both patterns affect economic analysis in the same way? Would you regard your own expenditure habits as falling primarily in these categories? Explain.
2. Can you think of any personal illustrations of irrational (inconsistent) behavior? Enumerate.

[8] Once the stocks held by others are stabilized, the indifference maps can be drawn and the technique brought into play. But if the external holdings are in continuous flux, the individual maps will themselves reflect this fact and become subject to constant revision.

3. From personal experience, how valid do you regard the hypothesis of: (a) constant tastes, (b) emulation demand, (c) "snob" demand, (d) interdependent preference phenomena.

The Theory of Revealed Preferences

A more recent approach to the formal theory of consumer behavior goes under the name of *revealed preferences*. Largely, this theory eschews any reference to utility and satisfaction, abandons the concept of indifference except as a very limiting case, and dispenses with the suppositions of continuous quantities embodied in the use of smooth indifference curves.[9]

This is the negative side detailing what is not in the theory: positively, the revealed-preference approach contains some "consistency" assumptions from which the fundamental theorems of demand theory can be deduced. Its axiomatic base may be stated as follows[10]:

1. A CONSISTENCY RELATION. If, with given income and prices, a combination of goods A (or ΣQ^a) are purchased rather than the combination B (or ΣQ^b), which is equally costly or less costly, the consumer must never be revealed to purchase B when A is less costly than B. In general, A must not be bought when it is higher priced than B, and B bought when it is higher priced than A.

Symbolically, if Q^a is bought when

$$\Sigma P^a Q^a \geqq \Sigma P^a Q^b \tag{6.4}$$

then, when

$$\Sigma P^b Q^b \geqq \Sigma P^b Q^a \tag{6.5}$$

combination Q^b is *not* to be purchased. If, under equation (6.5), Q^b is bought and, under (6.4), Q^a is purchased, inconsistency in choice is revealed, in a fundamental sense. (There is consistency, though, in the acquisition of the higher-priced basket! Snob behavior, when purchases move positively with price, is thus outside the domain of this theory, so that it is still a limited theory.)

2. A TRANSITIVITY RELATION. In the same way, if combinations of goods A, B, C, $\ldots$, Z are listed, and A is revealed preferred—chosen— rather than B, and B rather than C, $\ldots$, Y rather than Z, then Z must not be chosen in lieu of A. (Of course, this is also a consistency relation, but it goes farther in its inclusiveness.) If enough batches A, B, $\ldots$, Z

---

[9] The original statement, and much of the development of the theory, is due to Paul Samuelson, *Foundation of Economic Analysis* (1948).

[10] See Harvey Wagner, "The Case for 'Revealed Preference,'" *Review of Economic Studies* (June 1959).

were revealed, presumably a full preference field and, thus, an indifference map could be reconstructed.[11]

The analysis emanating from these axioms does not require that all income be fully utilized, nor does it require an expression of preference with respect to those combinations or varieties of goods that are never actually bought or sampled by consumers. Further, all of the argument runs in objective terms of observable prices and quantities.

From these relations, the normal law of demand can be derived. Take ΣQ^o as a batch of goods bought at prices ΣP^o and $\Sigma Q'$ as a batch bought at prices $\Sigma P'$. Symbolically, it follows that[12]:

$$\Sigma P^o Q^o \leqq \Sigma P^o Q' \tag{6.6}$$

$$\Sigma P' Q' \leqq \Sigma P' Q^o \tag{6.7}$$

Hence, it can be shown that

$$\Sigma \Delta P_i \, \Delta Q_i < O \tag{6.12}$$

In general terms, the inequality (6.12) must hold so long as greater quantities are bought at lower prices: the inequality itself refers to the sum of all changes in prices multiplied by changes in quantities. *If only the price of one good, the ith commodity changes, then equation (6.12) leads to the normal-demand law.* Hicks has referred to this as probably "the ultimate generalization of the theory of demand."[13]

Revealed Preference: The Theory of a "Grin Without a Cat"

Thus, the normal content of demand theory follows from some simple axiomatic relations, with a narrower basis than indifference analysis. It might be noted that, despite the postulates of consistency and thorough transitivity, some proponents of these views refuse to recognize a valuing subject behaving rationally—consistently—and refuse to impute any deliberate conduct based on expected satisfactions to his behavior.[14] It is

[11] H. S. Houthakker, "Revealed Preference and the Utility Function," *Economica* (1950).

[12]
$$\Sigma P^o Q^o - \Sigma P^o Q' = \Sigma P^o (Q^o - Q') \leqq 0 \tag{6.8}$$

$$= \Sigma (-P^o)(Q' - Q^o) \leqq 0 \tag{6.9}$$

$$\Sigma P' Q' - \Sigma P' Q^o = \Sigma P'(Q' - Q^o) \leqq 0 \tag{6.10}$$

Adding equations (6.9) and (6.10),

$$\Sigma (P' - P^o)(Q' - Q^o) \leqq 0 \tag{6.11}$$

[13] J. R. Hicks, *Value and Capital*, ed. 2, pp. 51–52.

[14] I. M. Little, *A Critique of Welfare Economics* (1950).

accepting the image of the grin without the reality of the Cheshire cat. This reticence might be adjudged as unnecessarily severe—as separating intelligent action from deliberate thought. Furthermore, when the consistency test is not satisfied, this theory has no way of deciding whether (1) it is observing irrational behavior, or (2) observing a snob phenomenon, or (3) witnessing a change in tastes. Its behavioristic straitjacket precludes any inference or commentary drawn from observed phenomena. Its ultimate demand generalization is, of course, consistent with indifference analysis for movements at least along a curve—and also compatible with the underlying cardinal-utility concept.

Wider Range of the Theory?

One argument advanced for the theory is that its narrower basis also allows it a wider range. That is, the full indifference map need not be postulated nor need choice patterns (outside of the observed market sequences) conform to a decreasing *MRS*. Further, the argument runs (realistically) in terms of discrete units and it does not employ the budget restriction that income need be fully allocated.

It is this last point that is, perhaps, the more dubious one. Conceivably, important income changes may invalidate the consistency patterns which, for smaller income movements, will be affirmed. Fundamentally, the $A > B > C \cdots > Z < A$ may be rearranged to $A > C > B$, etc., through the new consumption possibilities. In the older view, this was always recognized; the nature of substitute and complementary relations could be altered. It is not clear that these problems are really avoided, for large income changes, in the new approach.

A Summary Comment

From the foregoing, it is apparent that the empirical content of revealed-preference theory is purchased at a cost: it has no way of describing the notion of a change in tastes which most people would regard as a not uncommon experience even while admitting much underlying constancy of attitudes toward goods. Further, the consistency relations have a meaningful interpretation only in terms of some ultimate valuing subject—which the theory professes to ignore. The consistency relation can be violated, and with full, meaningful consistency (rather than inconsistency) in the case of snob purchases where price, rather than quality or quantity attributes, governs the purchase decision.[15]

Further, the assumption that a fall in price is tantamount to a rise in

---

[15] As another (trivial?) difficulty: how is a commodity to be defined? Are equations (6.4) and (6.5) to give way to equalities? If so, as in the red versus white tennis-ball case, might not indifference enter once again?

real income, so that demand for the lower-priced good rises, will elimi-nate inferior-good cases and, also, cases of zero income elasticity of demand—those on the borderland of inferior and superior goods. It may be ventured that this is an unnecessary—and artificial—restriction considering such items as salt, sugar, bread, etc., for individuals with incomes well above subsistence levels.[16]

Questions

1. Draw a budget line in a chart field and locate a combination Q' bought at the given prices. Vary the prices through Q' and locate another combination Q^2. Rotate the price line through Q' again, etc. If, at each price set, a different combination is purchased, demonstrate that preference curves and, in the limit, indifference curves and an indifference map can be constructed. (See Little, *Welfare Economics*, pp. 34–36.)
2. "Any good . . . that is known always to increase in demand when money income alone rises must definitely shrink in demand when its price alone rises." (Paul Samuelson, *Economica*, 1953, p. 2.) This has been referred to as *The Fundamental Theorem of Consumption Theory*. Prove it by means of budget lines alone.
3. Some proponents of the theory of revealed preference are unwilling to accept the notion of preference or satisfaction, even though they take the transitivity relation as axiomatic. How valid do you regard this procedure?

NUMERICAL UTILITY FOR CHOICES INVOLVING UNCERTAIN PROSPECTS

Another approach to the theory of consumer behavior that has been developing almost parallel in time with that of revealed preference has been a revival of a form of numerical utility, at least for choices in behavior in situations involving risk. Superficially, this has been regarded as a form of cardinal utility and a reversion to the older ideas—a conclusion hardly warranted by the facts of the theory.

Essentially, the theory derives from certain strands in thought in the famous work of Von Neumann and Morgenstern in the theory of games. We may quote some relevant lines[17]:

"Consider three events, C, A, B, for which the order of the individual's preferences is the one stated. Let X be a real number between 0 and 1 such that A is exactly equally desirable with the combined event consisting of a chance of probability $(1 - \alpha)$ for B and the remaining chance of probability α for C. Then we suggest the use of α as a numerical estimate for the ratio of the preference of A over B to that of C over B."

[16] See T. Majumdar, *The Measurement of Utility*, Chapter VII, for some interesting critical remarks on the theory.

[17] J. von Neumann and O. Morgenstern, *Theory of Games and Economic Behavior*, ed. 2, p. 18.

An Illustration

An illustration of these ideas will serve to show how a scale of numerical utility can be constructed. We are given that the utility of A is equal to that of B with a probability $(1 - p)$ plus that of C with a probability of p. Thus,

$$U(A) = p \cdot U(C) + (1 - p)U(B) \qquad (6.13)$$

That is, the utility of A, which is less than that of C (if C were certain) and more than B (if B were certain), is equal to some intermediate value of the two, depending on the likelihood of one or the other occurring. What combination of probabilities of drawing C or B would lead the individual to choose A rather than a chance of securing C or B? We are required, then, to find the probability values that would lead to the indifference relation (6.13).

Arbitrarily, we can assign the value of C to be 2 units of utility and of B to be 1. Thus,

$$U(A) = p \cdot U(2) + (1 - p)U(1) \qquad (6.14)$$

If a probability of 3/10 is attached to p, then

$$U(A) = \tfrac{3}{10}U(2) + \tfrac{7}{10}U(1) = \tfrac{6}{10} + \tfrac{7}{10} = 1.3 \qquad (6.15)$$

Linear Transformations

In this fashion, we could build up a scale of numerical utility values for any good for which a sure prospect of getting it was worth less than a sure prospect of C but more than B. Likewise, we could go outside the extremities for events more valuable than a certain C or, on the other hand, less valued than a certain B: the latter cases would require merely a rewriting of (6.13) so that $U(A)$, where $A > C$, is found through:

$$U(C) = pU(A) + (1 - p)U(B) \qquad (6.16)$$

$$U(2) = \tfrac{1}{5}U(A) + \tfrac{4}{5}(1) \qquad (6.17)$$

$$5(2) = U(A) + 4$$

$$6 = U(A) \qquad (6.18)$$

Hence, in this case, $A = 6$. Values of A which are less than B could also be derived in this general way.

It is to be noticed that the initial values assigned to B and C were quite arbitrary. Suppose, rather than $U(B) = 1$ and $U(C) = 2$, we had used 10 and 15, or 4 and 5, or 30 and 45, etc. Then, with the same probability values, $U(A)$ would appear as:

	I	II	III	IV
U(B)	1	4	10	30
U(A)	1.3	4.3	11.5	34.5
U(C)	2	5	15	45

In I, the incremental rise in the *A* value is 0.3 and 0.7; in II, the same. In III, 1.5 and 3.5 or 5(0.3) and 5(0.7). In IV, it is 4.5 and 10.5, or 15(0.3) and 15(0.7). Thus, while the choice of initial values, amounting to a starting point ("a zero") and a unit of measure ("a one") is quite arbitrary, the resulting scales are linear transformations of one another, so that by simple additive or multiplicative processes it is possible to move from one to the other, and establish the same relative ordering.[18] In this way, a full scale can be ordered and given numerical significance.

Numerical Utility Is Not Cardinal Utility

Although a scale of numerical utility can be constructed, this should not be interpreted as a return to the concept of cardinal utility: nothing in the scale indicates satisfaction as an *intensive* quantity. All that is disclosed is a ranking of alternatives in cases involving risk or uncertainty of outcome.

It is well to be clear on this last point. If *A*, *B*, or *C* can be chosen, and there is no possibility of this choice going astray, the numerical scale cannot be constructed: probability relations simply do not arise. If the expected satisfaction from *A* is uncertain but is equal to a chance of being satisfied by *B* or *C* according to some estimates of likelihood, then the scale of values offers a means of depicting the likely choices of the individual or consuming unit. As Messrs Friedman and Savage declare, for choices involving risk the hypothesis is that "individuals choose in such circumstances as if they were seeking to maximize the expected value of some quantity," and that "preferences . . . in uncertain situations to which probability applies are governed solely by the probabilities attached to each possible income (or outcome)."[19]

Apart from the question of whether risk is important in the usual run of consumer decisions, another difficulty with the theory is its inability to allow for the pleasure of gambling, or the positive desire of some indi-

[18] See A. Alchian, "The Meaning of Utility Measurement," *American Economic Review* (March 1953).

[19] See Milton Friedman and L. J. Savage, "The Expected-Utility Hypothesis and the Measurability of Utility," *Journal of Political Economy* (December 1952), pp. 463 and 467. See also their important earlier article on "The Utility Analysis of Choices Involving Risk," *Journal of Political Economy* (1948). Reprinted in *Readings in Price Theory* (American Economic Association, 1952).

viduals to undertake decisions and make choices against formidable, if not hopeless, odds in the mere contemplation of the untold joys of winning. At issue, too, is the question of the size of the opportunity and the degree of risk attached.

While reservations may be made about the whole scope of the theory to many, if not most, everyday consumer decisions—for the purchase of milk, bread, newspapers, or the usual staples—it does provide a useful approach for the more probabilistic outcomes. Still, it is not to be interpreted as involving a return to cardinal utility in the older sense.[20]

A Crowning Irony?

One final remark may be offered. The new theory of revealed preferences, or consistent "behavior" eliminates the concept of indifference; the latter is a forbidden word which we must drop from our vocabulary. The equally new theory of numerical utility searches out indifference equivalents and builds its scale of numerical values on the indifference concept!

To cap the confusion, there are those who accept both theories, protesting purity at each place.

Questions

1. In what respects does the Neumann-Morgenstern theory of numerical utility differ from the older views of cardinal utility? Does measurability follow for "riskless" choices or not?
2. Consider the usual run of consumer purchases, from your studies and your own experience. What importance do you assign to risk in the totality of the expenditure plan? What type of markets does the theory seem to fit best?
3. In equations **(6.13)** to **(6.15)**, use at least three different sets of values for $U(C)$ and $U(B)$. Compute the $U(A)$ value. What is the relation between your computations and those in the text? What happens to $U(A)$ in the numerical scale if A is acceptable only if the likelihood of C is smaller? greater?
4. Describe clearly the way in which the theory of numerical utility may be applied to the theory of consumption.

[20] On this, see W. J. Baumol, "The Cardinal Utility Which Is Ordinal," *Economic Journal* (December 1958), and Robert Strotz, "Cardinal Utility," *American Economic Review* (May 1953).

Chapter 7

The Pure Theory of Exchange and Optimal Resource Use

We now turn to an examination of several topics that are not only interesting and important in themselves but also will lie at the bottom of later analyses and evaluations of the economic efficiency or optimality of various market structures. Fortunately, because of the facility already acquired in the use of indifference diagrams, the exposition can be brief.

THE PURE THEORY OF EXCHANGE

We begin with a study of the pure theory of exchange. The basic problem is one in which there are two individuals, each possessing quantities of goods X and Y, so that we must decide whether or not there is any basis for exchange between them, what the terms of exchange—or relative prices—for the respective goods will be, and the quantities that can be exchanged to their mutual advantage. Essentially, this study harks back to the theory of barter, as Marshall long ago explained.[1] Is it possible for the relative well-being of each participant to be improved under these circumstances?

Potential Exchange: The Box Diagram

The problem can be analyzed by means of contract curves derived from the indifference field.

In Figure 7.1, the usual indifference curves are drawn with their axes transformed. That is to say, O_1 and O_2 are the origins and reference points for A's indifference map and B's preference field, respectively: we have thus altered the location of the origin and the measuring point for ordinal and abscissae quantities. Furthermore, the axes are so chosen that the quantities jointly possessed of commodity X (amount X_a by A

---

[1] Alfred Marshall, *Principles of Economics*, ed. 8, Appendix F and Mathematical Appendix, Note 12, pp. 844–845.

and amount X_b by B) equal the whole length of the unit line JK. Correspondingly, LM equals the combined total Y quantity held (Y_a and Y_b). Through this device, we are able to locate both individuals simultaneously at the common point Q on the combined indifference map.

For A, already at point Q, all equally preferred combinations are located along the indifference curve lettered I. For B, the equal indifference combinations are along II. Seller A will be glad to trade as long as he moves anywhere in the field to the right of I, and, preferably, as

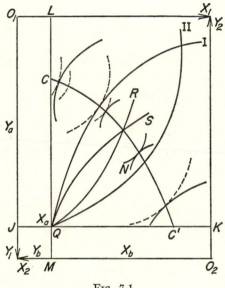

FIG. 7.1

close to O_2 as possible. B, on the other hand, would want to move toward O_1, or to the left of II.

For the moment, it is best to ignore the R and S curves, as well as CC'—we shall come to them in a moment. It ought to be obvious, however, that the entire chart field can be covered with indifference curves for individuals A and B. For the former, they will have the contour of I, and be convex to O_2. We have drawn only a few of these and have restricted ourselves to indifference curves lying *outside* the leaf pattern formed by I and II. Similarly, for B some indifference contours are also indicated by the dashed lines outside the I–II enclosure.

Consider, now, some possibilities of the ultimate exchange equilibrium. Is it possible that the final distribution of goods X and Y can be found to the right of II? Clearly, A would like this outcome, but, because B would be worse off than originally—for his starting point is on II—we can conclude that voluntary exchange can never lead our participants to this area of the diagram.

Similarly, we can dismiss resting places to the left of indifference curve I. To be sure, B would like a position in this area; nevertheless, as A begins at a satisfaction level I he wants to move toward O_2, and would never voluntarily consent to go back toward O_1.

Thus, the essential part of the analysis concerns the area included in the leaf pattern formed by the I–II curves. Within this area, trade presumably can occur to the mutual advantage of both participants: A could proceed in an indifference direction toward O_2 and B could drift up in an ascent toward O_1.

The Contract Curve

Within the I–II enclosure, therefore, we could draw the respective indifference curves within these bounds. Inevitably, we would find that there would be points of tangency between A's indifference curves and B's curves. Connecting all the points of tangency of the two families of indifference curves, whose members are traced in as dashed lines, the resulting locus is the *contract curve CC'*. The important property of the contract curve is that it connects the X and Y quantities at which the MRS for both parties coincides. Thus, $MRS_A = MRS_B$ at the quantities indicated along the contract curve.

Manifestly, whenever the $MRS_A \gtreqless MRS_B$, exchange is mutually profitable. If A regards $4Y = 1X$ and B deems $1Y = 1X$, then, so long as A gives up more than $1Y$ for $1X$, both parties benefit. Hence, any position off the contract curve (as at point N in the diagram) is less than mutually satisfactory: both gain by moving onto CC', thereby equating the MRS ratios.

Any movement off the contract curve permits the well-being of *both* to be increased. On the contract curve, however, a movement in either direction along it, toward O_1 or O_2, is accompanied by an *increase* in the well-being of one individual and a *decrease* in the well-being of the other: it is impossible to make both parties better off by movements along its path.

In this sense, the contract curve represents optimal exchange positions—the Pareto optimum, as it is called, after Vilfredo Pareto. Until individuals are located on it, an improvement for both is possible. Once on, further mutual benefit along it ceases. Thus, if the ultimate location is closer to O_1, B gains most; if the resting place is simultaneously on CC' and I, all the benefit of exchange accrues to B. On CC' and II, the sole benefit is to A. Where the actual resting place emerges depends, of course, on the terms of trade, or the rate at which exchanges take place. We turn now to some remarks on this subject.

The Offer Curve

Drawing a linear price line of any slope whatever through Q, and observing its point of tangency with some curve of A's and B's indifference system, we note that each individual could improve his real income by disposing of some Y for X, or vice versa, until a point of tangency of the price line and the indifference system was reached. Varying the slope of the price line and connecting the series of such points of tangency, we trace out A's *offer curve QS* and B's *offer curve QR*.[2] Appropriately enough, these intersect on the contract curve where a particular price line through Q is simultaneously tangent to both sets of indifference curves. This, we shall see, is the $D = S$ position—that is, where the demand quantities by A for the Y good, say, and supplies of X offered by A equal the demand for X wanted by B and the supply of Y offered by B. It is the position where the reciprocal supply-demand quantities are in balance.

So far, the offer-curve analysis has not elicited any new knowledge. Now, however, we are in a position to give it a new twist and extract information unobtainable from ordinary demand and supply curves. Suppose that exchanges occur not at a single price but rather at varying prices, each unit being sold at a different price by new bargains between our individuals. Say that some units are exchanged at an initial price. After the exchange, both A's and B's holdings fall within the possible area of exchange, within the shell formed between Q and the intersection of I and II. If the price is favorable to B, the new position is on the offer curve QS; if advantageous to A, on QR. If the full quantities demanded or offered at the given price are not sold, then some point outside the QS–QR circuit denotes the position of well-being. Nevertheless, the real income of both participants rises as compared to the initial position Q.

At the new location of the X and Y holdings, new offer curves similar to QS and QR can be constructed. They, too, intersect on the contract curve; the way, therefore, is open for further exchange. This is the significant point: no matter whether exchange takes place at one price or whether there are several prices at which limited quantities are transferred, the final exchange must carry both participants to some point on the contract curve CC'. The reason is that, until the contract curve is reached, the well-being of each individual can be augmented by further exchange; only on the contract curve is the MRS the same for both

---

[2] Conceiving Y as money, A's offer curve QS is an implicit demand curve, for each point indicates the sum of Y that will be sacrificed for an amount of X; QR would be an implicit supply curve, for each point indicates the total of X offered for a sum of Y.

parties, for the same total stocks of X and Y, and equal to the ratio of market prices. All subsequent movements from CC' will leave one party, or both, worse off than before.

Constant Marginal Utility of Money

The simplification wrought by Marshall's assumption of a constant marginal utility of money appears in this analysis, too. A typical indifference field is drawn in Figure 7.2, with commodity Y assumed to be the money commodity: for fairly obvious reasons, all indifference curves emanate from Y points denoting the purchasing power of money in terms of other goods. Viewing the marginal utility of money as constant, we find that changes in the MRS ratio between X and Y are the result of changes only in the X holdings, never in the Y amounts. Thus, as $MRS = MU_x/MU_y$, and as $MU_y = K$, then MRS changes only because of changes in amounts of X.

Consequently, the MRS equality along a contract curve is wholly contingent on the relative distribution of Y, for, given the Y holdings of each, the MRS of X and Y will be the same whether A or B has more of the Y item. The contract curve relating the consistent MRS ratios will thus be a vertical line. If a price ratio equal to this MRS ratio is immediately named, the equilibrium holdings of X and Y are, of course, determinate. Even if transactions are executed at several different prices,

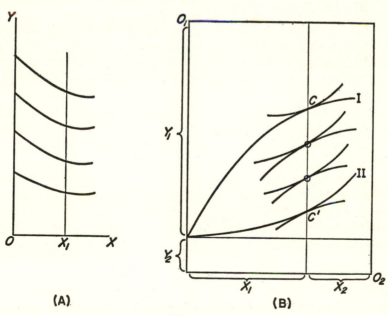

(A)   (B)

FIG. 7.2

each of which is inconsistent with equilibrium, so long as the equilibrium rate of exchange is finally announced *the total amount of X transacted is ultimately the same*. Despite the numerous exchanges at prices incompatible with equilibrium, the indeterminateness in the real income position extends only to the final distribution of Y (the money commodity) between the individuals—never to X.

The assumption of a constant MU_M thus leads to determinateness in the volume of trade even under the otherwise indeterminate situation of barter at multiple rates of exchange. As we proceed, we shall see many other interesting consequences of this innocuous-looking assumption.

The Pure Theory of Exchange

We turn, now, to the important proposition to which this analysis leads. Manifestly, it is that exchange can always be mutually advantageous to all participants until their respective holdings of goods is such as to equalize their respective marginal rates of substitution between any pair of goods. When MRS ratios (or, simply, the relative marginal significance of goods) differs among individuals, then the groundwork for beneficial exchange exists. In a price economy, therefore, optimal consumer adaptation requires that the MRS ratios for each be equal, and for each individual they also are to be equal to the ratio of market prices.

Shifts in the Distribution of Income

It should be grasped quickly that the Pareto optimal is an optimum position only within the given income division. For example, if the total of available goods were the same so that the length of the axes of Figure 7.1 was unaltered, but more of X and Y was available to individual A, then the area of possible exchange would be more closely narrowed and the contract-curve segment for ultimate equilibrium would be shortened. While the principle of optimality would be unaffected, the distribution of well-being would be altered almost inevitably, to favor A in the almost invariable case.

This points up an important qualification to economic analysis. Invariably, it does show the optimal solution within the given income, or, ultimately, the given wealth position. The optimality of the latter division itself is an issue that generally transcends economic analysis. Whatever solution is decided on at that stage, the Pareto optimum comes into play as indicating the exchange requisites for mutual benefit.

The Revealed-Preference Analysis

The foregoing analysis, running as it does in terms of "satisfaction" and "well-being," is not subject to interpretation by the revealed-preference approach. However, as the preceding argument ultimately led to equality of *MRS* ratios (or, what is the same thing, the existence of a common price set), through the revealed-preference approach it can be shown that a mutual improvement in purchase opportunities will always arise so long as the market prices facing the respective individuals differ.

Figure 7.3 contains a box diagram, with the respective origins indicated, with abscissae and ordinal lengths equal to the maximum quantities of each good that each individual can purchase, given their money incomes and market prices. Price lines *MN* and *CD* are drawn with

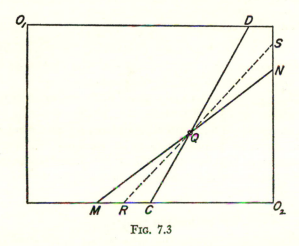

FIG. 7.3

different slopes for each individual, denoting the diverse relative prices faced by each. Both intersect at *Q*, for this represents the respective purchase quantities at the respective prices.

Suppose that each individual faced a common set of prices, intermediate between those initially faced: one good would rise relatively in price and the other would fall. Assume, too, that at the new prices the *Q* quantities could still be purchased with their respective incomes. The new common price line would resemble *RS*. Clearly, this would expand the purchase choice open to each, permitting *B* to move upward in the triangular area of *QSN* and *A* to move out toward *QMR*. Purchase possibilities for each are thus expanded to combinations that could not be achieved previously.[3]

The only difficulty with this analysis is that it never asks *why* individuals should want to purchase the new combinations within reach— unless it is willing to acknowledge that well-being ("satisfaction") is

[3] See K. Lancaster, "Welfare Propositions in Terms of Consistency and Expanded Choice," *Economic Journal* (September 1958), pp. 468–469.

increased in the process. On usual indifference interpretations, however, the analysis indicates that the removal of price discrimination can benefit both parties.

Questions

1. Draw a box diagram on the assumption that each man comes to market with only one good.
   a. What is the relationship between the general slope of the indifference contours and the possible extent of exchange?
   b. Under what conditions would exchange between the individuals be impossible? State the equilibrium relationship covering this result.
2. "The contract curve narrows the area of indeterminateness only under barter." Explain. Is the market solution for this case the most desirable solution or not? Discuss.
3. In the two-individual barter case, can you think of any reasons that would prevent the contract-curve solution being reached?
   a. Would envy, selfishness, or any other personal quality affect the result? If so, how?
4. What influence would greater numbers of traders have on the outcome? Would the position reached on the contract curve be affected or not?
5. What contribution is made by the hypothesis of a constant marginal utility of money? Does this or does it not solve the price problem under barter?
6. Explain why price discrimination is uneconomic.

OPTIMAL RESOURCE USE

Leaving the pure-exchange economy in which goods exist so that the problem is one of shuffling them about to those who place the highest relative valuations on them, we consider now the questions of optimal-production quantities and, ultimately, optimal-resource use. The ideas of this analysis will be required time and again in evaluating the felicity of market structures in accomplishing welfare ends.

The Transformation Curve and Opportunity Costs

We can begin this study with an examination of a transformation curve. In Figure 7.4, amounts of commodity Y are measured vertically and commodity X horizontally. The curve JK indicates the various amounts of the two goods that can be produced.

JK is a transformation curve: it shows the combined amounts of the two goods that can be produced either (1) within the firm or (2) in the economy at large. In the former application, a multiple-product firm is envisaged; in the latter, single-product firms prevail in the economy. Either interpretation will serve our purposes, but a little more generality may be secured by confining the argument to the full economic system rather than the firm.

As drawn, the curve indicates the maximum amounts of the two goods that can be produced with the given (available or used) amounts of productive resources. For example, the commodity combination at point 1 is X_1 and Y_1; at point 2, it is X_2 and Y_2. Either set can be produced. As drawn, the transformation curve illustrates a most fundamental truth; namely, that to produce more of one good (commodity X, say), less must be produced of another good (Y in the illustration). This is the basis of the theory of *opportunity costs* or *displacement costs;* with a fixed amount of productive resources the enlargement of any one output must involve the curtailment of another.

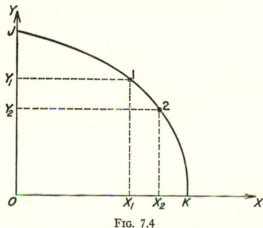

FIG. 7.4

It is ultimately this principle that is at the bottom of any *economic* problem, for it is the question of choice that gives birth to an economic issue. Using more productive factors to produce commodity Y, fewer are available for the output of X: the importance of the output gained must be evaluated against the production quantity lost. There is, then, an important choice to be made in the movement from point 1 to 2, or back again.

Increasing Marginal Rate of Transformation

Moving along the transformation curve, its slope at any point is described as the marginal rate of transformation

$$\left(MRT = \frac{\Delta Y}{\Delta X} \right)$$

It refers to the amount by which the output of commodity Y must be decreased for an increase (of 1 unit) of commodity X. As drawn, when viewed from the origin the curve is concave, denoting an *increasing* marginal rate of transformation. This, we shall now observe, is a reflection of diminishing (marginal) returns or the diminishing marginal productivity of productive factors.

Marginal Productivity and the Marginal Rate of Transformation

To associate the MRT and the marginal productivity (MP) of factors, write:

$$MRT = \frac{\Delta Y}{\Delta X} \tag{7.1}$$

For the simple case in which the only fluid and versatile factor is labor, and the amount required for 1 unit of output of either good is written ΔL, then

$$MRT = \frac{\Delta Y}{\Delta L} \Big/ \frac{\Delta X}{\Delta L} \tag{7.2}$$

But the quantities on the right are simply the symbolic statement of the marginal product of labor, for

$$MP_L{}^y = \frac{\Delta Y}{\Delta L} \quad \text{and} \quad MP_L{}^x = \frac{\Delta X}{\Delta L}$$

That is, $MP_L{}^x$ is the marginal product of labor in producing X and $MP_L{}^y$ is the statement for Y. Hence,

$$MRT = MP_L{}^y / MP^x \tag{7.3}$$

Marginal Productivity and the Increasing MRT

The relation between the increasing MRT and the decreasing-returns phenomena ought to be readily apparent from equation (7.3). The increasing MRT involves a rise in the ratio (7.1) or (7.3). Inevitably, therefore, it means that, as more of commodity X is produced and less of commodity Y (as in the movement from point 1 to point 2 in Figure 7.4), the marginal product of labor in Y increases—an implication of diminishing returns, for it signifies a higher marginal product at lower output levels—and the marginal product of labor in producing X falls, which is what we mean by diminishing returns. Hence, the commonplace hypothesis of economic analysis has been built into the transformation curve.

Optimal Resource Use

To approach the problem of optimal resource use, or the efficient allocation of productive resources, we can make a slight adaptation of Figure 7.4.[4]

[4] T. Scitovsky, *Welfare and Competition*, p. 161.

In Figure 7.5, the transformation curve JK is drawn as before. Superimposed on the figure, however, are the indifference curves of a particular individual. As drawn, the amounts OC_y and OC_x are produced and purchased by all other consumers. Hence, what is produced for a particular consumer along the range $J'K'$ of the transformation curve cannot affect their well-being: it influences only the economic position of the particular consumer whose purchases are being examined.

Suppose we consider point P. At this set of coordinates, the $MRS >$ MRT. That is, in consumption, the marginal rate of substitution is in

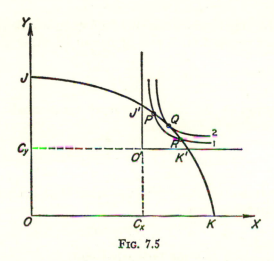

Fig. 7.5

excess of the marginal rate of production transformation. It is as if the consumer is willing to yield $5Y$ for $1X$ while production conditions require a sacrifice of only $3Y$ for $1X$. Well-being, thus, can be increased by producing less Y and more X.

At point R, $MRT > MRS$. In consumption, a sacrifice (say, of 1 to 1) is acceptable, while in production, a 2 to 1 ratio is involved. Producing more Y and less X can enhance well-being. The optimal resource use is indicated, therefore, at Q, where $MRS = MRT$.

For optimal resource use, we have

$$MRS = MRT \equiv \frac{MP_L^y}{MP_L^x} \qquad (7.4)$$

If we take the price of productive factors—labor, in this case as given (P_L)—we have

$$MRS = P_L \cdot MP_L^y / P_L \cdot MP_L^x \qquad (7.5)$$

Each term on the right, however, for the one variable-factor case, is simply the marginal cost of production.[5] Thus,

$$MRS = \frac{P_L \cdot MP_L{}^y}{P_L \cdot MP_L{}^x} \equiv \frac{MC_x}{MC_y} \tag{7.6}$$

Obviously, therefore, resources are best allocated when marginal-substitution ratios in consumption are equal to the relative marginal costs in production. This condition must hold for each consumer, and, thus, for *every* consumer. Unless it is satisfied, it is possible to increase the well-being of at least one consumer without reducing that of another. Hence, the Pareto optimum is not realized until (7.6) is satisfied.

The Market Relation

So long as prices are unaffected by the individual's volume of purchases in consumer markets, we saw that

$$MRS = \frac{P_x}{P_y} \tag{7.7}$$

This was the condition that had to be satisfied for maximum well-being in consumption. When production is introduced, the optimal allocation of resources requires that (7.6) holds good. As MRS is equal to both for maximum satisfaction, then

$$MRS = \frac{P_x}{P_y} = \frac{MC_x}{MC_y} \tag{7.8}$$

From this, we can conclude that resources will be allocated in conformity with a Pareto optimum whenever marginal costs are equal to market prices. Unless this condition is satisfied, the efficiency of the economy's resource-allocation mechanism admits of improvement.[6]

The relation (7.8) must hold, then, in the economy at large for allocative efficiency. Similarly, if one firm produces the two goods, the same relations must be satisfied. Further, the relation as written referred to one productive factor—any factor. Thus, it must hold for all versatile factors, which embraces all those having alternate uses. For economical production, or output at minimum costs, it was noted earlier that the

---

[5] See above, p. 103.

[6] Actually, (7.8) requires not the equality of price to marginal cost, but equiproportionality in all uses. Thus, $(P_x/MC_x) = (P_y/MC_y) = \cdots$ some common factor. When $MC_x = P_x$, etc., this proportionality factor equals 1. However, it can be shown that, if the ratio exceeds 1, then resources are not being properly allocated between leisure and effort. See M. Reder, *Studies in Welfare Economics*, pp. 31–38.

equiproportionality of marginal products to factor price (where the latter were taken as data) had to be observed.[7] This is tantamount to the marginal-value product for each factor being equal to marginal cost, and thus satisfying relation (7.8).

While (7.8) was developed by mounting an individual indifference field on an economy-wide transformation curve, the essential result could have been secured more directly. It is simply that a price, or budget line (such as those used in the consumption analysis), must be tangent to the transformation curve. When the ratio of prices is not equal to the MRT (that is, $P_x/P_y \neq MRT$), then well-being can be improved by a shift in resource use. This leads immediately to (7.8).

Questions

1. To what extent can the theory of transformation curves be used when unemployment is rife?
2. What is the effect of technological change and a growth in the stock of equipment on the transformation curve? the loss in fertility of land?
3. "The theory of opportunity cost is at the bottom of all economic analysis. In fact, it constitutes the very defining characteristic of an economic problem." Argue, both pro and con.
4. Would or would not the *condition* of optimal resource use be changed with a shift in the distribution of income? Would well-being be altered or not? If so, explain how. If so, explain in diagrammatic terms what would take place.

SOCIAL AND PRIVATE PRODUCTS

One major qualification must be put on the proposition that optimal resource allocation requires the equality of marginal costs to prices or marginal-value products to factor prices. We consider this now: the main ideas are derived from Professor Pigou's well-known distinction between private and social costs.[8]

Marginal Private Versus Social Costs

In the one-factor case, $MC_x = P_L/MP_L$. Taking the price of the product as given, and equal to MC, we have $P_x \cdot MP_L = P_L$. That is, the price of the product (P_x), multiplied by the marginal product of the factor, will be equal to the price of the factor when $MC_x = P_x$. The relation $P_x \cdot MP_L$ will be referred to as the *marginal-value product* of the factor: it is thus equal to the product price per unit multiplied by the number of units added at the margin by the factor. For a variation in use of one factor alone, it thus constitutes the marginal cost of production.[9]

[7] See above, p. 36.
[8] A. C. Pigou, *Economics of Welfare*, ed. 4.
[9] See above, p. 58. See also Samuelson, *Foundations*, p. 66.

Now there are cases, all of which involve more than two goods being produced in the community, where the marginal-value product of the factor to the firm is less than the marginal-value product to the community. For example, suppose that, by adding more of a factor and increasing output, this leads to the need for more factory inspectors, thus imposing a cost on the community. Or, in the more familiar illustrations, suppose that the smoke belched out of the factory chimneys results in damage to the health of the local populace, or deposits soot on their buildings which thus need more frequent painting, or discolors clothes hanging out to be dried, etc. Or rivers and lakes are polluted; or the transport needs require greater public maintenance of roadways and expanded school facilities to serve the enlarged population, or create losses in time and other costs for other local business men affected by the congestion through the expanded output of the firm.

All these illustrations can be multiplied and new ones concocted. But the point is clear: the additional output produced by one firm may make production more costly for others. Thus, the private-value product will be less than the *social-value* product. The increase in the one product is counterbalanced by the decrease in the other. Or, to maintain the output of the latter, additional cost must be lavished. This addition should, in some way, be regarded as part of the marginal *social* cost of expanding the firm's output.

Converse cases also abound. The opening of a new plant in a town can reduce the relief rolls, and, conceivably, even lower tax rates. The drainage or irrigation undertaken by one farmer can lower the cost of so doing for another. Education, or simple literacy, can reduce the private costs of on-job training for private firms. Health control, flood control, crime prevention, fire and police departments, etc., can reduce costs of operation for private business firms, lowering marginal private costs.

In all these cases of interdependence between the outlay of one producing unit and the production costs of another, the principle for optimal-resource use is clear; namely, that where marginal private cost is less than marginal social cost, production would be carried too far if $MC = P$. On the other side, where marginal social cost is less than marginal private cost, production could well be carried beyond the $MC = P$ relation.

Many of these illustrations were drawn from the realm of government activities, for which often no price is charged or for which it is not possible to price according to business principles. Still, the underlying principle is apparent: where social benefits are diffused through the government outlays, the net cost to the community is less than the apparent pecuniary outlay.[10]

[10] W. Baumol constructs an argument for government to confine itself largely to these situations. See his *Welfare Economics and the Theory of the State.*

Questions

1. Why was the elaboration of private versus social products confined to the *n*-good, rather than the 2-commodity case?
2. Cite some purely enterprise illustrations of private products differing from social products.
3. From even the limited remarks in the text, is the distinction between private and social products of the essence in many differences of views on the worthiness of government expenditure? Discuss at some length.
4. Is it possible for the effects to extend into the future or not? How would you handle such relations in a more thoroughgoing analysis?

MEASURES OF CONSUMER WELL-BEING

We now consider several questions related, in a sense, to the notion of a Pareto optimum, but even more closely connected to once popular Marshallian ideas on consumer's surplus. They can be included conveniently at this point.

A Price Change and Improvements in Well-Being

The indifference-curve approach does place the demand curve on a firmer footing besides underscoring the interrelations among tastes and thus among markets. To appreciate its applicability in many other questions, consider a fall in the price of one commodity, other prices remaining unchanged. We might ask, by how much does this price fall improve consumer well-being? This was the sort of problem incorporated in the older literature under the guise of "consumer's surplus." Analogously, we might want to discover the income rise at unchanged prices that would be as satisfactory to a consumer as a fall in P_x. Both answers, we shall see, are not quite the same. Indifference-curve analysis can illuminate this puzzle and enable us to extract more precise results than possible with the older methods.

Compensating Income Variations

The analysis can be simplified by measuring amounts of money (instead of a commodity) vertically and amounts of commodity X horizontally. This procedure is valid if we suppose that the prices of all other commodities are constant, so that each amount of money corresponds to a definite amount of other goods. Hence, the indifference curves now touch the vertical axis; for each quantity of money ("other things") connotes a definite level of well-being. Heretofore, as both X and Y were essential to life, the indifference curves did not touch the axes but instead became asymptotic to them.[11]

[11] A. G. Hart, "Peculiarities of Indifference Maps Involving Money," *Review of Economic Studies* (1941).

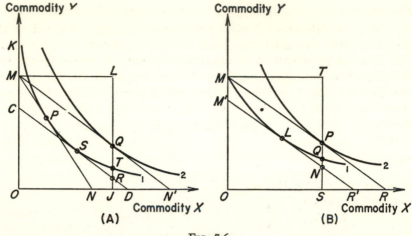

FIG. 7.6

In Figure 7.6(A), the original income and price relations are indicated by the opportunity line MN; the equilibrium adaptation is at P. The price line MN' informs us that P_x has fallen while other prices are unchanged; the new equilibrium is at Q. At Q, the individual purchases OJ of X and JQ of Y (other things), having parted with LQ of money for the OJ amount of X. If we measure the actual money value of the improvement in well-being resulting from the fall in P_x, one answer would be that the consumer benefits in amount equal to TQ, for this sum might be exacted from him, perhaps in direct taxation, without any diminution in well-being as compared to his original indifference status. The money sum TQ might, with propriety, be described as a compensating-income variation. Since it presumes that the OJ purchases will continue, TQ can be further distinguished as a *quantity*-compensating variation.

In fact, if TQ alone were expropriated, the consumer would be better off than he was originally, despite the tax payment. For, after the loss of TQ of money income, a price line parallel to MN' would run through T and would be tangent to a higher indifference curve than that carrying the index 1. If the consumer were to be restored to indifference level 1, a sum equal to QR ($= MC$) would have to be extracted from him after the price fall. For, when a money sum QR ($> TQ$) is recovered from him, the new price line CD is tangent to indifference curve 1 at point S, ensuring the return to the original indifference level 1; a price line passing through T and parallel to CD would raise the income status.

The sum QR, therefore, measures the change in income that exactly describes the gain in well-being occasioned by the price fall. This can be termed the *price-compensating variation in income;* it is the full measure of the income enhancement consequent upon a price fall.

Conceivably, if *CD* were tangent to curve 1 vertically below *Q*, which is the point of tangency of *MN'* with curve 2, then *QR* = *QT*. This would mean that the *MRS* was equal in both instances: at the amount *OJ* of *X*, a rise in income, if accompanied by more *X*, would reduce the *MRS*. The change in the demand for *X*, with respect to income changes, would then be zero.[12] In utility terms, the marginal utility of *Y* could be described as constant, for, even as the *Y* holdings alter (as we move vertically up or down on the indifference map), the ratio MU_x/MU_y (= *MRS*) would be unchanged.[13] Barring this exception, the price-compensating variation *QR* will exceed the quantity variation *TQ*

Equivalent Income Variations

Modifying the query, we may inquire what gain in income at the original prices would be equivalent to the fall in price represented by the rotation of the price lines from *MN* to *MN'*. The price change is presumed to be suspended and the initial prices embodied in *MN* are to rule; the consumer is to be lifted onto indifference curve 2 by a grant of money income in lieu of a price fall. This type of variation is termed an *equivalent-income variation*.

There are at least two ways in which the income level can be elevated. First, we can suppose that the quantity of *X* to be purchased after the income rise is indicated at *P* (or, on the indifference map, the commodity intake can be found vertically upward on curve 2). This change of income can be called a *quantity-equivalent variation*. Unless the *MRS* is constant for the fixed *X* regardless of the change in *Y*, the new price line will intersect curve 2 and well-being will exceed the level defined by curve 2.

Second, in contrast, the price line *MN* could be edged upward, always parallel to *MN*, until it became tangent to curve 2. The money sum necessary for this movement can be denoted as a *price-equivalent variation*. It may, in the one case of constant *MRS* ratios despite altered *Y* holdings, be equal to the quantity variation, but otherwise it will be smaller.

Although it can be proved rigorously that the equivalent variations exceed the compensating variations, the following simple fact can be adduced to corroborate this view. Since P_x is higher under the hypothesis of an equivalent variation than with the compensating variation, to lift an individual from indifference level 1 to indifference level 2 requires a greater sum than would be necessary at a lower P_x. If the lower price prevailed, and if an individual were already on curve 2, a given money

---

[12] The income elasticity of demand would be zero.

[13] In indifference terms, this is the meaning frequently attached to Marshall's premise of a constant marginal utility of money in drawing the demand curve.

sum taken from him which forced him down to curve 1 would be insufficient if handed to him to restore him to curve 2 when he was already on curve 1 and faced with higher prices. Thus, the quantity-equivalent variation, for a price fall, exceeds the price-equivalent variation, both of which exceed the compensating variations; of the latter, the price variation is the greater magnitude. Although we have looked at these measures from the standpoint of a price fall, if P_x rises then what were hitherto compensating variations now become equivalent variations.[14]

Further Applications

The analysis so far has been intricate largely because of the variety of measures turned to light; it is not possible, however, to declare which measure is best, for each has its use depending on the question to be answered. Some further applications of these ideas may be noted.

MR and $M'R'$ in Figure 7.6(B) represent price lines at varying income levels but with constant prices. Let us measure the gain in money secured by the presence of a commodity compared to the pecuniary value of the loss in well-being suffered by its complete withdrawal from the market.

When X is withdrawn, according to Figure 7.6(B), the maximum position of well-being is at M, on the vertical axis, of indifference curve 1. When X is available at the market price, well-being rises to the level indicated by indifference curve 2. By having commodity X at the given price, an individual enjoys an enhancement of real income measured by PN $(= MM')$. On the removal of commodity X, without a new substitute to replace it and with other prices constant, he would retain PT to spend on other things (the Y commodities), but his pocket would literally be picked in sum PN; the individual would be driven to the level of well-being represented by point M on curve 1. The sum PN is thus a measure of the economic importance of the commodity to him.

As an alternative problem, what is the maximum sum an individual would offer in order to purchase a particular quantity of a commodity as compared to the sum that he does pay in view of market prices?

This problem is interesting in connection with all-or-nothing types of bargains. Possessed of money income OM at the prevailing MR price structure, the consumer will purchase OS of commodity X, spending SP on all other commodities and PT on X. Confronting the individual with the alternative of paying a higher sum for the quantity OS of X or not being permitted to buy any of it at all, at a maximum he would tender the sum TQ for OS of X, or an amount PQ above his expenditure when

---

[14] See A. Henderson, "Consumer's Surplus and the Compensating Variation," *Review of Economic Studies* (1942) and J. R. Hicks, "The Generalized Theory of Consumer's Surplus," *ibid.* (1945–1946). Also, J. N. Morgan, "Measurement of Gains and Losses," *Quarterly Journal of Economics* (1948).

he is free to purchase at the market price. The sum PQ thus represents his *consumer's surplus* on being able to purchase at the market price rather than being compelled to submit a maximum offer for this quantity.

Questions

1. If prices move disproportionately, what is the effect of compensating wage earners according to a price-level index?
2. "If relative prices never change, it is possible to treat all other goods as if they were a single item." Why?
   a. Is this hypothesis equivalent to the assumption that all the goods are produced in a constant proportion or not?
3. Assuming a constant marginal utility of money, how many separate measures of income variation can be distinguished?
4. How do "all-or-nothing" bargains affect the level of consumer well-being compared to being confronted with a given market price with freedom to purchase as much as you wish?

INTRODUCTION

The analysis of demand and cost phenomena has provided a stepping-stone for investigations into the theory of price, for the market manifestations evolve out of the mutual interactions of consumers and firms. Considering the influence of the firm as paramount upon price, Part II is built about its equilibrium adaptation in various kinds of sales markets. Sometimes the firm cannot exert any perceptible influence on price; in other cases it can. In still other instances, it is able to affect price but chooses not to do so. Hence, we shall have to classify several types of market situations faced by the firm. That it is the actions of the firm which command the major share of the attention in the theory of price determination, constituting the bedrock of the analysis, is an important departure from older views according to which prices were conceived to be a resultant of impersonal and mechanistic market forces.

Unfortunately, the question of classifying market positions is still an unsettled issue; it has aroused a substantial amount of controversy for more than 20 years.[1] Perhaps this conflict was inevitable in view of the practically simultaneous appearance of the two epochal works, on the equilibrium of the firm in nonperfectly competitive structures, by Mrs. Robinson and Professor Chamberlin. The discord which, it was hoped, would evaporate with the curative effects of time, considering the substantial harmony in technique and results by these two investigators, has persisted; classificatory issues thus go deeper than personalities and appear irreconcilable by current standards and insights. Rather than attempt another restatement of the respective positions, emphasizing major differences and exaggerating minor nuances, it would seem better, at this point, to confine ourselves to explaining only the mode of classification adopted for our own work. The price analyses to come treat of basic problems acknowledged by all.

The Classification Adopted

Historically, from the seller's side, the presence of a large number of sellers offering a homogeneous product, with any one seller providing only a very small portion of the total output, has formed the backbone

[1] The main works on the classificatory controversy are, of course, those of Professor Chamberlin and Mrs. Robinson, in *The Theory of Monopolistic Competition* and *The Economics of Imperfect Competition*, respectively. In Chapter IX of the later editions of his book, Professor Chamberlin summarizes his views and describes the earlier discussions.

of the idea of competition. Professor Chamberlin has aptly termed this *pure* competition, while to others it is homogeneous competition or atomistic competition. As there are n firms in the field, where n is a very large number, and as the products are homogeneous, the elasticity of substitution between the firm's product and the products of the remaining $n - 1$ firms is infinite. Hence, any one firm that named a price higher than that of its competitors would see its sales slump to zero. At the market price, its demand curve would thus be infinitely elastic. Also, as its production outpourings are but a minute portion of the total supply, either lowering its price below that of the rest of the market, or raising it above, for all practical purposes would fail to affect the sales of the other firms; the cross-elasticity of demand between the firm's price and the sales of the other $n - 1$ firms (conceived as a total) would be zero.[2] As the firm could not drive the other firms' prices up by withholding its output, and as it would be unnecessary to lower prices below the market level to secure sales, the firm would abide by the market price. Chapter 8 is devoted to the equilibrium problem of the firm selling under these circumstances.

Alternately, the firm may recognize that the elasticity of substitution between its product and that of other firms is, for many consumers, less than infinite, with the exact degree of substitution contingent on the relative prices. Here the firm is producing a commodity differentiated from the rest; it now has a measure of market independence, for there is no longer a definite market-price ceiling above which its sales sharply and discontinuously shoot back to zero. If the cross-elasticity of demand between its particular product and that of any other firm is nil, this situation can be described effectively as a case of monopoly or polypoly, the latter being a case where market cross-elasticities are small, even though individual preferences establish many close substitutes. Not only is the firm's demand curve relatively inelastic, but also the situation is devoid of any important interrelations between the price policy of the firm and the market behavior of other firms. Chapter 10 is built on these premises.

Conceivably, two (or few) firms may be producing a product that, from the standpoint of consumers, is homogeneous, so that the MRS between them is constant (and E_{ss} infinite). As n is now a small number, the supply offerings of any one firm may comprise a significant portion of the total; the cross-elasticity of demand between the price policy of

---

[2] Robert Triffin compares the atomistic firm to another firm so that the cross-elasticity is infinite. I have criticized this position at another place. See his *Monopolistic Competition and General Equilibrium Theory*, Chapter III. Also, my article on "The Classification of Market Positions," *Quarterly Journal of Economics* (1942), with Dr. Triffin's reply.

any one firm and the sales of the remaining $n-1$ firms is finite. This is the characteristic problem of duopoly and oligopoly that comprises most of the subject matter of Chapter 11.

Similarly, the elasticity of substitution for consumers between the firm's product and that of other firms may be high but finite, rather than infinite, with the cross-elasticity of demand between the firm and other firms also important. These instances are described as typifying monopolistic or heterogeneous competition, discussed in Chapter 12. Whenever the cross-elasticity of demand is finite, as in oligopoly or monopolistic competition, we are in a network of circularity in market relations where the mutual interdependence of the respective firms must be stated.

The classification thus hinges on the two criteria, of the size of the elasticity of substitution and the cross-elasticity of demand. Schematically, the plan adopted can be represented in the accompanying two-way table (Table II.1).

TABLE II.1—CLASSIFICATION OF MARKET POSITION

E_s \ E_x^y	O	*Finite*
Small	Pure monopoly	Partial monopoly
Large	Polypoly	Monopolistic competition
∞	Pure competition	Duopoly—oligopoly

In the monopolistic situations where $E_s < \infty$, the opportunity is always open to the firm to enlarge its market by means of a sales campaign, as through advertising. This element furnishes part of the content of Chapter 12. Similarly, because of a high cross-elasticity of demand, the firm may perceive the impracticality of a price reduction in advancing its sales because of the price retaliations of other firms; prospects of varying its product and modes of nonprice competition may appeal to it as more feasible methods of expediting sales. These phenomena are elucidated in Chapter 13.

Although most of the analyses of Part II are conducted with special reference to the firm, in some cases a buyer may dominate a particular market. If there are numerous sellers and but one buyer, we have monopsony, or buyers' monopoly. Two or few buyers occasion duopsony and oligopsony patterns. The conjunction of one buyer and one seller re-creates the traditional conception of bilateral monopoly. Problems of this sort provide the content of Chapter 14. Curiously, the classificatory problem from the buyer's side has largely been ignored, although many of the same intricacies that mark monopoly positions undoubtedly would obtrude. The lack of devotion to these problems can be attributed to the intuitive belief that pure monopsony structures are less prevalent than monopoly structures. To balance out the discussion of Part II, and modify the typical hypothesis that different firms producing a homogeneous technical commodity are significantly influenced by even trivial price changes on the part of other firms, Chapter 12 deals with the geographical separation of firms and the spatial interdependence of prices. Besides contributing some realism, this analysis opens up some new matters.

An Alternative Classification

An alternative classification, developed by Professor Bishop, may also be presented here as an indication of a strong effort to draw sharp classificatory lines.[3] The separation is based on the point elasticity of demand (E_i) for the product of the i-th firm and the point–cross-elasticity between the relative change in P_i and the relative change in $Q_j^{(E_ij)}$. The accompanying two-way table (Table II.2) is a copy of the original presentation.

TABLE II.2—A MARKET CLASSIFICATION BASED ON ELASTICITY CONCEPTS

Numbers Equivalent of Suppliers \ *Nature of Product*	*Near-Homogeneous* $E_i \to \infty$	*Significantly Differentiated* $E_i < \infty$ (*Significantly*)
$\dfrac{E_i}{E_i{}^j}$ large	Near-pure competition	Significantly differentiated competition or pure monopoly
$\dfrac{E_i}{E_i{}^j}$ small	Near-pure oligopoly	Significantly differentiated oligopoly

Where the cross-elasticity is large, the cases of oligopoly, pure or differentiated, arise: this is close enough to our cases of oligopoly and monopolistic competition. The smaller cross-elasticity and the smaller elasticity lead to somewhat greater interpretative problems: it is hard to distinguish "differentiated competition" from "pure monopoly"—the

---

[3] R. L. Bishop, "Elasticities, Cross-Elasticities, and Market Relationships," *American Economic Review* (December 1952), p. 799. Also, see the comments by W. Fellner and E. H. Chamberlin, and Bishop's reply, in the December 1953 issue.

latter category actually remains undefined. The one more curious omission from the table is the case of pure competition which, unfortunately, cannot be included because $E_i/E_i{}^j$ becomes indeterminate: both numerator and denominator becoming "infinite." Strangely, for "near-pure" competition the value of this ratio is "large," while it is "large," "zero," or "unity" for pure competition. Most other classifications flounder on the monopoly definition; this bogs down at the competitive end.

One final note should be appended on all classifications dwelling on incremental price or output changes: the value of cross-elasticities, say, may differ substantially for a finite as against an infinitesimal movement, and look rather different for a price fall as against a price rise. Simple tests by the student can establish the point. Classification-wise, the firm may thus jump about, from one relationship to another. Inevitably, a classificatory position which is held only tenuously may be regarded as not held at all.

Some Terms and Equilibrium Concepts

We shall have to make reference to *static, stationary,* and *dynamic* equilibrium, and to *long-* and *short*-run equilibrium. As these terms are usually as germane to one market structure as to another, we might clarify them here, to indicate the usage intended. It is not a breach of faith to confess that equilibrium concepts are always unrealistic. And yet, whatever violence such abstractions do to our sense of reality, the analysis is incomplete until it depicts the final position toward which individual markets, and the economic system, are impelled by the underlying forces.

Briefly, static analysis abstracts from time. The demand curve and the cost curves are taken to refer to the same time interval. Although there may be a past, future periods are disregarded, blacked out: such studies may better be termed *single-period* analysis. The stationary state, on the other hand, envisages constant and repetitive supply and demand forces through time. Economic life is not really stilled: there is unvarying motion, with a constant output flow, constant consumer purchases, constant factor hire, and constant factor incomes.[4] In dynamic analysis, change in the taste, income, and productivity data is of the essence: in a dynamic temporal equilibrium sequence, in each time interval the new changes are equilibrating. This involves a study of multiple time intervals.

The concept of long and short periods is due to Alfred Marshall. To Marshall, whether price problems were of the immediate, short-run, or

[4] Professor Pigou has characterized this model as the stationary flow equilibrium, to emphasize the attribute of motion (*Employment and Equilibrium,* Chapter 10). To Professor Schumpeter it is the "circular flow" economy (*Theory of Economic Development,* R. Opie, trans., Chapter I).

long-run variety revolved about the nature of supply. In the easiest case, where supply consists of a fixed stock of goods, there is an immediate market-price problem. Regarding supply as a rate of flow from existing equipment or "facilities"—the productive resources within the industry—the price problem is viewed as a short-run phenomenon. Allowing more time, so that the stock of equipment and the number of firms could grow or contract, the price problem is a long-run conception. The construction thus has little to do with clock time; instead, it is erected on the degree of fluidity and finality in production adaptations.

Allusion will also be made to the concept of comparative statics. In this type of analysis, it is assumed that a (slight) change in demand or supply has occurred and that the system responds to the movement, frictionlessly clicking into equilibrium. The task, then, is to depict the final influence of the change, tracing the differences between the equilibria and ascribing these to the variation in the determining data.

Questions

1. "Any classification of market positions based on elasticity concepts holds at best within a range of price relationships." Evaluate.
2. What is the difficulty of defining the concept of pure monopoly?
   a. Is the concept of a good "without any substitutes" a valid one? Explain.
3. How would the competition of sellers of complementary goods appear in a market classification? What happens to the cross-elasticity of demand?
4. For short periods of time, would the concept of a stationary state be reasonably appropriate, as a realistic matter? If not, give some idea of the magnitude of change in important variables.

Chapter 8

252525252525252525252525252525252525252525252525252525

Pure Competition

Under pure competition, the firm is unable to influence market price. The first analytic problem is that in which (1) the firm acts to dispose of the most profitable amount of its fixed holdings at the externally determined market price. Next, the problem is (2) one of producing with its present facilities the most profitable output volume. Finally, through time (3) the firm must reach a decision on installing the volume of equipment and producing the amount of output that promises it maximum profits. These several aspects of the adaptation of the firm under competitive conditions will be discussed in this chapter. Since the individual firms which sell the same commodity comprise an industry, we shall also be interested in the equilibrium of the larger group as well as of the firm.

FIXED STOCKS OF GOODS

The first of the equilibrium analyses is that in which supply consists of a fixed stock of goods. The problem is to define the conditions of equilibrium for the firm and for the industry.

Equilibrium of the Individual Seller

For a simple problem in the theory of exchange under pure competition, let us suppose that an individual comes to the market with commodity Y and wishes to trade Y in return for commodity X. Being only one buyer among the numerous buyers of X, and just one of the multitudinous sellers of Y, the individual is presumed to be powerless to influence the terms of the trade. The sole question, then, is one of ascertaining the number of units of Y that will be proffered and the quantity of X purchased at each of the possible price ratios.

The indifference curves and the price-consumption line can aid us in solving the problem. The indifference map expresses the individual's preferences for the two commodities. Assuming his stock of commodity Y to be OM, his income or purchasing power consists of OM of Y.

Rotating several linear price lines from point M on the vertical axis, the price lines will indicate the purchase possibilities with respect to X and Y at the several prices.

At each possible exchange ratio, the sales and purchases most satisfactory to the seller will be those quantities indicated at the point of tangency of price line and indifference curve, with the difference between the original OM amount of Y and the equilibrium amount of Y comprising the quantity exchanged at the market rate of exchange for commodity X. When a series of price lines thus emanate from point M, the price-consumption curve thus describes the amounts of X bought and the amounts of Y retained (and also sold) at the successive prices. If Y is a superior good which the seller could not afford to consume when its price (and thus his income) was relatively low, or if X is an inferior good, the price-consumption curve may curl up toward OY, revealing that the seller will offer fewer units of Y as its exchange value rises. This is tantamount to a smaller supply being offered at a higher price and is explicable in terms of a strong negative income effect for X. The amount of Y that is *retained* by the individual can always be regarded as a market purchase of Y by the seller *from himself*.

Supply Curve Derived from the Price-Consumption Curve

Rather than trading one commodity for another, the firm's typical problem is to exchange goods for money. If we measure the goods on the vertical axis and fix this quantity at OM, and measure amounts of money along the horizontal axis, indifference curves for goods and money can be designed. For each possible P_y (where $P_x = 1$), a price line can be rotated from M to OX showing the maximum money proceeds for OM of Y at the going P_y. The sales offerings of Y can be observed at each tangency point of price line and indifference curve so that, by following the course of the price-consumption line, which indicates the amounts of Y unloaded at each P_y, the familiar supply curve of the firm can be elicited.

If the indifference curves between the Y commodity and money form vertical lines, indicating an infinite rate of substitution of money for the Y commodity, and implying that well-being can always be raised by a pecuniary enhancement, regardless of price the full Y commodity will then be sold. The firm's supply offerings at the various possible prices will be constant and equal to OM; the firm's supply curve will be perfectly inelastic.

Market Equilibrium; Fixed Stocks of Goods

Turning to the market equilibrium where stocks of goods are fixed, the demand quantity of commodity X for each individual at each P_x

can be read off at the tangency points of the system of price lines to the successive indifference curves. By totaling the quantities wanted by each individual at each successive P_x, we can construct the market-demand curve.

For the market to be in balance, the price must equate the quantity demanded, D_x, and the quantity available, S_x; if sellers' demands for their own commodity are nil, the equilibrium price for the sale of the full stock must evoke a demand quantity for just that amount, neither more nor less. If sellers have their own demand at the respective prices, a supply curve can be built out of the quantities that they wish to dispose of at each price (the difference between the quantities offered and the full stock on hand will measure their withholdings at each price, evidencing a preference for the goods rather than for the money and other goods obtainable from the sales proceeds). Familiarly enough, the intersection of the demand and supply curves indicates the equilibrium price at which quantities wanted for purchase and quantities offered for sale are equal.

Individual and Market Equilibrium Conditions

Whatever the price and quantity sold, so long as consumers and sellers are informed of the going prices in the numerous markets and are impotent individually to affect market prices, the marginal rates of substitution among each pair of goods will equal the ratio of prices among the commodity pairs. This relationship must obtain at the equilibrium price, for it prevails *at each price point* on the demand curve for, say, commodity X. In marginal utility doctrine, this condition of consumer equilibrium is expressed as the equiproportionate ratio between marginal utility and prices at each possible price. Thus,

$$MU_x/P_x = MU_y/P_y = \cdots MU_n/P_n = M \qquad (8.1)$$

where MU refers to the marginal utility of a commodity and M is the additional utility of an increment of income (money). Shifts in consumer expenditure will develop whenever this condition is unfulfilled, so that the position cannot be one of equilibrium.

In short, there are the dual conditions of market equilibrium under competition: (1) the market condition of an equality of the quantities supplied (S_x) and the quantities demanded (D_x) at a common price, and (2) the individual conditions of equivalence between price ratios and marginal rates of substitution. Each consumer accepts the market price as a datum and orders his own purchase plan to conform to the price structure; the aggregate of consumers shapes the market-demand curve and, with supply (which is also compounded of individual elements), determines the market price. Price, a datum to each individual participant, is thus a variable for the market.

Diagrammatic Illustrations

These ideas may be illustrated diagrammatically. In all of the diagrams of Figure 8.1, prices are measured vertically and quantities horizontally.

Curve D represents the market-demand curve, denoting the aggregate quantities wanted by all consumers at each price. In Figure 8.1(A), supply is perfectly inelastic, implying that sellers want to discard their full stock OM regardless of price; being devoid of any taste for the good, they prefer money to any quantity of it. Market price must then settle at OP, for, if but one price is to rule, this is the only price that will clear the market without a remainder of supply offerings or demand quantities.

Some flexibility of supply offerings is indicated by the supply curve

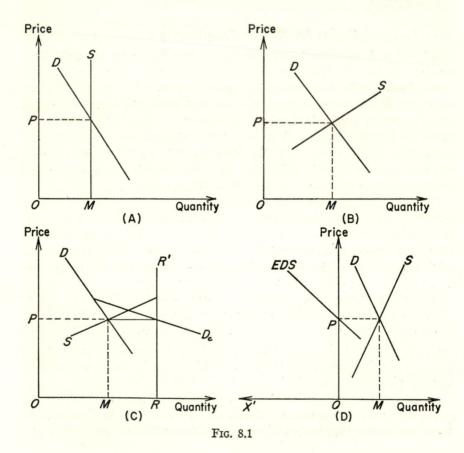

FIG. 8.1

in Figure 8.1(B); depending on prices, sellers will offer varying portions of their total holdings. At each price, some quantities will be withheld, either in the hope of more favorable future prices or because at the successive prices the stocks withheld are preferred by the sellers for their own use compared to the additional income obtained from the sale of their full holdings. As OP is the only price at which $D_x = S_x$, it is the sole equilibrium price position, assuming that sales occur only at a single price within the time interval.

The facts implicit in the supply curve of Figure 8.1(B) are demonstrated in another form in Figure 8.1(C). The total stock of the commodity on hand is OR; a vertical line RR' is drawn through this amount. The curves D and S are drawn on the same premises as before. But at each price there is added to the market-demand curve the "own demand" of sellers; in amount this is always the lateral difference between the total available stock OR and the quantity reflected on the supply curve S at each particular price. Mounting the sellers' demand upon the market-demand curve (the buyers' demand), we derive the *communal-demand curve* for the commodity, the DD_c curve of Figure 8.1(C). This will intersect RR' at the price OP: quantity OM will be sold to buyers while MR will in effect be purchased, retained by sellers for their own use.[1]

Besides disclosing that the supply curve is an inverted type of demand curve, the analysis also reveals that each consumer will be able to command a greater stock of any good, and improve his own well-being, the closer the market-demand curve lies to the ordinate axis or the less the commodity is valued by other consumers. According to Figures 8.1(B) and 8.1(C), sales will be numerous, and *consumer* well-being higher, the lower the sellers' valuation of the stocks they possess.[2]

Figure 8.1(D) describes the *excess* demand (or supply) of buyers (or sellers) at each price height. When the S_x quantities offered exceed the D_x quantities wanted at some price measured horizontally, the locus of EDS (the excess demand-supply curve) lies to the left of the vertical axis. When $D_s > S_x$, the EDS quantity will lie to the right of the vertical

---

[1] A communal-demand curve drawn on this basis is likely to have some strange "kinks" if the supply curve bends backward to a positive income effect for the good by the sellers. The phenomenon of supply as reverse demand is often referred to as the "reversibility" of the supply curve. The sellers' own demand is also called the "reserve prices." See P. H. Wicksteed, *The Commonsense of Political Economy* (L. Robbins, editor), Vol. II, and H. J. Davenport, *Economics of Enterprise*, pp. 48–52.

[2] Thus, to Pareto the tastes of other consumers are an "obstacle" to the want-satisfaction of any one consumer (*Manuel*, pp. 155, 175). See also Irving Fisher, *Mathematical Investigations in the Theory of Value and Prices*, pp. 44–51.

axis; while, if $D_x = S_x$, the *EDS* curve will cross the axis. Although *EDS* is drawn as linear in Figure 8.1(D), its actual shape will depend on the nature of the D_x and S_x curves. The locus of *EDS* also corresponds to that of DD_c in Figure 8.1(C), but the excess D_x or S_x quantities are now measured from the vertical axis rather than from the *RR'* line, denoting the available market quantity.

The Equilibrium Position

In summary, let us review the results when the market-equilibrium condition of $D_x = S_x$ is not satisfied. If the same situation tended to repeat itself through time, and if at the market price there is excess demand, price will tend to go up as buyers strive to acquire more of the good and as sellers perceive higher price opportunities. With excess supply, it is the sellers who scramble to regulate their inventory position. Neither position would be able to endure and price would have to yield. Only that price which equated the quantity offered and the quantity demanded could equalize the D and S forces.

Questions

1. "By 'buying' we mean giving up money to acquire goods. Therefore, all valuable goods owned by individuals are continuously being bought by them." Comment. How is this related to the principle of opportunity-cost?
2. What is the connection between the supply curve and the price-consumption curve? In what sense is the latter both a demand *and* a supply curve?
3. In the fixed-stock case, all supply curves ultimately become perfectly inelastic. Why? Market-wise, under what conditions will this fact be important?
4. "Any price *may* be an equilibrium price." In what sense is this valid? Contrast with the statement that "only one price can be an equilibrium price."
5. What advantage do you see to eliminating the supply curve and using only the communal-demand curve? What information is provided by the supply curve and *not* by the communal-demand curve?
6. What virtue, and what shortcoming, do you see in the use of the excess-demand curve?
   a. Draw an *EDS*. From it construct the implicit D and S curves.

VARYING SUPPLIES OF GOODS

In the second of our competitive analyses, supply is regarded as a flow, with the amount of goods that sellers proffer for sale conceived as a variable, a resultant of the productive process. The amount of fixed factors engaged by the firm, which includes the stock of equipment, is posited as a datum so that the expansion of the firm is limited to the hire of variable factors. With this restriction on the firm, and if the number of firms is simultaneously held rigid, then the ultimate supply facilities of the industry are immediately bounded.

In short, the initial analysis is confined to a firm possessed of fixed equipment faced by externally determined product and factor prices. Our object is to describe the output volume that will be prepared for sale, assuming that the firm endeavors to maximize its profits.

The Output Equilibrium of the Firm

Overlooking any possible nonpecuniary motives, the firm will seek that output volume at which profits are a maximum. This is the equilibrium output, for, when profits are at their peak, the firm will be relieved of any incentive either to accelerate or to curtail its output flow, but instead will seek to maintain its production schedule. In principle, whatever the market structure, it will always be profitable to expand output whenever the addition to total revenue (TR) exceeds the addition to total costs (TC) caused by the output increase. Alternately, it will be lucrative to contract production when the total revenue drop is less than the dent in total costs.

The change in TR is, of course, simply the marginal revenue, MR, while the movement in TC is obviously MC. Hence, whenever $MR \gtrless MC$, production plans will be rearranged. Maximum profitability entails that $MR = MC$.

Recalling the formula for MR ($= P - Q\Delta P$), under pure competition where the firm can sell additional quantities of output without influencing market price, the $Q\Delta P$ portion of the formula vanishes (for $\Delta P = 0$), so that $P = MR$. The condition for maximum profitability of the firm under pure competition thus becomes

$$P = MR = MC \qquad (8.2)$$

This is the necessary condition of output equilibrium under pure competition on the presumption that the firm seeks to maximize its earnings: we can refer to it more succinctly as $P = MC$. It need not mean that each entrepreneur consciously thinks in marginal concepts, though it is, however, a property of the maximum-profit position. If profits are at a maximum under pure competition, whatever the computations are that led the firm to this output position, marginal cost *will be equal* to price.

To make sure that the output volume is one of maximum short-period profits rather than minimum losses, there is a supplementary proviso that must be attached; namely, that price also exceed average variable costs.[3] Thus, the full condition for maximum short-period profits under pure competition may be written as

$$P = MR = MC \geqq AVC \qquad (8.3)$$

[3] This also guarantees that marginal costs are rising. If $MC = P$ while marginal costs are falling, the position will be one of minimum profits, rather than one of maximum profits or minimum losses.

If the AVC curve sits everywhere above market price, the $(P = MC)$ position would be one of minimum losses rather than maximum profits.

On a rising MC curve, the full condition can be satisfied only to the right of the minimum AVC point. Through time, for the firm to remain in business under the ruling ownership and not succumb via bankruptcy, fixed costs must also be recovered. Otherwise, even if the firm continues production with its current equipment, its plant is unlikely to be replaced as it depreciates. The longer-period equilibrium would thus require the substitution of AC for AVC in equation (8.3).

Diagrammatic Illustration

To illustrate these relations, MC and AVC curves are drawn in Figure 8.2(A) along with price line PP', which is indicative of a market price external to the firm and beyond its control.

Output would thus be pushed to OM, for, at any other output level, the firm would fail to maximize its profits. Producing less than OM, the OP (price) addition to total revenue of a further unit of output would exceed the MC addition to total costs: it would be profitable for the firm to step up its output rate. Beyond OM, where $MC > OP$, the firm would deem it prudent to curtail its production schedule. OM, therefore, is the equilibrium output; at this output volume the impulse to advance or contract production disappears.

At all outputs greater than OL and less than OM, the supplementary condition of equilibrium is satisfied; namely, $P > AVC$. As short-period profits occur at all outputs between OL and ON, this condition by itself would hardly afford an unequivocal directive for the most profitable production policy, since it leaves the most profitable output level undefined; in contrast, as long as $P < AVC$ at all output levels, the firm would withdraw from production entirely.

The difference $(P - AVC)$ at the $P = MC$ output denotes the unit

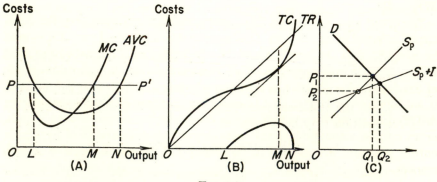

FIG. 8.2

earnings available to meet fixed costs and profits. The product OM $(P - AVC)$ represents the total earnings available for profits and fixed charges. There is no need to draw in the AC curve, which includes the long period fixed charges, for this cannot affect the equilibrium output. So long as $P > AC$ at output OM, fixed charges will be covered.

Total-Revenue and Total-Cost Curves Solution

Clearly, it is uninformative, so far as the position of maximum profits is concerned, to advocate that the firm produce an output at which $P > AC$; as this is true at numerous outputs, it leaves the solution overly determinate. Frequently, it is suggested that the firm ought to produce the volume of output at which its AVC (or AC) is a minimum. But this would be valid only if the aim of the firm were to maximize its unit profits rather than to maximize total profits. The output indicated at the minimum point on the AC curve will be the most profitable one only if market price is at the minimum AC level: AC will then be tangent to PP' at the output at which $P = MC$.

The output of maximum profits can also be described by TR and TC concepts and curves. The problem can be posed as one of rendering

$$TR - TC = \text{maximum} \qquad (8.4)$$

In Figure 8.2(B), as price to the firm is constant, TR is linear and rising.[4] TC, of normal form, is also included. Subtracting the vertical differences of these two curves, the total-profit curve, the LN path, emerges. This reaches its maximum at output OM, although profits are present between output volume OL and ON. At OM output, the slope of TC is the same as TR, signifying that $MR = MC$. This is a characteristic of maximum profitability, whether the business man makes his computations by subtracting totals or calculates first unit profits and then total profits, or thinks in marginal terms. If profits *are* maximized, *then* $MR = MC$.

We could also insert the TVC curve in Figure 8.2(B). As the TVC curve is parallel to TC, at OM output its distance from TR would be greatest and its slope would be the same as TR, indicating that $MC = MR$. In commonsense terms, this emphasizes the subordinate role of fixed costs. For, insofar as a firm maximizes the difference $TR - TVC$, it will obtain the largest sum possible for covering fixed charges and for distribution as profits. As TFC is the same whether output is zero, 1 unit, or an infinite amount, the fixed costs cannot influence the most profitable output position. Movements in TVC and TR are alone decisive in this respect.

[4] For each possible price, another linear TR curve can be drawn.

Equilibrium Factor Hire

The condition of equilibrium factor hire for the firm selling in a competitive market is also worth elucidating. Essentially, it is an alternative mode of expressing the output equilibrium condition for the firm, because, once we have determined the factor hire, the output volume is implicitly decided, and vice versa.

As in the earlier expansion-path analysis, factor prices are assumed constant. Variable factors are hired at each output in the amounts indicated along the expansion path.[5] Consequently, at each output level we have

$$\frac{MP_a}{P_a} = \frac{MP_b}{P_b} = \frac{MP_c}{P_c} = J \tag{8.5}$$

Multiplying each marginal product by the market price of output, P_x, we have

$$P_x \frac{MP_a}{P_a} = P_x \frac{MP_b}{P_b} = P_x \frac{MP_c}{P_c} = P_x J \tag{8.6}$$

We shall refer to each $P_x \cdot MP$ as the *marginal-value product* (abbreviated *MVP*) of each factor.

It will pay the firm, under competitive conditions, to hire additional factors so long as their marginal-value product exceeds their price, or whenever the J ratios exceed unity, for then the factor will add more to the value of output than to total cost. Hence, if $MVP_a > P_a$, more of factor A will be hired.[6] Conversely, if the marginal-value product lies below the factor price, some units of the factor will be released. Maximum profits thus require an equality of MVP_a and P_a or a value of unity for the J ratios. It can be shown that this entails $P = MC$: it can be quickly recognized to be so for the one-variable factor case where $MC = P_a/MP_a$ so that $P_x \cdot MP_a = P_a$.

Market Equilibrium

Building from the idea of the output equilibrium of the firm, we can deduce the market-supply curve.

Whatever the market price may be, we now know the output volume that will be rendered by each firm. Guiding the horizontal price line PP' of Figure 8.2(A) parallel upward or downward would reveal that output

---

[5] See pp. 35–37, above.

[6] As *MVP* is equal to the marginal product of the factor multiplied by the selling price of the product, when other factors are fixed the *MVP* curve is the marginal-product curve of Figure 4.2, transformed in the chart field only by the market-price multiplier. See p. 49 above.

volumes greater or less than *OM* would be offered in the market as the market price rises or falls. The *MC* curve is thus, literally, the firm's supply curve under competitive conditions.[7]

This will be true of each firm. By aggregating at each price the quantity offered by the individual firms, we can construct the market-supply curve: this is compounded out of outputs along each firm's *MC* curve at each particular price. It should be noted, however, that this unique association of the market-supply curve and the aggregate of the individual-firm *MC* curves is valid only on the maximum-profit hypothesis, and in stationary conditions, where the anticipations are that price will remain unchanged; for then, whatever the price, the firm will produce its maximum-profit output volume and proffer all of it for sale on the belief that the price will persist. Another attribute of the market-supply curve that should be stressed is that each point on its course refers to *a rate of production per unit of time* and that at each market price $P = MC$ for each firm. In the fixed stock analyses, the supply offerings came from existing stocks at each price; now each price is conceived to evoke a particular quantity of output. Construed as representing output flows, a new dimension and a new vitality are imparted to the supply curve, enhancing its use in realistic problems.

The condition of market equilibrium when supplies are variable and buyers and sellers are numerous can be summarily described. Figure 8.1(B) contains the appropriate diagram. The market-equilibrium price is located at the ordinate height of the intersection of the *D* and *S* curves. But, whereas the earlier price analysis pertained to a fixed stock of goods, the system has now been opened to output flows: each price point is conceived to evoke the corresponding rate of production on the supply curve in each unit of time, while each point on the demand curve shows the amount of purchases at each price over the same time interval. Thus, the $D_x = S_x$ position refers to an equality in the rate of purchase and production over the same time span.

The Influence of Inventory

Let us consider the relations between marginal-cost and market-supply curves in somewhat more detail.

In Figure 8.2(C), the *D* curve is drawn along with S_p, where the latter refers to industry output at the respective prices: the S_p curve is thus a composite of individual firm *MC* curves. The $S_p + I$ curve represents the effect of inventory withholding or unloading. At prices above OP_2, there is a net flow from inventories; below OP_2 there is inventory accumulation. In the case illustrated, the effect of drawing existing stocks

[7] A firm holding part of its output for its own consumption can be viewed as *buying* at the market price.

down is to reduce market prices and enlarge sales. In this illustration, while each firm does equate MC to P, there are simultaneous market increments to supply so that the analysis pertains simultaneously to both stocks and flows. Pricewise, the $S_p + I$ curve is relevant.

If the $S_p + I$ curve were to cut the S_p curve from the left—if the S_p and the $S_p + I$ curves in the figure were reversed—then, conceivably, current output for some (or all) firms might go beyond the $MC = P$ intersection. Later on, we shall examine the circumstances in which this may occur.[8]

Summary

The condition of output equilibrium for the firm under pure competition thus requires that $P = MR = MC \geqq AVC$, while for the industry we must have $D_x = S_x$, so that the flow of output from all firms at a particular price equals the rate of purchases of all buyers. In order for the output decisions of firms to be consistent with the market equilibrium, it must be assumed that all firms estimate, as the basis for their output volume, the price that actually does rule later as the equilibrium price for the industry.

Questions

1. Explain:
   a. Why $P = MR$ under pure competition.
   b. Why $P > AVC$ must also hold good as a further condition for maximum profits.
   c. The nature of the output at which $P = MC$ when $AVC > P$ at each price.
   d. Why the slopes of TR, TC, and TVC are the same at the $MR = MC$ output.
2. How do you measure profits in Figure 8.2(A)? in Figure 8.2(B)? Which is a better diagram for this purpose?
3. What output would be produced if the firm were to seek to maximize unit profits? What significance do you attach to this output? Does it have any "long-run" significance? Explain why or why not.
4. Prove that when $MVP_a = P_a$, $MVP_b = P_b$, ... etc., then $MC = P$ under pure competition. (Hint: use the analysis of Chapter 3, p. 59.)
5. "Fixed costs are of decisive importance in determining price and output policies in mass production industries." Evaluate, at the present stage of your training.
6. Why must correct anticipations be introduced even in the simple case of pure competition?

VARYING AMOUNTS OF EQUIPMENT

The analysis so far has been confined to the output equilibrium of existing firms. Besides neglecting the entry of new firms, the analysis

---

[8] See pp. 331–332, below.

has been silent on the matter of the current firms' augmenting or depreciating their equipment mass. In introducing these elements, we are immediately thrust into long-run price analysis. While heretofore the output forthcoming at each price was associated with a particular equipment array, we now recognize the opportunities for firms to penetrate into or to depart from the industry, or for old firms to augment their facilities or to allow them to deteriorate.

Alterations in the plant facilities available to the industry will exert a profound effect on the supply curve. In general, an expansion in the number of firms and in the stock of ready equipment ought to push the supply curve to the right. Price, through time, ought to fall unless there is a counterbalancing expansion in demand. To show this is to embark on the third of our price analyses.

The Maximum Layout: Stationary and Competitive Conditions

Let us study the problem as it presents itself to a firm considering the plant and equipment volume that is most profitable prior to ordering its erection and installation. At this stage, we assume that the product price in the output sector contemplated by the firm is subject to pure competition and that, as conditions are stationary, the firm envisages that this price will remain constant over time.

Recalling the planning curves of Figure 4.4 in Chapter 4, we can superimpose on any of the diagrams a horizontal line to depict the level of market price. Typically, profits will be maximized at the output and for the layout at which the MCP curve intersects the price line. It would be to the entrepreneurs' advantage, therefore, to erect the layout indicated on the ACP curve at the $P = MCP$ output. If the ACP is discontinuous, there may be several intersections of P and MCP; we would then be interested in the one involving maximum profits. One further restriction must be imposed so that the size of the firm under pure competition is not indeterminate; namely, that the ACP curve be of U shape, reaching a minimum and then rising. Figure 8.4(B) contains a valid illustration.

Manifestly, even under competition, the layout chosen may be "larger" than the plant that minimizes ACP.[9] The minimum ACP point is important only because new firms would abandon efforts to enter the field unless price promised to exceed this minimum sum. But, if price was expected to be permanently higher than this minimum ACP sum, conceivably a larger profit sum could be amassed with a larger layout. But

---

[9] Really minimum unit costs occur by not building a plant and not producing at all—unit costs are then zero! But this result hardly yields any profit. However, it does indicate that the minimum ACP point is an inadequate criterion for selecting a layout.

this would entail that other firms are unable to acquire the equipment consonant with the minimum ACP point, and thereby drive down market price while securing a permanent niche for themselves in the field. Hence, the selection of an equipment volume to the right of that embodied in the minimum ACP point foreshadows differences in entrepreneurial abilities or opportunities, or mistaken calculations about the entry plans of other firms.

Expansion of Existing Firms

The planning curve has been linked to a firm considering entry and building a new plant. A firm already operating and possessed of productive facilities may also ponder whether it should augment (or diminish) its stock of equipment. The problem of organizing a new firm involves a movement from zero plant to a positive plant size; the problem now is that of altering the plant size.

In this analysis, we must assume that one of the AC curves that molds ACP is already a reality, and that the successive AC curves and the final ACP curve evolve from the combination of new facilities plus old. Starting from any individual AC curve along ACP, if we include the old plus new capital costs (besides all other costs) in the new AC curve that lies to the right of the old, the expansion will be warranted if total profits with the new plant exceed those with the old. Ultimately, what is involved is the theory of obsolescence and replacement which, in a way, is merely expansion in a new guise. The problem will be treated at slightly greater length later on.[10]

As an alternative formulation of the problem, if new capital charges on borrowed sums are excluded from the cost calculation (although depreciation is included), and if the additional earnings with the additional equipment exceed the rate of interest, the installation will commend itself. The effect of the plant construction, however, will be to shift the entire AC curve from its previous position to a new location.

Entry Equilibrium of the Industry

There is a further aspect of the theory of competitive entry that ought to be unraveled—namely, the conditions of equilibrium with respect to entry. Normally, it is declared that the entry of additional firms will cease when the new firms are unable to earn "normal" profits. Including normal profits as a long-period cost (and thus assuming them to be contained in the cost curve), when the current number of firms are earning normal profits the U-shaped AC curve of firms acting under the rule of competition will be tangent to the price line, as in Figure 8.4(B), with the tangency occurring at the minimum AC point.

[10] See pp. 258–259.

Again we run into the chronic antithesis—that between the expected and the actual, between estimates and events. It may be that new firms cannot earn normal profits, so that, by objective criteria, we can declare that the industry is in equilibrium. Yet, despite the current level of profits, however "normal," or even abnormal and on the low side, this fact may well be irrelevant. For, so long as entrepreneurs of new firms *believe* that a profitable level of earnings will ensue, they will not cease their efforts to enter. Contrariwise, the facts may disclose abnormally high profits. Nevertheless, entry may be stifled through ignorance, erroneously pessimistic forecasts, or impediments in the loan markets.

Judged, therefore, by the number of implemented decisions to enter, the industry may suffer perpetual shocks and chronic instability as entrants endeavor to create a spot for themselves despite subnormal profits of existing firms. An immanently normal profit structure may well be destroyed and transformed into losses by the efforts of new firms to penetrate the field. *Hence, the concept of equilibrium,* in the sense of an absence of inherent forces that attract new firms and new entrants, *is not amenable to objective description in terms of an absolute level of profits.* In the commonplace version, the industry will be in equilibrium when only "normal" profits are being earned. But this entirely overlooks the motives underlying entry, the mental attitudes and prognostications of entrepreneurs. Rather than being susceptible to meticulous arithmetical calculation, everything hinges on the vision of the individuals who appraise the future prospects in the diverse fields. Situations that would be unattractive to most bystanders might still act as a powerful magnet to others. Or, whatever the truth of actual profits, entry will be deferred and numbers in the field will be "normal" and in "equilibrium," entirely aside from the actual facts on profits. Objective criteria are meaningful only in a stationary world where the future was expected by all interested participants to remain unchanged and where unfolding events proved the correctness of their judgments.

Exit as a Subjective Phenomenon

Just as the level of profits that invite entry is a subjective phenomenon dependent on forecasts, the forces conditioning the exit and the economic demise of a firm are likewise mental estimates of the future. There are, however, certain differences; for, when a firm is in the conjectural stage, its ability to enter depends not only on its profit projections but also on its capacity to command capital funds—something usually taken for granted in the literature. Once in the field, however, the firm will continue production so long as sales proceeds can be made to exceed at least total variable costs by a margin equivalent to earning prospects on the current market value of the fixed equipment in an alternative field. Even if earnings are "normal" or "subnormal," in the sense that a given entrepreneur would feel that prospects would not be conducive to his entry if he were again faced with the opportunity of coming into the field, the level of earnings at which the same individual will leave the field is probably lower. *The expected level of profits that fosters entry is probably greater than the sum that compels exit.*

Pure Competition and Entry

The matter of entry must not be confused with that of the purity of competition. As long as there are innumerable buyers and sellers of the product acting individually rather than in concert, a purely competitive price will be the upshot. If homogeneous entry into the field is possible, and if new firms do embrace the opportunities, the effects of the entry of innumerable new firms will betray themselves in a rightward shift in the supply curve and thus in a fall in market price and in profits of firms already ensconced in the industry.

Entry then can be associated with the degree of perfection of the equilibrium and competition; it is superfluous, however, to the concept of pure competition itself. Likewise, if present members of an industry dissolve and disappear, closing out their productive activities, unless the exit is on such a scale that the remaining sellers are too few for competitive price making, the exit also is irrelevant for the concept of pure competition. Questions of the opportunities for homogeneous entry, of the obstructions placed in the path of new firms, of aversions to and preferences for heterogeneous entry, will have their implications on the level of prices, on the level of profits for the contemporary firms, and on the nature and variety of goods produced to satisfy consumer wants. For, if homogeneous entry is fettered, new firms will resort to the production of imperfect rather than perfect substitutes. If we agree to categorize the perfection of competition by examining the conditions respecting entry, any obstacles to new firms, whether they be psychological or objective, will occasion imperfections in competition. The equilibrium can then be described as one of pure but imperfect competition. For price making, however, the theory of pure competition is ample.

The Irreversibility of Supply

Whatever the forces which provoke it, the expansion of the stock of equipment within the industry will shift the entire market-supply curve; the effects of the additional equipment on the economy will linger until it wears out and disappears from the productive scene.

Thus, as equipment expands in response to a rise in price ensuing from a rightward shift in the demand curve (say, from D_1 to D_2), the supply curve in Figure 8.3(B) is successively dislodged to S_1, S_2, S_3. Connecting

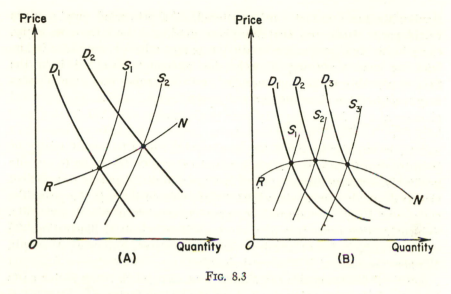

FIG. 8.3

the various equilibrium points of intersection of each D and S curve, we derive the "long-run" path of adjustment of supply to demand, represented by the curve RN. This need not be a continuously upward-sloping curve, for, as new firms enter (or old firms expand), production costs may fall; the curve RN of Figure 8.3(B) is but one possible picture of falling long-run supply price. If, after its initial growth, the market-demand curve shifts leftward because of a sudden aversion to the product, so long as the equipment remains on hand S_3 will be the relevant short-period supply curve.

As the stock of equipment in the industry is likely to depreciate and be withdrawn from the field in a manner different from the order of its introduction, RN is unlikely to represent the path of contraction. Hence, RN, the long-run supply curve, is "irreversible" as compared to the reversibility implicit along each S curve which portrays the actual facts of price-quantity relations for both expansion and contraction with the existing array of equipment. Each point on RN should be interpreted as the "long-run" output associated with the corresponding price so long as the latter is perpetuated over time.

External Economies

Undoubtedly, it is perplexing to find that RN, the long-run supply curve, is downward-sloping. When we study this phenomenon, we see that it is attributable to very special causes. For example, there appears to be little reason why resources required by the firms decline in price as the industry widens; the contrary would appear to be the more logical results. Moreover, if factor prices altered, *all* short-period supply curves would move rightward—not only those attributable to the new entry. Conceivably, however, as the industry expands, a host of specialist industries may come into being to service the common needs of this industry: in a sense, the growth, improvement, and cheapening of factor supplies may constitute the ultimate source of production economies. Technological changes also make an impact; their consequences are thus treated only implicitly in the "long-run" analysis. Perhaps, because of indivisible agents, demand for specialist services may have been too small before the industry growth to permit any firm that catered to the trade to operate profitably. Lawyers cannot survive in a town until it becomes of sufficient size to demand their services in sufficient volume through the year; the same would hold for doctors, carpenters, repairmen of all sorts, etc. Sub-contracting firms provide a more obvious industrial illustration. All this may explain the falling long-run supply curve. Following Marshall, to whom the concept is due, we designate these cost changes as "external economies." Diseconomies can similarly be charged to rising factor costs because of more intensive demand for productive factors.

Diagrammatically, the effect of external economies can be visualized by aid of Figure 8.4(A). Suppose that industry output is $Q_1 = 10,000$ units. Then, MC_1 is the marginal-cost curve of a typical firm in the industry. If industry output goes to $Q_2 = 15,000$ units, the firm's marginal-cost curve shifts rightward to MC_2. In the figure, OQ_1 and OQ_2 represent the firm's output points equivalent to Q_1 and Q_2 industry production. The "long-run" MC curve for the firm is thus the broken line MC_i^2.

External diseconomies would require that the cost curve shift leftward, from MC_2 to MC_1. One other point appears clearly in the diagram: it is quite possible to have external economies with *rising* "long-run" marginal cost phenomena.

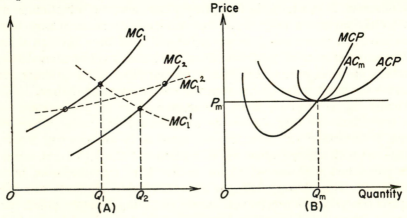

FIG. 8.4

The Long-Run Equilibrium: A Critical Note

It is well to observe again the arbitrariness in the analysis of the long-run equilibrium position: everything depends on the degree of shift in supply curves in response to underlying demand changes and, more immediately, the market-price changes. If firms are optimistic that the price rise heralds an upward trend, entry may be rapid and expansion of existing firms may be vigorous. If it is believed that the demand and price rise are ephemeral, little or no expansion may be stirred.

A demand rise accompanied by substantial technological innovations in the industry can likewise have effects rather different from a demand movement which occurs in an environment in which entrepreneurs are hampered by an inability to acquire essential personnel or facilities. Thus, while the concept of the "long-run" adaptation is an important notion designed to separate more ultimate from more immediate effects, the precise lines of the long-run adaptation depend on the incentives, the expectations, and even the motivations and personality of the entrepreneurial movers. The actual time pattern of the adaptation will also be influenced by these factors. A long-run adjustment reached steadily will also have implications for the economy that are different from a movement that runs in fits and starts. A steady adaptation at a slow pace is not equivalent to one that flows quickly. For all of these reasons, the long-run adjustment, though real, is not one that permits safe and precise quantitative forecasts. Finally, the fact that new disturbances are always intervening as long-run adaptations take place inevitably contributes to the uncertainty of entrepreneurial adjustment—even to some erratic and confused responses—while serving to place the economist on guard against attributing a too definite reality to such analyses.

Unfortunately, these precautions and admonitions have not been usually observed in much of the literature where long-run adaptations are not merely presented to indicate that ultimate phenomena may differ from the more immediate, but are delineated as if they have an actual reality and relevance of their own. Such a position involves several question-begging assumptions, particularly its postulate of an ultimate constancy even while it is resolving merely one problem of change.

Finally, as we shall see later, the adaptation of an entrepreneur—or any individual, for that matter—in an economy of change where the future is uncertain will never be the same as in an economy without change, or with change when the dimensions of the latter are certain. Acts performed with conviction inevitably differ from behavior under uncertainty. This element, too, has been overlooked by those who offer long-run analysis with precise cost curves and sharp features, rather than the more blurred and tentative descriptions that are closer to the facts.

The "long-run" is a mental construction; reality will conform to it only in an unusual concatenation of circumstances.

Before closing this discussion, we ought to examine Figure 8.4(B). This diagram is often used to portray the long-run equilibrium of the firm. As drawn, it shows the ACP curve just tangent to the market price of OP_m at output OQ_m. Hence, it is argued that the firm will select and actually utilize that bundle of equipment implicit in AC_m. This sort of adaptation is held to be typical for old firms.

Clearly, this analysis is valid if: (a) the identical ACP experience is commonplace to all firms; (b) price through time, and factor prices over time, are expected to hold constant so that AC_m is always the least costly layout per unit of output; (c) entrepreneurs hold these views with absolute conviction. Merely to state these conditions is to appreciate the rather stringent assumptions on which so many analyses are predicated. Scant wonder, therefore, that predictions from them are often scarcely applicable to real world events.

Questions

1. "Under pure competition, with unrestricted entry, a new firm will always build a plant and equip it so that unit costs are at the lowest level on the ACP curve." Discuss conditions in which this proposition would or would not be valid.
2. Draw an AC diagram for the problem of expanding the facilities of an existing firm. Demonstrate that the ACP curve then depends substantially on the original starting point.
3. Discuss the concept of "normal" profits. What is the relation of profits to entry and exit? Explain the extent to which these categories are objective and measurable.
4. "Long-run supply depends on all the accidents, enthusiasms, fears, and personalities of entrepreneurs in an industry. Hence, the equilibrium portrayed is not unique and, instead, depends on the time dimensions and the path of adaptation." Evaluate.

STABLE AND MULTIPLE EQUILIBRIA

After the study of the equilibrium position, questions of the stability of the equilibrium relationship and the possibility of multiple equilibrium values invite our scrutiny. In the stability analysis, we inquire whether or not the system contains forces strong enough to restore the equilibrium relationships when either output or market price accidentally deviates from the $D_x = S_x$ equality.

Fascinating though it is, the stability study is not an end in itself. Instead, by exposing the recuperative forces in the system when once the structure is pushed slightly ajar, we ought to discover how the economy responds at least to minor shocks in the form of slight changes in either the D or S data. Unless the system can right itself for small disturbances in the guise of nonequilibrium prices and quantities while the underlying forces are unaltered, there can be little assurance that an eventual $D_x = S_x$ position will be forthcoming when there is a real modification in D and S. The stability analysis thus constitutes an introduction to economic dynamics.

There are two possible minor disruptions to the equilibrium in particular markets that we shall want to unravel; generally, we can deal with them simultaneously: (1) a shock to the equilibrium structure by way of a price slightly above or below that indicated at the $D_x = S_x$ point; (2) output slightly greater or smaller than the quantity represented at the $D_x = S_x$ position.

Briefly, the equilibrium will be perfectly stable if both the slight price or quantity disturbance sets forces in motion to restore the original $D_x = S_x$ price-and-output pattern. It will be completely unstable if, after either shock, the immanent D and S forces urge the system ever farther from the initial $D_x = S_x$ point; it will be but imperfectly stable if movements in one direction are self-correcting while a departure in the other direction renders the system unstable. A system in neutral equilibrium will permit the new price-output location to perpetuate itself; the initial dislodgment invokes neither recuperative forces to restore the original position nor a further oscillation to a new point of rest.

Stable Equilibria

As we visualize the conventional downward-falling D curve and the upward-rising S curve, an accidental price fall from the equilibrium price (while the $D_x = S_x$ output continued to be offered) would release forces tending to restore the equilibrium price. As $D_x > S_x$, or as there is excess demand at the lower price, the market pressures in a free market would drive the price upward. An increase in output would also carry its own corrective; the supply price would exceed the demand price for this larger output volume, and the fall in price and consequent disappointment of sellers' expectations would restrain future output, thereby serving to re-establish the earlier equilibrium. A price rise or output decrement would also disclose stabilizing tendencies. We conclude, therefore, that the normal D and S field, with the demand curve downward-falling to the right and the supply curve upward-rising to the right, will presage a perfectly stable market.

Unstable Equilibria

A complete reversal of the normal position of the S and D curves, shown in Figure 8.5(a), is the most obvious illustration of a completely unstable equilibrium. A rise in price, with output at the $D_x = S_x$ level, will reveal an excess demand; despite the market shortages at the higher price, the subsequent decreased production would intensify the rising price tendencies. Similarly, with an initial price fall, the departure from

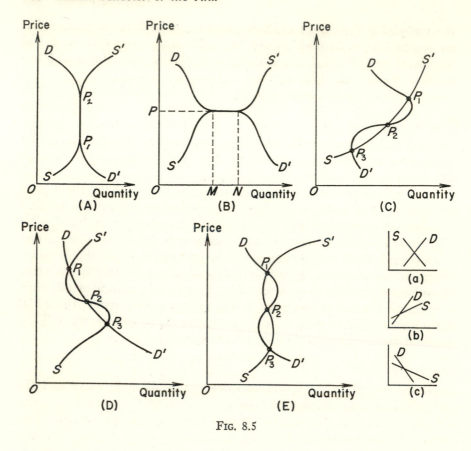

Fig. 8.5

$D_x = S_x$ would involve unsold stocks; despite the excess supply and falling price pressures, each fall in prices would further unbalance the situation. Like results follow from either an increment or a decrement of output.

Strangely enough, if both *D* and *S* have the same directional slope, as in Figure 8.5(b), with the *D* slope steeper than that of *S*, the equilibrium will be fully stable for a price dislodgment despite the incongruous *S* curve, for at a price in excess of (below) the equilibrium level, output will rise (fall) and the excess supply will drive the price back. However, if output, rather than price, were accidentally to rise or fall from the equilibrium output quantity, the results would be destabilizing: for the demand price exceeds the supply price to the right of the equilibrium output, and lies below it to the left of this. If the *D* and *S* letters are interchanged in Figure 8.5(b), the configuration is *unstable* for a price dislodgment but stable for an output aberration.

If the demand curve is of normal form while the supply curve falls, as in Figure 8.5(c), the instability arises from a price departure from the equilibrium level with stability for an output departure. Again, if the letters D and S are interchanged in Figure 8.5(c), the results are reversed. Thus, there may be price stability with output instability, or price instability with output stability.

Neutral Equilibria

Figure 8.5(A) contains an example of neutral price equilibrium; $D_x = S_x$ over the full price range P_1 and P_2. Any price in this area is possible, and so the actual market price is indeterminate: neither a price rise nor a price fall would stir any ameliorative forces. An example of output rather than price indeterminateness is portrayed in Figure 8.5(B); for an output change, the system is in neutral equilibrium between OM and ON, while for price movements it is stable.

It is easy to draw rather grotesque curves purporting to evidence instability. But the display is merely of diagrammatic interest unless we have reason to suspect that it represents some reality. In general, we can surmise that, whenever the income effect is normal on the demand side, or whenever negative I effects for one portion of the consuming public are counterbalanced by positive I effects of the remainder of the consumer body, the normal D curve will describe the course of market demand; from this side the stability conditions will then be fully satisfied. Analogously, when each firm's MC curve is rising because of diminishing productivity, stability from the cost side will ensue. When personal services are sold, a positive income effect from those providing the service is a prerequisite for a normal rising supply curve.[11] When these conditions are not satisfied, the market may be either partially or entirely unstable.

A Symbolic Statement

Symbolically, the condition for perfect stability can be written as follows. Denote the excess D or S at a price P as D_E, and denote D_p as the

---

[11] Although a rising market-supply curve is usually likely, it is possible for the volume of services rendered to decline as price (and, thus, producer's real income) rises. Sellers may consume part of their own product, which they could not afford to do at a lower price and low income; for labor services, workers may prefer more leisure at a higher hourly wage rate to exerting the normal quantity of effort, thus decreasing the number of hours worked. For example, if an individual's demand for money is relatively fixed, an increase in wage rates may decrease the amount of labor available, because each wage earner would want to work fewer hours. Complaints against absenteeism in war industries in 1942 may show evidence of a strong positive income effect for leisure and relatively small income demand for more commodities. The supply curve, where hours of work are measured on the horizontal axis, would tend to turn back to the vertical axis. (See SS' in Figure 8.5 [D].)

difference of demand and supply price for some output quantity X. Hence, $D_x - S_x = D_E$ and $D_p - S_p = D_p$. The former way of looking at the stability question is associated with the name of Walras, with the emphasis on excess supply at a price in excess of the equilibrium level. Emphasis on a positive D_p to the left of the equilibrium output is essentially Marshall's approach to the question.

For perfect stability with respect to price and output dislodgments, we must have

$$\frac{\Delta D_E}{\Delta P} < 0 \tag{8.7}$$

$$\frac{\Delta D_p}{\Delta Q} < 0 \tag{8.8}$$

With perfect stability, both values are negative. From the $D_x = S_x$ position, a fall in price must widen the excess demand and an increase in output must raise the gap between supply and demand price. To be sure that the simultaneous price adaptations in other markets do not derange the stable equilibrium, a price movement in some other commodity Y must help eliminate the excess demand for commodity X, or leave it unaffected. Thus,

$$\frac{\Delta}{\Delta P_y}\left(\frac{\Delta D_E}{\Delta P_x}\right) \leqq 0 \tag{8.9}$$

If the equilibrium is perfectly stable, with D and S curves of normal form, it follows inevitably that, if D shifts to the right with S unchanged, P will rise and sales and output will be greater. Likewise, if S shifts to the right with D unchanged, the equilibrium P will be reduced while sales and production will be enlarged.

The stability analysis thus conveys some meaningful results for comparative statics where only equilibrium positions are compared. A problem of dynamics, however, is to trace the path by which the new equilibrium is reached, emphasizing the time required before the new balance obtains. Building on these ideas, it becomes possible to regard the stability analysis as a small excursion into dynamics. If we write ΔP for the change in price, and Δt for the passage of time, if the equilibrium is perfectly stable and without any tendencies to fluctuate over time, then

$$\frac{\Delta P}{\Delta t} = 0 \tag{8.10}$$

Thus, the stability analysis develops into an exercise in dynamics in which the value of this ratio will normally differ from zero; this relation between economic dynamics and stability analysis has been termed the *correspondence principle.*[12]

Multiple Equilibria

The examination of neutral equilibrium disclosed some instances of multiple equilibrium. It is useful to pursue this analysis farther, for it portends certain indeterminacies and certain elements of arbitrariness in even the competitive order. Figure 8.5(C) furnishes an illustration, with an abnormal backward-bending D curve typical of inferior goods. The normal supply curve, SS', thus intersects it at the three points— P_1, P_2, and P_3.

All three positions satisfy the equilibrium condition $D_x = S_x$. Depending on the price arrived at, the chain of substitutes and complements will be differently affected in this overdeterminate situation. Stable equilibria, however, are located at the extremities, at prices P_1 and P_3. At either position, an increase in price would render $S_x > D_x$, while a slight fall would leave $D_x > S_x$. At P_2, on the other hand, a slight accidental price or output movement would set in motion a train of events that could not be deflected short of P_1 or P_3.

Multiple equilibria might also be ascribed to an abnormally shaped supply curve cutting a normal demand curve; Figure 8.5(D) is illustrative. Suppliers, perhaps, prefer leisure to income; consequently, at higher prices they offer fewer services. Stable equilibria obtain only at the end points, P_1 and P_3, where an accidental rise in price would reveal an excess supply quantity and would exert pressure for a return to the original equilibrium position. When, as in Figure 8.5(E), both D and S are abnormal, the end points are stable for a price rise but not necessarily for a (slight) output modification; for the latter the price adjustment might shuttle between P_1 and P_3. Parenthetically, it is to be observed that an abnormal S curve must, in its uppermost region, revert eventually to normal form as income opportunities become immensely attractive to present suppliers or to new suppliers entering the output fold. The same may be said for the lower stretches of the D curve: lower income classes enter as buyers while previous purchasers, with only a slight outlay, can obtain a large amount of the commodity and, by substituting it for other products, release income for diversion to other "superior" goods.

Questions

1. Explain the connection between stability analysis and comparative statics.
2. What is the distinction between the Marshallian and the Walrasian stability conditions?

[12] P. Samuelson, *Foundations of Economic Analysis,* Part II.

3. Why need we bother with the stability conditions? Isn't the location of the equilibrium position sufficient? Explain.
4. What would be the typical market responses to D or S changes if neutral equilibria were commonplace?
5. If such conditions are common, "multiple equilibria go far to destroy the arguments for noninterference in market phenomena." Discuss.

PURE COMPETITION AND OPTIMAL RESOURCE USE

Before concluding, some remarks ought to be made on the relation between a purely competitive economy and an optimal economic order. It was observed in the preceding chapter that an optimal system would have as characteristic the equality of MRS ratios in consumption for household purchasers; this could be assured through uniform, nondiscriminatory prices in purchase markets. In production, marginal costs would be equal to price, and, in factor use, marginal-value products would be equal to factor prices.

In all these respects, a purely competitive order gets perfect marks, so much so that too often pure competition is regarded as *the* optimal order rather than being viewed as *one* form of economic and social organization that does promote a Pareto-type allocation of resources.

It is necessary to make this distinction between pure competition and the optimal economy for several reasons. In the first place, when external economies are recognized, clearly it is possible for marginal private and marginal social products to differ so that a purely competitive order will no longer be optimal. Perhaps this discrepancy is a minor one, but this is a question of fact, not one for theory or general reasoning. Observing that this problem is at the base of much of the clamor for government action, it may be surmised that its dimensions are large rather than insignificant.

Further, in determining (a) the volume of investment, (b) the variety of products, (c) the degree of advertising, (d) the rate of growth, (e) the rapidity of technological innovation and transmission of new ideas, and (f) the division of income, it may well be that a purely competitive order may evidence serious shortcomings. Perhaps they may still be less than those of other modes of economic organization. Still, so long as they exist, they ought to deter the too-facile identification of pure competition with the optimal or ideal system of resource use.

SOME NEGLECTED POINTS

The chief topics discussed in this chapter have been the demonstration of the equilibrium output of the firm under pure competition and the exposition of the market-supply curve as compounded out of the cost curves of individual firms. The competitive equilibrium was then redefined as entailing an equality between the rate of flow of purchase and production at the market price, or at the quantity at which demand price and supply price were equivalent. The stability analysis was supplementary to the basic analysis of the market behavior of the firm.

In surveying the ground covered, it is appropriate to remark on some of its implicit assumptions. In the output equilibrium of the firm, it was presumed that the aim of the entrepreneur was to maximize pecuniary profits. Of course, this presupposes that the entrepreneurial effort accompanying greater output is a costless psychological phenomenon. Undoubtedly, this is in error. Conceding the irksomeness of organizing greater output volumes, it is unlikely that the $P = MC$ output will be forthcoming if, to the left of this output amount, the valuation of leisure exceeds that of the extra income to be derived from the greater production. Conversely, if the entrepreneur derives pleasure from production, even though profits are thereby diminished, output will transcend the $P = MC$ profit-maximization norm. We may infer that the latter conduct will be relatively rare compared to the inertia leading to output below the profit-maximization level.

Manifestly, other motives for departing from the $P = MC$ output position would not be absent even under pure competition. We shall be able to distill even more reasons for nonmaximum profit output under monopoly; hence, we defer the formal presentation of the theory of nonpecuniary profit maximization until the ensuing chapter.

Another hypothesis vital to the theory is a familiar but neglected one; namely, *that the firm is able to command enough financial resources to equate MC to P,* granting the absence of nonmaximum profit motives. Now, even if all markets were purely competitive, in the sense that nowhere in the economy could a firm influence price, this hypothesis seems unwarranted. Before output can be produced, materials must be purchased, variable factors must be paid in advance of the sales of their output, and even fixed costs must (usually) be paid before the output is sold and cash is received. Even if interest rates were competitively determined, there might still be barriers to the firm's borrowing the amounts appropriate to its profit maximization. With borrowing conceived of as entailing the sale of securities (that is, promissory notes of one kind of another), the market lenders may refuse to purchase the offerings of the particular firm. Lack of finance thus becomes a stringent limitational factor, indeed.

A theory of competitive output equilibrium that presumes unlimited borrowing opportunities, ignoring the obstacles in the way of securing funds to float the maximum profit output volume, is surely incomplete. Although we do nothing to repair the deficiency currently, it is well to note it and to be explicit about it. Pure competition in factor markets and product markets, while access to funds is limited, is an insufficient guarantee of the $P = MC$ output volume.

Analogously, in the theory of plant selection it is generally assumed that the firm is able to command whatever financial resources are necessary to enable it to order the volume of equipment that will maximize its profits. Merely stating this as the implicit proposition is sufficient to throw it under a cloud. Pure competition in selling products and hiring factors would never assure, by itself, access to funds for all entrepreneurs. Although more work remains to be done to demonstrate the economic significance of these limitations, it is an easy matter to see that they may prevent the erection by a new firm of the $P = MCP$ layout and restrain the $P = MC$ output tendencies of an active producing unit.

Chapter 9

꧀꧀꧀꧀꧀꧀꧀꧀꧀꧀꧀꧀꧀꧀꧀꧀꧀꧀꧀꧀꧀꧀꧀꧀꧀꧀꧀꧀꧀꧀꧀꧀꧀꧀꧀꧀

Equations of General Equilibrium:
Input-Output Analysis and
Linear Programming

This chapter makes a minor detour in our study of particular markets, for it is concerned with the equilibrium of the entire economic system. For the equations of general equilibrium analysis, fathered by the great Walras, purport to show the simultaneity of the total equilibrium adaptation, where happenings in one market are substantially contingent on events in surrounding markets.

We shall not follow this essentially mathematical study very far; it is the sort of investigation that appeals to mathematicians turned economists—and vice versa. Most concrete problems require only an acquaintance with the main equilibrium concepts, to provide protection against cruder omissions in basic arguments or the neglect of complications developing from seemingly insubordinate connections. Because of a rather obvious affinity, the chapter contains a sketch of input-output analysis and linear programming.

The Reality of General Equilibrium

Few would quarrel with the proposition that an equilibrium between decisions to offer certain quantities for sale and decisions to purchase an identical quantity at the same price is possible in particular markets—in the sense that the price that sellers are willing to accept (while continuing to produce the same quantity) tends to coincide with the price that consumers are willing to pay. That there is a balance between production and expected sales is attested to by the fact that new output is generally sold, with unplanned inventory fluctuations being fairly small. Although this is only an indirect and tenuous evidence of economic order and competitive balance—for the world has its fill of monopolistic prices —there is good reason to suspect that an approximate balance of expected and actual prices and outputs would be commonplace in particular markets, especially if the more violent swings of the business cycle were eliminated.

Presumably, we might be ready to concede that particular equilibrium analysis divulges some fundamental tendencies in the economy, the end-results of market processes that secure a balance. But we are much more reluctant to concur in the view that all markets are in balance simultaneously, admitting that the tendency in individual markets is still a long way from subscribing to the proposition for all markets simultaneously, over any period of time. But, once we acknowledge that, in each particular sector of the economy, there are equilibrating forces at work, there is less reason to shrink from the view that the entire system can settle down in an equilibrium of supply and demand. In this light, the "famous fiction" of the stationary state is not without interest, for it describes the price and output tendencies within the entire economy over (short) periods of time when the fundamental data remain as postulated. Nevertheless, whatever violence the idea of general equilibrium does to our sense of reality (and even if we entirely reject it as an artificial image of the economic world), it is still incumbent upon us to demonstrate the conditions that need to be satisfied for the general equilibrium of production and consumption.

The Equations of General Equilibrium

The delineation of the equations of the general equilibrium of the economic system, based on the theory of the interconnectedness of all parts of the economic universe, was the crowning accomplishment of Leon Walras.[1] His teaching revealed that an economic event in one market, however minor its magnitude, would have repercussions in other markets. Because of this perception, the simultaneity and mutual dependence of economic phenomena have come to be widely appreciated.

Walrus organized his analysis into a series of equations which, with occasional modification, have persisted until this day. His approach is most definite in application to the special *stationary* problems he envisaged, but the difficulties of economic theory are associated with time and the concomitant changes of technology and capital equipment. There is a good deal less unanimity on how these may best be incorporated into economic analysis.

[1] See Leon Walras, *Elements of Pure Economics* (London, 1954), William Jaffee, trans. For further reading, the following may be recommended as informative on a nonmathematical level: Gustav Cassel, *Theory of Social Economy* (London, 1932), Chapters 3–4; E. H. Phelps Brown, *The Framework of the Pricing System* (London, 1936). Other references appear below, in the programming discussion.

Goods, Factors, and Consumers

Suppose that there are produced in the economy the different commodities $A, B, C, \ldots, M$. Each good is produced in amount X, so that we have

$$X_a, X_b, X_c, \ldots, X_m :: \text{amounts of particular commodities}$$

There are various factors of production in the economy, 1, 2, 3, $\ldots$, in number N. Let Y represent the amount of (the services of) each factor of production used in the production process. Thus,

$$Y_1, Y_2, Y_3, \ldots, Y_n :: \text{amounts of services of productive factors}$$

How we choose to distinguish factors of production is often a matter of convenience; for example, Y_1 may refer to men under forty, Y_2 to older workers. Yet, for purposes of production, they may be of equal efficiency, so that their age or other noneconomic characteristic is unimportant from the immediate point of view. The greater the recognition of factor heterogeneity, the larger the number of factors in our listing.

Our system also contains consumers, in number j, with each consumer having tastes or a utility function represented by U. Thus,

$$U_1, U_2, U_3, \ldots, U_j :: \text{individual utility functions}$$

The Endogenous Variables

Thus, our model contains goods, in number M; productive factors, in number N; consumers, in number J. In an economy of pure exchange, where goods are conceived to be in existence independently of production, the equations involving the productive factors drop out, leaving only a need to consider equations for U and X. In a continuing economy, where consumption is contingent on production, the X quantities are a resultant of the efficient application of the Y productive services.

Essentially, the economic process involves *a matching of productive resources to satisfy tastes* through the intermediary of produced goods. In this complex contest, the particular volumes of output—the various $X_a, \ldots, X_m$ quantities—and the attached prices of goods and productive services evolve. These are the *endogenous* variables, the determinates, the outcome of the basic economic data of tastes and resource quantities which govern the mechanics of the economic process. Thus, the variables solved are the prices $(P_a, P_b, \ldots, P_m)$ for the respective commodities, the prices $(P_1, P_2, \ldots, P_n)$ for the respective factors, and the produced quantities of goods $(X_a, X_b, \ldots, X_m)$. For simplicity, we impose the assumption that all factors are in perfectly inelastic supply and all are employed.

Of course, actual prices and quantities are determined in the market-place. What Walras did was to show that the solution could be achieved mathematically, if only we had the requisite information. Equationally, we then have to derive:

$$X_a, X_b, X_c, \ldots, X_m \;::\; \text{quantities of commodities}$$

$$P_a, P_b, P_c, \ldots, P_m \;::\; \text{prices of commodities}$$

$$P_1, P_2, P_3, \ldots, P_n \;::\; \text{prices of services of productive factors}$$

As a convenient simplification, we take one price as the common denominator of value (the *numeraire,* as Walras termed it); thus, $P_a = 1$. Prices of all other goods are thereby expressed as multiples of P_a. Equationally, we have to determine the quantities of M-different commodities, the $(M - 1)$ associated commodity prices, and the N prices for the productive factors.

Consumer Equations

For each consumer we have a utility function, in form:

$$\left.\begin{aligned}
U_1 &= U_1(X_a{}^1, X_b{}^1, X_c{}^1, \ldots, X_m{}^1) \\
U_2 &= U_2(X_a{}^2, X_b{}^2, X_c{}^2, \ldots, X_m{}^2) \\
U_j &= U_j(X_a{}^j, X_b{}^j, X_c{}^j, \ldots, X_m{}^j)
\end{aligned}\right\} \tag{9.1}$$

In the parentheses, the subscripts refer to the particular commodities possessed by the respective consumers, identified by the superscript.

From Equations (9.1) it is possible to derive equations of marginal utility, involving partial derivatives obtained for each good, and written as $\phi_{1a}, \phi_{1b}, \ldots, \phi_{1m}$; there would be m-equations for each consumer, one with respect to each good for each consumer. Therefore, there are $(j \cdot m)$ marginal utility equations. With 1,000 consumers and 100 commodities, the marginal-utility equations would number 100,000.

For utility maximization, each consumer must bring the ratio of marginal utilities into line with prices:

$$\frac{\phi_{1b}}{P_b} = \frac{\phi_{1c}}{P_c} = \cdots \frac{\phi_{1m}}{P_m} = \phi_{1a} \tag{9.2}$$

The ratio ϕ_{1a}/P_a, where $P_a = 1$, represents the marginal utility of "money"—conceived simply as the numeraire commodity.

For each consumer there is also a budget equation, or budget constraint; geometrically, this limitation was embodied in the price line. Analytically,

$$X_{1a} + P_b X_{1b} + P_c X_{1c} + \cdots + P_m X_{1m} = P_1 Y_1 + P_2 Y_2 + \cdots + P_n Y_n \tag{9.3}$$

Equation (9.3) merely declares that, for each consumer, the purchase outlay must equal the income from the services of productive factors; some of the X's and Y's may well be zero.

If the amount of services of productive factors provided by each household is known, so that the Y's are given, and assuming that product prices $P_a, P_b, \ldots, P_m$, and factor prices $P_1, P_2, \ldots, P_n$, are known, then Equations (9.2) and (9.3) determine the consumer's purchase plan. We have to solve for the purchase quantities $X_{1a}, X_{1b}, \ldots, X_{1m}$, involving m-variables in all.

For m-goods, from (9.2) we have $(m - 1)$ equations. With (9.3) there are m-equations in all; the number of equations equals the number of unknowns. In principle, therefore, the system can be solved.[2]

Market-Demand Equations

For each consumer, and for each price set, the purchase intake $X_{1a}, X_{1b}, \ldots, X_{1m}$ is determined. Given the prices, the total purchases by the market group become

$$\sum_{i=1}^{j} X_{i_a}, \sum_{i=1}^{j} X_{i_b}, \cdots, \sum_{i=1}^{j} X_{i_m}$$

Purchases thus depend on the ruling set of prices. Aggregating the individual market purchases, the market-demand schedules are written as:

$$\left. \begin{aligned} X_b &= f_b(P_b, P_c, \ldots, P_n; P_1, P_2, \ldots, P_n) \\ X_c &= f_c(P_b, P_c, \ldots, P_n; P_1, P_2, \ldots, P_n) \\ X_m &= f(P_b, \ldots, P_n; P_1, P_2, \ldots, P_n) \end{aligned} \right\} \tag{9.4}$$

There are $m - 1$ demand equations here, each being a function of m-product prices and n-factor price (or income) variables; there are only $(m - 1)$ equations because, as we shall see, if we know the purchase quantities of $(m - 1)$ goods, we immediately can learn the remaining mth equation. The unknowns are $2m - 1$ in number, consisting of m of quantities of X and $m - 1$ prices (remembering that $P_a = 1$).

While we shall not need them, m-supply equations can be written as functions of the same unknowns; each supply equation is then equated to demand.

Budget Equation

Summating the individual budget equations, we establish the aggregate income and outlay function:

$$X_a + P_b X_b + \cdots + P_m X_m = P_1 Y_1 + P_2 Y_2 + \cdots + P_n Y_n \tag{9.5}$$

[2] The marginal-utility equations contain variable items involving $X_a, X_b, \ldots, X_m$. With the P's known, the values of these must be so adapted to satisfy equations (9.2) and (9.3).

Treating the Y's as known,[3] this adds one new equation, making m in all (with 9.4), and n new $(P_1, P_2, \ldots, P_n)$ unknowns, making $2m + n - 1$ unknowns in all. From (9.5) it is clear why the demand equation for X_a is superfluous; given $X_b, X_c, \ldots, X_m$, then X_a follows.

Unit Cost Equals Price

Next, are the equations involving the *coefficients of production,* and the stipulation that unit costs equal prices; this was Walras' way of declaring that neither profit nor loss was realized in production.

$$\left.\begin{array}{l} P_1Y_{1a} + P_2Y_{2a} + P_3Y_{3a} + \cdots + P_nY_{na} = P_a \\ P_1Y_{1b} + P_2Y_{2b} + P_3Y_{3b} + \cdots + P_nY_{nb} = P_b \\ \text{- - - - - - - - - - - - - - - - - - - -} \\ P_1Y_{1m} + P_2Y_{2m} + P_3Y_{3m} + \cdots + P_nY_{nm} = P_m \end{array}\right\} \quad (9.6)$$

The interpretation of equations (9.6) is rather direct. For example, Y_{1a} refers to the amount of Y_1 factor service, and the Y_{2a} term denotes the amount of Y_2 factor service, etc., in 1 unit of product A. Thus, the Y_{1a}, $Y_{2a}, \ldots, Y_{na}$ terms represent the coefficients of production, where each is regarded as fixed and unvarying, regardless of factor prices. Multiplying factor amounts per unit of output, by unit factor prices, yields the average cost per unit of output. In (9.6) we have m new equations without any new unknowns; recall that the Y-coefficients are regarded as exogenous, as data given us by technology. This yields $2m$ equations against $2m + n - 1$ unknowns.

Output Equations

As prices become determined, according to (9.6) the amounts of goods demanded can be ascertained, in (9.4). However, it is necessary that there be at hand enough productive factors to produce the quantity of goods wanted.

$$\left.\begin{array}{l} X_aY_{1a} + X_bY_{1b} + X_cY_{1c} + \cdots + X_mY_{1m} \leqq Y_1 \\ X_aY_{2a} + X_bY_{2b} + X_cY_{2c} + \cdots + X_mY_{2m} \leqq Y_2 \\ \text{- - - - - - - - - - - - - - - - - - -} \\ X_aY_{na} + X_bY_{nb} + X_cY_{nc} + \cdots + X_mY_{nm} \leqq Y_n \end{array}\right\} \quad (9.7)$$

These equations stipulate that the total amount of Y_1 required for the production of X_a, of $X_b, \ldots,$ of X_m, is equal to or less than the amount of factor Y_1 that is available. To eliminate any problem of involuntary

[3] We could, if we wished, treat them as unknown at this stage and later stipulate full employment; this comes to the same thing.

unemployment, and any implication that this has for factor prices,[4] we stipulate that factors are available in precisely the right amount; hence, we eliminate the inequality sign in (9.7).

Equations (9.7) yield n new equations, without any new unknowns.

So far, therefore, we have $2m + n$ equations, and $2m + n - 1$ unknowns.

The Redundant Equation

The summary yields one equation in excess of the number of unknowns; for a well-behaved set of equations it appears that the system is overdetermined. Since Walras' day, however, it has been known that there is one equation that is redundant. Let us consider this.

Suppose we have the following equations:

$$a_1 X_1 + a_2 X_2 + \cdots + a_n X_n = C_1 \tag{9a}$$

$$m a_1 X_1 + m a_2 X_2 + \cdots + m a_n X_n = m C_1 \tag{9b}$$

Actually, from elementary algebra, it is clear that (9a) and (9b) are not independent equations; they are the same equation, one being a multiple of the other.

Something of the same nature can be done with our system of equations. In proof, multiply the first equation of (9.6) by X_a, the second by X_b, etc. Thus,

$$
\left.
\begin{aligned}
X_a(P_1 Y_{1a} + P_2 Y_{2a} + \cdots + P_n Y_{na}) &= P_a X_a (\equiv X_a) \\
X_b(P_1 Y_{1b} + P_2 Y_{2b} + \cdots + P_n Y_{nb}) &= P_b X_b \\
\text{------------------} \\
X_m(P_1 Y_{1m} + P_2 Y_{2m} + \cdots + P_n Y_{nm}) &= P_m X_m
\end{aligned}
\right\} \tag{9.8}
$$

Equations (9.8) tell us that total factor outlay equals total sales receipts.

Multiply (9.7) by factor prices:

$$
\left.
\begin{aligned}
P_1(X_a Y_{1a} + X_b Y_{1b} + \cdots + X_m Y_{1m}) &= P_1 Y_1 \\
P_2(X_a Y_{2a} + X_b Y_{2b} + \cdots + X_m Y_{2m}) &= P_2 Y_2 \\
\text{------------------} \\
P_n(X_n Y_{na} + X_b Y_{nb} + \cdots + X_m Y_{nm}) &= P_n Y_n
\end{aligned}
\right\} \tag{9.9}
$$

The set (9.9) tells us that *the factor payments from each industry equal factor income.* Now, if we add the left-hand side of equation set (9.8), involving factor outlays, and do the same for the left-hand side of (9.9), we see that they are the same: all that was required was a convenient

---

[4] For the price of factors in surplus supply could be zero or negative unless the supply curve were perfectly elastic at some level.

multiple for each equation. Thus, the respective right-hand portions of the two sets are also equal.

But this indicates that the budget equation (9.5) is actually redundant; it is not an independent equation but is implicit in (9.6) with (9.7). Eliminating (9.5), we are left with $2m + n - 1$ equations and $2m + n - 1$ unknowns.

Some Mathematical Implications

The last discussion should warn us that mere equality of equations and unknowns is insufficient for a solution: the equations must also be independent.[5]

Further, the equations may be independent and equal in number to the unknowns, yet yield several solutions: such systems are generally regarded as indeterminate. For example:

$$a_1 X_1 + a_2 X_2 = 0 \tag{9c}$$

$$a_3 X_1 + a_4 X_2 = 0 \tag{9d}$$

These are linear equations of degree zero. A solution of the equations appears as:

$$\frac{X_1}{X_2} = \frac{a_4 - a_2}{a_1 - a_3} \tag{9e}$$

Innumerable *relative* solutions of X_1 and Y_2 emerge. These equations are particularly instructive because often, in demand theory particularly, it is argued that equations are of precisely this form—that demand depends only on relative prices; a major problem concerns the implicit theory of money that is incorporated into this theory. This can occasion economic and mathematical difficulties for the determination of the full system. These are intricate matters better pursued in an analysis more fully oriented toward the mathematical aspects of the subject.[6]

Some Conclusions on General Equilibrium

In an avowedly mathematical treatment, the equations presented here can be modified and altered; the assumption of fixed-production coefficients, for example, could be dropped and a system permitting factor substitutability contingent on factor prices could be inserted. Likewise,

[5] For an extended discussion, and references to the literature, see R. Dorfman, P. A. Samuelson, and R. M. Solow, *Linear Programming and Economic Analysis* (New York, 1958), Chapter 13.

[6] For detailed exposition, see Don Patinkin, *Money, Interest, and Prices* (Evanston, Ill., 1956).

the nature of factor-supply conditions could be elaborated and the simplifying hypotheses of full employment abandoned. The theory of interest and the dynamics of changes in the stock of capital could also be attempted. In so doing, a full mathematical treatment of economics, in all its intricacy, could be essayed by one with sufficient technical prowess.

Of course, different students would make the emendations differently: this would restore the same ultimate controversies to economics, but largely confining participation to the mathematically adept, rejecting the aid of those proficient in economics but deficient in mathematical skills. This could be a heavy price to pay; there is scant justification for the proposition that all good ideas—that all good analyses—emanate only from mathematical skills.

But this line of inquiry, provocative as it may be, can be dropped; indeed, having peeked at the house in which Walras lived, just what permanence and value does it seem to possess?

Of course, it indicates at least the possibility of mathematical solutions for economic phenomena. Yet, even in the era of computers, when we realize that for 100 million consumers and only 100 commodities there are 10 billion equations of merely type (9.1), it seems that the marketplace is in no great danger of being superseded! Furthermore, we have not even begun to speak of the enormity of the task of gathering the data—of giving vitality and substance to the equations. Despite the development of statistics and the amassing of information, this remains too formidable a problem for the near future: almost everyone would have to become engaged in data-gathering; there would be no assurance that the information would not be obsolete by the time it was organized and processed for calculation!

Essentially, what Walras and subsequent equation builders have shown is the interdependence of economic quantities—the locking of the full nexus of economic phenomena in what seemed to be separate and distinct sectors of the economy. This is the main contribution of general equilibrium analysis.

If the demand for each commodity were independent of prices in other markets, or if alternative modes of expenditure were not a fact, or if each consumer modified his expenditure only slightly in response to price changes while outlay was transferred by each individual to a different commodity, then the hypothesis of market independence would indeed be serviceable although it would ignore some very definite (if small) interrelations. But it is not only taste interdependence that gives credence and vitality to the general equilibrium concept: there is the fact that ultimately all entrepreneurs draw resources from the common pool of productive factors—this is at the bottom of the principle of opportunity cost, a major proposition drawn by the tradition of literary economists and implicit in the general equilibrium equations of mutual dependence.

That the equations have attracted mathematically minded scholars to the theory of economics has been an accomplishment of a different nature, involving the development and the evolution of the science in its present state.

INPUT-OUTPUT ANALYSIS

The boldest and most audacious attempt to use the equations of general equilibrium has been in the development of *Input-Output Analysis*, originated by Professor Leontief. The practical problems in application, in extracting data, in industrial classification and computation, as well as the many steps toward creating a more dynamic scheme, belong to a specialized study: the literature is already fairly massive.[7] Our own task is the more modest one of demonstrating how the central theme is tied to the main corpus of economics. Full-sized courses are already devoted to the subtleties and perplexities in building input-output tables.

From the central idea that industrial outputs in our economy become the inputs of other industries, or that purchases of factor services are made in order to make sales of more finished outputs, the theory was born and grew: for a time it attracted so much attention that it tended to dwarf the pursuit of ordinary economic analysis. Time has lent perspective, so that now it is discerned primarily as of major interest and importance in organizing data and systematizing the presentation of the output flow through the economy, disclosing the major and minor ramifications in the structure.

The Closed System

The original, and still basic, conception for didactic purposes involves a complete circular flow, descendent from the ideas of the Physiocrats and the Tableau Economique.[8] For example, we can view the economy as comprising agricultural and manufacturing firms, and households. Agricultural output, say, is sold to the manufacturing industries (for processing) and to households directly. Manufacturing firms sell materials to agriculture for farming and the remaining output to households. The latter buy from both—and also sell their labor services to each.

[7] The original statement is in W. W. Leontief, *The Structure of American Economy, 1919–1939* (New York, 1951, ed. 2). A recent textbook, with further extensions and references, is H. B. Chenery and P. G. Clark, *Interindustry Economics* (New York, 1959).

[8] A. Phillips, "The Tableau Economique as a Simple Leontief Model," *Quarterly Journal of Economics* (February 1955).

In this mechanistic conception, workers sell their services to derive income to buy the industrial outputs of the economy, etc.: household purchases thus become the inputs necessary for labor outputs. Consumption is thus visualized merely as an intermediate process on the road to production, rather than as an end in itself.

Schematically, the thought can be illustrated in Table 9.1.

TABLE 9.1—INPUT-OUTPUT TABLE

Output \\ Input	Agriculture	Manufacturing	Households	Value of Outputs
Agriculture......	...	$50	$50	$100
Manufacturing...	$20	...	$60	$80
Households......	$80	$30	...	$110
Value of inputs...	$100	$80	$110	...

Manifestly, the dollar sum of outputs as revealed in Table 9.1 is exactly equivalent to the value of inputs: inputs are bought to produce goods for market sale, to buy inputs, to produce goods, etc. Circularity is the obvious characteristic.

Analytically, the construction builds from the earlier equations (9.7); this is its association to general equilibrium analysis.

Write:

$$a = \text{inputs embodied in each unit of output}$$
$$X_i = \text{output of industry } i$$
$$i = \text{factor-input subscript}$$
$$j = \text{industry-output subscript}$$
$$i = j, \text{ in the closed model}$$

Thus,

$$
\left.
\begin{aligned}
-X_a + a_{ab}X_b + a_{ac}X_c + \cdots + a_{aj}X_j &= 0 \\
a_{ba}X_a - X_b + a_{bc}X_c + \cdots + a_{bj}X_j &= 0 \\
a_{ca}X_a + a_{cb}X_b - X_c + \cdots + a_{cj}X_j &= 0 \\
\text{-- -- -- -- -- -- -- -- -- -- -- --} \\
a_{ia}X_a + a_{ib}X_b + a_{ic}X_c + \cdots + a_{ij}X_j &= 0
\end{aligned}
\right\}
$$

(9.10)

The interpretation should be self-explanatory: the *a*-coefficients merely replace the Y's of (9.7), while the $(-X)$ values denote the total "output" of productive services.[9] Thus, a_{ab} refers to the amount of factor A in 1 unit of product B; X_b refers to the total output of B. Similarly, a_{aj} refers to the amount of factor A in 1 unit of product J, etc. The *a*-coefficients can be understood to mean either physical amounts, as ounces, pounds, tons, or gallons—or man-hours of work—or dollar amounts of the factor, per unit of output. The X's would also have to be read in a compatible fashion; in computational representations of the economy, the Leontief flow-charts must inevitably be in dollar sums (or fractional components of money totals).

The Open Model

In the "open" model, some purchases of output are represented as "final," or conventionally interpreted as such. Consumers are regarded as providing a purpose for production, not as an industry or a slave being maintained at minimum cost; the same point of view holds true for government purchases and for investment activity in the year in which capital goods are created and installed. Foreign trade is also regarded as an exogenous source of final demand, outside the model; imports are purchased as intermediate products by the several industries or are purchased directly by the final demand sectors.

In principle, so far as the equations go, it is no longer necessary for the number of industries and factors to be equal: ordinarily, where the final demands of consumers, government, and investment comprise a form of exogenous industry, then $j > i$. A more difficult and important problem in the open model—for the closed one is utterly inadequate for practical application—is the classification of industries. For, depending on whether, say, automobile toolshops are included in metalworking, or woodworking, or electrical, or automotive, etc., the size of the respective coefficients will be affected. Further, the fewer the industries in the classification, the greater the loss of detail; also, the less meaningful the calculated coefficients. With more numerous industries, the classification decision becomes more vital.

Simultaneously, as the number of industries is enlarged, the computational complications are multiplied: 100 industries signifies 10,000 possible entries for coefficients—and 100 simultaneous equations to solve; some simplification occurs when some entries take a nearly zero value. Also, when industries are regarded as homogeneous (e.g., the "agricul-

---

[9] Mathematically, what is interesting in this model is that all equations are linear and homogeneous of degree zero, as in **(9c–9d)**. Thus, the solution yields only *relative* values.

tural" industry of large rancher or grower, or sharecropper and family garden, put in the same industry pot), then the main diagonal in the table is no longer zero: wheat farmers buy corn products, or metal-working firms buy from non-rival metalworking firms. Challenges are posed by the treatment of capital depreciation, the inclusion of inventories, the division of wholesale and retail trade, transportation, the classification of imports, etc.; the resolution of these vexing matters and a host of many kindred applied problems is elaborated in the specialist literature.

Recognizing that, over the long view, capital equipment is created as an output to serve as a source of future inputs, there have been many efforts to incorporate this idea in dynamic models. These have received more cautious acceptance than the stationary-flow models.

Conclusions

As observed, input-output analysis represents a bold and ingenious attempt to utilize the ideas of general equilibrium theory. It has already contributed enormously to organizing and relating data in ways that would have been thought impossible prior to its appearance. It has contributed greatly to an appreciation of coefficient magnitudes, and to the disclosure of degrees of interdependence within the economy. Thus, it has been able to express the innumerable ramifications of public policy on the activity of particular industries and particular levels of demand.

The formidable problems of growth, of industrial heterogeneity, of variable production coefficients, still constitute major problems, supporting the conclusion that we are unable to reduce all of economic activity and interdependence to a few pages of tables; surely, so long as technical change is at least partly exogenous or autonomous, the calculations cannot be presented as eternal verities. Complications of prediction, of forecasting, still remain to plague us, just as in more aggregative and less detailed approaches to the economy in historical evolution.

LINEAR PROGRAMMING

Programming—another extension, and direction, of economic analysis —also at one time threatened to swamp the more conventional theory; time has lent some greater perspective on this, too.

All that is intended here is to lay out the formal structure of a programming problem, contrasting it with the traditional maximization analysis and illustrating some programming situations geometrically and algebraically. Both thin, inviting books and formidable, alarmingly thick, textbooks are available in abundance on the subject.

The Maximization Problem

The typical maximization problem in the theory of consumer behavior, in its formal essence and in the simpler utility terms, involves the following:

Maximize:

$$U = U(X_1, X_2, \ldots, X_2) \tag{9.11}$$

subject to:

$$P_1 X_1 + P_2 X_2 + \cdots + P_n X_n = Y \tag{9.12}$$

Technically, this is described as a restrained maximization problem, for the utility ascent is limited by the budget restraint. In the theory of the firm, the formal question is nearly the same: maximize output subject to a specified total cost restraint.

Suppose, in the utility maximization problem, we had imposed additional restraints of the following sort: (1) that the consumer's outlay on food was to be limited to one fourth of income, or on clothes to one tenth, etc. Suppose, too, that these rationing rules were effective in holding outlay below free market patterns. Imagine that there were further restrictions in force compelling the purchaser to acquire specified *limited* amounts of each good, surpassing, for some commodities, the free market quantities. Imposing these additional conditions, and stipulating that answers must be at least of certain size, we are constructing a programming problem.

An example prepared by Dorfman for the theory of the firm[10] can be provided.

An Illustration of Limiting Processes

Suppose that a firm can produce stampings for 40,000 automobiles or 20,000 trucks per month, involving a 2/1 ratio. Thus, the production transformation curve appears as AT in Figure 9.1.

Suppose that the auto assembly lines can run at a maximum of 35,000 units, and of trucks, at 15,000. Immediately, limiting factors appear in the lines A_1 and T_1. Too, we can take it that, for engine assembly, 45,000 autos and 17,000 truck engines can be installed each month, shown by the EA and ET lines.

Effectively, therefore, with these limitations the transformation curve is bounded by points 1, 2, 3, 4, 5 in Figure 9.1, approximated in the inset diagram (9.1[a]). As can be seen, there are now sharp edges and discontinuities, rather than a uniform linear relationship. Each "ceiling" is

[10] Robert Dorfman, "Mathematical or 'Linear' Programming," *American Economic Review* (December 1953).

explicable in terms of a particular production limit; each restraint is of a linear nature.

As another illustration, suppose that it is possible to produce output by two processes, perhaps in two plants (see Figure 9.2). In one plant, the ratio of capital to labor (measured in dollar costs per output unit) is 2 to 1, and in the other plant it is 1 to 4. These become the only expansion paths possible; output can be produced with the one process or the other.

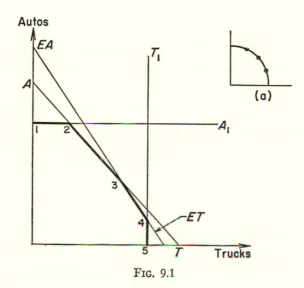

FIG. 9.1

Lines such as *AA*, *BB*, ..., can be drawn connecting equal amounts of output produced by each process: they are our isoquants of earlier study. What is of interest is that *factor combinations along these lines can also be hired, resulting in the identical output volume.*[11] This is an unexpected and vital conclusion—namely, that intermediate combinations of the factors can be used, divided between the two plants to keep them both operating. It suggests that, depending on costs, capacities, or other restraining factors, output can be divided among the plants in literally innumerable ways, so that the 2/1 and 1/4 restraints are less onerous than at first sight.

Among the interesting problems to which linear programming has been applied are the "diet" problem—one of minimizing total food outlay in such a way that the basic nutrients (of calories, vitamins, etc.) are ob-

[11] For proof, see Dorfman, *op. cit.*, p. 806n. The factor-use levels in each firm would be given by a parallel to the respective expansion paths from *AA*, *BB*, ..., etc.

tained; of course, this is a special sort of rationing situation. International trade, where the respective outputs in the different countries are produced at constant cost, can also be interpreted as a programming situation. Illustrations from the theory of the firm abound; two have already been given. The famous transportation or assignment-type problems were among the earliest, and led to the pioneering investigations: for example, a firm with several factories must supply numerous markets; there are varying productive capacities in each factory. Ships of varying capacity, carrying tonnage to several ports, might have to be

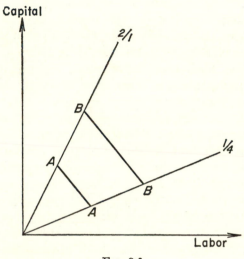

FIG. 9.2

routed to other ports to pick up tonnage for return at a total minimum cost—or days in transport, as under wartime conditions when time is at a premium. A variety of other problems, often subtle versions of a typical specimen, have also been devised.

The Formal Statement

Formally, the linear program problem is of the following sort:
Maximize:
$$Z = P_1 X_1 + \cdots + P_4 X_4 \tag{9.13}$$
Subject to:
$$
\left.
\begin{aligned}
a_1 X_1 + \cdots + a_{14} X_4 &\leq C_1 \\
a_2 X_1 + \cdots + a_{24} X_4 &\leq C_2 \\
a_3 X_1 + \cdots + a_{34} X_4 &\leq C_3
\end{aligned}
\right\} \tag{9.14}
$$
With values restricted to:
$$X_1 \geq 0, \ldots, X_4 \geq 0 \tag{9.15}$$

The affinity to the simpler calculus problems (9.11)–(9.12) of economics should be apparent; there is also the linear aspect of all equations. With the restriction on solutions, so that a "foolish" computer, for example, should not turn up negative answers for shipments, or prices, or nutrients, etc., as well as in the number of side conditions and variables, the novelty of the mathematics becomes appreciable.

A sidelight on these problems is that, in every programming statement, a maximization problem can be turned around to one in minimization; perhaps this is not so surprising when one realizes that from the ground the top of the mountain is the nearest point to an airplane in the sky—everything depends on the vantage point. Mathematically, this ability to turn the problem about possesses the advantage that it is often more feasible to solve the "dual" problem, as the alternative statement is called. Sometimes the economic interpretation of the dual is immediately meaningful; in other cases, it establishes some strange conceptions.

Solving the programming problem, especially when variables and conditions are numerous, can be a frustrating business; several computational procedures have been devised. Nonlinear programming problems, for simpler situations, are also well developed currently: for economic problems this is important especially when returns to scale problems involve increasing or decreasing returns. Integer programming has also evolved, for situations where only discrete values are meaningful: it makes no sense, for example, to say that a firm should ship to 4½ markets! It must sell to either 4 or 5—or some other integer number. The curious student is recommended to consult any of several fine treatises on these subjects.[12]

[12] For simpler statements, aside from the Dorfman article, see W. J. Baumol, "Activity Analysis in One Lesson," *American Economic Review* (December 1958); J. R. Hicks, "Linear Theory," *Economic Journal* (1960).

A "thin" book (in size) and mathematical in style, is S. Vajda, *Theory of Games and Linear Programming* (London, 1956); a "thick" and lucid volume is the Dorfman, Samuelson, and Solow volume. Another account is provided in *Linear Programming and the Theory of the Firm* (New York, 1960), K. E. Boulding and W. Allen Spivey, eds.

Chapter 10

꒱꒱

Monopoly

In this chapter we begin our studies of monopoly markets. So long as a firm produces a commodity regarded by consumers to be distinct from other products, the door to monopoly pricing is open. The seller—or, impersonally, the firm or income-maximizing unit—will perceive that its demand curve departs from the horizontal and that its sales are a function of the price named. To forestall the characteristic features of monopolistic competition, the degree of market interdependence between the firm's product and that of any other firm is assumed to be virtually nil. It will then be the entrepreneur's privilege to name that price which maximizes the firm's income; no longer is it merely a matter of producing to sell at a price determined by the external, impersonal forces of the market. The task of price policy that devolves upon the entrepreneur will be a matter as vital from a profit standpoint as that of economical resource management.

A Methodological Comment

A methodological comment is in order at this point. To impart a comparative flavor to our results, we shall assume that the firm whose pricing policy is under scrutiny formerly adjusted "competitively," equating MC to P, and that now it undertakes to wield its monopoly power by naming a price more productive of profits.

This is the method of comparative statics. This approach is warranted not only because of our familiarity with the $P = MC$ pricing model but also because it enables us to detect immediately some of the economic derangements caused by monopoly pricing. An unqualified analysis of monopoly price policy by one firm divorced from the concept of general competitive equilibrium, and extrapolated to the case of n firms, implies ultimately an entirely monopolistic world. More realistically, our procedure assumes that the world is partially competitive, with $P = MC$ firms not uncommon, and partly monopolistic. This is closer to the facts—a more rewarding field for study.

Initially, aside from the monopoly-pricing venture, we suppose that other conditions are unchanged: consumer tastes and incomes, factor prices, and input-output data are presumed to be constant. Also, the number of firms, the variety of outputs, and the stock of equipment of firms remain as before. Most of these hypotheses will be shelved as the analytic structure is opened.

Monopoly Is a Matter of Opportunity

It should be underscored at the outset that monopoly pricing is a matter not of motive but rather of opportunity. The objective of the firm is to maximize its earnings, whether it is selling in a competitive or a monopoly market. The difference is that, under competition, the firm is impotent to alter its market price, so it accepts the fact and adjusts its behavior in the light of it. Under monopoly, the firm enjoys the power to name its sales price. In this sense, all firms would like to be monopolists, but, in the nature of things, such aspirations cannot be realized in certain fields. Nonetheless, the motives are the same—the pursuit of maximum profits and the diversion of as large a flow as possible of the income stream to the firm. Under competitive conditions, the fulfillment of this objective through pricing policy is denied to the firm. Profit ends are the same for competitors and monopolists; it is the *opportunities* for fulfillment which differ.

A corollary of this proposition is that it is an error to insist that monopoly is purely a consequence of the size of firms. Large firms, in industries that can absorb but few large firms, are likely to be monopolists.[1] But monopoly is not an attribute of the capital strength or the productive capacity of the firm. Small firms, measured in terms of either volume of employment or the asset value of plant and equipment, may well be monopolists in the fundamental sense of price power. Small monopolies of this sort may, in the aggregate, cast a greater economic spell than the industrial giants whose price policies are open to public scrutiny and responsive to public reaction, and for whom it is thus often incumbent to moderate their price exactions. But the strength of these patterns can be appraised only by empirical inquiry.

These remarks should set our perspective: to focus on price policy rather than size. Size is frequently a source of productive economy; it would be a hollow improvement, say, to correct monopoly pricing by limiting the size of firms, only to find that prices are then higher because of the diseconomies of small-scale production.

By the same token, the enormity or the insignificance of profits has little to do with the notion of monopoly, even though the two are so frequently confused in public discussions of monopoly. Large profits may

---

[1] Or oligopolists, as we shall later describe them.

accrue under pure competition. Conversely, the number of worthless patents and copyrights is legion; the losses of business firms with acknowledged monopoly power are also common. One proposition that might safely be made respecting monopoly and profits is that, if demand is such as to assure profits to firms that price according to competitive formulas, then profits will be even greater with monopoly pricing. If production is unprofitable under competitive arrangements, it *may* be profitable under monopoly. But this is as far as we can go. It is far-fetched, however, to describe monopoly as a guarantor of profits.

MONOPOLY EQUILIBRIUM

Monopoly price and output can be portrayed neatly and summarily as a result of the insight afforded by the marginal-revenue curve.

The Condition $P > MR = MC$

In pure competition, the firm can sell as many units as it cares to at the going price; its demand curve is a horizontal line at a price height corresponding to the market level. Price (or average revenue) and marginal revenue are, to the firm's way of looking at them, identical. Recalling our formula for MR, since the $Q \, \Delta P$ component is zero in pure competition, $MR = P$. Equilibrium output, then, is determined by the relation $P = MR = MC$. A monopolist, on the other hand, will perceive that the demand curve confronting him possesses some inelasticity so that $P > MR$ (for $P = MR + Q \, \Delta P$, where ΔP is not zero). Lacking a settled market price to which he must conform, the monopolist must choose both the output and the price that will maximize his income.

A demand curve D_1 and the corresponding MR curve are drawn in Figure 10.1(A) along with a curve of constant marginal costs. Our guid-

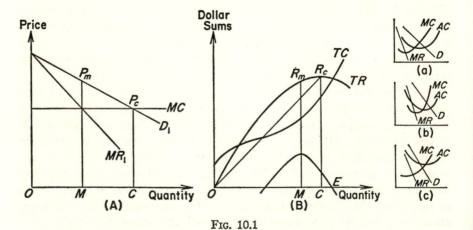

Fig. 10.1

ing principle is that a firm able to name its price will enlarge its output, and hence lower its price, so long as the additions to total proceeds (MR) exceed the additions to total cost (MC). The equilibrium condition for the maximum price-output adjustment is still $MR = MC$, the equality of the increment to costs and sales proceeds. As $P > MR$, the complete rule becomes $P > MR = MC$.

In Figure 10.1(A), this would be at output OM and price MP_m. As a supplementary condition, total revenue must exceed the total costs— either the full total costs or the full variable costs, depending on the time length under discussion: thus, $P \geqq AC$. Curiously, AC bears no determinate equilibrium relation to MC; P, however, must always exceed both AC and MC. In contrast to the competitive equilibrium, in which MC was rising and greater than AC, now MC may even be falling (and AC necessarily falling) at the $MR = MC$ intersection (see Figure 10.1[a]). More will be made of this point later.

The condition for maximum profits is thus as before, that $MR = MC$. While under pure competition $P = MR = MC$, under monopoly $P > MR = MC$. That P exceeds MR under monopoly is, of course, attributable to the fact that $Q \Delta P > O$. As an implication of this analysis, if a monopolist wanted to dispose of a fixed stock of goods, the price that yields maximum profits would maximize total revenue; MR would be zero and E_d would equal 1.

The monopoly equilibrium can also be depicted by total cost and total revenue curves, as in Figure 10.1(B). Monopoly output will be at OM, where a tangent to TR is of exactly the same slope as a tangent to TC; the rate of change in total costs and revenue being of the same order evidences an equality of MR and MC. Once more, the relation $MR = MC$ stands revealed as a property of the output of maximum profits, whether business men think in these categories or not. The vertical spread between TR and TC will, of course, be greatest at this output, denoting maximum profits: hence, the profit curve E, also drawn in the figure, reaches its maximum value at this output. A $P = MC$ price would appear at output OC where average revenue equaled marginal costs; a vector from the origin to TR would be of the same slope as a tangent to TC.

It is often convenient to refer to the output at which $P = MC$ as the "competitive" output and to refer to the $P > MR = MC$ position as the "monopoly" output. Generally, no harm will be done by this use of terms. However, with only one firm in the field, any use of the term "competition" is a misnomer; a single firm would scarcely have any incentive to produce the $P = MC$ output. The reference to competition is intended only to convey the fact of $P = MC$ and is not to be construed as signifying that, if the monopoly firm were decomposed into numerous atomistic units and pure competition evolved, the composite supply curve of the industry would be an unimpaired projection of the monopoly firm's *MC* curve.

Decreasing AC and Monopoly Pricing

In Figure 10.1(A), while *MC* was portrayed as constant, the *AC* curve was omitted completely from the discussion. Under pure competition, with a U-shaped *AC* curve, maximum profits would emerge when $P = MC \geqq AC$. Under monopoly, a unique and consistent equilibrium pattern of *AC* and *MC* is lacking, except that both must be less than price.

Consider Figure 10.1(a). Market demand is such that $MR = MC$ at an output at which *AC* is still falling. Consequently, in equilibrium $P > AC > MC$. In Figure 10.1(b), both *AC* and *MC* are falling at the output of maximum profits. Again, $P > AC > MC$.

In both Figure 10.1(a) and Figure 10.1(b), $P > AC$ at the intersection of the demand curve and the *MC* curve. In Figure 10.1(c), however, if a firm—by desire, accident, or legal compulsion—produced the $P = MC$ output, as $AC > P$, losses would ensue. Short of subsidies or charitable designs, a firm could not engage in business very long under these circumstances. Although we could still term the $MR = MC$ output as the monopoly position, the "competitive" output would have to be redefined as, perhaps, the $P = AC$ output level.

The declining *AC* was demonstrated earlier to be a consequence of the laws of proportionality and size in factor use, generally the presence of indivisible or "lumpy" equipment. If demand is so limited that only one firm (or few firms) can exist in the field, then monopoly or oligopoly will be the upshot, even without limitations on entry. A rightward shift in demand can, conceivably, rid the commodity sector of its monopoly aspects.

Equilibrium Factor Hire

An alternative condition of output equilibrium for the firm under competitive conditions involved the equality of the factor's marginal-value product and its price. The corresponding rule for monopoly requires multiplying each factor's contribution to a unit marginal product by the marginal revenue derived from the further unit of sales, terming the result the *marginal-revenue product*, equating this to the factor price. As before, it will be profitable for the firm to expand its hire of factors until the factor's marginal-revenue product equals its price. This can be shown to entail $MR = MC$. Thus,

$$MR_x \cdot MP_a = P_a$$

where P_a is the factor price, MP_a its marginal product as a fraction of a single unit of output, and MR_x the marginal revenue of a further unit of product X.

Questions

1. "Monopolists are unethical. Competitive firms, as exemplified by wheat farmers, say, demonstrate higher standards of ethics." Comment.
2. Why is it unrewarding to measure monopoly power by the presence of abnormal profits?
3. Prove that, for costless output, the price of maximum profits entails an $E_D = 1$. What would be the competitive price?
4. At the output of maximum profits, can unit costs be falling under pure competition or not? under monopoly? Explain your answers.
5. For equilibrium factor hire under monopoly, explain why the marginal physical product of a factor must be unity or less. How must the MR be interpreted if $MP > 1$?

OUTPUT RESTRICTION

It is interesting to assess the possible magnitude of monopoly-output restriction as compared to a $P = MC$ price policy. The degree of restriction will depend on the shape of the cost and demand curves in the region between the $P = MC$ and monopoly output.

The Demand Curves

It was observed that the MR correspondent to a convex market-demand curve intersected a line parallel to OX at an abscissae distance less than one half the intersection of the same parallel line with the demand curve.[2] Viewing the parallel line as a curve of constant MC, the conclusion is that, with a convex demand curve and constant MC, monopoly output will be less than one half the $P = MC$ total, evidencing a really serious degree of output restriction. On the other hand, when the demand curve is concave, the monopoly output will approach more closely the $P = MC$ norm; it will at least exceed one half the latter level. For a linear demand curve and a constant MC curve, monopoly output is precisely one half the $P = MC$ figure. This last case is shown in Figure 10.2(A); OL is the monopoly output and ON is the competitive level. Thus, the curvature of the demand curve is an important determinant of the degree of monopoly output restriction and, consequently, of the height of monopoly price.

Clearly, if numerous buyers are very sensitive to a price change from the ruling market price, with a price rise driving them to buy a wide

---

[2] See above, p. 16.

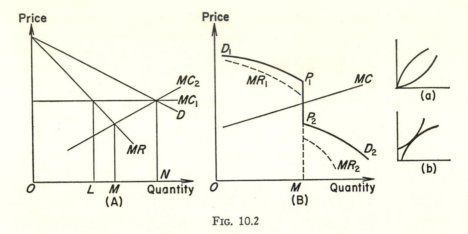

FIG. 10.2

array of substitute products and a price fall attracting custom from the entire commodity field, then the market-demand curve will be extremely elastic in the region of the market price; this will lead to what amounts to a competitive adaptation of $P = MR = MC$ despite the fact that the full demand curve for the firm is not perfectly elastic. A number of price-conscious buyers can accomplish this result even if the demand of other buyers is inelastic. Recalling the earlier formula,

$$\frac{P}{MR} = \frac{E_d}{E_d - 1} \qquad (10.1)$$

it is clear that, as elasticity rises, marginal revenue approaches price.

The MC Curves

So much for the demand curves: let us now consider the effects of the MC curve on output restriction.

Assuming the demand curve to be linear, like D in Figure 10.2 (A), it can be seen that, when MC is constant, the degree of output contraction will be more serious than when MC is rising between OL and ON, assuming that both MC curves intersect D at the same point.

From the standpoint of comparative output totals, a combination of (fairly) constant costs and a convex demand curve threaten the gravest departure from the $P = MC$ position. The conjunction of a concave demand curve and a rising MC curve should cause a lesser output derangement. Likewise, if a constant MC curve lies above a rising (linear) MC curve until the $P = MC$ output level, the concave-demand, constant-MC pair will draw output closer to the competitive form than the convex-demand, rising-MC pattern.

Examining the canoe-like MC paths in Figure 10.2 (a), it is clear that the lower curve (the convex path), is conducive to output expansion while the upper curve exerts a strong contractionist pull, at least over the range drawn. If the curve positions were reversed, as in Figure 10.2(b), the conclusions would have to be modified. Strictly speaking, the concavities and the convexities of MC are devoid of significance until we fix the position of the cost curve with respect to a demand curve.

Equality of Monopoly and Competitive Output

Occasionally, monopoly output may coincide with the $P = MC$ level. For example, envisaging a perfectly inelastic demand curve, monopoly and competitive output would be fully equivalent. There could be, however, a substantial divergence between the prices: the competitive price ought to equal MC (so long as the latter was constant or rising; if falling, price would amount to AC). The monopoly price would, in principle, reach the highest point on the inelastic demand curve.[3]

A less obvious case is depicted in Figure 10.2(B). For the moment, we need not probe too deeply into the cause of the inelastic kink at output OM: under oligopoly conditions, we shall have a plausible explanation for it. Meanwhile, we may regard it merely as a firm's demand curve with sales being elastic just above the P_1 price height although the firm's sales are almost completely insensitive to a price fall until P_2; as MC intersects MR at output OM, competitive and monopoly price will be at P_1.

Because of the discontinuity in MR, it is, in this case, a little far-fetched to describe the equilibrium condition as one at which $MR = MC$; instead, it is best to say that, to the left of the maximum-profit output, $MR > MC$, and to the right, $MC > MR$. In all but discontinuous cases, therefore, $MR = MC$.

Similarly, if the firm is producing its maximum output so that its MC curve becomes vertical and perfectly inelastic, while MR is greater than MC, a similar modification is required. At the capacity output, the gap between MC and MR will usually be less than when output is to the left of the capacity volume; but these verbal modifications to allow for discontinuities involve common-sense interpretations of the formula.

Questions

1. "The extent to which monopoly price exceeds the $P = MC$ price depends *solely* on the elasticity of demand." To what extent would you limit the implications of this proposition; namely, that demand alone matters?

[3] Perfectly inelastic demand, at least for more than a small range, is inconsistent with the basic assumption of the indifference system which presumes substitution among commodities and rejects the hypothesis of an absolute desire for one good to the exclusion of other goods.

2. Prove that, if the MC curve is horizontal, the proximity of the monopoly output to the $P = MC$ output level depends on the shape of the demand curve.
3. In several situations, output under monopoly is the same as when $P = MC$. Enumerate as many such cases as you can. Will price be the same in the different market structures or not? Why?
4. Demonstrate that it is meaningless to argue that the *shape* of the MC curve, rather than its position, determines the spread between monopoly and the $P = MC$ output level.

PRICE AND OUTPUT INTERRELATIONS

Let us consider briefly the reverberations in the rest of the economy consequent upon the monopoly-price policy of the firm under review. We can assume that there is, initially, a $P = MC$ adaptation for each firm. Let us set out some of the immediate repercussions of a monopoly price by one firm even if, under our special assumptions of monopoly, the impact effect on any single other firm is small.

Substitute-Complementary Relations

A price rise, we have learned previously, will invite a transfer in demand to substitutes: they should rise in price while complementary goods should fall.[4] On the simplest view, *assuming unity aggregate elasticity of consumer expenditure,* the higher the arc elasticity of demand for the commodity from the competitive to the monopoly price, the more likely it is that alternate outputs will expand and their prices will rise, for there is now less expenditure on the monopoly output and more on other goods. If the arc elasticity is inelastic, suggesting a greater expenditure on the commodity despite the higher monopoly price, other prices and outputs will fall.

Normally, if substitutes are available, the arc elasticity of demand should exceed unity. Thus, the demand and output of other goods will expand as the firm prices monopolistically. If the diverse firms to which demand is transferred adhere to a $P = MC$ policy, their prices will rise only if their MC curves are rising: the general output expansion will be more limited the less elastic are their MC curves. If the firms to whom demand is transferred are themselves monopolists, even with constant MC curves in these firms their prices will also tend to rise.

Manifestly, there is increased output and employment in the rest of the field to set off against the monopoly diminution. Over the whole field, however, the tendency will be toward higher prices. Consumer money incomes being posited as constant, and, considering the diversion of

---

[4] In view of the unpredictable income effect, rather than speak of substitutes and complements, we should stress that, for some goods, the cross-elasticity will be positive, and for others, negative.

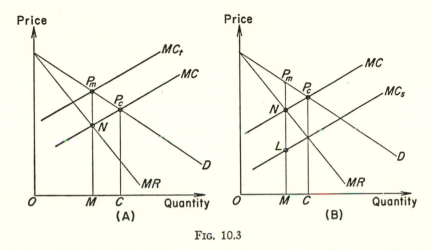

FIG. 10.3

income to monopoly-profit recipients, important implications for relative well-being lurk just below the surface.[5]

Extension to N-Monopoly Firms

The results can be extended to more impressive proportions. When we assume that the new monopolist is not one firm but, rather, innumerable independent firms producing dissimilar commodities, the analysis attains a new significance; the sum total of the little bits of monopoly contractions may be of major significance, deflecting the general equilibrium farther from the competitive price-output configuration. It would thus be erroneous to conclude that, from the standpoint of want-satisfaction, the economic importance of the alternate-output expansions exactly offsets the monopoly contractions. *Even if the employment total is maintained, the monopoly pricing will disrupt the relative division of income and the composition of aggregate output.* It is in the relative distortions of the output structure that monopoly pricing wreaks special havoc.

Monopoly Pricing as an Indirect Tax

Some added insight into the nature and consequences of monopoly pricing can be derived by comparing it to an indirect tax, such as a sales tax or an excise tax per unit of output levied under competitive conditions.

In Figure 10.3(A), suppose that D is the demand curve and MC the supply curve under competitive conditions. The competitive price would then be P_o and output OC. Suppose that a unit excise tax were imposed

[5] Compare my article on "Monopoly Pricing and Unemployment," *Quarterly Journal of Economics* (1946).

equal to NP_m per unit; the new supply curve under competition would be lifted to MC_t and price would finally settle at P_m, with output falling off to OM. The price rise would equal $P_m - P_c$ and the output diminution would equal $OC - OM$.

Modifying our hypothesis, we can visualize MC as the marginal-cost curve of a monopolist, and D and MR as the demand curve and the marginal-revenue curve, respectively. Obviously, under monopoly conditions, output will advance only to OM and price will be fixed at P_m. But these are precisely the results that would ensue under the imposition of a tax in competitive circumstances. *Monopoly pricing can thus be likened to an indirect tax, with the important distinction that the tax proceeds, in amount $OM \cdot (P_m - N)$, are amassed by the monopolist as income rather than by the Treasury as a tax collection.*

A Device to Secure Optimal Output

To carry this analysis a step farther, an ingenious use of subsidies has been suggested to ensure the $P = MC$ output and price and, at the same time, to check the monopoly income.[6] In Figure 10.3(B), if we draw D, MC, and MR, the competitive output will be OC and monopoly output, OM. In these circumstances, if a subsidy of NL per unit of output were granted to the monopolist, it would lower the marginal-cost curve to MC_s. As MC_s intersects MR at output OC, output would go to the latter level and the competitive price immanent in the real data would be announced. After this output level was achieved, the subsidy could be recouped, via an appropriately designed income tax in equivalent amount; as the most profitable output is not affected by an income tax, output would stay at the OC level.

Undoubtedly, the suggestion is more tantalizing than practical, although, during World War II, subsidies such as those on meat, together with heavy rates of excess-profits taxation, tended to operate in the same way, so that the scheme is perhaps not so fanciful as might appear at first sight. Nevertheless, an economy intelligent enough to apply the device would possess the wisdom to eliminate monopoly pricing by more straightforward processes if this were deemed salutary.

Conclusion: The Impact of Monopoly

In sum, we can conclude that monopoly will have a definite impact in the economy upon: (a) the composition of output, diverting it from quantities and, perhaps, varieties that would otherwise be produced and (b) the distribution of income. These aspects of the equilibrium will be altered. Whether price levels, national income, and employment will be

[6] Mrs. Robinson, p. 163. The suggestion is credited by her to Mr. E. A. Robinson.

affected or not will depend on some supporting hypotheses of over-all economic policy. Thus, we can state the following two points:

1. If national income levels are held constant along with wage rates, monopoly pricing will lead to unemployment in amount equal to the monopoly profits divided by the average wage rate. Some offset will result from any fall in profit or rent levels in the economy, counterbalanced by nonmonopoly rent and profit increases induced in the competitive (or other monopoly sectors) through the diversion of demand. Income distribution and relative outputs must change.

2. If employment is maintained through national economic policy while money wages are kept constant, price levels will be higher through the monopoly pricing; monopoly incomes will, of course, emerge, as well as some changes in other rent and profit amounts. Nonwage income, in general, will rise, so that the income change is to the detriment of labor. Again, the content and composition of aggregate production will alter.

These are the general conclusions with respect to monopoly in the economy. Some further considerations will be unfolded later on. Yet, we make no mistake in emphasizing the inroads on output composition and income distribution.

Questions

1. Explain how monopoly alters the composition of the output total. Under what extreme conditions would this argument be *invalid?*
2. In what respect would you criticize the analogy of monopoly pricing to an excise tax?
3. Trace through as best you can the effect of monopoly on employment if total expenditure remains constant and money wages hold rigid. Suppose that total expenditure rises so that employment is constant. How is the income distribution changed?

MEASURES OF MONOPOLY POWER

To impart some precision to the concept of monopoly power, the following measures have been devised. They pertain solely to the particular firms practicing monopoly pricing or output restriction. The first measure stresses the discrepancy between MC and P as an indicator of the price distortions attributable to monopoly power.

The Discrepancy $P - MC$

A measure suggested by Professor A. P. Lerner is grounded in the divergence between price and marginal costs. Thus,

$$M_L = \frac{P - MC}{P} \qquad (10.2)$$

where M_L is the degree of monopoly power, P is the price, and MC the marginal costs. When $MC = MR$, the typical monopoly equilibrium, the measure is equivalent to the reciprocal of the elasticity of demand, $1/E_d$.[7]

Obviously, the measure could be extended to encompass all deviations from the $(P = MC)$ equation, as in cases of pure competition but imperfect foresight where entrepreneurs fall short of the optimal result. In some circumstances, as with a rising demand curve or unwitting overproduction, the measure may be negative, so that $MC > P$. Normally, the measure will fluctuate between zero and unity. When $MC = P$, the deviation from the competitive result will be zero. At the other end, for costless output the measure will become unity, indicating the ability of the seller to charge a price for a free good.[8]

The Difference $(P_m - P_c)$

For many purposes, a more apt comparison than that between P and MC would relate monopoly price (P_m) and competitive price (P_c). While Lerner's measure fits perfectly for the one case of constant marginal costs, it breaks down when the MC curve either rises or falls.

A provisional measure of the discrepancy between P_m and P_c can be constructed on the assumption that demand and marginal-cost curves are linear in the region between the monopoly output and the competitive figure. The linearity hypothesis affords some idea of the possible price distortion. Thus,

$$P_m - P_c = \frac{(X_m b_1{}^2)}{b_1 + b_2} \tag{10.3}$$

where X_m is the monopoly output while b_1 and b_2 represent the numerical values of the slopes of the D and the MC curves, respectively.[9]

---

[7] See p. 19 above.

[8] One weakness of the measure would be its failure to distinguish between Cournot's illustration of plentiful mineral water flowing without cost and Marshall's case of hard stones, limited, valuable, costlessly produced, but irreproducible.

[9] To derive the formula, simply equate a linear demand to a linear MC curve, then solve simultaneously for the competitive price (P_c) and output (X_c):

$$X_c = \frac{a_1 - a_2}{b_1 - b_2} \, ; \quad P_c = a_1 - \frac{b_1(a_1 - a_2)}{b_1 + b_2} \tag{10.4}$$

Likewise, deriving MP and equating MC to MR for monopoly behavior,

$$X_m = \frac{a_1 - a_2}{2b_1 + b_2} \, ; \quad P_m = a_1 - \frac{b_1(a_1 - a_2)}{2b_1 + b_2} \tag{10.5}$$

Subtracting P_c from P_m and substituting for $(a_1 - a_2)$, we derive the result stated in the text. In all this, a_1 and a_2 refer to the demand- and cost-curve intercepts on OY. The measure based on linear curves is suggested by Bowley, *Mathematical Groundwork*, p. 60.

Clearly, when b_1 is zero—as in infinitely elastic demand—the difference between P_m and P_c is zero. On the other hand, the larger the slope of the demand curve relative to MC, the greater the divergence of the two prices; with perfectly inelastic demand, the difference between the prices is enormous. Also, a rising MC curve beyond the monopoly output tends to keep the two prices more closely aligned. When marginal costs are constant, b_2 is zero and the $P_m - P_c$ spread depends on the exact slope of the demand curve. Further, the larger the monopoly output, the greater the price distortion occasioned by monopoly.

It is wrong, of course, to pretend that the D and MC curves will, in fact, be linear. For a convex demand curve and a linear MC curve, the measure will overstate the discrepancy; it will understate the gap if D is linear and MC is concave. Where both curves are convex, exaggeration is again likely, while, if both are concave, the difference will be understated.

Suitable diagrams can be drawn for all these cases. Dispensing with analytical finesse in the face of factual ignorance, an even rougher approximation might often suffice; it might be surmised simply that P_c lies midway between P_m and MC.

A Measure of Output Restriction

Frequently, we will want to have some idea of the degree to which monopoly output falls below the competitive level; the simple divergence of P and MC is uninformative on this aspect of the equilibrium.

A relative measure of the output difference X_c and X_m, for linear curves, works out neatly. Thus,

$$\frac{X_m}{X_c} = \frac{b_1 + b_2}{2b_1 + b_2} \tag{10.6}$$

where b_1 and b_2 have the meanings assigned to them previously. For costless output, or for production under constant MC conditions, b_2 is zero and X_m becomes exactly one half the X_c amount.[10] A steeply rising MC curve will lift the ratio, carrying X_m somewhat closer to X_c.

Questions

1. If the elasticity of demand is equal to 8, what will be the value of Lerner's measure of monopoly power? Why? If the firm does not equate MC to MR, will this still be the case?
2. Under what conditions would the Lerner measure fail to reveal the extent of monopoly?
3. Prove that, if the demand curve lies closer to the OX axis, the $P_m - P_c$ discrepancy will be smaller. (Hint: To illustrate, take demand curves of the form $P = a - b_1x$.)

[10] See pp. 177–178, above.

4. Why is the slope of the demand curve more important than the slope of the
   MC curve in influencing the size of $(P_m - P_c)$? Illustrate by some sample
   values.
5. How important is the slope of the (linear) MC curve in determining the ratio
   of monopoly to competitive output? What influence does the slope of the demand curve have on the importance of MC in affecting the output ratio?
   a. Is the OY intercept of MC of any importance on the result or not? Explain.

SPECIAL EQUILIBRIUM CASES

It is instructive to consider some special cases of monopoly equilibrium,
such as those in which supply and demand are interdependent and the
phenomena of rising demand curves, as well as instances in which multiple equilibria arise.

Interdependent Supply and Demand

The theory of the firm is generally predicated on the supposition that
supply and demand are independent phenomena. From the standpoint of
the economic system, however, it is an ancient truism that both cost and
demand phenomena are interdependent: the classical statement of this
truth became known as Say's law of "supply creating its own demand."
Sometimes, however, the assumption of independence, even from the
standpoint of the firm, is misleading. Though it would be wrong to suggest that illustrations of interdependence of demand and supply for the
firm abound, they are not uncommon; employees may, for example, purchase from the firm some of the goods which they help produce—
purchases which would not be made if they were not employed by the
firm. Or they may buy standard items in a company store; the firm
would have to assess the importance of such factors when hiring personnel. For the moment, we shall evade the latter type of multi-product
problem and concentrate only on the former.

In Figure 10.4(A), the demand curve d_1 is the market purchase schedule even before the firm starts producing. As it makes one batch of output
ready for market, the d curve shifts to the right—to the new position d_2
—because either those engaged in its production now have income with
which to buy the product or the information acquired in its production
makes them wish to own it, thereby supplementing the original market
demand. A second batch of production gives birth to d_3, etc. Working
with a rising marginal-cost curve, which implies that successively more
wage earners are hired at the given wage rate to produce further units of
output, the lateral distances of the d_1, d_2, d_3, ... curves are likely to
spread farther apart as production expands.

To ascertain the sales price of 1 unit, we would seek it on d_2 at the
ordinate above the abcissae of 1 unit of output; for 2 units, on d_3; for

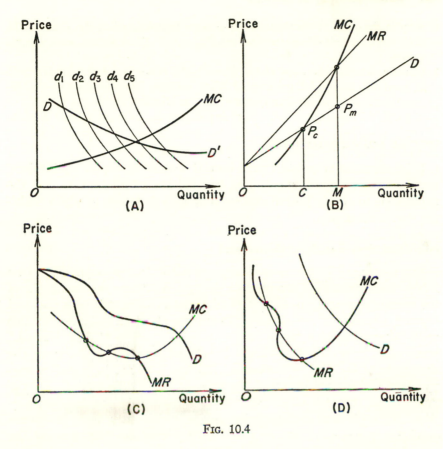

FIG. 10.4

3 units, on d_4, etc. Connecting these actual demand points for the corresponding outputs, we trace out the cross-cut curve DD', which describes the effective market-demand relations from the standpoint of the firm. To determine the equilibrium price and output, a curve marginal to DD' would have to be drawn and equated to MC.[11]

Rising Demand Curves

Earlier, we referred to rising demand curves for commodities of "conspicuous consumption," where consumers were prone to buy more at higher rather than lower prices. This is a reversal of the fundamental theory: tastes become dependent on prices rather than prices being dependent on tastes.

In Figure 10.4(B), the demand curve is D, while MR and MC have

[11] There are many twists that we might give to the d_1, d_2, d_3, . . . field, depending on the particular circumstances of each case. The preceding analysis should suffice for the general case.

the customary meanings. Monopoly pricing in this circumstance is unquestionably conducive to larger sales and output than a $P = MC$ policy: the usual norms are upset. No matter how irrational the procedure appears to an outsider, the consumers themselves regard their well-being improved by the "high-price distinction" conferred upon them. Lower prices will decrease the "well-being" of those afflicted with a high-price psychosis.

Aside from the "Veblen case," a few other instances of rising demand curves can be developed. The backward-falling (Giffen) demand curve will be recalled. If goods that follow this pattern are also subject to monopoly, the output may also exceed the competitive level; this will depend on the exact position of the two curves. Rising demand curves can also evolve from the interdependent supply and demand constructions of the preceding section: maybe as more workers are hired and employment prospects brighten, there is a strong current of "sympathetic consumption."

One final case may be mentioned here; namely, the situation in which purchasers judge quality according to price. That is, they may prefer a necktie selling for $3.00 rather than $1.50 merely because of their assumption that the higher price connotes higher quality. This, too, is a distortion, if not a perversion, of the economic process where, instead of prices being determined on the basis of "quality," quality is judged as dependent on price. This case, too, smacks of the "snob" case or Veblen situation. It is probably more common than many of us may care to admit.[12]

Multiple Equilibria

Corresponding to the possibilities of multiple equilibria in a competitive order, several points of intersection of MR and MC curves are also conceivable.

In Figure 10.4(C), the elasticity of demand veers sharply, perhaps as new layers of market demand are uncovered, with lower-income groups entering the market discontinuously; uninterested in automobiles, say, at $2,000, they suddenly find the purchase attractive at $1,500, so that there is a marked extension of demand at this last price. At $900, say, another substantial income tier is tapped. Examining the several $MR = MC$ positions, we find that the end-points represent stable equilibria while the middle $MC = MR$ point is a minimum and unstable position. Which end-point yields maximum revenue will depend, of course, on the precise shape of the MR and the MC curves.

Figure 10.4(D) describes a not unlikely market relationship, in which marginal costs fall irregularly until they finally turn upward. Here, too,

[12] See T. Scitovsky, *Welfare and Competition*, pp. 403–406.

the end-points are stable while the middle equality is a minimum position; a movement in either direction will swell profits.

Questions

1. What is your estimate of the importance of cases of interdependent supply and demand? If these cases are common, is there much point in separating demand from supply analysis? Explain.
2. What is your guess on the importance of rising or Veblen demand curves in our economy? If this case is common, how does it affect the conception of resources being adapted to consumer desires?
3. Are situations of multiple equilibria likely to be more common under monopoly than under competition, or not? Explain.

NONPECUNIARY MOTIVES

Our analyses have relied for their solution on the fundamental assumption of the pursuit of maximum pecuniary profits. Although it is probably accurate as a general principle of business conduct and as an indicator of the ultimate results, the shortcomings of this assumption are commonly acknowledged; no one will deny that it fails to describe *all* the facts. Public utility corporations, for example, are prohibited by law from applying the maximum formula; the modifications called for in the analysis can at least be outlined. Besides conscious restraint from the maximum rule, it is also true that, to attain the maximum-income position, economic subjects must be capable of performing the proper computations. Ignorance and incompetence are all too rife—a brief quizzing of a business man on the effect of taxes and fixed charges on his behavior will generally corroborate this fact. Certain practices that may be cited as violating the maximum rule, such as retail mark-ups and full-cost pricing, will be treated briefly.

Although motives would not be lacking for producing an output at which $MC \neq P$ under pure competition, there are many more compelling reasons under monopoly for $MC \gtreqless MR$, despite the sacrifice of some immediate monopoly profits. Occasionally, even actual losses may be sought, braved with complete equanimity. In a competitive régime, it would be foolhardy for firms to invite losses.

Nonmaximum Motives

Some of the factors that may impel a monopolist to forgo the maximum current income may be listed briefly. For one thing, "just price" notions often prevail and condition price policy, invoking a "fair" price code rather than a maximization standard. Or the monopolist may be anxious to deter the market inroads of producers of substitutes. Or the policy may be designed to forestall government regulation, or to retain consumer good will. Or, being human, entrepreneurs may like to boast of their output level and of their productive prowess, contenting themselves with a "fair" rather than maximum profit. More rationally, the entrepreneur may be deterred by the additional entrepreneurial output exertions incident to procuring additional profits. Another idea that we shall develop later is the fact that current losses may be consciously planned to influence consumer tastes for the future, at which time a more thoroughgoing monopolistic price policy can be instituted; comparable action by an atomistic firm selling in a competitive market would be inconceivable.

Whatever the particular forces are that prompt a departure from the $P > MC = MR$ rule, price and output will deviate from that implicit in the maximizing principle.[13] This must not be overlooked in deriving propositions and drawing comparisons between the monopoly world and an optimal arrangement.

Graphic Analysis

The range of motives that guide the monopoly firm can be crystallized ultimately in a system of indifference curves. Measuring profits or money income vertically and output horizontally, there is associated with each combination of income and output a certain amount of irksomeness, an apprehension of potential competition, or perhaps a governmental regulation, or a certain welfare attitude of a fair price, etc. Each indifference curve will connect a series of income-output combinations representing a definite preference level; at each point, the marginal rates of substitution between output and income can be computed, while the ascension from one curve to another denotes successively higher preference levels.

According to a convex contour system, shown in Figure 10.5(a), an entrepreneur will substitute output for income at a decreasing MRS: the concomitant advantages of enlarged production—perhaps the prestige of a large production volume, or the fear of government punitive action with restricted output, or the sales losses to market usurpers at higher prices—outweigh the profit diminution consciously suffered by output expansion. Output forces then dominate. Drawing the locus of a profit curve on the same diagram, found by subtracting the total costs from the total receipts of each output, it will usually prove to be bell-shaped, with the maximum height at the $MR = MC$ point, as in Figure 10.5(b).

Output equilibrium will be found at the point of tangency between the profit curve and an indifference curve, for this will be the highest level of well-being open to the firm. Output, when the output-income indifference curves are convex, will exceed the quantity shown at the simple $MR =$

---

[13] When output forces predominate, the monopolist will be less reluctant to lower price the more elastic are the demand and supply curves, for the profit position will then be rather well maintained despite the lowering of price. See Bowley, pp. 25, 60. Also see the discussion of Baumol's position, below.

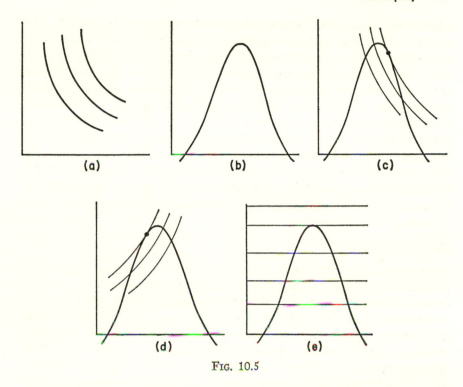

FIG. 10.5

MC equality reflected at the top of the profit bell, for the tangency is now to the right of the summit of the profit locus (circled in Figure 10.5[c]). Conversely, the entrepreneur may find additional output irksome and may prefer the peace and quiet life associated with less output: only the prospect of increased profits can move him to produce more. Here, the indifference contours are of the form of Figure 10.5(d), so that contractionist forces predominate. As restraining forces are in the saddle, the equilibrium output lies below the amount indicated at the equation of *MR* and *MC*.

Maximization Psychology

Even under competitive market conditions, where the firm is unable to affect price, with the usual cost curves the profit locus would also assume a bell shape; given the indifference field for the relations between income and effort, we can determine whether expansionist or contractionist motives predominate. Evidently, the type of indifference system implicit in the conventional assumption of the pursuit of maximum pecuniary profits, translated into profit-output indifference contours, assumes indifference curves that are parallel to *OX*, as in Figure 10.5(e); that is, the entrepreneur is visualized as motivated solely by profits, regardless of the effort and output entailed: the MRS between effort (and output) and income not only is constant but also is always *zero*. The entrepreneur is depicted as utterly indifferent between small- and large-scale production, not even appraising his labors as more arduous because of greater production. On this postulate, the point of tangency between the indifference lines and the profit bell must be at the top of the latter curve, where $MR = MC$.

Interpreted in this way, it would appear that the behavior implicit in the Fundamental Assumption is but a special case that probably errs in overstating the output even under inherently competitive conditions. While the fundamental assumption illuminates the business mechanism, it must be regarded as exemplifying not the whole facts but only an important first approximation.

There is one other direction in which the sharp edge of the fundamental assumption must be tempered. Just as the assumption of the pursuit of maximum pecuniary profits explains less than the full facts, it was disclosed earlier that, for each level of output, the firm may fail to hire the minimum-cost factor combination. Just as profits can be reduced through price restraint, they can also be lost by uneconomic factor hire. The minimal total-cost curve may thus fail to describe the actual cost path of output expansion, given a disinterested and a nonpecuniary entrepreneurial attitude.[14]

Pricing in Regulated Industries

Good illustrations of nonmaximum pecuniary forces under monopoly can be drawn from the field of regulated industry, where, for a variety of reasons, the state has been impelled to place the field under its regulatory surveillance. Invariably, the price policy of the public utility is moderated toward the end of "fair" rather than maximum profits; nonmaximization precepts are implanted by law to guide the adaptation of the firm. The rule of regulation is encompassed in the broad court directive of a "reasonable return on prudent investment value."

There are two major problems involved here: (1) first, the content of "prudent investment" must be ascertained. There is no need, for our purposes, to recount the endless controversies encountered on this route; its calculation becomes a ubiquitous nightmare for the regulatory authorities seeking the appropriate valuation of nonmarketable capital

---

[14] Some writers contend that competitive markets must compel the adoption of minimum-cost methods of operations through the pressure of entry on profitability. But this argument is shaky in fact as well as in principle. Competitive price making and homogeneous entry are by themselves insufficient to ensure minimum cost modes of production. At best, as in agriculture, they prevent costs from becoming "excessive"—which is not the same thing at all.

assets. (2) After "prudent investment value" is decided, concurrence is sought on the volume of earnings which will yield the firm a "reasonable" return on the fixed investment. Ultimately, this is a price decision: the price approved by a regulatory commission leads to earnings through the relation $Q(P - AVC)$.

The line separating investment and variable costs is, itself, frequently a vague one. Still, if the utility property is valued at a "prudent" sum V, then the ratio $Q(P - AVC)/V$ must promise a "reasonable" rate of return.[15]

Visualizing the usual D, MR, and MC curves, and from them the profit locus of Figure 10.5, it is clear that, if all the information were at hand, it would be a simple matter for the regulatory commission to approve a price which allowed "reasonable" earnings. Whether this requires the monopoly price, the competitive price, an intermediate figure, *or even one higher than the monopoly price or lower than the $P = MC$ price*, is, *a priori*, indeterminate.[16] Conceivably, only the monopoly price may ensure reasonable earnings, although, occasionally, even the $P = MC$ price might exact more than the "fair" earnings so that the only tenable price, according to the legal mandate binding the regulatory body, will be below the $P = MC$ level.

Full-Cost Pricing

Practical men are often impatient with the economists' view of business men adjusting marginal costs and revenues. Instead, they contend that industrial firms ordinarily estimate their average cost and add to it, for "good measure," a sum to guarantee "reasonable" profits.

Symbolically, it would mean that the specified price is $P = k(AC)$ or $P = k(AVC)$, where $k > 1$ and represents a mark-up factor. The allegation of the pervasiveness of this practice raises several issues. Analytically, (1) it conceives demand to be completely inelastic and the production scale to be rigidly fixed, for then entrepreneurial costs, to which a "fair" profit is added, would be unique; (2) the conception may visualize the firm as always preparing goods to order, or always operating at capacity, so that the output level is completely known. Otherwise, AC fluctuates with the level of output, so that price and output policy entail estimations of demand, not of costs alone.

Once we concede some demand and cost flexibility, we are thrown back to some mode of connecting MC and MR, but recognizing irration-

[15] The rate problem is further complicated by the fact that the regulated firm produces more than one output.

[16] Despite the indeterminateness, it is strange that public-utility writers almost invariably suggest that the regulated price is normally intermediate between the monopoly and the competitive figure.

ality—calculating incompetence—and nonpecuniary pricing motives. As another avenue of full-cost pricing, if, despite fluctuating demand, the *AC* curve is flat so that average costs are constant, the firm may adhere to its "full-cost" price: this is about the strongest theoretical bulwark in support of the supposed phenomenon. Still, with *given* demand conditions, full-cost pricing would denote the presence of irrationality or nonpecuniary motives.

Obviously, after prices are named, they must equal profits plus other costs: "full costs" undoubtedly are facts of arithmetic. *But they are not a theory of price determination; there is no explanation of why the "full costs" change, or why they are larger rather than smaller, or why prices are sometimes below costs.*

Whenever either *D* or *MC* is perfectly inelastic, it is a matter of indifference from the standpoint of economical resource allocation as to whether a high or a low price is charged: output will be the same in either event, with only the income distribution among sellers and purchasers affected, and some (secondary?) reverberations in other markets.

Maximum Sales

The view has also been put forward that the aim of the monopoly (or oligopoly) seller is "maximum sales," as represented in sales receipts.[17]

In terms of total revenue curves, as in Figure 10.6(A), output of maximum profits is at Q_1. However, the firm is interested in sales receipts and will push production to Q_2.

Of course, this can be visualized in terms of the profit-output indifference contours of Figure 10.5(a). However, there is a danger in pushing this kind of argument too far: if the *TC* curve cuts the *TR* curve to the left of the maximum on the latter, as in Figure 10.6(B), the policy will entail losses. There are, thus, obvious limits to the argument. Furthermore, it is likely to be most meaningful when the profit locus tapers off slowly, as in Figure 10.6(C), so that the profit deterioration in expanding output beyond the profit maximum OQ_1 is rather nominal. Demand, thus, would have to be highly elastic and average costs rather constant—or decreasing.

While there may be good reasons for the policy under monopolistic competition (e.g., to forestall competitors from entering so that profit gains are preserved over time), it hardly appears sturdy enough to serve as a general case. However, once the maximization position is analyzed, the argument can be extended to include such phenomena whenever they occur.

[17] W. J. Baumol, *Business Behavior, Value and Growth,* p. 47.

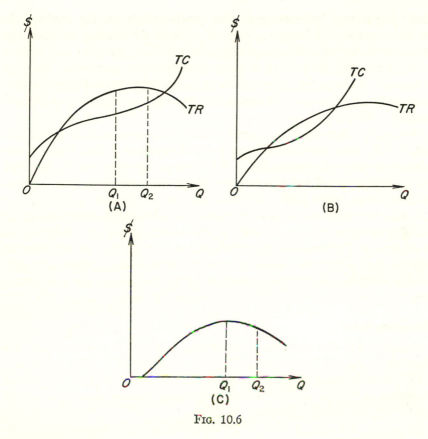

FIG. 10.6

Retail Mark-Ups

A concrete discussion of price making demands some comments on retail mark-ups which seem so remote from either competitive or monopoly price theory. Briefly, mark-ups are the retailer's description of his practice of price making—of determining selling price by adding, say, 10 per cent to merchandise cost.

Visualizing an urban department store, a policy of maximum price making would counsel that each division of the store cover at least its full separable expenses, including the direct variable cost of sales help, wrapping paper, floor space having an alternative use value, and storeroom and warehouse facilities, where these must be specially rented or where they have valuable alternate uses.[18] Normally, as the merchandise is purchased at a single price for resale, the major component of MC is

---

[18] Ultimately, all divisions compete with one another for store locations. Bids by individual departments depend on neighboring counters; substitute and complementary profit maximization relationships abound. See pp. 317–320.

constant; if variable "merchandising" costs were zero, the buying price at wholesale would represent the full height of MC. When the selling costs are rising, the MC curve will be upward-rising.

Fitting a demand and an MR curve into the picture, the maximum price can be computed. After computing maximum price in this fashion, obviously the difference between sales price and merchandise cost can be termed a "mark-up" and, superficially, merchandise cost appropriately "marked up" has determined price. But this fails entirely to explain the differences in mark-ups in different stores—or even departments of the same store—or why mark-downs and clearances are commonplace phenomena. Undoubtedly, business men are often confused on the best mode of securing maximum profits, so that, instead of engaging in minute cost calculations, they may employ a rule-of-thumb *average mark-up* in the belief that a typical variable cost accompanies each unit of sales. If the intersection of the marked-up cost curve and MR were to occur to the right or to the left of a more rational cost calculation, a reconsideration of pricing policy would be remunerative. In this sense, mark-up tactics are ill suited for the attainment of maximum profits.

Questions

1. Enumerate all the reasons you can think of for a firm failing to maximize immediate profits.
2. a. How would you draw the output-income indifference curves for a "pure philanthropist"?
   b. What shape profit contours and output-income contours would facilitate output expansion? What connection would these have to the elasticity of demand?
3. "It is possible that, without damage to the public utility firm involved, price might sometimes be reduced rather substantially." Discuss conditions in which this may be a valid proposition.
4. Public-utility pricing designed to secure a "fair" profit has been likened to a competitive adaptation. Discuss circumstances in which this analogy is mistaken, if not far-fetched.
5. What difficulties do you see in the hypotheses of "full-cost" pricing and pricing to maximize sale receipts as general hypotheses for the economy? (It may be helpful to examine statistics of profits to gross national product for business corporations.)

MONOPOLY AND OPTIMAL RESOURCE USE

Following our earlier analysis of the nature of optimal resource allocation, and the fact that a system of pure competition would satisfy the optimal content of $MRS = P_x/P_y$ for each consumer, and $MC = P$ for each producer, it will be self-evident that, under monopoly, there are distortions in resource use.

So long as $MC \neq P$, or the ratio of $MC_x/MC_y \neq P_x/P_y$, it can then be shown that it is possible to divest resources from outputs of relatively low MC to higher MC and increase well-being in the process. The interesting part of this demonstration is that, even with income division constant, so that the monopolist's income is unaffected, everyone (including the monopolist) can experience an enhancement in well-being. This was part of the earlier proof and, hence, need not be repeated here.[19]

Monopoly—or all departures from $MC = P$—thus receives bad marks from an allocational standpoint. We must be clear on what this means: it signifies that, with constant tastes and factor productivities, general economic improvement is possible. Nevertheless, when we consider other aspects of the adaptation, we may want to qualify this conclusion. Just ahead lie questions of altering tastes—of widening varieties of goods available—of introducing new items in the economy—of altering the technology and productivity of factors, etc. Some of these questions will occupy us in successive chapters. The incidence of monopoly may be less devastating in a changing framework than in a constant structure.

[19] See above, pp. 108–113.

Chapter 11

Duopoly and Oligopoly

We now consider cases of duopoly and oligopoly, where two or more firms produce perfectly substitutable goods and each individual firm is able to influence, but not to determine, the price of the commodity it sells. Here, too—as numbers are presumed too few for the competitive result—in the final equilibrium $P \neq MC$. But the analysis takes many peculiar turns.

In our duopoly and oligopoly analyses, we suppose that the firms comprising the market are producing an undifferentiated, perfectly substitutable, good. To hold any part of the market, each seller must at least meet the price of his competitor.[1]

This much of the discussion might be anticipated: briefly, we must not be surprised to learn that, from an *a priori* standpoint, there are *multiple* price-output solutions. When one firm must look to the actions of another, and must weigh several alternative reaction patterns, there are just too many eventualities. Games of chess (the usual simile goes) can be played in many ways, depending on the strategy, the psychology, and the prescience of the participants.[2] Analytically, all that we can do is to lay out some prospective developments and leave it to empirical study to isolate the model which best represents a particular market situation. Hence, to say that duopoly problems are indeterminate is to say that they are overly determinate—that there are too many potential solutions. Whether or not an equilibrium will be reached, its exact content when reached and its stability will depend entirely on the special data of the particular market environment.

[1] That is, unless the "low"-priced seller rations sales, thereby leaving some custom for others even at higher prices. If the commodity can be profitably resold by those who purchase in the lower-price market, ultimately only one price can prevail.

[2] The theory of games has been applied to these problems, following the great work of J. von Neumann and O. Morgenstern. See M. Shubik, *Strategy and Market Structure*, for an extended discussion.

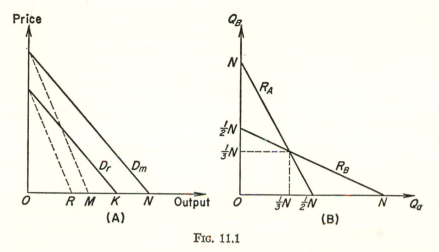

FIG. 11.1

Before we become too distraught with these problems, it should be underscored that, so long as ultimately $P > MC$, the usual strictures on monopoly pricing apply, whatever the minutiae of the particular equilibrium solution.

OUTPUT FOLLOWERS

Suppose, first, that firm B's output (and sales quantity) is known to firm A, together with the full curve of market demand: both are so much data to A. As an additional simplification, we assume that output is costless, as in Cournot's mineral spring.[3] Market demand is also assumed to be linear, as D_m in Figure 11.1(A).

As production is costless, if there were numerous owners of mineral springs the competitive output would thus be ON and price would be zero. On the other hand, if there were but one firm, so that monopoly prevailed, the output would be OM, or $\frac{1}{2}ON$.

Under duopoly, firm B, let us suppose, decides to produce an amount equal to $\frac{1}{2}OM$, or one half the quantity that a monopoly combine would offer for sale, doing so on the presumption that A will do the same and that the maximum aggregate profit obtainable will then be shared equitably between them. As B will sell $\frac{1}{2}OM = KN = \frac{1}{4}ON$, we must subtract this quantity laterally from the market-demand curve in order to ascertain A's maximum sales possibilities at each price. Doing so, we obtain the curve D_r, which can be termed a *reduced* demand curve for firm A's output.

---

[3] This is the celebrated problem of Augustin Cournot, *Researches into the Mathematical Principles of Wealth*, N. T. Bacon, trans., Chapter VII.

The Equilibrium Solution

Just as a marginal-revenue curve can be drawn to D_m, the market-demand curve, a marginal-revenue curve can also be drawn to D_r, the *reduced* demand curve. So far as firm A is concerned, it is the MR to D_r which is relevant to its profit position. According to the usual principles for a linear demand curve, the marginal-revenue curve associated with D_r will fall twice as fast as the latter: thus, $OR = \frac{1}{2}OK$ in Figure 11.1(A).

By the usual principles of $MR = MC$, the output of firm A will settle at $\frac{1}{2}OK$ or $\frac{3}{8}ON$. Total output in this case, therefore, will equal $\frac{5}{8}ON$, with B producing $\frac{1}{4}ON$ and A producing $\frac{3}{8}ON$. Interestingly, this exceeds the monopoly figure by $\frac{1}{4}ON$. The combined duopoly output, on the assumptions we have made, thus *surpasses* the simple monopoly level.

This solution was contingent on the assumption that B produced and sold $\frac{1}{4}ON$. If B, which had expected A to produce $\frac{1}{4}ON$, now revises its policy and assumes that A's production will continue to be $\frac{3}{8}ON$, we can then derive a reduced demand curve for B: this will cut the horizontal axis at $\frac{5}{8}ON$. Then B's reduced MR curve will cut OX at $\frac{5}{16}ON$, which will become its most profitable output. Firm A, if it revises its policy, will then produce $\frac{5}{32}ON$. Firm B, then A, then B, etc., etc., will then revise its output policy. It will be found, however, that total output on these assumptions will approach closer and closer to $\frac{2}{3}ON$.

This last result is significant. For, if B (or A) produces $\frac{1}{3}ON$, the D_r for the other will intersect the horizontal axis at $\frac{2}{3}ON$, and the reduced MR curve will cut at $\frac{1}{3}ON$. The total output resulting from this mutual interaction, where each firm believes that the other firm's output will persist into the next period at the same level as in the past period, will be two thirds of the competitive production volume. This is the solution (1) for linear demand curves, (2) for constant marginal-cost phenomena, (3) where each firm is an "output follower." (Each firm is tagged a "follower" because each takes the other's output as a datum, with each believing that it is powerless to influence or alter the other's output.)

Reaction Curves

If, from the market-demand curve, as in Figure 11.1(A), we deduct each possible output of B, we can thereafter find A's maximum profit output for each corresponding B quantity. If we list all these related quantities, a *reaction curve* for A can be derived. Let us develop this concept more systematically, for it will be found to have many uses.

In Figure 11.1(B), the reaction curve R_A associates amounts of output of A to each level of B's output. To illustrate, if B's output is at ON, then A's output is zero. On the same assumptions as those surrounding Figure 11.1(A), ON is the competitive output, so that price is zero. With the linear market-demand curve, every time B's output falls by 1 A's output will increase by one half unit. Ultimately, with $Q_B = O$, A's output is $\frac{1}{2}ON$, or equal to the monopoly level.

A similar reaction curve, R_B, can be drawn for firm B, resting on th hypothesis that B is a follower-firm taking Q_A as a datum. The two curves intersect at a position of mutual equilibrium, where each will produce $\frac{1}{3}ON$.

Profit Contours

The full theory of the reaction curve involves slightly more detail. Curve 1 in Figure 11.2(A) is a *profit-indifference curve* for A, consisting of all outputs of A which, in conjunction with outputs of B, yield A a fixed amount of profit. Curve 2 indicates profits somewhat greater than those depicted along curve 1, and curve 3 indicates still higher profits. Hence, a system of profit contours can be formed with profits ascending as we approach the horizontal axis under the mantle curve 1. The lower contours are more profitable for they assume lower output by the B firm.

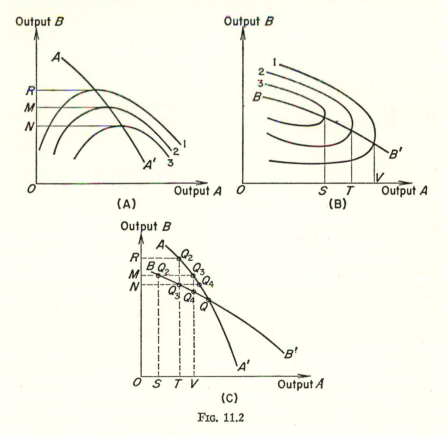

Fig. 11.2

On the arguments surrounding Figure 11.1(B), a zero profit for A will appear at N on the vertical axis, while, at $\frac{1}{2}N$ on the horizontal axis, profits will be at a maximum, amounting to the monopoly sums. At both these extremities, therefore, the profit "contours" are points rather than curves. In between, however, the profit contours are usually dual-valued, for, at each output of firm B, it is possible for firm A to earn the same profit sum by either a smaller or a larger output level. This is, after all, a consequence of the multi-valued profit contour at any but the output of maximum profits. As B's output rises, the profit contour for A is pinched-in, until, at some maximum of B's output, only a unique output for A will yield an equivalent amount of profit. This is at the peak of each profit contour in Figure 11.2(A). These peaks, it may be observed, are important, for they represent the output of maximum profit for A with each Q_B.

We can show this as follows: drawing lines parallel to the horizontal axis from R, M, and N to denote a given output of firm B, and noting their tangency to the profit-indifference curves, we can extract the successive outputs of firm A that yield A *maximum* profits. When we connect these various points by a continuous line, A's *reaction curve* appears, lettered AA' in Figure 11.2(A). The reaction curve, thus, is the locus of the most profitable output adjustments of A to each and every B output. It is negatively inclined, for (aside from complementary goods), as B's output diminishes, it is always profitable for A to expand production. The gradient of AA' will, for followers, be less than unity, implying over its course a lesser A expansion than B's contraction.

A similar reaction curve can be derived for B, based on B's adjustment to A's output. B's profits rise as the contours approach the vertical axis in Figure 11.2(B). If the two firms are vastly different in size, with B the smaller firm, then A's reaction curve will be rather steep, largely uninfluenced by B's output, which is presumed to be almost constant.

The Equilibrium Solution

The reaction curves reveal the equilibrating tendencies when both A and B act as output followers. Drawing only the reaction curves AA' and BB' in Figure 11.2(C), suppose that B's output was OR and A's output was OS. In the subsequent period, OT will be produced by A and OM by B—points Q_2 on the reaction curves in the figure. In the third period, the outputs will be, respectively, ON for B and OV for A—points Q_3 on the reaction curve. Then each will advance to the Q_4 points, until, finally, their successive adjustments will carry them to the intersection of the reaction curves at point Q. Here, at the "Cournot point," the equilibrium balance will be stable, for, once attained, neither firm will have any incentive to depart from it—under the assumptions made thus far.

The firms being of equal size, the respective outputs at the Cournot point should be the same, since the output equation of MC to the MR on the reduced demand curve of each firm should be identical. For the linear-demand case, and costless output, each firm ought to produce $\frac{1}{3}X$, where X is the competitive output, or a combined duopoly total of $\frac{2}{3}X$.

The special, and strange, premises of this argument need not be labored. It is almost inconceivable that entrepreneurs, seeing their predictions of continuing behavior on the part of their rivals falsified time after time, are nevertheless so unimaginative and obtuse as to impute this behavior pattern to their rival each time. Hence, we do well to scrutinize some alternate and more plausible hypotheses.

Questions

1. If the demand curve is linear and costs are zero, assuming that the competitive output is 9 units and A's initial output is 2, show the successive outputs through 8 adjustments. Does the combined total approach more closely to 6 units or not?
2. Given the market-demand curve as linear, of the form $p = a - mq$, where p is the price and q denotes total output while a and m are constants (also, for duopoly, $q = q_1 + q_2$), find the total revenue curve.
   a. Write the marginal-revenue curve for the market.
   b. Write the marginal-revenue curve for firm A.
   c. Prove that marginal revenue for firm A falls more slowly than that for the market. What is the significance of this for duopoly, as compared to monopoly, output?
   d. Show that the output of firm A is given by

$$q_1 = \frac{a - mq_2}{2m}$$

   How is this related to the reaction curve?
   e. Write the reaction curve for firm B.
   f. Find the equilibrium outputs for the duopolists.
   g. Write the competitive and the monopoly outputs.
   h. Compare total *profits* in the respective situations.
3. What would be the general form of the reaction curve if the demand curve were of the form $p = f(q)$?
4. Enumerate all possible circumstances where the output-follower case is a realistic portrayal of market phenomena.

OUTPUT LEADERS

As one alternative possibility, B may act as an *output follower; A* may know this and may therefore hasten to produce that quantity which evokes such a reaction in B as to maximize A's profit. Firm A may then be designated as an *output leader.*

In Figure 11.3(A), BB' is firm B's reaction curve, *which is known to A.*
The output of maximum profit for A will then appear at a point of tangency between A's family of profit contours and the reaction curve BB',
at point N in Figure 11.2(A). All contours above 1 would be less profitable for A; in seeking the more profitable lower contours, those *below* 1,
as A fixes an output greater or smaller than indicated at point N, B's
output reaction will be such as to place A on a less profitable contour—
one higher in the chart field than that with index 1. The output-follower,
output-leader pattern is, therefore, perfectly determinate.

If we visualize the problem in terms of a linear market-demand curve

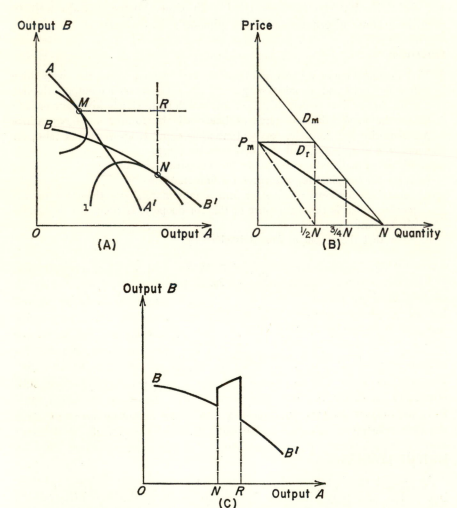

Fig. 11.3

and zero costs once again, the answer can be made more concrete. Firm *A* will know that *B* will, at most, produce the monopoly output and charge the monopoly price. Thus, in Figure 11.3(B), the market-demand curve being D_M, the highest possible price is OP_M: firm *B* will produce $\frac{1}{2}N$ and *A* will produce nothing. Thereafter, according to the earlier argument, for each unit expansion by *A*, the output of firm *B* will contract by one half unit. The D_r curve for *A* will thus run from P_M to *N* in Figure 11.3(B). By familiar rules, *A* will decide to produce $\frac{1}{2}N$ and *B* will thus produce $\frac{1}{4}N$. Total output will thus be $\frac{3}{4}N$, which exceeds the $\frac{2}{3}N$ produced under the output-follower solution.

Firm *A* is thus in a position to determine its most lucrative output opportunity by forcing *B*'s response. Of course, if *B* is a large firm which hardly responds to output changes in *A*, a smaller rival, the reaction curve *BB'* will be fairly flat and nothing that *A* can do will be likely to alter *B*'s output.

Indeterminateness with Contending Leaders

Suppose that *B* vies with *A* for output leadership. Just as *A* endeavors to produce the output indicated at *N* in Figure 11.3(A), *B* will seize upon the amount noted at point *M*. Consequently, the combined output culminates at point *R*.

This is obviously unprofitable to both firms; while a revision of anticipations undoubtedly will follow, the final equilibrium settlement is indeterminate without more data on the new reaction pattern. Thus, although the output-follower, output-leader case converges to a determinate equilibrium, when both firms contend for the leader position a behavioral change on the part of at least one firm is ultimately in order.

A mixed pattern might also be sketched. For the most part, *B* may be content to act as an output follower, although it may refuse to be pushed beyond a certain output; rebellious, it can threaten retaliatory price warfare. *B*'s reaction curve is thus the discontinuous locus *BB'* in Figure 11.3(C). Until an output *ON* of firm *A* has been reached, firm *B*'s reactions are normal. But, if *A* insists on an output between *ON* and *OR*, then *B* may make one last stand and, by increasing its production substantially, slash the market price. Firm *A* will thus have to weigh carefully an output decision in this area; the price fall may be more than the firm relishes or is able to withstand. Beyond *OR* output by *A*, however, *B* may restrain its combativeness, for the ensuing losses may be regarded as too severe.[4]

---

[4] Parenthetically, in these problems the output leader will probably have to wait at least one period before its market policy bears fruits in generating the appropriate output response on the part of the follower.

Conjectural Variations: Indeterminacy and Games

We might explore some further samples of conjectural variations—as A's guess of B's output, which is necessary in planning A's output policy, is termed.[5]

It was shown that, if both A and B expect each other's previous output to be repeated, an equilibrium is eventually attained. Contrast this with the results forthcoming when each seller presumes that the other is altering its previous output level, without being certain of the direction. Thus, if A expects B to expand in the second period and B expects A to contract, both may be surprised—B pleasantly and A adversely—for the actual output of B may exceed what was expected while A's output may fall below B's expectations. As A prepares to contract his output again because of B's expansory proclivities, he may impute some knowledge of his future behavior to B. In contrast, B might merely extrapolate the past output of A for the future.

This is likely to mean new indeterminateness: equilibrium cannot prevail unless the respective forecasts are realized. Even if the forecasts of a rival's behavior are accurate, the equilibrium will not automatically perpetuate itself, for revisions in anticipations can unloose a completely new cycle of fluctuations.

It can be observed that, if the output of A falls short of B's expectation, then B's production for the period will be, in retrospect, too small and the market price too high. Demands for substitute products will be stimulated. An exceptionally large output, exceeding even the competitive volume, is likewise not beyond the realm of possibility.

Cases of "bluff" tactics can also be envisioned: one firm may overproduce in one market period in order to impart a spirit of caution in the rival's production policy for subsequent periods. Stultifying problems are also conceivable: each firm may create the impression that it is going to produce the competitive output volume. In theory, both will then abstain from producing. Clearly, therefore, the content of duopoly analysis rests on conjectural hypotheses of behavior.

Questions

1. Given the linear market-demand curve of (2) in the last exercise on page 203, the marginal-revenue curve for firm A, and the reaction curve representing the output of firm B as

$$q_2 = \frac{a - mq_1}{2m}$$

   show that:

[5] Symbolically, the conjectural variation for A refers to the value of dQ_b/dQ_a. This may be $\gtrless 1$. Is it an objective relationship? Is it a prediction? Is it an estimate with much uncertainty involved? Explain.

a. the output of maximum profit for firm A is given by

$$q_1 = \frac{a}{2m}$$

b. Find the output of firm B.
c. Find the combined output and total profits.
d. Compare this with the follower solution, the monopoly solution, and the competitive solution.

2. Explain why the leadership hypothesis is likely to be short-lived.
3. The conjectural-variation term refers to the output variation for firm B with output changes for firm A. Write the various forms and magnitudes that this term can take.
4. Give several reasons why the reaction curve may not be smooth and continuous.

JOINT MAXIMIZATION ANALYSES

Because the monopoly-output level permits the maximum *joint* profits in the market, many have attached an especial importance to this out-put position.[6] The reason for this should be readily apparent: if the combined duopoly output runs in excess of the monopoly output, and if each firm shares equally in the outcome, then it is possible for both firms to increase their profits. Even if the market is not shared equally, it is always possible for one firm to increase its profits while the other firm is left at least as well off—though this may require some side pay-ments—until the monopoly position is established.

The No-Gain Locus

In Figure 11.4(A), profit contours are drawn for the two firms, after the fashion outlined previously. If we connect points of *tangency of the profit contours,* we derive the "no-gain" curve of Figure 11.4(A). For the linear-demand, zero-cost curve, the tangency points occur on a line running from $\frac{1}{2}N$ on the vertical to the same distance on the horizontal axis. Obviously, the "no-gain" line is situated below the separate reaction curves.

Consider the significance of this line. If we take any point in the chart field off this line, it is always possible by reducing (or increasing) at least one firm's output to *increase* the total profits of the pair. If agreement can be forthcoming in the sharing of the augmented profits, both firms can be made better off. In this sense, the "no-gain" curve is a contract curve containing the profit-optimum points. Once on the curve, the profits of one firm can be augmented only at the expense of the other firm.

[6] For example, see H. Gregg Lewis, "Some Observations on Duopoly Theory," *American Economic Review* (May 1948), and W. Fellner, *Competition Among the Few.*

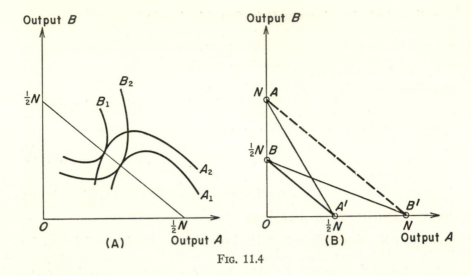

Fig. 11.4

Comparative Solutions

Figure 11.4(B) contains the reaction curves running from $\frac{1}{2}N$ on one axis to N on the other. The output-follower solution, we have seen, falls at the intersection of the two curves, amounting to two thirds of the competitive output for the simple linear-demand, costless-production case. Each firm produces one third of the competitive aggregate.

On the other hand, for the joint maximization solution, output must fall along the "no-gain" curve, running from $\frac{1}{2}N$ on the vertical axis to $\frac{1}{2}N$ on the horizontal axis in the same simple illustration. The output distribution is indeterminate without further information—unless we assume that, somehow, each settles on one half the monopoly amount— or one fourth the competitive ON total.

The competitive output is given along the line running from N to N on the respective axes. If the zero marginal cost is equated to price, also zero, the various output distributions are shown along this line.

The Duopoly Solution?

While strong forces would seem to be pulling the firms toward the monopoly solution, nevertheless it still does presume a particular behavior pattern on their part. It involves the joint solicitude of the firms in the profit position of the other; it fails to take account of desires to dominate the other, to bluff the other, or to be independent of it. Further, it fails to acknowledge the role of ignorance, innocence, or even stubbornness or willfulness. For all these reasons, while it is an important solution it is not *the* solution, in the sense of a sole possibility. If recognition of mutual fortunes were the paramount concern of business firms even with numerous sellers, as under competition, the monopoly price would be the upshot. As shown in the follower case, this does not happen, because, once output of one firm contracts, it becomes profitable for the output of the other firms to expand.

Questions

1. Discuss at length the *a priori* arguments favoring, and the arguments limiting, the universality of the joint maximization solution. Do you have any facts or partial evidence supporting your view? If so, what are they?
2. "The zero profit contour for each firm is formed by the triangle from the origin to the *N*-points on each axis, for the linear-demand, costless-output case." Explain how this is related to the boundary of the profit contours.
3. Draw some diagrams showing how the profits of one or both firms can be increased whenever the output point lies off the "no-gain" locus.

MARKET-PRICE ASSUMPTIONS

The exposition of duopoly theory so far revolves about the assumption that, however output decisions are reached, the full quantity produced is released for sale in the given market period. This is a restrictive hypothesis. Firms can sell from, or hold for, inventory; if carrying costs are prohibitive, they can destroy part of the output if to do so is more profitable than enlarging sales. To understand these cases involves not output but rather *market-price* hypotheses. Assuming that firm *A* announces the price and is thus the *price leader*, the assumptions with respect to market-price policy comprise at least three distinct types: (1) *A* knows that *B* will follow his (*A*'s) price policy whatever the direction, whether up or down; (2) *A* knows that *B* will not follow a price rise above some level, but will meet any price fall; (3) *B* will follow upward price movements but will object to downward price revisions below some stipulated level; if *A* should try to enforce such low prices, *B* will retaliate, say, by a 10 per cent price cut for every 1 per cent lowering by *A*. Supplementary assumptions can be made in each case; until we explicitly disclaim it, we assume that *A* possesses full knowledge of how *B* will act.[7]

Complete Price Follower

When *A* knows that *B* is a complete price follower, if both firms are of approximately the same size the price should finally settle at the

---

[7] This analysis should be applicable to "open-price" industries and to many real world cases; for one firm usually initiates a price movement; others follow with a minor or major time lag. Simultaneous action seems to be a more dubious hypothesis; when it occurs it probably evidences collusion rather than spontaneous behavior.

monopoly level, for this figure should maximize each individual profit share. If we assume a linear-demand curve and costless output, and the proviso that as price is the same and both firms are the same size they share the market equally, then if the market-demand curve D_x intersects OX at N, the demand curve for firm A will be $\frac{1}{2}D_x$, cutting the OX axis at $\frac{1}{2}ON$. The MR curve of A's demand curve will cut the OX axis at $\frac{1}{4}ON$. This is the most profitable sales volume for A; it is also B's sales. Total output is thus $\frac{1}{2}ON$, or equal to the monopoly amount.

Downward Price Follower

If A knows that B will follow any downward price revision from some presumed level, say OP_1 in Figure 11.5(A), but would never go higher, then A's demand curve will resemble the discontinuous path $P_1d_2d_3d_4$, where $d_1d_2d_3d_4$ represents one half of the market-demand curve. The latter would be A's demand curve if B were a completely servile follower, up and down, but sharing the market equally with A at identical prices.

There is a strong likelihood, in this case, that price will stick at OP_1; certainly it cannot go higher. Oddly, if A's MC were to intersect P_1d_2 to the left of d_2, then firm B would fill more than one half of the market-demand quantity. The outcome thus depends on the level of OP_1 and the reasons for B's attachment to it.

Price Cutting

Rather than merely follow downward, B may threaten to cut price by 10 per cent if A dares even a 1 per cent price reduction below a certain level—say, OP_1. Figure 11.5(A) also describes this situation. If B were

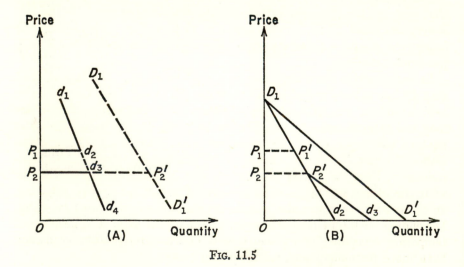

FIG. 11.5

a complete price follower, the reduced curve $d_1d_2d_3d_4$, one half the market curve D_1D_1', would be A's demand. As it is, A's curve follows d_1d_2 and then darts back to P_1, for, as A names a price even fractionally below OP_1, B cuts to OP_2. Thereafter, if A meets the OP_2 figure, and even lowers price farther, B may merely meet the new price cut. Should B refuse to sell below a price of OP_2, A's demand will spurt out and then coincide with the full market-demand curve.

The demand curve for firm A is thus $d_1d_2P_1P_2d_3P_2'D_1'$. Once more, the proximity to competitive or monopoly price is likely to depend on the price height at which B's defenses are set.

Limits on B's Sales

Another duopoly variation is outlined in Figure 11.5(B): D_1D_1' is drawn as the full market-demand curve. If B always concurred in A's price policy, then D_1d_2, which is $\frac{1}{2}D_1D_1'$, would appear as A's demand curve, with the remaining half of the market-demand quantities supplied by B. A may perceive, however, that B will not assent to a price above OP_1, so that, if A should list a higher price, B would capture the full market. Further, if B's full supply quantity equals the abscissae amount P_2P_2', subtracting this amount from the market-demand curve at prices below OP_1, we can define A's demand curve as the discontinuous path $P_1P_1'P_2d_3$: A's price will settle at the maximum profit position along this path. If B withholds some supplies from the market at prices below OP_1, $P_2'd_3$ will assume a more concave form.

Contesting Leadership

The argument of this section has been predicated on the supposition that firm A (the price leader) knows the reactions of firm B (the follower) and thus, by a suitable choice of price policy, can induce B to implement A's price pronouncement. This supposition is akin to the output-leader analysis.

In some market structures, one firm (not necessarily the largest one) may be the acknowledged leader to whom all others look for the price key. Tradition and little else may govern the relationship. The leader may estimate the price most lucrative to itself, on the basis of a sales analysis of other firms at each potential price. Barring an acknowledged leader to whom all eyes are turned, if the practice is to post prices simultaneously, then the lowest-priced firm will immediately be the leader, with the others having to conform after a longer or shorter time lag. In the interim, however, the normal distribution of sales may be upset. Depending on the market organization, leadership may be a position of temporary occupancy and a source of contention and conflict, or it may have more permanent and acknowledged roots.

Financial Strength and the Role of Inventories

One inference that may be drawn from this analysis, and that empha-sizes some unwholesome aspects in fields of small numbers, is that a disproportionately larger firm—one able to supply a greater quantity at a given average cost—and possessed of superior financial resources,[8] will have a preponderant influence upon price merely through its ability to instigate a session of price cutting of longer or shorter duration. A smaller firm (measured in the comparative terms of the output volume of mini-mum AC), or one that is financially impotent, would be unable to counter the threat. Contrariwise, where both firms are of approximately the same size, there appears a new motive for inventory holdings—namely, to ward off a rival's price-cutting propensities with the retaliatory weapon of sizable inventories. The costs of an excessive inventory carry-over may be less. than the income loss with a downward price revision.

Kinked Demand Curves

A few remarks on kinks or sharp corners in demand curves and the level at which they are found are in order: the discontinuous curves of Figure 11.5 contain "kinks" at P_1 and P_2. Often these features can be assigned to the entrepreneur's faithfulness to an old historical price and, through inertia and friction, to a reluctance to change. Perhaps long-run estimates of "spoiling the market" in the future by a current change have a bearing. Seeking a more rational explanation, perhaps when A raises his price B may refuse to follow because of a high degree of output elasticity, with production taking place under relatively constant or even falling marginal-cost conditions. New entry into the field might also be facilitated at but a slightly higher price; A's price-raising tactics are thus opposed by B. A converse set of reasons would account for the hostility to a price fall.

Wherever the discontinuity occurs, the marginal-revenue curve is likely to break sharply, probably to turn negative. This provides good ground for believing that output will settle at the kinked point. Thus, in Figure 11.6(A), the demand curve is $P_1P_1'P_2P_3$ and the MR curve is the dashed line jumping to negative, positive, and negative values. P_1 is thus likely to be the price except for a sharp drop in marginal cost.

A Cost-Curve Solution

Costs have been virtually ignored in duopoly analysis thus far. One suggestion of a unique and determinate solution of duopoly problems for firms of dissimilar size has centered about disparities in cost curves.

In Figure 11.6(B), D_1D_1' is the market-demand curve and D_1d_1 the

[8] As defined in the next section.

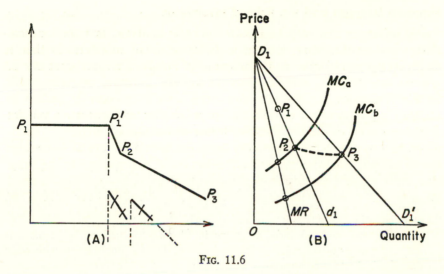

Fig. 11.6

demand curve confronting each firm, on the assumption that both charge identical prices and supply one half the market. MR is marginal to $D_1 d_1$. MC_a and MC_b are the marginal-cost curves of firms A and B, respectively.

Considering these relations, suppose that A possesses the power to name market price while sales are shared evenly. It will announce a price of P_1, for, at the output corresponding to this price, its profits are maximized. On the other hand, if A's minimum average cost equals P_3, say, then A will not offer any output at all below this price.

Firm B's MC curve intersects the MR curve at a price within the $P_1 P_2$ range. Sharing the market equally, B would post a price somewhere in this range; thus, it is argued, as B's price is lower, A will have to conform to it. Further, so long as the price named by B does not drop below P_2, A will satisfy one half the market demand. But, if price were to fall below P_2 but above P_3, A would equate MC_a to market price and serve *less* than one half the market-demand quantity.

B's demand curve, therefore, is $D_1 P_1 P_2 P_3 D_1'$; it will adapt itself to this curve and name its market price on the usual profit-maximization principles. Hence, it is averred, B will inevitably emerge as the price leader.

The flaw in this argument is that it assumes that A will abide by B's market price and will sell precisely the amount B proposes for him. To demonstrate its lack of generality, suppose that B posts a price in the range $P_1 P_2$ and produces an output equal to one half the total of market demand. If A *correctly predicts* B's production, and subtracts it laterally from the demand curve, A will produce more than the amount mentally allotted to him by B. The error thus lies in the neglect of A's output independence: B could inspire obedience to its price policy only through price-cutting tactics whenever A failed to submit to its plan for "collusive conformity." But, if B imposes its price through intimidation, it is superfluous to emphasize the shape of B's or A's marginal-cost curve.[9]

Questions

1. What further variations of the market-price behavior assumptions can you suggest, other than those contained in the diagrams of this section?
2. For each of the major behavior patterns, what reasons can you give to explain each type of possible reactions?
3. Considering the odd demand or sales curves of this section, how valid is the "law of demand," involving the downward-to-the-right "normal" demand curve?
4. Discuss circumstances in which price leadership may be a durable position, and other situations in which it may be extremely temporary.
5. With a kinked demand curve as shown in Figure 11.6, under what conditions will a change in costs lead to a change in price? Draw your diagram with some care if one is required to answer this question.
6. How would you define the notion of a "cost advantage"?

ECONOMIC WARFARE

We pass now to issues of economic warfare. Economic warfare refers to those duopoly or oligopoly situations in which the aim of one firm is to lower prices in such degree as to drive a rival from the field. In price-cutting campaigns, in contrast to warfare, the aim is more limited—to secure a greater volume of sales or to punish rivals for certain price actions, but not to eliminate them from the field. Economic warfare as a means of reducing numbers in the field also belongs to the theory of entry and exit; merely the occasional brandishing of the big stick is apt to render entry extremely uninviting.

Bankruptcy and the Durability of Equipment

Discerning its rival's intentions, a firm about to be assaulted may submit without a struggle; foreshadowed losses will often breed a docile attitude and the quietude of an alternative output may well be preferred. Nevertheless, while its equipment exists as a productive entity, its mere presence constitutes a damper on the monopoly price, for some part of the market could be regained whenever the price went high enough to make the foray lucrative. This raises the extremely important question of whether forcing a firm into bankruptcy accomplishes the ends of battle.

Suppose that, because of the struggle, the defeated firm undergoes reorganization proceedings, with the claims of old owners and creditors

[9] Fundamentally, this duopoly solution relies on B's knowledge of A's reactions, which thereby molds the demand curve $D_1P_1P_2P_3D_1'$ for B. The argument is a special version of the theory of conjectural variations.

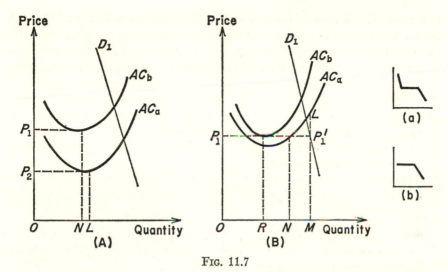

Fig. 11.7

reduced, but that plant and equipment do not pass into the hands of its belligerent opponent. Hence, regarding the firm as a bundle of equipment, it will be preserved as a going entity despite the changes in ownership rights. Unless it regards discretion as the better part of valor, production with its equipment will cease only when the bellicose firm makes it impossible for any management to cover average costs, including in the latter the costs of all factors that have alternate uses.[10] This condition goes much beyond the legalistic phase of bankruptcy.

Cost Assumptions

There are two sets of vital assumptions in analyzing the problem of economic warfare. The first pertains to the cost structures of the contending firms, while the second has regard to the financial strength or the capital positions of the dueling firms.[11] We shall at first postulate identical financial strength for each firm, both of whom produce identical commodities.

Assume, first, that the attacker A possesses the cost advantage, interpreting this to mean that the minimum point of firm A's AC cost curve lies below that on B's cost schedule. The cost structures are represented

[10] Full contractual overhead costs would have to be included in the curve of average total costs to indicate the price the firm would have to receive for each output level to cover its full operating charges. But remembering that revisions of contracts are constantly made (and would have to be made after bankruptcy), only the lowest sum that would be accepted by factor owners need be included in the relevant "longer-period" AC curve.

[11] The financial-strength aspect has occupied the attention of M. Shubik in his discussion of "games of economic survival," *op. cit.*

in Figure 11.7(A). D_1 is the general market-demand curve for the commodity; cost curve AC_a belongs to firm A and cost curve AC_b to firm B. Least-cost outputs are, respectively, at OL and ON. Examination of the diagram makes it evident that B can be driven from the field without any loss to A, for, by announcing a price slightly below OP_1 (the minimum point on B's cost curve), A can envelop the entire market while escaping any loss to itself. Firm B can produce only by impairing its capital position and foregoing the more lucrative alternate uses of factors under its control.

The cost structures depicted in Figure 11.7(B) are perhaps more probable. Here, although A's least-cost output is below B's, the entire market demand can be filled by A at a price below the minimum AC_b only if A is willing to face losses on its part.[12] To supply the full market at a price below B's minimum cost would involve a loss of at least LP_1' per unit for A. Actually B, the besieged, could punish and impose greater losses upon A by producing some quantity and driving the price lower still. So long as B stays at or to the left of its point of minimum costs, A's total losses on the greater volume might be so overwhelming as eventually to threaten it with bankruptcy.[13] If B simply announced that it was willing to sell an amount OR at a price equivalent to OP_1, and A announced a lower price, the ultimate upshot would be that A itself would be forced from the field.[14]

Sales Rationing

Conceivably, A can drive B from the field without serving the full market. Suppose that, at a price just below OP_1, A agreed to sell all the output it could produce without loss to itself: amount ON in Figure 11.7(B).[15] Then a demand quantity slightly greater than NM, at a price slightly below OP_1, would remain unsatisfied and open to B. Unless this "left-over" demand for B, resulting from A's "rationing" policy at the lower price, is tangent to or lies above some portion of B's cost curve, B will have to succumb.[16]

[12] B might produce the minimum-cost output even though actual sales in any period do not warrant it, holding as inventory the unsold portion of output from one period to another, perhaps producing a by-product in the interim idle periods. Of course, carrying charges would have to be included. See below, p. 358.

[13] Recall in this connection our postulate of equal financial resources.

[14] This kind of announcement by B which does not result in sales of the particular product, while it occupies itself, say, with by-products, might be called "sideline" pricing.

[15] The A firm would have to ensure that the goods went into the hands of final consumers to avoid the growth of secondary markets.

[16] The demand schedule facing B would be discontinuous; in Figure 11.7(a) there would be a horizontal segment at OP_1, for at this price B could share the

Similar Cost Structures

Assuming similar cost structures, with the minimum AC being identical for each firm, then, in order to render production unprofitable to firm B, the A firm would have to declare its willingness to sell at a price below its own minimum AC. Warfare would be a costly business and eventually A itself would have to fall, on the hypothesis of equivalent financial strengths and sideline pricing by B at its minimum AC level.

Finally, the cost advantage may lie with B. In Figures 11.7(A) and 11.7(B), AC_a now belongs to firm B and AC_b to A. Formidable losses would be in the offing for A in attempting to monopolize the field; it could not hope to succeed, for, whatever losses B might suffer, A's losses would always be greater. Thus, it is only with a decided cost advantage that an attacker can compel a rival with relatively equal financial strength to abandon its operations.

Financial Strength

It is time to discard the hypothesis of equal financial resources. Suppose, first, that the balance of financial strength, including in the latter both cash and the ability to command cash by borrowing or disposing of other assets, lies with the attacker. Possessing a cost advantage along with financial strength, it should be able to bully its way into sole dominance—depending, of course, on the margin of its financial resources. Even if it is at a cost disadvantage, it may still succeed if its financial strength is adequate, for, so long as it can withstand losses, it can make the field unprofitable for its rival. Should preponderant financial strength reside with the besieged firm, barring extreme cost advantage to the attacker, the former should be able to weather most warfare struggles.

Thus, financial strength is a crucial factor in economic warfare. Undoubtedly, vast financial disproportionalities can ensure victory and dominance in the field. Still, it is only a sharp cost advantage that is likely to be permanently successful in deterring rivals from challenging a firm's position and, by each conflict, weakening it. For, if a firm is defeated despite economically superior equipment—if it merely announces that it will always fill orders at its minimum cost—the financially strong firm will incur chronic losses; it will never receive an opportunity to exploit its monopolistic position and, sooner or later, it too will dissolve and disappear. Because of irretrievable losses, decisions to launch a costly internecine strife will be carefully weighed.

A more apparent way for the financially strong firm to become the

---

market with A. If the upper portion of the demand curve allowed profitable output to B, then A would have to offer more than ON units for sale at OP_1.

sole monopolist seller is, after the first test of strength, to acquire the equipment of the bankrupt firms at "bargain" prices. It thus buys its way into a monopolist position.[17] New entrants, thereupon, have to compete with a firm that, in a period of struggle for the market, does not have to plan to recover interest and amortization charges on its capital investment—costs that must be included by new entrants on a parity with wage and material costs.

Cost Interdependence

The analysis has concentrated on the case of an aspiring monopolist forcing price below its rival's costs in order to eliminate it from the field. Precisely the same result might be accomplished by raising the rival's costs above the sales price.

Let us say that the A firm, looking beyond the throes of battle, desires to keep price rigid at the historic level in order not to "spoil the market" for the future, realizing that even a temporary low price will prevent a later price rise. If there are certain strategic factors of production required by the rival firm, the bellicose firm could bid up their price so high as to inflict losses upon the B firm if the latter were to emerge as the successful bidder for them.[18]

A single firm could seldom hire enough of a large factor class to raise their price and make production costs prohibitive to a new entrant. This suggests that, in carrying out its policy, a firm will generally concentrate upon heterogeneous factors as objects for action. If substitute agents can also be employed, they too may have to be blocked to the rival, by contract, by hire, or by bidding up of their price. The particular resource owners would be the principal beneficiaries of the contest between the warring firms.

Questions

1. Does bankruptcy "destroy" a rival firm or not? Explain.
2. If a firm lowers price but rations sales, derive the "left-over" demand curve to the rival firm. Is this perfectly elastic at the price named by the sales-rationing firm?
3. Financial strength is an institutional phenomenon. Can social policy prevent its use in economic warfare? Discuss.

[17] We thus acknowledge implicitly the importance of access to wealth and loan markets, which may debar an economically superior firm from competing on equal terms with one inferior economically, but with capital market contacts and a superior liquidity position comprised of readily salable assets.

[18] Conceivably, say, in lumbering, where timber stands are necessary for survival, this may be possible. Wage rates may also be affected in small-scale business operations of a service variety where there are limited supplies of skilled labor.

4. Can you think of any situations in which warfare can succeed through driving up a rival's cost? Do these situations lend themselves to some principle of classification or not?

MARKET AGREEMENTS

The probability is strong that overt collusion will be the upshot in fields of small numbers. Price-follower–price-leader, output follower, and, generally, all passive market patterns are a tacit form of collusion, at one remove from connivance for restrictionist ends. However, their effectiveness may be as sure as a straightforward agreement among the participants. Let us discuss briefly the types of collusive agreements that may be sought to introduce order in oligopoly markets.

Output Agreements

One obvious form of agreement covers the output level of each firm; frequently, the participants will protest with an air of injured innocence when it is suggested that they conspire to fix price. Price, it will be demurred, is left to the "market." Manifestly, the relevant analysis in these circumstances is that of pricing a fixed stock of goods—that is, the market quota.

If the restrictionism accomplishes its ends, the monopoly-output level may be approached—assuming that the agreement covers a perfectly substitutable good for which a full market-demand-and-supply curve can be drawn and competitive and monopoly outputs contrasted. In general, if each firm knows the output permitted to others, and assumes that they will produce it, this quantity can be subtracted laterally from the demand curve and the reduced demand (D_r) curve derived; the firm can then calculate whether it should produce its full allotment, or less, or seek to surpass it: it would be strongly tempted to expand its output and surpass its quota if, for the production of the latter amount, $MR_r > MC$. The success of the agreement for the full market comprising all the firms is thus likely to depend on: (1) whether each firm is fully apprised of the total output quota; (2) whether estimates of the market-demand curve are uniform; (3) whether for all firms $MR_r = MC$, so that they could be trusted to abide by their quota quantities, neither to surpass them nor to fall below. In essentials, the analysis tends to coincide with the output-dependence case.

The bases of quota assignments are literally legion, though, in practice, either historical norms or percentages of imaginary capacities seem to exhaust the ingenuity of the architects of restrictionism. Practically, unless there is an enforceable system of punishments for breaches of contract, and of rewards for compliance, the arrangement is likely to disintegrate unless in each firm $MR_r = MC$.

Price Agreements

Price agreements are at least a frank approach to the monopoly objective without the equivocation of "orderly output" agreements; for the moment we presume that the agreement fails to stipulate output. The price may likewise be a historical one, or it may be deemed "fair," or it may be sanctioned by law, or appear most profitable, etc. If each member complies, a sort of pseudo-competition evolves; for each firm will detect that the demand curve facing it is perfectly elastic at the agreed price. In contrast to the perfectly competitive case, where the market-demand curve turns downward at an output far beyond the economic capacity of any one firm, each firm now discerns that the demand curve has a sharp corner at an attainable output level, depending on the random sharing of market sales.

If, in each firm of the member group, the MC curve cuts the MR curve directly under the demand-curve discontinuity, the full market demand at the conspired price will be served. If the gap between P and MC is extremely large, and if this is true in each firm, there is a likelihood that a lower price and extended output will prove profitable for the full market. Quality improvements, selling pressure, surreptitious discounts, and price shading are all likely to appear as each firm tries to expand its share of the market. If the gap between P and MC is narrow, higher prices may prove profitable. If the MC curve cuts the horizontal price line to the left of the discontinuity, higher prices are probable, with all firms concurring. If the avenue of higher prices is closed, the individual firms caught in this particular predicament may refuse some custom or ration sales; if the firms feel honor-bound to fill all purchase requests, we have a curious situation in which $MC > P$.

This is probably all that we need to say about collusion, at least on a general plane: each output and price scheme is likely to have some special features which must be treated individually, for they are the product of the arts of compromise and business diplomacy for which general principles cannot be advanced. Moreover, the degree of durability and compliance is always an indefinite matter. Still, so long as the result is a price policy in which $P > MC$ for each of the participating firms, the usual criticisms of monopoly will apply.

Coalitions and Compensations

In addition to overt collusion, there is always the possibility of coalitions among certain members to drive others out of the field. Forms of economic bribery, consisting of compensations by one firm to another to deter the latter from lowering price or to induce it to increase price, are also within the realm of possibility: it is always profitable to offer "compensatory" payments when the amount of profit to be gained exceeds the amount of disbursements to be made. But the amounts and the direction of payment are vague and indeterminate, depending on the individuals who play the oligopoly game, their resources, their prospective profit gains, and their personal psychological traits. Furthermore, since such payments may be traceable, prosecution under the antitrust laws would appear to be a powerful deterrent to their universal adoption, even though economic forces invite their use.

Questions

1. If you were to recommend market agreements, what advantages would you see in price rather than output agreements? disadvantages?
2. Enumerate the problems that would have to be faced in recommending agreements of either form to duopolists; to a half-dozen oligopolists.
3. Under what conditions is an agreement between two firms likely to secure compliance? Suppose that there are about half a dozen firms: what new difficulties appear in the way of compliance?
4. What is the problem of "pooling profits" through market agreements?
5. What is the relation between agreements and new entry?
6. Explain how coalitions can arise and how they can affect oligopoly solutions.

DUOPOLY INSTABILITY

Stability in monopoly markets in stationary conditions of demand and cost requires that, for each firm, $MR > MC$ to the left of the equilibrium output and $MC > MR$ to the right: running beyond the $MC = MR$ output level will reduce pecuniary income in precisely the same way as falling short of this output. The latter production level, therefore, will tend to be maintained.

In contrast, under duopoly, even in fundamentally stationary supply-demand conditions, one seller or both may alter its output in the quest of greater profits. As one firm's behavior will depend so much on what it expects of its rival, and as both may move simultaneously from any adjustment already reached, each position is at best unstable: the equilibrium has been aptly described as of the "cat and mouse" variety.[19] Each firm's movements will provoke the other; neither will stir without prejudging what the other will do. As the profit balance may be radically transformed by the mutual action patterns, any stability postulates become extremely tenuous; they could be posited only if one firm's output was unalterably rigid or its mental processes prejudiced against even a consideration of change.

The Temptation for Corporate Consolidation

There is one additional matter that renders suspect any "stable equilibrium" solution of the duopoly problem. Manifestly, the firms cannot

[19] E. A. G. Robinson, *Monopoly*, pp. 24–30.

help but apprehend the mutual interactions of their policies and their complete interdependence for a profitable life. Ultimately, the appreciation of their common interest in a monopoly policy would tend either to foster collusion of an overt kind or to encourage efforts toward a consolidation of the firms and reorganization of the field. Ruling out the possibility of combination, the agreement may evolve by mutual consent, through intimidation in the form of warfare or through bargained compromise in a live-and-let-live, let's-be-friends atmosphere.

A duopoly field, therefore, contains elements of perpetual instability, with prospects for a continual regrouping in a way not typical of firms in a competitive or monopoly structure. In a world in which dynamic changes incessantly interrupt the stationary flow, the manifestations of duopoly instability are undoubtedly lost in the sea of change; they are likely to be of only minor importance as compared to the effects of shifts in demand and costs. The flighty nature of its oscillations would become more apparent in quieter times.

Extension to Oligopoly

After this survey, the argument can be readily extended to oligopoly configurations of three or more sellers; assumptions of precisely the same type utilized in the duopoly analysis are again suitable. Normally, it can be surmised that each seller lumps together the output of all other sellers, treating them as one—a procedure that simplifies and imparts greater determinateness to our solutions. Firms probably do view their rivals in this way, observing most intently the projected plans of the larger rivals and compounding them with the probable policies of smaller firms.

The output-follower case can be treated briefly. A small firm of a compact oligopolistic group is likely to act according to our output-dependence postulates. In planning its output policy, it is likely to view the probable outputs of other firms as a datum. Recalling the case of zero costs and linear demand, if there are 100 firms in the field with 99 firms each producing $(1/101)Q$ (Q being the competitive total of output), then the remaining firm will tend to produce[20]:

$$\tfrac{1}{2}(Q - \tfrac{99}{101} Q) = \tfrac{1}{101} Q$$

Total output for the 100 firms will thus be 100/101 of the competitive amount. If there are 1,000 firms it will be 1,000/1,001 and, if 1,000,000 firms, 1,000,000/1,000,001 of the competitive amount. As the number of firms increases, the approach is closer to the competitive position.

Output-leader roles will probably devolve only upon the larger firms

[20] Any other solution, for the output-follower case, would be a nonequilibrium position, leading to further oscillatory adaptations.

of the oligopolistic group. The principles are as before: if two or more firms embrace this course simultaneously, it will probably culminate in an unsatisfactory profit level for each until at least one of them succumbs to a follower role.

Price leadership, which can be associated with output dependence, presupposes adherence by others, the price followers. The price leader will have to compute the quantities that others will unload at each price before naming the most profitable figure. If the firm is a small one, any attempt at price leadership (apart from institutional structures in which others are guided by the small firm by tradition or by some ingrained reason or other[21]) is generally doomed in advance. The small firm cannot succeed, for one thing, in inducing a price rise by withholding output. On the other hand, its output quantity of minimum average cost would probably be too small to force price downward.

In the output-dependence case, it was seen that, with larger numbers, total output approached competitive levels more closely. Another reason for expecting prices more closely approximating competitive norms with oligopoly would be the knowledge of each of the larger firms that, as they withheld production to force up prices, smaller firms, individually too small to affect output substantially, would take up the slack: the smaller firms would thus be the prime beneficiaries of the output restraint and price-raising proclivities by the larger firms.[22] Consequently, unless the production capacity of small firms is fairly rigid and inelastic, or unless an output policy can be imposed upon them, the price-raising propensities of the large firms will be severely circumscribed. The ease of entry of new firms thus also operates as a restraint.

As oligopoly also involves assumptions as to rival's price or output policy, and as many of the firms may modify their plans simultaneously, the instability noted for the duopoly model will have a counterpart here. Overt or tacit collusion, and a merger of some portion of the field, is a likely development, presaging a more markedly monopolistic structure. But this control can be perpetuated only if new entry and expansion by smaller firms can be blocked.

Questions

1. Why is a duopoly market "inherently unstable" in a way not true of a competitive market?

[21] As is possibly true of gold, silver, or foreign-exchange dealers where historical factors may introduce a traditional leadership element having almost the sanction of law.

[22] In a sense, this may happen when one country attempts to control the output of its own producers without power to control other producing areas; for example, our cotton program and the impetus given to Brazilian growers.

2. Defend essentially the converse proposition; to wit, that the duopoly market may be the more "stable" one. Are the terms being used in the same way in each argument?
3. We read of corporate mergers. How common would they be in a purely competitive economy? Would you or would you not favor mergers, as a general rule? Why?
4. Prove that, as numbers increase, the purely competitive result tends to obtain.

A CONCLUDING REMARK

Duopoly and oligopoly, it is clear, do not lend themselves to the simple, determinate analysis characteristic of pure competition and monopoly. To understand the price-output outcome involves an investigation of market facts. No one hypothesis is likely to be all-embracing, to fit each market pattern. It is in this area that realistic studies are required, to at least develop the facts on the rules of behavior common in some of the major industrial sectors.

Nonetheless, so long as $P \neq MC$, the general effects on well-being are equivalent in nature, if not in degree, to those emanating from any monopoly or nonoptimal position. Of course, from the standpoint of well-being, and of economic policy generally, the matter of degree, and not of kind, may be the persuasive factor, counseling action or recommending caution as the greater part of wisdom. So much more information will be required before our answers to these questions can be purged of an unbecoming bias—or the philosophies that are always ready to fill a factual vacuum.

Chapter 12

𝕫𝕫𝕫

Monopolistic Competition

The monopoly concept revolved about a firm producing a commodity for which perfect substitutes were nonexistent and, as a secondary condition, the lack of any substantial market interdependence between the firm's price policy and either sales or prices of other commodities, so that this aspect of the structural adaptation could be ignored.

Under monopolistic competition, the first condition is retained while the second restriction is abandoned; the cross-elasticity and the coefficient of price interdependence are so large that to omit these interrelations is to miss a vital part of the problem. The analysis is thus reminiscent of the duopoly relations of the preceding chapter, with the distinguishing proviso being that now the interdependence is presumed to be between sellers of imperfect rather than perfect substitutes. Some of the impediments to entry that serve to explain the multiplicity of products and the heterogeneity of competition will also be considered. The peculiar dilemma of monopoly and innovation also constitutes a topic for this chapter.

Sales outlays and product variation, especially in circumstances of nonprice competition, flourish in monopolistically competitive markets. Hence, these matters will occupy part of the main discussion.

MARKET INTERDEPENDENCE

The circle of interdependence was quite definite for perfect substitutes; it is more difficult to prescribe similar bounds for differentiated products. In the oligopoly group, the firm was in complete competition with firms producing the identical commodity, but a clear gap in the chain of substitutes separated it from the remainder of the structure; now, however, the firm finds its bearing only relative to the full system. To throw a cordon about any two (or few) firms is always arbitrary, defensible only because of a presumed higher elasticity of substitution of their goods or cross-elasticity of demand than between either of them and other commodities at roughly the going price ratios and aggregate income level.

For the most part, we shall look only at the interdependence between two firms. Of course we can isolate from the full system any number of firms whose mutual study appears interesting, examining their interdependence while overlooking their relations with the rest of the structure: this will do as the formal extenuation of our procedure. It is better to fix our sights somewhere and get some results for closely related firms, rather than to abandon the project on perfectionist grounds of incompleteness because it evades some side relations.

A Classification

We can distinguish between structures of passive and resistant reactions. These may be likened to a price-leader, price-follower situation as against a contesting leadership pattern. Thus, B is a *passive* price follower if, after A has named his price, B regards it as immutable and proceeds to adjust MC to the MR of its new forthcoming demand curve. This assumption is similar to the output-leader, output-follower case. In contrast, a resistant firm will not acquiesce so supinely if it is dissatisfied with A's price. Instead, through price pressure, it may strive to compel A to alter its ways: by lowering P_b sufficiently, the announced P_a can be rendered unprofitable to firm A. In short, the passive pattern relies on A's initiating price changes. Differences in the size of the firms would be an adequate reason for the asymmetry in their behavior.

Some cases do not fit neatly into this scheme. For example, suppose that the B firm adheres to its old price despite the change in P_a, even though its new $MR \gtrless MC$. Firm B reacts neither actively nor passively, but, rather, quite inertly. Also, B may react passively to some price movements of A and actively to others.

Passive Reactions: Leader-Follower

The theory of passive reactions for two closely substitutable goods, A and B, can be clarified by means of a pair of interrelated demand curves. In Figure 12.1(A), suppose that firm A originally announces a price of OP_1. The demand curve for firm B is thus D_1 in Figure 12.1(B). Realizing its impotence to influence P_a, firm B equates its MC to the MR correspondent of D_1. Firm B's price thus settles at P_1' and sales at OM'. Once P_b is known, the demand quantity of A at price OP_1 is also determinate, at OM. As A raises price—to OP_2, say—the demand curve for B moves out to the right, to D_2. For simplicity, even assuming constant marginal costs (MC_1) in firm B, P_b will rise, to P_2', with sales at ON'.[1] A's sales become ON. Whereas A's sales *must* fall off if P_b rises less than

---

[1] For the elasticity of demand on D_2 at each price is lower than on D_1. From $P = MR(1 - 1/E)$, the result follows.

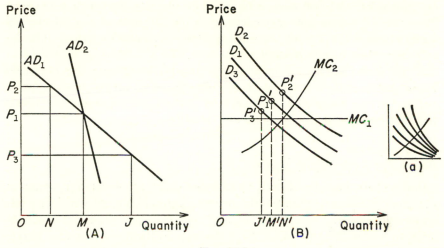

FIG. 12.1

proportionately, B's sales may even increase, despite its higher price, as some of A's former purchasers swing over to buy from B.[2] The effect on B's sales can be decomposed into its loss of custom to other sellers because of its higher price, and an increase due to the demand shift from A. If A is a large firm having a substantial body of price-sensitive customers, then almost certainly $ON' > OM'$.

Conversely, if A lowers price to OP_3, the demand curve for B will fall back to D_3. Price in B will descend to P_3' with sales at OJ'. A's sales will advance to OJ. If B's price fall is relatively less than A's, then B's sales may narrow while A's market expands. Conceivably, the sales of both A and B may expand at the lower prices named by the respective firms.

As P_b is determinate once P_a is announced, and as A's demand quantity is then determinate, the full demand curve for firm A (AD_1 in Figure 12.1[A]), can be constructed. On the basis of this demand curve, A will name the most profitable monopoly price. Once A does so, it settles the demand curve evolving for B; then P_b and B's sales are determinate, as well as A's demand quantity.

If the marginal-cost curve for the B firm is rising, as is MC_2 in Figure 12.1(B), then, with curves to the right of D_1, price will be higher than P_2'. With demand curves to the left, as D_3, the price will be lower than P_3'. The demand curve for A will be relatively inflexible, as illustrated by AD_2 in Figure 12.1(A). An interesting conceptual possibility is that

---

[2] The conclusions are provisional, for they depend on the exact shift of the demand curve.

in which firm B's price may be constant despite A's price maneuvers even while B's marginal cost curve is rising: in these circumstances, the demand curve for A becomes the familiar one drawn on the assumption of other prices being constant.

Thus, with passive reactions, $MR = MC$ for both firms, the difference being that one firm's (A's) demand curve is drawn on the basis of other prices varying with each P_a, while B's demand curve evolves on the basis of other prices being constant. It will be A's task to decide on the price configuration that is most profitable to itself.[3]

Active Reactions: Vying Leaders

Turning to the case of active reactions, or vying leadership instances, the analysis takes a more novel turn when B, disgruntled with A's price moves, disregards the equation of MR and MC and bends its efforts to compel A to name a price more satisfactory to itself, to B. Generally, B will seek a demand curve farther to the right, thus securing a higher price *and* greater sales.

Referring to Figure 2.1 in Chapter 2, through cutting P_b disproportionately for any P_a below P, the demand curve for A will be of the discontinuous form D_1PD_3 as compared to D_2D_2', predicated on proportionate price movements in P_b to any change in P_a. Firm A may well eschew a contest that is unprofitable and instead adhere to the price indicated at P.

Conditions of Active and Passive Reactions

Departing from the purely formal plane of analysis, passive reactions are likely whenever the B firm is so remote from A as to dispel any illusions of influencing the latter significantly by a counter price cut; as this condition is very close to our definitional image of monopoly, it largely evades the peculiar problems of monopolistic competition. Perhaps, instead, B is convinced of A's adamancy to either guile or temporary price pressure; it would then be futile for B to launch an active but temporary price-cutting policy. More lasting conflict might be unsatisfactory to B on contemplation of the disparity in financial strength or in cost conditions.

Active opposition is probable when the markets are so closely intertwined that there is a sharp fall in B's sales if B does not meet A's price fall proportionately while, if it does, it can only maintain but scarcely augment its previous volume of sales: the general "market" demand, so

---

[3] If B's MC is falling, so that a ΔP_a actually *lowers* P_b, the demand curve for A will be extremely elastic in the upper reaches, practically eliminating the chances of a price rise by firm A.

If firm B produces an item that is complementary to that of A, the foregoing analysis can be reversed, with D_b shifting to the left as P_a goes higher.

far as *B* visualizes it, is believed inelastic, with the fall in P_a and P_b scarcely enlarging total sales.[4] The demand-curve family that confronts *B*, based on the different P_a prices, thus tends to converge at low prices, as in Figure 12.1(a). As a condition for active reactions, *B* must also believe in *A*'s amenability to a display of resistance. Financial strength looms as a factor of the utmost importance in determining whether a firm's reaction is of a passive or an active variety.

Warfare with Differentiated Products

The analysis of economic warfare is simplified when the products are differentiated. For *A* to banish *B* from the field, it will be necessary for *A* to dictate a price that moves D_b at all points under *B*'s curve of average costs. It is conceivable that some consumers may be so attached to *B* that, despite *A*'s strongest efforts, the demand remaining to *B* may be large enough to accommodate it and enable it to subsist in the field. In the duopoly relations of perfect substitutes, given a more satisfactory cost position and adequate financial resources, the aggressive firm could always bend its rival to its will, pushing it from the field if it set its mind to do so.

Mutual Interdependence

It is possible to draw *price-reaction curves* to picture the process of mutual price adaptation where *both* firms act passively, taking the other's price as a datum. The curves are analogous to the output-reaction curves of duopoly theory.

In Figure 12.2(A), iso-profit contours for firm *A* are drawn, with each point on a curve indicating the price P_a that, given the associated P_b, allows a given profit level. The curves tend to be circular: at each P_b, two values of P_a might yield identical profit results. Only the lower portions of the curves are drawn on the figure. As we move up the field to higher contours, *A*'s profits rise, for, as P_b goes higher, *A*'s demand curve moves farther to the right. (Similar profit contours can be drawn for *B*.) Connecting the minimum points on each profit curve, *A*'s price-reaction curve, AA', is elicited: it relates *A*'s price adjustments of maximum profits to the various possible P_b prices. Normally, it should rise to the right,

---

[4] It might be objected that, if *B*'s sales are insensitive to a price fall, *A*'s demand will also be inelastic, thus checking *A*'s price experimentation if *B* allows price to fall roughly proportionately. Two explanations are possible: (1) either *A* or *B* may be mistaken as to the degree of demand elasticity, with *A* imbued with the idea of elasticity and *B* obsessed with the fear of inelasticity; or (2) as the products are dissimilar, if *B* appeals to a higher income class it may lose the sensitive, price-conscious purchasers if it fails to cut price while failing to gain any important additional custom when it does slash its sales price.

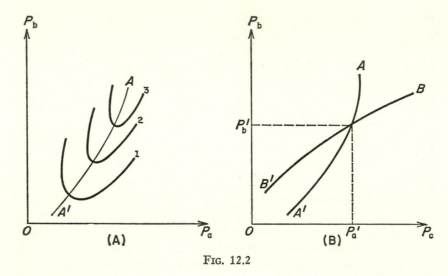

Fig. 12.2

though ultimately it will become perfectly vertical when a further price rise in A will be unprofitable despite the lift in P_b. The reaction curve BB' can be constructed in the same way. The separate price reaction curves, AA' and BB', are placed in juxtaposition in Figure 12.2(B).

If each firm acts passively, taking the market price of the other as a datum, just as in the output-follower case, the equilibrium is given at the intersection of the two curves: each firm presumes, in effect, that its demand curve is drawn on the hypothesis of other prices being constant, so that P_a' and P_b' in Figure 12.2(B) represent the equilibrium price set.

Follower, or passive, patterns thus are equilibrating. Leader relationships may be described in a way equivalent to those under duopoly: if both vie for leadership, the ultimate outcome is indeterminate without further information on how the relationship is modified through experience. Combined patterns of passivity over some range, and then active reactions, would generate a discontinuous price-reaction curve.

Cost Phenomena

Probing the implications of Figure 12.2(B), both firms are apparently producing under conditions of rising marginal costs; as P_b rises, P_a rises and vice versa. In Figure 12.3(A), both firms are producing under conditions of falling marginal costs; here, too, the movements are equilibrating. In Figure 12.3(B), B is producing under conditions of falling MC while A operates under rising cost conditions. A mutually satisfactory equilibrium is still possible, as the numbered points along the adjustment path indicate. In all these cases, at the intersection of the two curves the demand curve of the firm, erroneously conceived by each firm

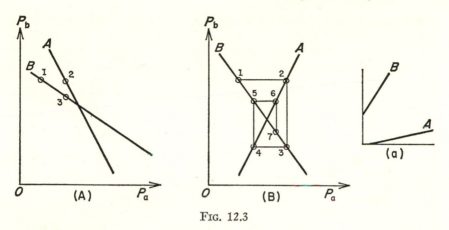

FIG. 12.3

as resting on the postulate of other prices constant, is intersected by the actual demand curve which is of the other-prices-adjusted variety.[5]

If reaction patterns follow the course of Figure 12.3(a), equilibrium is impossible. At each price named by B, A names such a price as to encourage B to raise his price; then A proceeds once again to do the same. The curves depict the absurd spectacle of both firms pushing skyward in their price policy—presumably despite the total disappearance of buyers!

Complementary Goods

When A and B are complementary commodities, we have another variety of interdependence among differentiated commodities. Reaction curve A in Figure 12.3 shows A's response to any given P_b, while B's reaction curve to any P_a is the B curve. The reaction curves for falling MC among substitutes apply. In general, a fall in B's price should evoke a less-than-proportionate rise in P_a, and vice versa. As before, an equilibrium is possible at the prices shown at the intersection of the two curves. Profit contours can also be inscribed onto the figure; as A's profits will increase with a lower P_b, a profit contour closer to the horizontal axis will signify higher profits for A. Follower-leader patterns can be analyzed along the usual lines.

Questions

1. How would you define a "group" of firms under monopolistic competition?
2. How can the analysis surrounding Figure 12.1 be extended to more than two firms?
   a. As P_a rises, in the leader-follower pattern, can the follower's price *fall*? Discuss.

[5] See below, p. 345.

    b. If constant costs prevail for B, what will happen to its price as P_a alters? Why?

    c. Discuss the factors influencing the elasticity of demand for both A and B, remembering that the products are differentiated. Explain important differences in the location and the slope of the curves.

3. With contesting leaders, or active reactions, discuss the possible relations of MC and P.

    a. Discuss the elasticity of demand for A.

    b. When will an active or resistant response have most chance of success? Include the nature of demand interdependence and cost and financial advantage in your answer.

4. Discuss at some length, and diagrammatically, the warfare analysis.

5. Draw profit contours with some care for price-reaction curves.

    a. Locate the maximum contour. Explain.

    b. Is the full contour relevant to the analysis? Why?

    c. Analyze the price-leader pattern in terms of tangency of the contour to the price-reaction curve.

    d. Do the same for contending leaders. Is a follower position ever more profitable than a leadership position? Discuss.

    e. Have you considered the case of falling average costs in your answer? Why?

6. Apply all of question (5) to the case of complementary goods.

SELLING COSTS

Sales outlays must be incorporated into our study as an additional attribute of a monopoly world and as a determinant of the equilibrium of the firm. Advertising expenditures constitute the most interesting, though not the sole, manifestation of sales outlays. The use of salesmen, public-relations expenditures, and gifts to purchasing agents are all to be included as sales outlays, although, generally, we will view sales outlays as synonymous with advertising.

It is not an exaggeration to say that the procedures of advertising simultaneously accomplish commodity homogeneity and heterogeneity. To encroach on the market preserves of other sellers, the firm must demolish the notion of a sharp differentiation of other products from its own. Advertising with this objective will restore a larger degree both of substitutability among goods and of market homogeneity. In the same act, however, the firm must inculcate an attitude of the superiority of its own product, to instill in consumer consciousness the idea of a greater heterogeneity than exists in fact.

In an economy where advertising flourishes, we cannot be unmindful of the fact that these outlays fit rather awkwardly into the concept of a social order in which productive resources are deployed strictly according to consumer desires; advertising operates to reshape desires, even after we concede that some advertising campaigns are notoriously unsuccessful. The traditional portrayal of the economic process, of producers acknowledging the inviolateness of consumer tastes, and adapting to them, is not wholly accurate. Resources are not merely adapted to given consumer ends; instead, tastes are partially shaped to producer ends, depending on consumer receptiveness to sales appeals and entrepreneurial ingenuity, initiative, and imagination in creating them. Although sales pressures modify our views on the motivating forces of economic activity, it is by no means tantamount to the conclusion that all sales techniques are inexorably iniquitous. Ultimately, advertising must be considered as a venture in political liberty—an exercise of the right to influence the opinions of one's fellow men. Advertising is analogous to education in that the purpose of both is to increase or modify knowledge and thereby influence the individual's sense of values; yet it differs from education in that it is a one-sided appeal rather than an intellectually complete presentation of the facts.

Advertising is usually associated with the impersonal sales appeals. Often the same objective of influencing purchase decisions is sought through direct contact with prospective buyers. Letters, house canvassing, and trade salesmen are illustrative; their object is to create a favorable sales climate. Sometimes the precise line of demarcation between selling and production costs is difficult to draw; still, the idea of producing to fill an existing scale of preferences, and of activities devoted to changing the preference structure, is clear in principle and acted on in practice.

Advertising, Entry, and Product Variation

It is not easy to divorce the theory of advertising from that of entry and the legal protection accorded sellers by trade-mark laws enacted to safeguard their infringement. Motives for advertising would all but vanish in an atomistic competitive world where entry was open to all, for only a fraction of the benefits (an amount quite disproportionate to the aggregate advertising outlays) would redound to the favor of the firm incurring the expenditure.[6] Consequently, it is only the legal protection against commodity trespass in conditions of demand expansibility that provides the sustenance for the familiar fabric of the advertising world. Cooperative advertising of the tamest sort, by an industry in an "Eat More Bread" or "Drink More Milk" campaign, would flourish under atomistic competition. Even then, it would be undertaken not by a single firm but rather by the united group—a monopolistic type of organization combined to differentiate the industry's product from all the rest.

---

[6] With "millions of producers," everyone would be aware of the good, to begin with.

It is likewise hazardous to separate the study of advertising from the theory of product variation. In the light of the subjective definition of a commodity adopted earlier, we observe that, as advertising alters consumer valuations, it literally places a new product in the commodity chain. Puristically, the logic of this view is unassailable, yet for our present purposes we can distinguish advertising from the other costs of producing a *technical* commodity, defined from the seller's standpoint, and witness its ramifications.

Advertising as a Productive Agent

Earlier, a distinction was made between output factors and income factors.[7] Both factors are paid for because they are productive of income to the entrepreneur. The output factors have a marginal physical product with a sales value; sales outlays, as an income factor, are incurred not for the physical productivity of, say, a $1,000 sales expenditure, but because it enables the demand price for any output quantity to be raised.

Considering the alternative types of sales outlay—such as billboards, daily and weekly newspapers, magazines, radio time, etc.—let us seek the conditions under which a further expenditure will be lavished on one sales medium rather than another. Writing ΔQ_1, ΔQ_2, ΔQ_3, $\ldots$, ΔQ_n, as the increase in sales at a given price from advertising media 1, 2, 3, $\ldots$, n, and ΔA as an additional sum of expenditure on any of the various forms of advertising (a sum of $1,000, say), then further sales expenditure on sales medium 1 (say, newspaper space) will be preferred to medium 2 (say, radio time) if

$$\frac{\Delta Q_1}{\Delta A} > \frac{\Delta Q_2}{\Delta A} \tag{12.1}$$

Just as marginal physical products, at any given level of output, had to be proportionate to factor prices, for any aggregate sum of sales expenditure the equilibrium condition for an increment of sales outlay must be

$$\frac{\Delta Q_1}{\Delta A} = \frac{\Delta Q_2}{\Delta A} = \frac{\Delta Q_3}{\Delta A} = \cdots \frac{\Delta Q_n}{\Delta A} \tag{12.2}$$

There is, thus, a strong analogy in the hire and economical use of income and output factors.

Diminishing Returns to Advertising

As advertising expenditure aims at changing tastes, ideally each increment in the sales outlay should dislodge the demand curve, pushing it

[7] See Chapter 3.

to the right. It is tempting, and it probably bears some degree of veri-
similitude, to cite a law of diminishing returns to advertising. But it
would have to be so burdened with qualifications as to belie its status
as a valid working principle; the subject affords abundant scope for
empirical investigation. The thought would be expressed in some such
way: as constant increments of advertising expenditure are made, the
demand curve is dislodged laterally to the right by ever less significant
amounts. Or, more precisely, at any given price the additional sales
quantities wanted diminish as further increments in sales outlay are
incurred. The ratios of equation (12.2) would thus fall as the total advertising outlay was increased.

This would signify that the measure of the elasticity of advertising,

$$E_a = \frac{A \Delta Q}{Q \Delta A} \qquad (12.3)$$

ultimately approaches zero.

The substance of this law could be sought in either of two premises:
(1) that the initial increments of sales outlay are designed to attract immediately the most receptive groups so that additional sales expenditures
fall on less sensitive ears; or (2) even if the entire group hears the first
sales plea, successive sales expenditures that canvass the same audience
are less effective in evoking additional demand, for to induce them to buy
more of the advertised product involves an increasing sacrifice of other
products: there is a type of decreasing marginal rate of substitution (or
increasing rate of resistance) in operation, rendering demand shifts more
unlikely.

Irregularity in Response to Mental Stimuli

A first qualification to any stubborn adherence to this "law" is that
the efficacy of an advertising campaign is dependent largely on the
general size of the block sum allocated to the purpose rather than to
minor increments or decrements about this total. For example, there is
seldom any way of knowing when advertising—or any type of education,
for that matter—will strike firm root. Minute gradations are likely to
make only a feeble impression, while a $100,000 "increment" of expendi-
ture from a zero level may have a marked result. The next few increments, by amounts even as large as $25,000 each, may fail to arouse any
additional desires at all until a total sum of, say, $250,000 has been
reached. Demand may then suddenly spurt sharply and vigorously to the
right.

Interminable discontinuities of this nature undoubtedly complicate the
maximizing effort of the firm. Probably all that can be safely concluded
is that, in any geographical area, beyond a certain expenditure, diminish-

ing returns to "education" will probably prevail, depending on the income position of the audience, their receptiveness to sales promotional devices, and the perspicacity and discrimination of entrepreneurs in waging the sales campaign. Sometimes, even the assumption that demand curves will move to the right when more advertising expenditure is lavished is not warranted.[8]

Selling-Costs Equilibrium

Let us diagnose the profit-maximization problem of a firm expending outlays for advertising. If we visualize D_1 as the demand curve prior to the inception of the advertising program, and MC as the cost curve exclusive of any sales expenditure, the monopoly equilibrium will settle at the usual $MC = MR_1$ output position. Introducing advertising outlays, D_1 now moves out to a new position, D_2. Once more the equilibrium condition must be satisfied, but this time of $MC = MR_2$. The advertising allowance will repay itself if the new *net* revenue exceeds the old net revenue by more than the sales outlays. In the final equilibrium, not only will $MC = MR$ in the usual sense along given MR and MC curves, but also the addition to total profits derived from creating a new demand and MR curve will equal the incremental selling outlays. For introductory purposes, the equilibrium conditions may be stated as

$$\text{(1)} \qquad P > MR = MC \qquad \qquad \text{(12.4)}$$

$$\text{(2)} \qquad \Delta R = \Delta A \qquad \qquad \text{(12.5)}$$

$$\text{(3)} \qquad P \geqq AC_p + AC_s$$

where MC is exclusive of any sales outlay, ΔR is the additional profits created by the demand-curve shift, and ΔA is the additional sales expenditure to move the demand curve to a higher total-profit level. Condition (3) refers to price exceeding the sum of both average production and selling costs. In both dimensions, of production and of sales outlay, maximization must take place,[9] the difference between them being that

---

[8] For example, an intensive campaign to popularize a certain item may actually offend upper-income groups without engineering a compensating improvement in the demand from lower-income groups. We can guess that an agency will not retain a contract very long under these circumstances!

[9] In terms of factor hire, the conditions also imply that, just as factors are used so that marginal revenue products equal factor prices, so that further profitable factor use is impossible, the marginal receipts from an increment of advertising is equated to the cost of a unit of advertising. Thus,

$$\frac{MRP_a}{P_a} = \frac{MRP_b}{P_b} = \cdots = \frac{\Delta R_1}{\Delta A_1} = \frac{\Delta R_2}{\Delta A_2} = \cdots = 1 \qquad \qquad \text{(12.6)}$$

different demand curves generate the TR_2 and TR_1 sums. Advertising outlays are omitted from the TC totals.

A Diagrammatic Analysis

Let us develop the equilibrium analysis diagrammatically and more systematically. The most general case seems to be one in which the advertising program centers about some prospective price—or range of prices. After all, to sell a product at $10,000 you would not utilize the same media or make the same outlay that you would for a 50-cent item.[10]

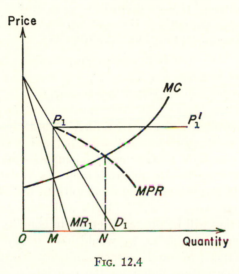

Fig. 12.4

Motor boats and mink coats, chewing gum and cigarettes, elicit different types of sales campaigns.

In Figure 12.4, D_1 is the firm's demand curve prior to any advertising whatsoever and MR_1 is the corresponding marginal-revenue curve. As always, MC is the curve of marginal production cost. In the absence of any sales expenditure, OM would be the monopoly output.

If the firm advertises at and adheres to a market price of P_1, its relevant demand curve is P_1P_1'.[11] If we subtract *the marginal sales outlay*—

[10] For a more complex diagrammatic technique which considers advertising outlay as devoted to shifting the full demand curve without stressing a particular price, see N. S. Buchanan, "Advertising Expenditures: A Suggested Treatment," *Journal of Political Economy* (1942).

For an indifference curve apparatus, which is more general but requires some facility in handling implicit ideas, see K. Boulding, *Economic Analysis*, pp. 776–780.

[11] Conceivably, after the sales outlay is expended, the firm might modify the advertised price. The new demand curve would then be of normal form at the level resulting from both initial tastes and advertising.

the outlay necessary to expand sales by 1 unit—from P_1P_1', the sum remaining will be the marginal production revenue (MPR). That is, MPR indicates the portion of price proceeds available to cover production costs. Thus,

$$MPR = P - MSO \tag{12.7}$$

where MSO is the marginal sales cost. Connecting the successive MPR points, they form the curve indicated in Figure 12.4. It builds on the assumption that there are diminishing returns to advertising.

Manifestly, at price P_1, the equilibrium sales volume is at ON, where $MC = MPR$. Stopping short of this output, or selling more, will leave $MC \gtreqless MPR$. The full equilibrium condition is

$$P = MC + MSO \tag{12.8a}$$

or

$$P - MSO = MPR = MC \tag{12.8b}$$

As in all monopoly problems, therefore, $P > MC$, where the latter embodies only production costs. Full profit maximization entails also, of course, that price exceeds average costs, including both production and sales cost in the average. As the diagram indicates, if MSO is small (say, practically nil), with the advertising accomplished by information passed along by consumers' word of mouth, MPR will practically coincide with P_1P_1' and production will be pushed literally to equality of MC and P.[12]

To calculate aggregate profits, we would have to superimpose a curve of average production (AC) and average sales costs (ASC) for each sales volume on our diagram and summate the two into a combined average cost, as CAC. Total profits would then be the difference between total sales proceeds, or $P_1 \cdot ON$, and total production and sales costs, calculated by multiplying the CAC at ON by ON.

By drawing a similar diagram for each price, we could then compute the total profits at each price selected as the vehicle for advertising, and then extract that combination of price and advertising outlay which maximized profit. The problem is thus one of finding the maximum maximorum—the "maximum of the maximums."[13] Of all the outputs

[12] This might also be the adjustment position if the firm allocates a fixed sum to advertising that stresses a particular price. This is an interesting conclusion, for it seems to be a not uncommon behavior rule.

[13] It is not an uncommon problem. In calling football practice, perhaps the best 100 men in the school out of 1,000 try out for the team. Then the best 33 are selected for the squad. Then the best 11, of the best 33, of the best 100, are named for the varsity team. Once the most valuable player is selected, he is the best one of the best 11, etc.

which ensure maximum profits at each price, it is necessary to select the most profitable output, price, and sales-outlay combination.

At very high prices, the firm probably would find few buyers; lavish sums spent for advertising would be wasted; the most profitable sales volume at a very high price might thus be extremely small, due to the enormous selling costs required for extending sales. Practically, therefore, some price ranges can be quickly eliminated in reaching a policy judgment. Conversely, because of rising marginal production costs, it would pay to spend very little on advertising at extremely low prices. The lower level of the average cost curve would set a limit in the downward direction.

Nonoptimal Sales Outlays: Lump-Sum Expenditures

Suppose that a lump sum is allocated to finance the sales campaign, based not on any deliberate calculations of the most profitable volume of sales expenditure, but rather, say, as a percentage of the previous year's profits. The demand curve at the advertised price would spurt out as a horizontal line to the right, to a sales total representing the market purchases at the ruling price. Conceivably, to fill the full market-demand quantity at the advertised price might carry marginal production costs well above price. If the firm refuses to push production this far, it may have to resort to some unobtrusive form of rationing; if it agrees to accept all orders at the stipulated price, we can be sure that its advertising expenditure has been excessive or that its market price is too low in the light of its outlays, so that it will have failed to maximize its profits.

Contrariwise, the lump-sum advertising outlay may leave price well in excess of the marginal production costs for the purchase quantity at the fixed price. Here additional sales outlay may be able to increase sales with $MPR > MC$, so that the advertising outlay is too small for profit maximization.[14]

---

[14] With corporate income taxes at 52 per cent of profits, and having been upward of 80 per cent during the war years under "excess-profits tax" legislation, it is sometimes alleged that advertising outlays are stimulated. That is, every $1 of advertising costs the firm no more than 48 cents, for, were the outlay not made, taxes would take 52 cents of the extra $1 of profit. Advertising not undertaken at a cost of $1 would be embraced if the cost were only about one half this sum.

This argument assumes that profits will be the same with or without the advertising. Unless the outlay is of an institutional variety, designed to promote "good will" but not directed to immediate sales, this argument is fallacious. It would be valid, however, if the firm seeks not to maximize profits but rather to achieve a "normal" level of profits.

Advertising Cross Elasticities and Price Cutting

The equilibrium analysis has been confined to the firm initiating the expenditure, and thus fits most properly into our monopoly analysis; when we widen our sphere of reference to include market interdependence, there are other interesting possibilities to be unraveled.

Briefly, there are three sets of reaction patterns to consider: (1) other firms can respond passively or actively, but only in terms of price policy, to the advertising outlay of the firm; (2) they can reply with an advertising program of their own; (3) they can answer with a product-variation measure designed to neutralize the inroads of the first firm's advertising. Only the first two forms of behavior will be discussed immediately.

Assuming some advertising originally by all firms, and writing A_1 and ΔA_1 as the sales outlay and outlay increment by firm A, and ΔA_2 and ΔP_2 for advertising and price changes by a firm influenced by it, in the first case we have a cross-advertising and price elasticity,

$$_pE_A = \frac{A_1 \Delta P_2}{P_2 \Delta A_1} \gtreqless O \tag{12.9}$$

and in the second case, a cross-advertising elasticity,

$$E_{A1} = \frac{A_1 \Delta A_2}{A_2 \Delta A_1} > O \tag{12.10}$$

Advertising and Price Interdependence

Let us pretend that, for several reasons, competing firms prefer not to imitate the advertising program with an advertising campaign of their own but accept it as a datum: the elasticity (12.10) is thus zero. Thereupon, the only problems that concern us are the reverberations of firm A's sales-expenditure policy on the rest of the price structure; this involves the magnitude of $_pE_A$.

Conceivably, firm A's advertising policy may be wholly unsuccessful so that, contrary to expectations, its demand curve remains frozen at the original position. Here the sole effect consists of a transfer of income from monopolist to advertising agency; there will be some effects in the economy so long as the expenditure pattern of the new income recipients for finished goods does not exactly coincide with that of the former monopoly-profit recipients.

Normally, the policy will be successful in a profit sense. Demand may be shifted to the firm at the expense of: (1) certain definite commodities —"near" substitutes; (2) more remote substitutes or the whole commodity chain; (3) individual propensities to consume may increase so that the added expenditure is against saving.[15] There can, of course, be some overlapping in these relationships, or a combination of effects.

The second case, which is a throwback to the monopoly hypothesis, may be disposed of summarily: it furnishes a sound reason for passive reactions by affected firms when firm A embarks on a sales program. For, when A's advertising affects only distant substitutes, with present customers of near substitutes remaining attached to existing firms, it is also probable that there will be a diversion of demand from the vast commodity field to the proximate substitutes for the advertised good. The awakening interest in the commodity class will be conducive to the sale of higher-priced substitutes and, for less affluent income groups, to lower-priced grades. The firm's advertising, therefore, will benefit all of the nearby firms. Unless the enlarged demand enables the firms to exploit latent productive economies, prices of the chain of goods favorably affected by the switch in tastes will evidence some rising tendencies, so that $_pE_A > O$; if the shift in demand has made inroads in the markets for some particular commodities, their prices will be depressed. If savings margins are alone contracted, only rising-price pressures are in the offing. Apart from the price and output ramifications, income is now earned in the advertising profession and their demands for finished goods now appear as part of the equilibrium structure.

Price Reactions and Profit Adjustments

More frequently, the shift in demand will affect a nearby chain of substitutes. This will probably signalize market inelasticity of demand for the commodity "class," inasmuch as the new purchasers of firm A's goods are habitual purchasers of similar technical varieties from competing sellers. The latter may persist in their previous price policy in the belief that the demand transference is but an ephemeral phenomenon, or they can retaliate through either a price fall or an advertising policy of their own, or else by a minor variation in their own product, perhaps publicizing some mythical attribute. In the latter event, the advertising will have caused a reorganization of the commodity belt for the entire interdependent group.

If the nearby firm (or firms) do reply through price action, we are confronted once more with a typical problem in monopolistic competition. As the products are differentiated, and the advertising has presumably shifted its demand curve, the advertising firm need not join in the game of price cutting (especially if, in embarking on the original sales outlay, it has weighed these responses). If the competing firms reduce their

---

[15] There are some implications here for the level of employment and the interest-rate structure.

prices, there will be a profit shift within the field, with a portion of the normal earnings of the group now being deflected to the advertising agency by the aggressive selling firm.

Price cutting is likely to be the retaliatory weapon with which to bludgeon an adventurous, or impetuous, firm that insists on advertising a commodity for which the demand over the entire commodity class is inelastic and insensitive even when all firms advertise, so that the aggressive firm's sales expansion is to the detriment of a few "near-by" firms. As for the nonadvertisers, they may have no other recourse, for production may be completely unprofitable after the transference in demand. In this case, $_pE_A$ may be large—and negative.

Cross-Advertising

Visualizing the monopoly case where the expanded demand after advertising is siphoned from the vast commodity field, suppose that all firms employ advertising as an instrument of sales policy. In this event, the sales of the firm are a function not only of its own price and all other prices but also of its own sales outlays and those of other firms.[16] Conceivably, *after the full round of advertising, demand curves may be in exactly the initial position*—not an inconceivable contingency when the interplay of cross-advertising is accredited its due weight. The sole beneficiaries of the selling program would be the advertising industry, to which there now accrue what would otherwise become monopoly profits. If the original sales positions are (practically) restored, we see a strange idiosyncrasy of competitive cross-advertising: the sole beneficiary is the advertising fraternity.

Advertising to Prevent Price Cutting

Rather than advertising being conceived as either an independent phenomenon or a counter measure to a sales program of a rival, it may be designed to fend off the price-cutting tactics precipitated by a competing firm. If both A and B are of vastly different size, with B much the smaller, it may be that firm A, visualizing the market demand as inelastic, poses no objection to a price rise by B. With P_a constant, the demand curve for B will be of normal form for a P_b price rise above P_1. For a P_b price fall, A may reply by an extensive advertising campaign destined both to expand the total market custom and to siphon demand from B.[17]

[16] Thus, $x = f(P_1, P_2, \ldots, P_n; SO_1, SO_2, \ldots, SO_n)$.

[17] The appropriate elasticity is of the form:

$$_AE_p = \frac{P_b \Delta A_a}{A_a \Delta P_b}$$

(12.11)

For the case described it is likely to be negative and much in excess of unity.

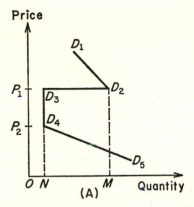

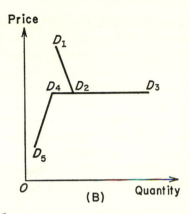

FIG. 12.5

With this onslaught, B's sales dwindle from OM back to ON in Figure 12.5(A). Thereafter, B cannot increase its sales unless P_b falls below OP_2. The demand curve for B thus assumes the extremely flighty $D_1D_2D_3D_4D_5$ drawing in Figure 12.5(A). Firm B will be under strong economic compulsion to name the price indicated at the elastic demand stretch, D_3D_2.

In a similar vein, firms A and B may be selling conventionally priced but imperfectly substitutable commodities, with the normal price indicated by the ordinate height of the $D_4D_2D_3$ horizontal line in Figure 12.5(B). At prices above the normal figure for the commodity class, B's sales may fall off precipitously, so that its demand curve in the upper area is as D_1D_2. If B tries to lower price below the market figure, rivals may resist by advertising, rather than reducing prices, imparting to firm B a reputation for purveying a "cheap" and inferior product variety. The discontinuous curve $D_1D_2D_3D_4D_5$ depicts the facts described. Firm B will deem it the better part of valor to conform to the price convention.

Advertising and Costs

At least a brief comment is expected on the ancient conundrum of whether or not advertising raises prices. In the light of the oligopoly background, a simple answer is impossible; the problem is indeterminate, for it contains several concealed assumptions. In the one case in which demand curves after advertising remain as they were before, prices are obviously unaffected.

When advertising greatly extends the demand for a commodity, there is a presumption that, through time, the price will be higher. But this is almost irrelevant; price will always be higher when demand for a product increases; the sole possible objection is that now the demand shift is "inspired" rather than "spontaneous." The issue here concerns the ethical right to advertise rather than the fact of a higher price. The only apparent exception to the rule that advertising, with the ensuing demand expansion, raises price—excluding advertising at the original price before advertising—is when AC is falling; the new demand may facilitate a price fall.

This last case cannot be ignored, for widespread economies of scale are often obtainable only after demand is augmented. If the demand shift also occurs to the detriment of a specified list of other commodities, unless their outputs are also marked by decreasing AC, their price should also fall.

Another way of examining this problem is to consider the effects of advertising on prices not only in a system where they are first introduced but also in a system from which they are withdrawn: we can speculate on the consequences if suddenly all sales outlays were prohibited. If nothing further happened, if tastes molded by *past* advertising were unaltered, then prices should be essentially uninfluenced. In the longer future, as tastes deviated from the pattern they would assume when subjected to sales pressures, the relative price structure would reflect these facts of a more somber world. Those goods whose demand relies strongly upon sales expenditure would sell at relatively lower prices: this envisages rising MC curves. But, in general, it is not possible to advance an unequivocal answer in terms of price relationships, for the forces influencing tastes would differ in both nature and intensity. Undoubtedly, the major readjustment would devolve upon the advertising field itself; as a supplementary matter, price reductions through diminished demands for the normally advertised products would, to some slight degree, be counterbalanced by higher prices for periodicals and the disappearance of some publications from the contemporary scene.

A Qualification for Nonpecuniary Motives

Although *a priori* conclusions on whether or not advertising raises prices must inevitably be vague, there is one qualification that must be stated. Frequently, if firms voluntarily forgo the full monopoly price and profits because of a variety of nonpecuniary motives, when pricing is undertaken with an eye to a "fair" volume of profits rather than *maximum* profits, then advertising can be charged with raising prices. For, with the removal of advertising, a firm whose demand curve is relatively unaffected by the sales outlays may find its profits unduly swollen by the retention of the usual sum of sales expenditures—so much so that its riches become a source of, say, political embarrassment. Making lavish advertising outlays, its ostensible monopoly profits can be dissipated, permanent "good will" created, and its hold on consumer demand irrevocably strengthened. To the superficial observer, the pricing policy accompanied by sales outlays would appear as innocuous, as a guarantor of but "fair" and not extraordinary "monopoly" profits. In instances of this nature, the more extreme criticisms of advertising as a price-raising factor cannot be summarily denied.[18] As borderline illustrations there are the wartime advertisements of firms which, despite the paucity of products to sell, made large outlays because otherwise the sums so spent would have had to be paid out in taxes. Normally, these sums would appear as profits.

Advertising and New Entry

There are other directions from which advertising can be charged with raising prices. Even arguing that advertising fails to affect demand curves, the combined average-cost curve, of selling and production costs, will be higher than if advertising costs were zero. This would entail a higher financial investment in initiating an enterprise, operating as an impediment to firms deprived of easy access to capital markets. As the financial scale of enterprise must be greater, this limitation upon entry is a handicap to greater competitiveness. Higher prices ought to be the upshot.

Questions

1. a. Would selling and promotional outlays be present under atomistic competition? Explain.
   b. If firms merely equated $P = MC$, could sales outlays be present? Explain.
   c. What is the difference between these cases?
2. "Advertising is ultimately a venture in free speech." Discuss.
3. Distinguish between: (a) news and propaganda; (b) advertising and education. Point up similarities as well as differences.
4. "Advertising flourishes in half-truths. Standards are not likely to be improved. 'Truthful advertising' is a contradiction in terms." Evaluate these statements critically.
5. Write an essay on the optimal aggregate amount of sales outlays for an optimal economy.
6. Would you argue that there are "diminishing returns to education"? to advertising? Use any factual information or personal experience you can bring to bear on the former subject.
7. Explain the equilibrium adjustment if sales outlays are designed to shift the full demand curve and are not optimally devised with a specific price in view.
   a. Show the shift in the demand curve with further increments of selling costs.
   b. Show the successive equilibrium prices.

[18] As an illustration, consider advertising by milk companies, electric power public utilities, and the public relations advertising of corporations whose radio broadcasts can hardly influence the demand for their product or deflect business from a (nonexistent) competitor.

    c. Show the successive equilibrium average *combined* costs, including sales as well as production costs.

    d. With the successive optimal prices, and associated average costs, show how the maximum maximorum price-output, selling-cost combination can be expressed in *marginal* terms. (Compare Buchanan's treatment with your own.)

8. An indifference-curve approach to the sales-outlay problem:

    a. Measure price horizontally and total revenue and/or total sales outlays vertically.

    b. Draw indifference curves showing given sales *quantities* at each price and selling-outlay combination. Why will they rise to the right? Why will curves showing greater sales lie to the left? Why do the curves get closer and closer?

    c. Draw production-revenue contours showing total revenue *net* of sales outlays for each price–sales-outlay combination. Why are these circular? Why will the largest production-revenue contour tend to lie in the middle of the system of curves?

    d. What is the significance of the tangency points of production revenue and sales-quantity contours? (Compare Boulding's treatment with your own.)

9. Will a given sum of sales outlays be as effective at high prices as at low? Explain. What is the significance of this for practical decisions on price policy and sales expenditures?

10. Assuming that advertising outlays were not determined optimally, how might they be chosen? Do any of these methods assure maximum profits?

11. Discuss at some length the meaning, and magnitude, of the cross-elasticity between advertising and (a) the firm's price; (b) the price of another firm; (c) the sales outlays by other firms.

12. "Retaliatory advertising is wasteful if it fails to affect sales. Promotional outlays are similarly wasteful." Discuss.

13. Discuss at some length the question of whether sales outlays raise or lower prices. Where do you think the weight of argument rests?

14. "An enterprise system cannot operate without advertising. It is a prerequisite for progress, an important element for a dynamic economy." Argue.

A Concluding Note

One further remark may be offered here on the place of sales outlays. Would we want to eliminate them? There is reason to doubt this: there is the need to stimulate purchases, to convey information, to influence tastes. For, with or without sales outlays, tastes *will* be influenced. The issue is one of the means to be used toward this end. Far too little attention has been devoted to this question in discussions of optimal forms of economic organization. The problem is of the same order as the question of the optimal amount of education, and the optimal degree of progress. Just as the content of the latter has scarcely been analyzed with the care the subject deserves, the same may be said with respect to the part to be played by sales outlays—and the manner in which it should be played. These are difficult questions and it is no use to pretend that the answers are obvious or command a large consensus, leading to the rather safe surmise that their forms are likely to be with us in the future in much the same way as in the past.

SPACE AND MONOPOLISTIC COMPETITION

Identical physical goods separated in space are *different* commodities in an economic sense, and they can sell for different prices. Analogously, it is possible to conceive of the theory of monopolistic competition in terms of locational separation with product differentiation being visualized as a form of physical distance. But the analogy can be pressed too far: as identical physical commodities can be brought together geographically, they do become perfectly substitutable goods. Physically differentiated goods can, at best, be made *nearly* full substitutes. Complete substitutability compels an abandonment of the theory of monopolistic competition.

Spatial Interdependence

Our discussion of spatial price relations will be conducted mostly in terms of the price interdependence among technically identical goods. Preceding chapters, in retrospect, can be described as embodying a simple locational pattern, with buyers and sellers clustered together, literally obviating spatial aspects. The analysis would be applicable in a world in which transport costs were zero and interest costs for transport time were nil.

Provisionally, we postulate that all prices are quoted f.o.b. factory by sellers so that buyers pay the full transport costs from the seller's plant to their own doorstep. This seems to be the customary assumption in economic analysis.[19]

If transport costs amount to one penny per product-unit, then each buyer's demand curve will have to be reduced by this amount; in Figure 12.6(a), if the continuous line represents an individual's demand curve in a world of free delivery, the lower broken-line curve forms the effective demand curve at the factory door. Obviously, the higher the transport charges, the greater the reduction in the effective demand curve. Where transport costs are proportional to distance, after a fall of a penny per mile in the basic transport rates, the demand curves of those consumers located at a one-mile radius will be elevated by one penny, while the demand curve of consumers located a thousand miles away will move up by $10 per unit. Transport costs can thus be potent factors in determining not only the geographical area served but also the volume of sales within the area.

Let us develop the notion of the market "borderland" served by two

[19] See Marshall, p. 325. F.o.b.-factory pricing is also "mill pricing" and "works pricing."

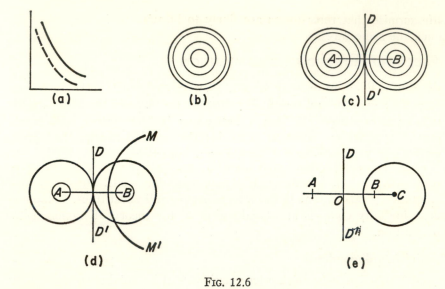

FIG. 12.6

firms in geographical competition. Suppose that A and B sell a homogeneous good at equal f.o.b. prices; transport costs we assume to be proportional to distance in all directions. The problem is to demonstrate the spatial area covered by each firm under these assumptions.

Places of equivalent transport costs are thus located on the circumference of a circle, with the firm enclosed at the center. Drawing a family of concentric circles, as in Figure 12.6(b), we can depict buyers by points in the encircled field. When the points are on the same circle, the full delivered price to each buyer is the same. At some point between firms A and B, buyers will deem it a matter of indifference whether they purchase from one or the other; these individuals are described as on the *equilibrium* border or the *indifference* boundary. With identical prices at works and with transport proportional to distance, the equilibrium fringe will be found along a perpendicular to a line connecting A and B, as DD' in Figure 12.6(c), where DD' is precisely midway between A and B. Purchases by the individuals situated along DD' will be distributed at random; individuals to the left of DD' will deal exclusively with A, while those to the right will direct their custom to B.

For each pair of firms in the field, we could draw a DD' perpendicular, demarcating the areas of patronage. Surrounded on all its borders by firms equi-distant from it, the A firm would be economically contained within a polygon whose sides would form the equilibrium boundaries; with an infinite number of firms within the immediate vicinity of A, the latter would be enclosed within a point circle.

Divergent Prices and Nonuniform Transport Costs

Visualizing firm A as lowering its price, individuals on DD' would no longer be indifferent as to the source of their purchases; there would be a deflection of demand from buyers along DD' to A. Curiously enough, the new isoequilibrium path would follow the hyperbola MM' in Figure 12.6(d). Firm B would retain all custom to the right of the MM' shield; it is an interesting result that a discrepancy in f.o.b. prices, with transport costs equal and constant in all directions, would restrict the higher-priced firm to a sales area bounded by a hyperbola.[20]

When f.o.b. prices are equal while transport costs are higher from B, then B's sales area will be inside a circle, with the center (C) lying at a greater distance from A in the horizontal plane than the actual door of firm B: in Figure 12.6(e) the length $AO = BO$. Outside the circle, firm A will absorb all the custom.[21]

More amoebic shapes would evolve if we supposed that transport costs varied with factors other than distance—if, say, only railroad transport were available in one direction and only water carriage in the other, or if the rate structure were distorted by rules of thumb, custom, and political pressure. If railroad rates are the same from point A to a surrounding zone, the effect is as if all consumers within the area are physically located at the same point.

An Alternate Diagrammatic Device

An alternate apparatus affords useful insight into the typical problems of spatial analysis. Rather than assume that buyers and sellers are scattered over the landscape, suppose that they are situated along a national highway, as OO' in Figure 12.7(A).

Writing A's price as OP, and B's as $O'P'$, with $OP = O'P'$ and transport costs the same per unit of distance from A or B, final prices to buyers can then be measured by the height of the Y-arms; firm A will sell to all buyers on its left who care to purchase at the f.o.b. price while B will serve those on its right—those in its "hinterland." A will also secure the custom of those living on the right fork of its Y and out to X, where X is midway between A and B. Conversely, B will control the market to the right of X. The NX vertical marks the isoequilibrium spot separating the markets of the two sellers.

In Figure 12.7(A), the slope of the PY and PN arms is determined by the transport costs per unit of distance: if transport costs are zero, the arms become perpendicular to PA, forming a T. If the f.o.b. prices and

[20] This can be proved rigorously by simple analytic geometry. See Allen, *Mathematical Analysis,* p. 81.

[21] See Allen, p. 84.

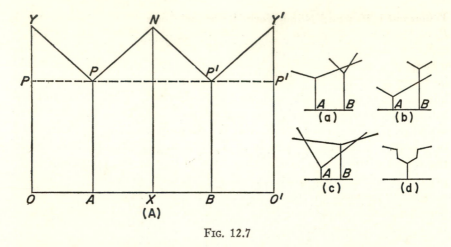

FIG. 12.7

transport costs are the same from either A or B, the intersection of the respective Y's will split the market area in two.

If it were less costly per mile to ship a unit of the good from A than from B, the Y-arm from A would rise more slowly and firm A would penetrate more than one half the distance between itself and B; it would dominate the market area on the far right of B, confining B to a limited sales area on its left and a somewhat larger area on its right: the relations are disclosed in Figure 12.7(a), which also assumes that $P_a < P_b$.

If P_a plus transport costs from A to B resulted in a net price at B below P_b, then B would have to relinquish all its custom: it would be driven from the field at these price relations, for the Y-arm of A's Y would always lie below the Y-arms of B, as in Figure 12.7(b). Finally, if $P_a < P_b$, and unit transport costs $T_a < T_b$, A will gain most, if not all, of the custom in the entire market area, selling on both sides of B and perhaps compelling B to leave the field. It could likewise be demonstrated that, if $P_a < P_b$ but $T_a > T_b$, A would supply part of the common market dividing the two while B's output would be diverted to buyers located at the extremities, deep in its own and in A's hinterland (see Figure 12.7[c]).

Hence, for control of neighboring market areas, the mill price and thus production costs are decisive; for "world" markets, transport costs are paramount. Access to the sea, rather than an innate commercial spirit, provides a simple explanation of the world-trading proclivities of the dominant export-import countries.

Changes in Transport Costs

We might ponder the effects of a change in transport costs. Only a disproportionate movement would create new boundaries. In terms of the

Y diagrams, an equivalent transport cost reduction from A and B, while $P_a = P_b$, would maintain NX unchanged. But it would be wrong to conclude that market demand would be unresponsive: the effective demand curve of each individual would be increased. Increased sales would be made by each firm, especially to the more remote regions where the burden of transport costs is more severe. Further, it has been implied hitherto that buyers were spaced continuously along OO', and that there would be purchasers even at X. But the diagram need not be interpreted in this way: although the people at X, for example, are indifferent as to the source of their purchase *if* they care to buy at the prevailing f.o.b. price, the ruling price might exceed any effective demand point on the individual demand curves. A fall in transport costs, therefore, might permit a fresh market layer—from A to X and B to X in Figure 12.7(A)— to be tapped by each seller.

As a reduction in transport costs will always elevate the market-demand curve, the f.o.b. price should ordinarily rise after a fall in transport costs; the rise in the f.o.b. price is likely to restrain the purchases of those in the immediate vicinity of the firm, with the result that the major implementation of purchases will come from the outlying regions. This is an unexpected conclusion; the purchases of those near the seller's establishment will decrease and their economic position will deteriorate with a fall in transport charges.

It is illuminating to reflect on the effect of transport costs that fluctuate disproportionately to distance; railroad schedules often include special lower long-haul rates. Thus, if transport charges move discontinuously after a certain distance from the f.o.b. point, the slope of the arms of the Y will break, as shown in Figure 12.7(d). Whenever the rate falls as the mileage traversed increases, the economic separation of buyer and seller narrows: the handicap of distance is partially suspended and the disparity in delivered prices diminishes. When there are economies of scale, lower transport costs can expand the market and cut the total number of independent producers of a particular commodity; high transport charges from efficient producing sectors permit local firms to survive despite higher production costs.

Questions

1. Analyze the effect on market price, and seller's f.o.b. price, if buyers are concentrated, as within a city, while sellers are dispersed outside the city. How would the analysis appear in terms of the Y-arms?
2. Suppose, in terms of the Y diagrams, that buyers are heavily clustered just to the right of firm A and at some distance to the left of firm B. What locational response is likely from firm B? Thereupon, from firm A?
3. Trace the connection between the problem of question (2) and the theory of duopoly.

4. Suppose that the equilibrium-border formed by the Y-arms is unoccupied. Does this increase or reduce the degree of price interdependence among the firms? Are the respective firms in competition with one another or with producers of differentiated products?
5. What is the spatial effect of a rise in price by one firm, with price of the other firm constant?
6. If firms agree to divide the territory, under what conditions can the agreement survive? When will it break down?
7. Suppose that buyers and sellers are dispersed but that all physical goods are carted to a central market and all transactions are consummated at the central market. How do transport costs affect the final volume of transactions? What institutional economies can be introduced in these circumstances?
8. Explain how "free delivery" is a form of price discrimination. What is its ultimate effect on local purchasers in the vicinity of the seller? on purchasers located some distance away?
9. Basing-point pricing refers to sellers in one city, say, quoting prices f.o.b. another city not identical with their plant. Thus, in the past, steel mills wherever located quoted prices f.o.b. Pittsburgh. Analyze the effects of this practice on final prices to consumers; on the volume of transportation charges. Why, do you suspect, firms followed this practice originally instituted by the United States Steel Corporation?

Chapter 13

꧁꧂꧁꧂꧁꧂꧁꧂꧁꧂꧁꧂꧁꧂꧁꧂꧁꧂꧁꧂꧁꧂꧁꧂꧁꧂꧁꧂꧁꧂꧁꧂꧁꧂

Product Variation and Entry Under Monopolistic Competition

Atomistic competitive theory presumes that there is a diversified list of commodities produced, as $A, B, C, \ldots, M$, with each of the commodities drawn from an infinite number of firms. In this model, it is plausible to omit the theory of product selection, for in stationary theory the commodity chain is fixed, limited to the M varieties; even in the long run new firms are able to enter only in these product sectors, and, in equilibrium, they perceive equal profit opportunities in all commodity directions.

Stepping outside the stationary confines, the gains of even commodity innovation will be short-lived once we admit the prospect of free entry for new firms. Envisaging impediments to entry, the theory of product variation assumes a new significance: trivial variations of old commodity types may be incessantly created, because differentiation can be handsomely remunerative. New firms must devise close substitutes for currently profitable commodity varieties. Similarly, in markets of circular interdependence, firms will seek to sever the price cord by introducing a new product variety to steal custom from other firms and mitigate the degree of market competition. Through time, however, other firms may match the variation by product improvements of their own.

One other motive for product variation ought to be underscored. To hasten obsolescence of existing commodities and induce a new wave of buying, firms will often perceive the advantage of introducing style changes, thus shifting the demand curve to a higher level. This is true of women's clothing as well as of appliances and other durable goods.

COMMODITY DIVERSIFICATION AND SEALED ENTRY

As a partial proof of the proposition that commodity diversification under heterogeneous entry surpasses that of homogeneous entry, it is instructive to consider a partially competitive case, where firms abide by the $P = MC$ rule but in which entry is obstructed by patent and trade-mark laws: this provides further corroboration that optimal pricing and entry are quite independent phenomena.

Heterogeneous Entry and Excessive Product Diversification

Although monopoly pricing is missing from this model, most of the other attributes of imperfection linger on. As direct encroachments on existing product preserves are prevented, the gestation of a new firm signalizes the birth of a "new" product. Normally, it would repay the firm to devise a product so much like others as to capture some of their demand, while simultaneously imparting certain commodity attributes as to make consumers reluctant to shift to other products for minor price differences. This would be the goal of policy: to build concomitant identity and difference. Impediments to entry place a premium on ingenuity and improvisation in small matters as well as on important pioneering innovations, for merely trivial differences enable new firms to penetrate the economic scene. The prospect of enduring profits to a successful innovation also encourages more frequent experimentation than under full freedom on entry. A chance of gain is less attractive if, when successful, it has to be shared with others while losses must be borne alone.

It is not really clear whether the likelihood of a greater diversity of products comprises an unmitigated waste or a positive gain: everything hinges on how wants are satisfied as a result; as entrepreneurs are provoked into experimenting, this spark of dynamism must be described as instrumental for progress. Consumers, however, are compelled to pay higher prices for the wares of a protected firm's product than would be necessary if others could proffer a perfect substitute.

Barriers to entry are costly in other ways. The lack of a standardized final product may entail the use of specialized equipment; capital costs are likely to be higher than if standard machinery were ordered by numerous firms. As part of the same theme, supplementary industries will not grow as rapidly to service the common needs of the firms producing the commodity "type" as they would if practices were more uniform.[1] The resulting higher price may alone enable new firms to secure a niche in the commodity belt despite inferior, imperfectly substitutable, goods.

MONOPOLY PRICING AND INNOVATION

Once we admit the possibility of monopoly pricing alongside sealed entry, there is even a stronger impetus to product innovation. Clearly, innovations that are lucrative with $P = MC$ pricing will be even more remunerative on a $P > MR = MC$ pricing policy. Hence, with monopoly pricing and closed entry, differentiation should be even more complete and the commodity network should be more extensive.

[1] These are Marshall's famous "external" economies (*Principles,* p. 266).

The same conclusion can be obtained in another way. If we assume that total employment is the same in the competitive and the monopoly-pricing worlds, as the individual firm's price is higher and output is smaller under monopoly pricing, there will be less employment generated by each firm. Consequently, for the same total employment there must be more firms, more entrepreneurs, and a greater diversity of products; the ubiquitous advertising trappings of a monopoly model will also appear. The advertising would be attributable to the protection accorded differentiation rather than to monopoly pricing as such.

The Order of Commodity Innovation

Besides innovations being more commonplace under monopoly pricing and heterogeneous entry, the innovations would not be introduced in the

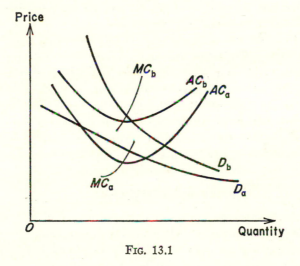

FIG. 13.1

same order or in the same time sequence as under competitive pricing. A simple illustration will demonstrate this. If a firm ralizes that it is able to shut itself in from the encroachments of homogeneous competitors, considering the product varieties and subject to a $P = MC$ pricing mandate, it will select that product and that plant layout which promises to maximize profits on this basis. Making similar profit computations, but now fortified with the right to name a $P > MR = MC$ price, it is likely to choose not only another layout but also *another differentiated product*. Assuming different average cost curves for each good, as D_a and D_b in Figure 13.1, the A commodity with its relatively elastic demand is likely to be introduced under $P = MC$ pricing while, with monopoly pricing, the B commodity will be the more suitable profit vehicle. Commodity B may be lavishly ornamented to convey prestige value but devoid of added functional use; item A may be unadorned but functionally serviceable.

Thus, there is the strong likelihood that, under monopoly, not only will the dates of commodity innovation be different but also the commodity universe itself will be likely to take on a hue other than that under competition, with products part of the one set-up excluded from the other. Undoubtedly, some goods profitable under a monopoly program will be unable to cover costs under a $P = MC$ arrangement.

Patent Sealing

A constricting aspect of monopoly is the practice of patent sealing, in which a firm registers patents not in order to use them but rather to prevent their use by others with consequent encroachment upon its market preserves. The effect is, of course, to narrow the degree of market interdependence and to instill a commodity gap by legal means. Commodity improvements can be effectively suppressed by this device.

Some would contend that, if the unutilized patents are for truly superior products, then the monopoly firm itself will introduce them. But this argument abstracts entirely from the element of time and the role of "changeover" costs; an existing firm will have to weigh the losses occasioned by the abandonment of equipment on the production of the new variety: a new firm would not be subject to the same restrictive calculations.[2] Patents registered to prevent their use by others can be an important factor in depressing the level of consumer well-being, if the practice is widely prevalent.

INNOVATIONS AND PRICE REPERCUSSIONS

Let us now consider the effects of the appearance of a new firm and a new item in the commodity belt upon the prevailing price structure. We can assume that the new commodity is priced according to competitive rules: the perturbations in the price structure, in kind if not in intensity, will be similar when the new product is subject to monopoly-pricing arrangements.

Taking consumer demand as a datum, with homogeneous entry and a new firm contributing to the supply of familiar commodities, there should be some downward pressure on price: price tends to fall because existing firms have been pushing production too far into stages of decreasing marginal physical returns; the entry of the new firm eliminates some higher-cost output proffered by existing firms.

Price repercussions are more complex under heterogeneous entry and

[2] Thus, it is possible that pure competition may be less than optimal in this respect, involving destructive capital costs. There has been very little discussion of this point in the literature.

a new product being tendered by a new firm. First, the new product might so siphon off demand from the current commodity types that the latter prices may fall; here the introduction of the new good confers an undisguised benefit upon consumers. To those who continue to buy the old variety, there is a direct enhancement of real income arising out of the price fall; the very fact that consumers include the new good in their purchase plan, despite the lowered price of the old good, indicates a preference for the new item and an improvement in well-being occasioned by its creation. A cogent argument can be adduced in favor of the innovation; consumers are better satisfied all around.

A Conflict of Interests

Conceivably, the new commodity may precipitate higher prices for some goods in the commodity belt; goods complementary to the new commodity may be a case in point. For those consumers who purchase only the complement which rises in price, there is a clear diminution in well-being as a result of the new good locating in the commodity chain.

Other causes of a rising price might also be cited. Frequently, the demand curve for an existing good may cross the AC curve to the left of the minimum point and hence may be too small to permit the equating of P and MC; only a $P > AC > MC$ price policy enables the firm to survive. Here a new innovation may, by driving existing demand curves leftward, elevate prices. Or, if the new firm requires a relatively large volume of productive factors employed by old firms, the use of common factors may entail a cost increase and a price rise.

In this event, the appearance of a new product presages a real conflict of interests. Those who hold to the purchase of the higher-priced item are undoubtedly deprived of some real income; those who would switch entirely to the new item even if the original prices prevailed enjoy an enhancement in their real purchase position. In general, the well-being of one group is improved at the expense of another. Conceivably, we can visualize the innovation attracting so much demand that substitute items are supplanted entirely and vanish from the commodity field. Those who are either repelled or unimpressed by the new variety will suffer a diminution in well-being.[3]

A tentative answer as to the most preferable position to the community might be sought on these lines. Perhaps, after the introduction of the new good, it is possible to recover from its purchasers part of their enhanced real income; transferring some of this sum to those who continue buying

---

[3] When the firm is driven from the field by economic warfare rather than by generally acknowledged product superiority, the significance of this point is even more poignant.

the old item might restore the real income of the latter groups so that nobody will be injured while others will benefit from the commodity innovation. The innovation would have everything to commend it if those who prefer the *original* commodity scale cannot reimburse those who approve of the innovation in amount sufficient to deter them from promoting the change. But, if even a smoothly arranged income transfer and rectification is insufficient to compensate consumers for the damage caused them via price rise, then the superiority of one equilibrium position over another could not be proclaimed with any great conviction. Only some convention—some noneconomic criterion—could be invoked to break the impasse.

The democratic principle of counting the numbers favorably affected and those adversely affected might constitute one standard. Or we could ask how different income groups fare after the change, and allow our biases to decide the issue. But the advocacy of any of these solutions will be entirely arbitrary, consequent upon our personal predilections rather than upon a standard of unequivocal benefit to all ensuing from the particular structural change.

PRODUCT VARIATION

The foregoing sections dealt with the greater diversity of products accomplished by the heterogeneous entry imposed upon new firms. A related problem is that of a going firm in the commodity chain deciding to vary the nature of its product; either the general preference of the consuming groups may have changed, or the competition of heterogeneous competitors may invite a commodity improvisation to relieve the degree of price interdependence. Cost changes may also render a new design more economical than formerly. Alternately, the purpose may be to make existing commodity varieties obsolete in recognition of the fact that demand from new users is small, so that, if current models are outmoded by the style change, demand from present owners can be enormously expanded—for example, by new fashions in women's dresses, new styling of automobiles, etc.

Differentiation and Maximum Profits

In essentials, the problem of product variation by a going firm is parallel to that of a new firm still in the planning stage, weighing the profitability of all the alternative product types open to it. The primary difference is that, as the firm already has its equipment, it must consider profitability in terms of its current plant, with additions, extensions, and modifications, rather than viewing the problem from the start as would a new firm: the commodity type most profitable to the one may not be most profitable to the other in view of going capital charges.

The nature of the "change-over" costs can be made more graphic by Figure 13.2. Assume that the firm is producing commodity A currently and that it is now more profitable to produce varieties B or C. In Figure 13.2, the curve D_b represents the demand for B while the curve D_c represents the demand for C. Assuming that a new firm was organized, the curve AC_1 may be the average-cost curve for producing commodity B. However, for the going concern, AC_1 can be assumed to represent the actual unit costs of producing commodity C. Hence, if the firm decides to switch to the production of B, unit costs are those shown by AC_2:

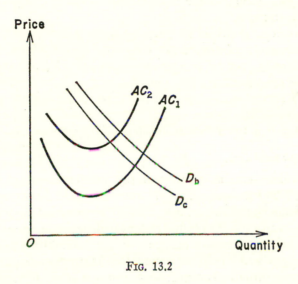

Fig. 13.2

the firm must abandon some equipment and incur expensive equipment modifications besides covering *capital charges on the abandoned facilities.* A new firm would thus undertake to produce commodity B, but the established firm would perceive the greater profitability of C. Average costs to an existing firm contemplating a variation of product will thus always have to include the fixed charges on its present layout plus those resulting from any plant additions, plus the full variable charges.

The Sales Function

Some aspects of the maximization solution implicit in the selection of a product by a new firm (or product variation by a going firm) can be clarified by the aid of the concept of the sales function. Viewing a commodity *from the sellers' standpoint,* we may say that it consists of a bundle of attributes that may be varied and profits thereby affected. The sales function x can thus be defined as follows:

$$x = x(P,p; A,a; C,c; W,w; T,t; D,d, \ldots)$$

where x = sales of firm A,

$\quad P$ = prices of all other products in the system,

$\quad p$ = price of product of firm A,

$\quad A$ = sales outlays of all other firms,

$\quad a$ = sales outlays of firm A,

$\quad C$ = "internal" contents ("quality") of all other products in the system,

$\quad c$ = "internal" contents ("quality") of firm A's product,

$\quad W$ = "external" attributes (such as styling, design of container) of all other products in the system,

$\quad w$ = "external" attributes of the product of firm A,

$\quad T$ = credit terms of sales of all other products,

$\quad t$ = credit terms of sales for the product of firm A,

$\quad D$ = delivery terms of sales of all other products,

$\quad d$ = delivery terms of sales of the product of firm A.

Of course this list of product attributes is by no means complete; a more detailed decomposition of C, W, T, and D is certainly possible.

It is within the province of the firm to alter any of the magnitudes indicated by lower-case letters; essentially, elements indicated by capital letters are beyond its control.

Rather than write sales (x) as a function of price, selling costs, styling, quality, etc., we can write profits (R) as dependent on largely the same variables. Thereupon, the condition for maximum profits is that the increase in profits (ΔR) must be zero (or negative) for product movements in any direction, whether it be a variation in sales, in price, in selling costs, in quality, in external structure, in credit terms, etc.

Hence, a variation in any dimension must yield zero profits before the commodity selected can be adjudged the maximum. Thus, where each variation assumes other elements unchanged, we have

$$\frac{\Delta R}{\Delta x} = \frac{\Delta R}{\Delta p} = \frac{\Delta R}{\Delta a} = \frac{\Delta R}{\Delta c} = \frac{\Delta R}{\Delta w} = \frac{\Delta R}{\Delta t} \cdots \leqq 0$$

If there are changes in the external economic structure, in P, in A, etc., then a new and varied product *may* become more profitable to the firm; the firm will ordinarily be unable to influence these variables, except in circular cases of monopolistic competition. If the product does not lend itself to continuous (probably trivial) modifications, then some of our conditions for a maximum disappear; if it is not possible because of the chemistry of the ingredients to vary the internal composition, say, then Δc is simply nonexistent. Likewise, if terms of sale are regulated by law, then Δt vanishes. Some of the more interesting problems arise when the firm finds it impractical to vary its price. This gives rise to the phenomenon of nonprice competition.

If the commodity types are substantially discrete so that there are gaps in the commodity chain with the maximum total revenue and the maximum total cost of producing commodities A, B, C, D, ... being vastly different, then it seems best to abandon the concept of marginal-product variations and marginal-profit changes and instead to refer to the product selection being governed simply by the prospect of greatest profits among the available commodity alternatives.

Diagrammatic Analysis

Some further idea of the problem of product differentiation can be conveyed graphically. In Figure 13.3(A), the curves R, S, and T represent the average-cost curves of producing these commodities, all of which are close but imperfect substitutes. If the market price is held constant at OP, the quantity demanded of R is OL, of S, OM, and of T, ON. From the diagram not only is unit profit on commodity T greater than profits on either R or S, but also the total profits that can be amassed on T are much more enormous. At the constant price, therefore, product T would be produced.

Yet, when we permit price to vary, then product R may emerge as most profitable. In Figure 13.3(B), the full demand curves for the three products have been drawn: at a price of OP, points OL, OM, and ON are the respective demand quantities for the three commodities, and are located as a point on the full curves. In the lower price ranges, the three curves may tend to converge; although product T enjoys more stylistic and quality embellishments than S, which similarly is more appealing than R, as the price of each falls the demand comes largely from lower-

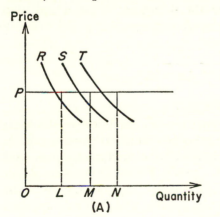

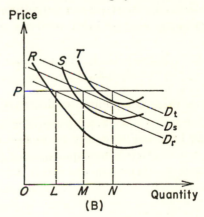

Fig. 13.3

income groups on whom the stylistic aspects are lost. Moreover, good R may lend itself better to operating economies than either of the other two, which, let us say, require some handicraft labor to impart their more distinctive features. From a profit standpoint, therefore, commodity R will be produced.[4]

NONPRICE COMPETITION

The theory of nonprice competition can also be associated either with the entry of a new firm or with a going firm which varies its product because of the nature of its market structure.

If we assume that a new firm is organized to market a fairly close substitute for some current varieties of goods whose production is limited to one or few firms, the new entrant is bound to affect the present oligopoly members. Ruling out any move to lower prices, after the field is reorganized, sales are redistributed, with the new firm draining off custom from among the former firms. As an illustration, we may think of new nickel candy bars, or $50 suits of clothes, etc. Hence, we have more varieties of the particular "class" of goods without any decrease in price.

There are innumerable ways in which demand may be redistributed. The newcomer might siphon sales entirely from the older members of the close group: we can deduce that the reorientation of sales will enhance consumer well-being, for the survival of the new firm indicates that wants are better satisfied than formerly.

The new firm may also thrive at the expense of a wide array of other products; consumers who were insensitive to the virtues of the former product types may buy the new innovation. Prices of all of the goods from which demand is deflected ought thus to trend downward, reinforcing the conclusion that consumer well-being is improved.

Suspension of price competition might thus lead to useful and more frequent quality advances. Existing firms will pose fewer objections to this form of competition than to price reductions, especially if market demand is inelastic; to the innovator the quality variation serves to protect it from attack by mere price reductions by present sellers.

Nonprice Competition and Excess Capacity

Some implications of nonprice competition on excess capacity may be noted. Suppose, in Figure 13.4, that price is held at OP by firms in the field; AC represents the curve of average costs of a "typical" firm while sales for each firm are OM.

[4] Professor Chamberlin, in Figures 11 and 16 (pp. 79 and 95) draws the prototype of Figure 13.3(A), above. But these curves should, for the true maximum-product solution, be accompanied by Figure 13.3(B).

If new entrants are successful in winning consumers away from the former firms, their sales will slump back from *OM* toward *ON*. At a sales volume *ON* we have a profitless equilibrium position for each of the older firms. Obviously, the result of the new entry is not to reduce prices but rather to redistribute sales, enabling consumers to be better served. But the rise in average operating costs is an aspect of excess capacity, implying that, with lower prices and the withdrawal of some firms from the field, the remaining facilities could be exploited more in-

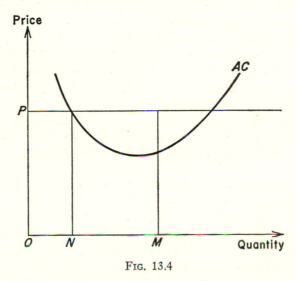

FIG. 13.4

tensively, with general improvement in consumer well-being. Nonprice competition thus appears as a likely cause of excess capacity and uneconomic resource use.[5]

Nonprice Competition Among Existing Firms

Besides a new entrant having to subscribe to a ruling price for a particular type of good, an existing firm may realize that it is caught in a rigid oligopoly price mesh and is unable to extend its sales and avail itself of operating economies through a price fall; the adamancy of existing firms may block this course. To extricate itself, it must either increase its sales outlays or proceed to differentiate its product anew relative to other commodities in the field. Figure 13.3(A) contains the relevant argument.

Thus, when market price is stabilized, we are likely to witness frequent changes in products; the innovations could be charged as uneconomic when consumers would have preferred lower prices to "su-

[5] See the original argument in Chamberlin, pp. 104–109.

perior" products. Often, the innovations or improvements may be prized more highly than lower prices; occasionally, because of the limited divisibility of the monetary units or the aversion to carrying small coins, consumers may prefer goods at customary prices (for example, chewing gum, candy bars, sandwiches, soaps) to the same goods at lower prices. Quality improvements are undoubtedly commendable in these situations.

Fair Price Laws and Nonprice Competition

Nonprice competition has also been fostered by state laws permitting manufacturers to fix minimum prices of their wares at the retail level, ostensibly to outlaw "loss-leader" sales and "cut-rate" stores which arouse the hostility of conventional retailers. Inevitably, the results of price-maintenance practices must be to switch competition to a new channel in order to earn the liberal price spread conceded by manufacturers. The sales rivalry thus manifests itself in the form of: increased services at the retail level, longer credit terms, delivery service, improved tone of the shop, surreptitious loss-leaders in the form of attractively priced menus in department-store restaurants, etc. Goods bought at the retail level must then be conceived as a hybrid composite of a technical good and "surrounding conditions of sale"; the effect must be to make the latter services more lavish and forestall lower prices.[6]

Other simple examples of nonprice competition are those of a firm granting elongated credit terms, or instituting a system of free delivery (within limits) to consumers; or the practice of granting samples and souvenirs to customers, or advertising "buy one at the regular price and get another [perhaps unrelated] good free." Liberal trade-in allowances may also be viewed as a variety of product differentiation and nonprice competition, where the standard price is overtly maintained but surreptitiously reduced through generous trade-in terms. The publication of list prices from which discounts are universally granted can be viewed similarly; this also permits a degree of price discrimination in favor of some buyers while lending itself easily to plans to restore the "normal" price level by reducing the average discount level. Premium stamps are likewise a form of differentiation and nonprice competition. Undoubtedly, the list of practices can be amplified.

---

[6] Manufacturers are often anxious to prescribe fair prices because of the socially perverse habit of judging quality by price; to preclude any possibility of their product's being stamped as "inferior," they are willing to accede to retail price fixing. Also, retailers must be cultivated; unless retailers accept their line (which is usually promoted by a liberal mark-up margin), their own productive endeavors will be frustrated. The arbitrament of the retailer is thus often more persuasive than the final judgment of consumers.

The Monopoly Installation

When the plant is in the conjectural stage, monopoly, inherently, does nothing to affect the ACP curves of Figure 4.4 in Chapter 4. However, we are no longer entitled to draw the horizontal price line indicative of a competitive, externally determined, market price; instead, it is a demand curve that ought to be poised as a counterweight to the ACP curve. If we insert D and MR curves in the diagrams of Figure 4.4(B), Chapter 4, the equipment implicit at the equation of $MR = MCP$, where $P > MR$, will be the optimal layout open to the firm.

Analytically, the theory of monopoly plant selection runs parallel to the competitive theory of installation in much the same way as the analysis of monopoly and competitive output. But there are some deeper implications: just as competitive output could never be to the left of the minimum AC point on a U-shaped cost curve—while in monopoly structures it might be—this arrangement is also conceivable when we consider the ACP curves; the intersection of MR and MCP may occur to the left of the minimum ACP output.

Hence, a dual set of forces is operating to restrain output in a particular monopoly market: (1) the volume of equipment installed is smaller than if price were adjusted on a $P = MCP$ basis; and (2) after the equipment is installed, output is less with monopoly behavior than it would be if the firm proceeded to equate P and MC. Curiously, as the firm erects too small a layout there is underinvestment in the field; as the layout that it does install is underutilized, there is excess capacity, measured by the difference between the $P = MC$ and $P > MR = MC$ output volumes.

Against this output restraint of the firm, however, must be set the expansion of substitute outputs to fill the void as demand is transferred to them by the monopoly-pricing practices.

Sales Outlays and Plant Selection

We can examine the influence of advertising on the size of layout. The solution follows established lines, the only complication being that there are the alternate methods of forcing the demand curve rightward, by stressing a particular price in the sales campaign or by merely conjecturing the demand-curve shift consequent upon definite sums of selling expenditure. The equilibrium price and output, and equipment implicit in the maximum-profit equation, can be located in the usual way. Assuming that advertising does succeed, as a general rule, in expanding demand, then the ability to exercise sales pressure is responsible for the installation of a *larger* mass of equipment and, ordinarily, for a higher volume of output and employment than would occur with the suppression of these instruments of economic persuasion. The production expansion, as a long-run matter, can be viewed as a substitute for involuntary unemployment, for greater leisure, or for greater output of staple, unadvertised commodities. Nevertheless, plant size and output level will be smaller than if the *same* amount of sales outlays were incurred with $P = MC$ pricing.[7]

That the size of plant will be larger with sales outlays than without promotional expenditures points up the difficulty of making direct monopoly and competitive comparisons. To make some sense of these, it is necessary to indicate first the nature of the sales outlays that would be permitted in an optimal (*not necessarily competitive*) world. Unless these outlays are parts of the system, it is conceivable that the size of firms, for products whose use does require persuasion and information, will be larger than when selling expenditures are prohibited entirely.

Profitless Monopoly

Let us suppose that heterogeneous entry is universal, that new firms must always offer a new product for sale; also, that the repercussions on the demand of existing firms, while small, are still positive. The old firms will be denoted as A, B, C, while N is the new entrant. After N is organized as a heterogeneous competitor, the effect is to dislodge the demand curve of firm A and push it to the left. This may engender a price *rise* in P_a; because of falling average cost in the production of A, it may be that a higher P_a is alone profitable after the transfer of custom to firm N. As more and more new firms make their appearance in the commodity cosmos, with limited inroads on the established firms by each new firm, it may be that the final demand curve is just barely tangent to A's average-cost curve, so that profits are nil even though P_a is higher than before.[8] Despite the annihilation of profits, the other symptoms of monopoly remain—too many firms, too many products, too many entrepreneurs, and too low a level of output by each firm, and, thus, too high a level of average costs, with each firm operating to the left of the minimum AC.

Envisaging entry into all those commodity sectors in which $P > AC$, so that the demand curves of all profitable firms are constricted until they just touch the AC curves, it is possible to conjure a model in which monopoly pricing prevails but which, because $P = AC$, is devoid of

---

[7] Interestingly, if firms were permitted to advertise but were compelled to subscribe to a $P = MC$ pricing formula, a firm producing under conditions of constant costs would never advertise. This suggests that advertising engenders an income shift from profits and rents.

[8] This is Professor Chamberlin's celebrated theorem.

monopoly profits although all the other features of monopoly remain. But this image depends on the ability of new firms to concoct product varieties which entice demand solely from firms enjoying excess profits. Occasionally, this profitless equilibrium has been portrayed as the "long-run" monopoly equilibrium, analogous to the normal profit equilibrium of perfect competition. Entry in both worlds will cease, it is claimed, when profits are normal. We can agree that the analysis itself is fascinating, indicating that the major consequences of monopoly may be present even without abnormal profits.

That all the characteristics of monopoly may prevail without excess profits, while puzzling at first sight, is amenable to common sense, for many monopolies are notoriously unprofitable; for example, many items are patented but are never exploited. Also, many items can be produced (barely profitably) only because of the suppressed competition and the opportunity for monopoly pricing. Profitability, then, is not the hall-mark of monopoly; it is only one, and not always the most important, of its consequences.

Limits to Profit Absorption

Monopoly profits could be annihilated only if new firms could penetrate the curtain of consumer resistance and absorb custom from going profitable firms. When we consider that a new firm will usually attract custom from the vast commodity network, the unreality of the profitless-monopoly conception is manifest. Although some consumers will purchase the new good because the older *functional* variety failed to accommodate them at the prevailing price, usually the demand curve for the new commodity will be compounded of many transfers of demand. Once we acknowledge that the substitutionary relations among goods differ for each consumer, it is futile to argue that new goods can always be created to reduce demand and profits of *only* profitable commodities. Good substitutes may be devised in some cases; it may be more difficult in others and quite impossible for still other goods. Technical limitations, or the animadversions of consumer tastes, may defy commodity emulation so that the prevailing monopoly profits may be substantial and enduring, diffused in disproportionate amounts among the several firms.[9]

This must not be construed as signifying that profit opportunities do not encourage commodity innovation; they do. But we should hardly be astonished to learn of the persistence of abnormal profits, for it would be unreasonable to expect them to be eliminated by every clumsy imitative maneuver.

[9] See the restatement by Chamberlin, ed. 5, pp. 201–202.

MONOPOLY AND PROGRESS

Progress is a matter of change—although the converse would not always be true. Economic progress, in the main, is marked by change in either the commodity varieties or the technological processes of producing the known commodity types. Once new equipment has been conceived, or a new product devised, the entrepreneurial promotional measures to place it on the commodity belt will undoubtedly be quickened if the innovators enjoy sole right to exploit their creation by sealing off entry and exercising the unitary monopoly powers within their grasp.

It would be wrong to conclude that innovation would vanish from a fully competitive world; in the time lag between the innovator's first actions and the entry of imitators, an important volume of profits may be amassed. Even after the appearance of homogeneous competitors, the equation of MC to P may leave an excess of P over AC adequate to cover depreciation and warrant the replacement of equipment; indubitably there would be innovation if homogeneous entry prevailed. But it is true that many products just barely profitable on a $P > MR = MC$ policy will not be lucrative on a $P = MC$ pricing stipulation. Both the order of commodity innovation and the diversity of products in a monopoly pricing system are thus likely to depart significantly from that obtaining in a competitively pricing universe.

This is the dilemma of endeavors to eliminate monopoly. For, by stimulating innovation and accelerating the pace of progress, monopoly has some wholesome aspects. For resource allocation, as manifest in the relative amounts of production, the results deviate from those that would be experienced in a competitive world. We would have to separate and weigh these elements in considering the welfare aspects of the diverse modes of price behavior. In a static world, the arguments favor pure competition; in dynamic circumstances the simple conclusion is less warranted.

ENTRY IMPEDIMENTS AND HETEROGENEOUS COMPETITION

Let us consider some of the factors responsible for the heterogeneous competition among firms; the multiplicity of products can be ascribed in part to the factors that impede entry. If all obstructions to entry were to vanish, each spot in the commodity belt would be occupied by as many firms as felt they could earn satisfactory profits at that particular station in the commodity universe. There would be commodity diversification in that innumerable commodities would be produced. But, when entry into a field is sealed, with new firms unable to duplicate an existing product, then the birth of new firms is contingent on their ability to devise new products for varieties currently remunerative. Even if all barriers to penetration were whittled away, new firms testing their ingenuity would profit by stealing a march on other firms in creating new products. Thus, although there is always an urge to innovation and differentiation in the commodity world, this motive is intensified, and the diversity of the commodity belt multiplied, by obstructions to entry. Typical imitators are compelled to become superficial innovators when opportunities to duplicate are closed to them.

Monopoly itself may sometimes be attributed to an undue pessimism constraining new firms from embracing opportunities in the commodity chain that would prove profitable to more optimistic spirits. Some of the uncertainty might be allayed through repeated testimony of the facts on profits by detailed and punctual earning reports by firms currently in the field.

Foundations of Monopoly Power

Let us summarize the chief methods by which entry is impeded. The more durable causes of monopoly power can be confined to a few distinct classes of phenomena, although their disguises are legion. To enumerate:

1. There may be consumer resistance to the products of new firms, despite technological superiority or technical identity with present goods; this resistance is often a consequence of consumer ignorance, inertia, or bias. Because of these factors, the demand curve for current firms will be less than perfectly elastic.[10] Although these barriers may be eroded over time, doubtless they hinder effective competition.

2. Demand may be too small, in the light of technological facts, to support more than one (or few) firm(s). This factor looms as the basis of the "natural" monopolies, of which public utilities afford the common illustration.

3. Certain types of output are contingent on the possession of rare skills or unique natural resources. Control over a natural resource, such as iron ore, may establish a *strategic* monopoly foothold. Financial domination of security and loan markets may serve the same purpose.

4. Legal privilege and restraint may exist. Although numerous firms can be supported in a particular industry, entry is blocked through public policy. State-licensing schemes, patent and trade-mark laws, public-utility franchises—all exemplify the principle. Also, the state may arrogate certain productive functions to itself; state tobacco and liquor monopolies immediately come to mind.

5. There may be physical terrorism and violence. Threatening newcomers with physical punishment may dampen their enthusiasm for entry. Apart from the notorious episodes of the Prohibition Era, Ameri-

[10] Why is General Motors so large? It has been suggested that we should look at the car occupying our garage!

can industry has largely been free of these more pernicious practices, which is a tribute to the law-abiding nature of the citizenry and the strength of the legal processes.

6. There may be economic coercion. Price wars, trade-union boycotts, dealer boycotts, denial of access to capital markets, and collusive compensation constitute important limitations upon entry.

7. Collusion and combination may establish monopolies. Bribery of a newcomer may also suffice to bar entry. But these phenomena will be of only transitional importance unless accompanied by a deep-rooted monopoly force. Many of the situations that can be classified within these groupings are frequently characterized as frictions. They cannot legitimately be dismissed as ephemeral phenomena in view of their tenacity and power of survival.

Advertising, be it noted, is important as a cause of monopoly only insofar as it wins consumers and stiffens resistance to substitutes or implants a trade-mark advantage impeding homogeneous competition. Because advertising relies on the accompaniment of (1) and (3) above, it is not entitled to separate status as a creator of monopoly power. Numerous concrete illustrations can be cited for all these causes. Undoubtedly, among the myriads of monopoly manifestations, there are cases that almost defy classification; generally, the salient characteristics will be found amid the list of our several categories.

Usually, the same forces that permit only one firm to flourish in a particular sector of the industrial belt can also be cited as an explanation of the small numbers of duopoly and oligopoly.

Chapter 14

Buyer's Domination and Bilateral Monopoly

Just as sellers can violate the competitive maxims, the price structure can also be controlled from the purchase side whenever buyers are in a position to dictate market price; the theory of monopsony embraces this set of phenomena as the analogue to monopoly from the buyer's side.[1]

The criterion of monopsony is the ability of the buyer to impose an effective price in the particular market. Lacking full control over price, the purchaser may still wield some *influence* on price: the circular cases of duopsony and oligopsony conform to this pattern. Advertising outlays by purchasers may also appear in some monopsony situations: witness the advertising of *buyers* of diamonds, old gold, and used automobiles. Forms of purchase differentiation may also develop: some purchasers will grant sellers loans for future production, give the seller access to the legal and technical advice of the purchasers' staff, offer them gifts, and, in countless other ways, make selling more attractive to them than to alternate purchasers who pay the same (or even slightly higher) prices. Nonpecuniary motives also guide purchase-price decisions; notions of a "fair" purchase price and of welfare solicitude for labor might be cited. Obstructions to buyer's-entry can also be enumerated: through contracts for the full output of producers, new purchasers may be frozen out of the particular purchase market. Clearly, a striking parallel to the monopoly patterns can be discovered for the monopsony categories.

MONOPSONY EQUILIBRIUM

While it was the demand and the marginal-revenue curves that contained the heart of the monopoly solution, in monopsony the analysis turns about the supply curve (S) and the marginal-supply curve (MSC).

---

[1] Virtually the same classificatory issues that becloud the monopoly concept could be resurrected here.

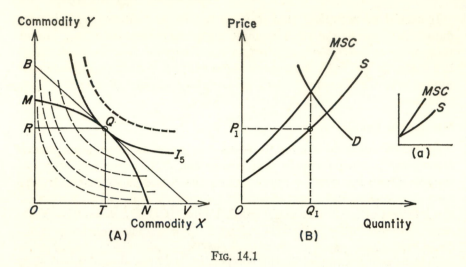

Fig. 14.1

The Marginal-Supply Curve

With one buyer among many, as the market price is a datum, the market-supply curve facing each buyer is envisaged as perfectly elastic: the price tags on merchandise in an urban department store provide an illustration. For monopsony, the S curve facing the purchaser departs from the horizontal: in many cases it may be positively sloped, rising with added purchases. Corresponding to the notion of marginal revenue, where each additional unit sold made imperative a price fall per unit, now a purchase expansion will lift the price paid on all smaller purchase quantities. The *marginal-supply price* (MSP) is thus defined as

$$MSP = P_2 \Delta Q + Q_1 \Delta P \qquad (14.1)$$

In contrast to MR, where $Q_1 \Delta P$ was subtracted from $P_2 \Delta Q$, it now represents an additive sum as long as the S curve rises positively with output.[2] The MSC curve connecting all the MSP points, therefore, will lie above the S curve, as in Figure 14.1(a). Under competitive purchase, ΔP is, of course, zero.

[2] Let $P_2 X_2$ be the new expenditure and $P_1 Q_1$ the old, where $P_2 > P_1$ and $Q_2 > Q_1$. Hence,

$$\begin{aligned} MSP &= P_2 Q_2 - P_1 Q_1 \\ &= P_2(Q_1 + \Delta Q) - Q_1(P_2 - \Delta P) \\ &= P_2 \Delta Q + Q_1 \Delta P \end{aligned}$$

When the supply price falls as purchase quantities increase, so that $P_2 < P_1$, the MSP formula resembles that of MR, and MSC lies *below* the S curve.

It should be remarked that *MSC* is not to be confused with a producer's *MC* curve: the market-supply curve may ultimately be a lateral summation of the individual producer's *MC* curves.[3] But the *MSC* curve is a reality solely from the buyer's standpoint: it is a curve of marginal-supply price or marginal "cost" as visualized through the eyes of the purchaser.

Monopsony Equilibrium

Given the demand curve, to wrest the equilibrium solution under monopsony is comparatively simple once the *MSC* curve has been extracted. Mounting demand curve *D* and the *S* and *MSC* curves in the normal price-quantity chart field, the monopsony equilibrium occurs at the intersection of *D* and *MSC*, as in Figure 14.1(B). Below the intersection of the curves in the conventional diagram, the monopsony purchase volume is located on the horizontal axis, while the purchase price is sighted at the ordinate height corresponding to the supply point on *S* directly *below* the *D = MSC* intersection: the monopsony price lies on *S* rather than on *D* or *MSC*.

Naturally, as *MSC* runs above *S*, the intersection of *D = MSC* is to the left of the purchase volume at which *D = S*. The important exception is of an industry producing in conditions of falling supply price, where the path of the *S* curve follows a normal *D*-curve course and the *MSC* curve appears *below S*; the *D = MSC* intersection then occurs to the right of the *D = S* position, and the monopsony behavior portends an augmented sales volume.[4]

MONOPSONY IN CONSUMER MARKETS

Once the demand curve has been drawn, the equilibrium solution follows in the manner described, with the *D* and *MSC* curves enabling us to pry open the answer. Yet, when we ponder the monopsony adjustment, it appears that the demand curve pertinent to the theory of the consumer market differs from the ordinary demand curve.

To demonstrate this, let us reconstruct the consumer-monopsony analysis in terms of the indifference system. On all of the earlier convex indifference maps, we recall that the price line that was superimposed on the chart field was always linear, signifying a constant price ratio P_x/P_y: in real terms, it meant that the market facts compelled the

---

[3] See pp. 136–137.

[4] A measure of the degree of monopsony power (M_s), corresponding to the formula for monopoly power, can be written as $M_s = (D_x - S_x)/D_x$, where D_x is the demand price for the quantity purchased and S_x is the supply price for the same volume. The deviation $D_x - S_x$ is the ordinate difference of the demand and supply prices at the $D = MSC$ intersection.

sacrifice of a constant decrement (ΔY) to obtain the constant increment (ΔX). The slope of the price (or budget) line was

$$-\Delta Y/\Delta X = P_x/P_y \qquad (14.2)$$

implying the exchange relations along the price line

$$-P_y\Delta Y = P_x\Delta X \qquad (14.3)$$

With P_x rising along the path of a positively sloped S curve, following each ΔX acquisition the sum $P_y\Delta Y$ disgorged in payment would mount as more X was acquired. Rather than equation (14.3), the new relation would be

$$-P_y\Delta Y = P_x\Delta X + X\Delta P_x \qquad (14.4a)$$

or

$$-P_y\Delta Y = MSP_x \qquad (14.4b)$$

for ΔP_x is no longer zero. Instead of being linear, the budget line will now become concave to the origin, for to procure ΔX requires larger ΔY amounts. (If the S_x curve were negatively sloped, with MSC_x below S_x, the budget line would be convex and resemble an indifference curve.)

The Equilibrium Position

Our next concern is with the equilibrium position. The budget line embodies the external market facts while the indifference system displays the subjective taste attitudes. The two must be locked and balanced.

When prices were constant, the condition of equilibrium involved the tangency of the linear budget line and the indifference curve or, more fundamentally, equality between marginal rates of substitution and relative prices. The same condition must prevail now: the concave (or convex) price line must be tangent to the indifference curve, occasioning the equality $MRS = MSP_x/P_y$, for otherwise the individual could enhance his level of well-being by a reshuffle of his holdings. Apparently, if the budget line edges out gently from OY, so that the ΔY decrement is small relative to the ΔX increment, the higher the ultimate level of well-being. When the concave dip of the budget line from OY is sharp and immediate, connoting a steeply rising supply price for X, the monopsony potentialities are likely to be less remunerative—though more satisfactory than paying the full demand price for the self-same quantity of purchases.

A graphic picture of the consumer monopsony equilibrium is provided in Figure 14.1 (A); the concave curve MN is the budget line, so that the purchase equilibrium is at Q, on I_5; OT of X and OR of Y will be bought.

The Marginal-Demand Price

In indifference terms, the monopsony analysis is hardly formidable. But, in translating the mechanics of the adaptation into demand-curve terms, still another variety of demand curve is born, composed of the various *MRS* ratios of Y for X extracted from each of the points at which the budget line intersects the indifference map. It is illuminating to follow the process of equilibration in detail until the tangency position is reached.

Using a linear budget line to illustrate the point, suppose that the individual has spent his full $100 income on $100Y$ and now ponders the wisdom of reselling some Y to acquire some X. As a simplification, we can postulate that $P_x = P_y = \$1$, so that the slope of the budget line is

$$\frac{P_x}{P_y} = -\frac{\Delta Y}{\Delta X} = 1 \tag{14.5}$$

Also, $P_x \equiv MSP_x$ and $P_y \equiv MSP_y$, because for competitive buyers the market price is the same as the marginal-supply price. Suppose that, on the initial indifference curve running through $100Y$, the *MRS* of X and Y is 10/1. Hence, to maintain well-being, the individual would be willing to offer as much as $10 to acquire $1X$; we can describe the *marginal-demand price* (MDP_x) for the first unit of X to be $10. Since only one tenth of a unit of X is necessary to maintain the level of well-being, and as, according to market prices, $P_x = P_y = \$1$, a full unit of X can be secured by relinquishing $1Y$, so the individual moves higher on the indifference hill by executing the trade.[5]

On the indifference map, the individual is now on the higher curve containing the coordinates $99Y$ and $1X$. The same problems arise now: as an exchange of $1Y = 1X$ can still be arranged, so long as the *MRS* of X for Y exceeds the 1/1 market-exchange rate, the transaction is advisable. If the *MRS* is now 8/1, then the MDP_x for a second unit will be $8 while the MSP_x ($= P_x$) will still be $1. Manifestly, each exchange of ΔY for ΔX pushes the individual onto a higher indifference curve. With each exchange, the *MRS* tends to be reduced until, at the tangency position, the 1/1 market exchange rate will equal the *MRS* ratio.

While the argument has been conducted in terms of a linear budget line, the reasoning does not rely on such a line. If the budget line is concave, the only modification is that now the market rate of commodity exchange is MSP_x/P_y. So long as $MRS > MSP_x/P_y$, it will be preferable to part with the decrement ΔY to acquire the increment ΔX, with an equilibrium when $MDP_x = MSP_x$, at point Q in Figure 14.1.

---

[5] See Chapter 1. Commodity Y can, of course, be money, implying constancy of prices $P_y, P_z, \ldots$

Two points merit further elucidation. At each indifference point inter-sected by the budget line, the *MRS* of *X* for *Y*, when translated into money terms, is the marginal-demand price (MDP_x); this denotes the sum that the individual will offer at each indifference point on the budget line to acquire ΔX. In the competitive purchase market, S_x is horizon-tal and perfectly elastic, enabling the MDP_x to be equated to market price.

As a second matter, as we move down the budget line, from point *M* in Figure 14.1(A) toward point *N*, it has been argued that each succes-sive acquisition of *X*, accompanied by the loss of *Y*, lowered the *MRS* of *X* and *Y* and, hence, lowered the MDP_x. This requires some explana-tion, for hitherto the rule to which the indifference curves had to comply was one of a decreasing *MRS* along a *given* indifference curve, but not from *one curve to another*, which introduces changing income levels into the picture. Normally, despite the income change, as *Y* was lost and *X* acquired, the *MRS* of *X* and *Y* would fall. But there is no inexorable necessity here; conceivably, *X* may be more important in the consump-tion plan as income levels rise, so that the new *MRS* exceeds the old. This would happen if *Y* was an inferior good; the MDP_x sum would thereupon rise as the *X* holdings were augmented.

The Monopsony-Demand Curve

If we assume commodity *Y* to be money, *each MRS point intersected by the budget line indicates the sum of money*—the marginal-demand price—*that will be surrendered for a further unit of X*. Each MDP_x point is thus contingent on the exact combination of *X* and *Y* possessed. Plot-ting each successive MDP_x point on the price-quantity chart field, we elicit the demand curve appropriate for consumer-monopsony analysis.

The assumptions of the MDP_x demand curve are: (1) the initial in-come of the individual; (2) the preference system; (3) the price of *Y* (representing all other commodities); and (4) the supply curve of *X* which, with P_y, shapes the course of the budget line.

It is this last premise (4) that distinguishes the (MDP_x) demand curve appropriate for consumer-monopsony analysis from the conventional de-mand curve. For the normal competitive-purchase demand curve, each demand point is *independent* of any previous commitment to spend an aggregate sum on *X*; each point enjoys a vitality even when divorced from the consecutive series of alternate points. Now, however, *the points are not alternate likelihoods but an interrelated sequence; one point is meaningless without all of the others*. For, in drawing the customary de-mand curve, it is assumed that the buyer is confronted with a *family* of horizontal supply curves and, from the ensuing *MDP* curves attached to each perfectly elastic S_x curve, *only the equilibrium-demand prices are isolated and combined into the continuous normal demand curve;* it will be recalled that, in competitive purchase, the demand curve was derived from the price-consumption curve embodying a series of alternate price opportunities. Nothing of this nature exists here. Under monopsony, the relevant demand curve is not compounded in this way: it comes from only one, rather than from a family, of supply curves. Because of this discrepancy, it will be convenient to describe the consumer-monopsony demand curve as an MDP_x curve.[6]

We must conclude that, as the demand curve appropriate for consumer-monopsony problems is distinguishable from the normal demand curve, it is improper to draw quick comparisons between monopsony and competitive-market purchases unless the convenient fiction of a constant marginal utility of money is explicitly stipulated. That purchases would be greater if the monopsony price were announced externally and regarded by the monopsony buyer as immutable seems to be an accurate enough proposition; but the analysis has confirmed that the exact extent of the enhancement cannot be read off the chart field merely by glancing at a unique demand curve.

MONOPSONY AND THE COST CURVES

Strangely enough, the theory of monopsony price in factor markets is less formidable than in consumer markets; most of the preceding difficulties can be attributed to the fixity of money income: factor-cost outlay is never limited in this way.[7] To trace the consequences of monopsony in factor markets, where the problem is more important and the situations more genuine, let us analyze the effects of a rising factor-supply curve on the expansion path, for, once this is fixed, the TC, AC, and MC curves can be extracted mechanically.

Varying Factor Prices and the Expansion Path

With a rising supply curve (S_x) of factor X, and P_y for factor Y constant, the factor-isocost curve will be concave.[8] Writing MP_x and MP_y

---

[6] As to the relationship between the MDP demand curve and the simple demand curve, it can be shown to the left of the monopsony equilibrium that the normal demand curve rests *below* the MDP demand curve.

As an exception to this rule, if the marginal utility of money with respect to income is constant, the MDP demand curve relevant for monopsony coincides with the simple demand curve. Likewise, if X is an inferior good, the MDP demand curve may lie *below* the normal demand curve, at least near the relevant equilibrium phase. For the analysis see my article, "The Theory of Consumer Monopsony," *Review of Economic Studies* (1951). Also, *Price Theory*, pp. 254–255.

[7] See Chapter 8, p. 153.

[8] See Chapter 3, p. 36.

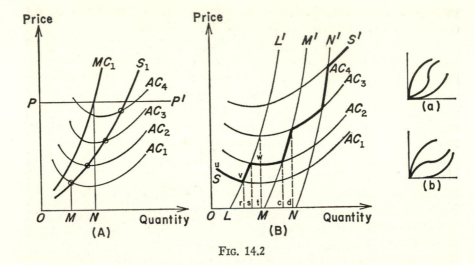

Fig. 14.2

for marginal products, and MSP_x for the marginal-supply price of factor X, the minimum-cost volume of factor hire occurs where

$$MRS = MP_x/MP_y = MSP_x/P_y \qquad (14.6)$$

With a larger outlay on factors, with P_y and S_x posited, there is an upward transformation in the isocost; covering the isoquant map with a family of isocosts, the expansion path can be traced by linking the various points of tangency. As S_x is rising, so that factor X becomes more expensive relative to Y, the expansion path will veer toward the upper ridge line, as in Figure 14.2(a).

The logic of this distortion in the expansion path should be apparent. Earlier, it was developed that, when factor prices are constant, the expansion path coincided with a definite isocline.[9] Now, as P_x rises as more X is hired, there are operative forces to discard X and substitute Y; this explains the edging toward the top ridge line, crossing over onto new isoclines. At the ridge line, despite the mounting P_x, more of X must be used when output expands—for MP_y tends to approach zero—indicating that the substitutionary limit has been reached.

To balance out the analysis, when P_y rises relative to P_x as more Y is used, the expansion path approaches the lower ridge line, as in Figure 14.2(b).

Monopsony and the Cost Curves

Each isocost, and thus each point on the expansion path, represents a definite output and outlay on factors; the implicit TC, AC, and MC

[9] See Chapter 3, p. 37.

values can thus be distilled. Let us examine some of the effects on the cost curves when monopsony pricing of factors is rife.

A family of AC curves appears in Figure 14.2(A). First, to expand output, assume that variable factors X and Y must be used in fixed proportions; the curves are U-shaped, we can agree, because of the presence of a third fixed factor.[10] Along each AC curve we postulate that factor prices P_x and P_y are constant. Climbing from curve to curve (from AC_1 to AC_2, say), we presume that P_y remains unchanged while P_x increases, so that P_x is the parameter responsible for the curve family.

Commencing at output OM and curve AC_1, and thus the implicit P_x of curve AC_1, as output advances and more of X is hired, P_x rises; the relevant AC is situated on a higher curve. For $1X$, say, the relevant AC point is located on AC_1; for $2X$, on AC_2, etc. Connecting these average cost points, the locus S_1 appears, with each point on its path signifying the actual AC experienced at the particular output level. Consequently, with a rising supply curve of factor X, it is the S_1 curve that will be crucial in the firm's output calculations. Drawing a curve marginal to S_1, as MC_1, in Figure 14.2(A), we find that the output equilibrium in a competitive sales market involves the equality of MC_1 and P. This is at output ON. To ascertain the AC at the equilibrium output, we would have to glance at the S_1 point directly above ON.

Observing the particular curve of the AC family through S_1 at ON, reflecting a constant P_x on AC equal to that paid in the monopsony equilibrium, and then drawing the MC correspondent of AC, we can draw a comparison between monopsony output and a competitive output based on an unchanging factor price P_x equal to the monopsony level. Apparently, if S_1 traverses a path to the left of the minimum AC, the monopsony contraction will be more serious than when the S_1 course is to the right of the minimum point.

Substitution Among Factors

Limited as the foregoing analysis is to fixed proportions of X and Y (like 1 skilled plus 5 unskilled laborers for every output addition), it does, nevertheless, convey the correct impression. Normally, factors X and Y are substitutable, so that the factor whose price has increased tends to be supplanted by relatively lower-priced factors at each output level. The output effect, however, tends to sustain its use by operating to expand the employment of all productive factors as production is increased.

Let us consider a case in which the substitution effect outweighs the output effect. In Figure 14.2(B), at the P_x implicit in AC_1, suppose that $10X$ are used, along with definite amounts of Y, until output Or is

[10] See p. 57.

reached. Beyond *Or*, more *X* will be demanded if P_x remains constant. On AC_2, as P_x is higher, the $10X$ are utilized until an output of *Os* is reached, with more *Y* replacing additional *X* between output *Os—Or*. On AC_3, $10X$ serves until output *Ot* is reached.

If we run the line *LL'* through the maximum outputs for which $10X$ are employed as P_x rises, the path *LL'* indicates that ΔX becomes economic to the right of *LL'* despite the higher price of *X*. Likewise, the *MM'* and *NN'* paths partition the *AC*-curve system according to the amounts of factor *X* implicit in the cost curves over each output range. Under fixed proportions, the *LL'*, *MM'*, and *NN'* paths become vertical lines.

Suppose that output is at *Or*. As output expands, if P_x is constant, more of factor *X* will be hired. As P_x rises, it may be feasible to apply more of factor *Y*, holding *X* at 10 units. Soon, however, more *X* must be hired despite the higher price; the relevant *AC* path follows the ratchet-course *uvw*, or *vw* between output *Or* and *Os*. Beyond *Os*, however, more *X* must be hired; the ΔX, plus the $10X$, will serve until an output of *Oc*. But the important point is that, between *Or* and *Os*, the output effect working to increase the use of factor *X* is dwarfed by the substitution effect, stifling its use in view of its price rise. If the lines of constant factor use, such as *LL'*, have a very gentle slope, the output effect will be weak; if *LL'* is practically upright, the output effect will be decisive. Assuming that P_x rises whenever the use of factor *X* is expanded, the *AC* curve will follow the *SS'* staircase of Figure 14.2(B). A curve marginal to *SS'* becomes the effective-monopsony *MC* curve. In Figure 14.2(B), it would be discontinuous, merging with the separable *MC* curves attached to each of the *AC* paths in the family over outputs such as *Os* to *Oc*, then breaking off erratically as the *SS'* curve shifts on to a higher *AC*.

MONEMPORY

An elementary extension of this technique depicts the equilibrium of a firm invested with monopsony power over some productive factors and monopoly power in its product market. Rather than designate this position "monopoly-monopsony," the term *monempory* has been suggested.[11]

Diagrammatic Analysis

The *D* and *MR* curves for final output are drawn in Figure 14.3, along with S_1 and MC_1, where the former are the market curves for the final product of the firm and the latter curves are to be interpreted as in the last section. Monempory output of profit maximization, therefore, is at *OM* and price at P_1, for these are the values at the $MR = MC_1$ inter-

[11] A. J. Nichol, review article, *Journal of Political Economy* (1943), p. 83.

section. The average cost of OM output is found on S_1 below the $MC_1 = MR$ intersection. Through this S_1 point, a curve such as AC_2 can be drawn, denoting the AC path on the abandonment of monopsony pricing of factors, but with the factor price fixed at the monopsony level. MC_2 is marginal to AC_2. Let us appraise the separate output influences of monopoly and monopsony.

Removing monopsony pricing of factors, while retaining monopoly selling in final output, AC_2 and MC_2 are the relevant cost curves: the

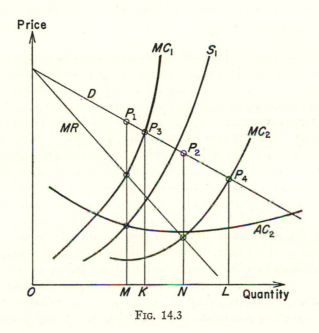

FIG. 14.3

equilibrium will be at P_2 ($< P_1$) and output at ON ($> OM$). Similarly, with monopsony devoid of monopoly, output will be OK ($> OM$); price will be P_3 (for here MC_2 intersects D). Deprived of both monopsony and monopoly power, price will settle at P_4, with output surging to OL: price will be lower and output greater than in any of the single-control cases.

This last position suggests the effects of a competitive-type adaptation. But we must be wary of hasty conclusions, for, by using more of X in producing the greater output, there could be a rise in the price of the factor, so that the curve AC_2 would be unstable; only if its rigidity were assured could the competitive and monempory comparisons be posited with confidence. Although monopoly in the sales market, without monopsony in factor markets, cuts output from OL to ON, while monopsony pushes it back to OK, supporting the inference that a monopsony structure is more deleterious than monopoly elements, this conclusion lacks inevitability; the test of its validity hinges on the exact shape of the MR and MC curves.[12]

In contrast to consumer monopsony, the demand curve for a factor under monopsony is the same as the demand curve in competitive hire, inasmuch as the product price, the input-output ratios, and the prices of other factors are unchanged. The difficulty in drawing the demand curve of the consumer is occasioned by the consumer having a fixed income sum to spend; in factor hire this restriction is superfluous.

Monopsony and Advertising

A few remarks may be injected on advertising under monopsony. These expenditures to shift the supply curve facing a monopsonist will normally accompany monopoly in the sales market—the monempory case. Advertising outlays to induce more sellers to deal with the buying firm will always be remunerative if the ensuing shift in the S_1 curve enlarges profits by more than the sum of advertising outlays.[13]

As in monopoly, nonpecuniary motives will often influence a monopsonist in his purchase policy so that the full degree of monopsony power may not be exercised in any particular period of time: once more this imparts an air of indeterminateness to any *a priori* solution. Motives for moderation and restraint in exploiting the monopsonistic position resemble the list enumerated for monopoly power; there may be mere inertia in using the power, ignorance of its full potentialities, or the monopsonist may have ideas on a "fair" buying price; or he may want to forestall government decrees and enactments; or he may desire to ensure future supplies, etc. Any of these reasons constitutes a plausible excuse for foregoing maximum pecuniary income in any single market period.

High-Wage Policies

Empirical study often discloses that firms with acknowledged monopoly power pay higher wages than their competitive brethren. This may be a consequence of paternalism and social welfare concern on the part of the management; it may also mask other motives. In essence, although the supply curve of labor is perfectly elastic to the firm, it views it as

[12] See J. Dunlop and B. Higgins, "Bargaining Power and Market Structure," *Journal of Political Economy* (1942), p. 13.

[13] Rothschild argues that "welfare" outlays of firms to attract larger and permanent working forces are an aspect of monopsony hire. See "Monopsony, Buying Costs, and Welfare Expenditure," *Review of Economic Studies* (Winter 1942–1943).

higher than its actual level; this can be visualized as a partial monopsony problem.

Paying higher than market wage rates will shift the firm's entire *MC* and *AC* curves up on the chart field, above the minimal levels. Consequently, in all the usual cases output will be reduced and sales price raised through the ostensibly benevolent policy. The implicit monopoly power, measured from the *MC* curve on which factors are valued at market prices, will probably be increased. From this point of view, the wage payment in excess of the market level is a form of monopoly profit sharing, with ramifications upon output. Employees are made effective partners to the monopoly, perhaps even becoming vociferous champions on the management's behalf in defense of its policy. This may be an inexpensive form of insurance for the firm, preferable to government regulation and a protection against potential "wage-sweating" entrants whose offense may consist of paying market wage rates.

DUOPSONY PROBLEMS

Duopsony and oligopsony denote markets dominated by two or more buyers, respectively, but too few to nullify each firm's influence over purchase price. We could resurrect the reaction-curve apparatus, and also distinguish between "leaders" and "followers," separating those instances in which the quantities that other firms buy are fixed as against those cases in which their purchases depend on one's own purchases. Only two simple cases of duopsony, however, will be discussed. Purchase differentiation analyses, by monopsonistic competitors, are by-passed.

Some Illustrations

As a first duopsony sample, firm *A* may expect firm *B* to purchase a fixed amount of the good. Admittedly, this is a most unreasonable hypothesis, for, with any insight at all, *A* will know that *B*'s purchases are not unrelated to price. Nevertheless, we can examine this case in order to demonstrate the principle. Visualizing an ordinary market-supply curve, and then subtracting *B*'s expected purchases laterally from it, we derive another supply curve, from which we in turn derive an *MSC* curve. With a linear demand curve representing *A*'s demand, *MSC* intersects it at a higher price than would be paid to the sellers if *A* were the only buyer. The duopsony price, as can be seen from Figure 14.4(A), is more favorable to the sellers than the monopsony price.

As a more realistic hypothesis, *A* may feel, in view of *B*'s demand, that there is a floor under the minimum market price. *B*'s purchases, however, contract as supply price rises, tapering off and narrowing until they become zero, as in Figure 14.4(a). Thus, the supply curve confronting

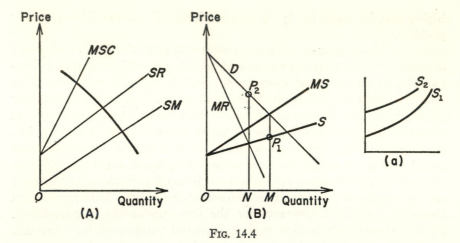

FIG. 14.4

duopsonist A will be the S_2 curve on the left, with the lateral area between the curves signifying B's demand intake at the successive prices. Drawing an MSC to S_2, and following through to the final adjustment, if S_2 is fairly elastic the purchase adaptation will not deviate too far from the competitive price.

Rather than pursue duopsony situations through all their ramifications, so long as the demand price $D = MSP > S_x$, in the final adaptation the same remarks that pertain to all monopsony departures from the competitive price still apply: the sole difference is one of the degree of derangement of the structure from the competitive alignment. Again we must recognize the possibility of direct agreement and collusion between duopsonists and oligopsonists, and compensation of one participant by others may be the outcome. Solutions for these "game" problems are, in general, numerous and inconclusive.

BILATERAL MONOPOLY

Bilateral monopoly—a monopsonist opposed to a monopolist—is an extreme case of conflicting interests, strength, and strategy.

In Figure 14.4(B), the demand curve D and the supply curve S are drawn. If the buyer were in a position to announce the price—a monopsony price—we could draw a curve marginal to S, as MS in the figure, and determine its intersection with D, indicating a price P_1 and output OM in Figure 14.4(A). On the other hand, if the seller named the price, we would have to sketch in the MR curve of D; market price now would be higher, at P_2, while output would be less—only ON. The nature of the price conflict is obvious. Price determinateness, therefore, is confined to the range $P_2 - P_1$; market price is limited to this range, for neither higher nor lower prices are profitable to either participant. If D represents a demand curve for an intermediate factor, and if the two firms mutually agree on price to maximize their *joint* profit, the output appearing at the intersection of D and S will be exchanged.[14] But this assumes harmonious attitudes and precludes either firm's seeking to exploit the other's weakness in bargaining.

It is a commonplace in economic analysis that market price under bilateral monopoly is indeterminate, in the sense that there are no *a priori* principles that enable us to judge precisely which price will be forthcoming on the usual maximization hypotheses. It will depend on compromise and strength and on the bargaining wiles of the participants —including carrying costs to the seller, the threat of future competition, and the nature of future demand; for the buyer there is the intensity of present demand, considerations of future supply prospects, alternative sources of gratification, etc.

Contract Curves

The problem of bilateral monopoly can also be analyzed in terms of the contract curves employed earlier. (See Chapter 7.) For what is essentially involved here is a trade between two individuals, though in collective-bargaining negotiations each "person" may be envisaged as acting for a collective group.

As demonstrated earlier (p. 105), on the assumption of a constant marginal utility of money a greater degree of determinateness is imparted to the bilateral monopoly analysis: the final volume of exchanges runs out to the amount indicated at the intersection of the demand and supply curves—where $D = S$—but the market price, and thus the income advantage to the participants, still remains indeterminate.

[14] Price could lie between the *average* supply price for this quantity and the maximum demand price, as in an all-or-nothing bargain, for this quantity. See *Price Theory*, p. 269, for references to the extensive literature.

PART III
Extensions of Price Theory:
Multiple-Product Firms and an
Introduction to Dynamics

INTRODUCTION

The firm whose equilibrium adjustment we have examined produced but one product. This is, of course, a simplification of reality, for real firms usually produce a diverse array of products. In the ensuing chapters, we attempt to remedy the shortcomings of previous analyses in this respect. Chapter 15 is devoted to the natural and economic causes of multi-product firms, with the emphasis placed on the cost interdependencies conditioning joint production. Some aspects of the theory of integration are also discussed. Chapter 16 discloses certain demand phenomena conducive to multiple-product production. The topics that fall under this heading comprise a highly assorted list—discriminatory monopoly and monopsony pricing, pricing goods in substitutionary and complementary relations, and pricing goods linked in both production and demand. Once these new complexities are unraveled, we shall indicate some dynamic extensions of price theory, to nonequilibrium situations and to the modifications inevitable when the passage of time is explicitly recognized.

Chapter 15

Cost Interdependence

In this chapter, we examine some aspects of the theory of cost inter-dependence; the theory of integration can be tackled as part of this development.

The complication in multiple-product analyses is that, normally, the expansion of one product will affect the firm's ability to produce other goods. Envisaging its list of $A, B, C, \ldots, N$ commodities, the marginal-cost curve for any one product, such as A, is contingent on the quantities of $B, C, \ldots, N$ being turned out. If the production of one good fails to influence the MC curves of other commodities, all of the preceding analysis can be preserved intact even on recognition of multi-product firms. Conceivably, the firm may assign an entire factory building, or an entire wing of a plant, to producing commodity A, another to B, etc., thereby mitigating the common pressures on identical productive facilities. In this event, the assumption of independent MC curves conforms very well with the facts.

If a firm does produce several products whose marginal-cost curves and demands are independent, the condition of equilibrium for each output is, of course, $P \geqq MR = MC$. If we view the firm as the vehicle for allocating factors among its several outputs, the relevant ratios to be satisfied for each pair of outputs are

$$\frac{MR_1}{MR_2} = \frac{MC_1}{MC_2} \tag{15.1}$$

In competitive sales markets, the MR's, of course, coincide with prices.

Multiple-Plant Firms

As an analogous problem, a firm will often erect independent plants for a particular product variety, choosing to expand its layout horizontally, with some geographic separation among plants, rather than to enlarge its facilities at a given site. Assuming that the identical product is sold in identical markets, it is clear that the volume of production in all plants will proceed until marginal production costs in each plant are equivalent; all *MC*'s, eventually, will be equated to the composite marginal revenue, with the one proviso being that, if marginal (and thus average) costs are falling in any one plant, output will tend to be concentrated there. Hence, with a sharp fall in market demand, there is a good likelihood that some plants will be kept idle—closed unless a by-product commodity type can be conceived. Production in several independent plants owned by a unitary parent firm can thus occasion a search for suitable by-product opportunities.

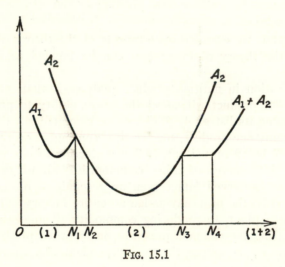

FIG. 15.1

Problem

Suppose that the *AC* curves of the respective plants are as A_1 and A_2 in Figure 15.1. Explain why production would definitely be concentrated in plant 1 for an output ON_1, in plant 2 for an output of ON_2 to ON_3, and combined between them for outputs beyond ON_4. What about outputs between ON_2 and ON_1? between ON_4 and ON_3?

Draw linear *AC* curves, one rising and the other falling. How will output be allocated between the two plants of the firm?

JOINT PRODUCTION

Joint products are those whose production is combined for natural causes. Illustrations are plentiful: there are the textbook examples of cotton lint and cotton seed, wool and mutton, zinc and silver, etc., produced in either fixed or variable proportions.

Just as the specialized literature becomes engrossed in the study of natural joint products, popular writings bestow their affection on "by-products" and "waste" products. For example, soap is described as a by-product of meat packing. What is intended is that, despite the major preoccupation with the slaughter of animals for meat, certain portions of the carcass are salvaged for other uses. Frequently, the classification between by-products and main products is highly arbitrary: if we have become accustomed to classify certain firms as meat packers, then all but meat products are by-products. If prices move in such a way as to render the incidental outputs more valuable to the firm than its presumed major occupation—if, say, certain medicinal extractions from the cattle become more remunerative than the sales proceeds from meat—it would be more accurate to describe meat packing as the by-product. But this is solely a question of suitable names; it is indubitably an instance of joint production in that several distinguishable outputs ensue from a unified series of operations.[1]

Fixed Proportions: Competitive Conditions

If goods are producible only in a fixed ratio—for example, if 2 pounds of cotton seed are always and inseparably fused with 1 pound of cotton lint—the condition of output equilibrium assumes a slightly novel guise: marginal costs in competitive markets must be equated to the *sum* of the price proceeds derived from the independent sale of each commodity. Thus,

$$MC_{x+y} = rP_x + sP_y \qquad (15.2)$$

where r is the number of X units and s is the number of Y units which form the combined output. (For simplicity, hereafter we assume that $r = s = 1$. Modifications, where this is not so, are obvious.)

It is interesting to unravel the effects of a rise in demand and price for one good (X) with the demand for the other good (Y) constant, where the goods are unrelated in consumption. The augmented joint proceeds after the higher P_x will stimulate further production of both products; the upshot will be that the increment ΔP_x leads to a decrement ΔP_y. In equilibrium, if the total output is to expand, the sum of the $P_x + P_y$ proceeds must be greater than before, so that

$$(+\Delta P_x) > (-\Delta P_y) \qquad (15.3)$$

Just as it is impossible to compute separable marginal costs for each product when they are produced in fixed proportions, it is likewise futile

---

[1] Waste products, generally, are materials eliminated after a set of operations and are not necessarily valueless even in the form in which they first emerge. After further fabrication and refinement, the "waste" products may become an integral ingredient of final output. They are simply by-products, often conducive to further industrial integration.

to endeavor to compute separable average costs. Hence, the full competitive output equilibrium conditions are

$$P_x + P_y = MC_{x+y} \geqq AC_{x+y} \tag{15.4}$$

Fixed Proportions: Monopoly Conditions

For a monopolist selling both X and Y, the firm will produce further units of the joint output so long as the combined marginal revenue exceeds their joint marginal cost. Equilibrium will involve

$$P_x + P_y > MR_x + MR_y = MC_{x+y} \tag{15.5a}$$

$$P_x + P_y > AC_{x+y} \tag{15.5b}$$

One point, however, should be underscored: a monopolist will withdraw goods from any market in which marginal revenue is negative; it could enhance profits by destroying or withholding the excess supply, depending on the cost of each maneuver. Thus, for other than costless output, only one marginal revenue of the joint pair may be zero.

With the proviso of positive MR's, our views on the consequences of an increase in the demand for one of the goods must be revised. Under competition, this would always entail a fall in the price of the production complement; under monopoly, only if the marginal revenue of the production complement is still positive will its price fall. Otherwise, the monopolist will prefer to eliminate the excess output of the complement rather than deplete total income through its sale. Costs of destruction or withholding, however, will be weighed against the loss by sale.

Variable Proportions

We consider now the more intricate case of variable proportions under which commodity X must be produced in conjunction with Y, although the ratios of the fused production unit can fluctuate, with more of X produced in lieu of some Y, or vice versa. The classic illustration is that of sheep bred more for their wool than for their meat, although it is not possible to displace either product entirely. In a sense, the aggregate output of the economy can be conceived as produced in variable joint proportions for, with full employment, producing more of one product requires displacing some quantity of another output. But the peculiarity of variable proportions is that it is technically impossible to abandon one product entirely.

Suppose that $10X$ and $30Y$ are produced at a total cost of $100 and that, in a competitive market, $P_y = \$6$. Further, we can imagine that it is also possible to produce $31Y$ with $10X$ at a total cost of $101. Substantially, therefore, $MC_y = \$1$; the firm would apprehend the profitability of producing more Y, with X constant, whenever P_y exceeded $1. Fixing the output of X, profits could be increased whenever the additions to total cost made by a further unit of Y were less than the additional proceeds procured from its sale. In competitive equilibrium, therefore, we would have $MC_y = P_y$ (or MR_y under monopoly).

Precisely the same analysis would be relevant for X. If the Y output were fixed, with $MR_x > MC_x$, more X output would be in order. Equilibrium would require that the addition to total cost, with the associated output constant, equal the addition to total receipts. Ostensibly, when the proportions are variable, a type of marginal cost can be deduced once the volume of the other output is stipulated.

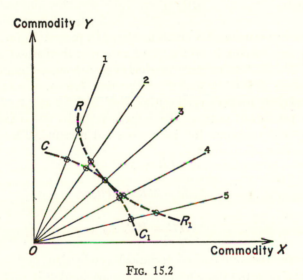

Commodity Y

Commodity X

FIG. 15.2

Diagrammatic Solution of Variable Proportions

The problem can be illuminated by an adaptation of the indifference- and transformation-curve technique. In Figure 15.2, we measure the output quantities of commodities X and Y along OX and OY. Production is possible in any of the proportions indicated by the paths 1, 2, 3, 4, ... Ultimately, the only restriction for the case of joint production in variable proportions is that the paths cannot coincide with OX or OY—it is not possible to produce one good to the exclusion of the other. The more numerous the possibilities of variation, the greater the density of the paths; joint production in fixed proportions implies that production can expand along only one path, as that with index 1, and no other.

A total-cost curve, CC_1, can be mounted on Figure 15.2 to combine all those outputs that can be produced at a given total-cost outlay; a constant total-sales revenue curve (as RR_1) can also be constructed to connect all those output combinations that yield a given total revenue.[2] The revenue curve will be linear when sales markets are competitive and convex (or irregularly concave-convex) under monopoly; the constant total-cost contour ought always to be concave.

From earlier discussions it will be perceived that, for each total-cost outlay, a firm will produce the output combination that is indicated at the tangency of a cost and revenue contour, for, at the tangency position, the total revenue obtainable for the cost outlay will be at a maximum, touching the highest-revenue curve. Sketching in the cost and revenue field, and then connecting the points of tangency, we could construct a type of output expansion path where each combined-output volume is contingent on a given total-cost outlay. At each point on the expansion path, the marginal rate of transformation of product X for Y, for any cost outlay, would equal the marginal rate of substitution in the sales markets of X for Y as revenue producers of a fixed volume of receipts. This, of course, implicitly embodies equation (15.1).

As this relation holds at each outlay level, for the full equilibrium the increase in total-cost outlays—the joint marginal cost—must equal the increase in total revenue—the joint marginal revenue. Thus,

$$\Delta TR = \Delta TC \tag{15.6a}$$

where

$$\Delta TR = MR + MR_y \tag{15.6b}$$

and

$$\Delta TC = MC_{x+y} \tag{15.6c}$$

Conceivably, the number of technical production paths may be so few as to preclude the drawing of continuous total-cost or total-revenue curves. Nevertheless, the principle is clear: for each total-cost outlay the output combination that maximizes sales revenue will be chosen, while in the ultimate equilibrium configuration the joint MC will equal the joint MR. As before, the marginal revenue of each good must be positive. A shift in demand or a realignment in costs is likely to alter the expansion path and the equilibrium-output combination. Inferentially, the more numerous the possibilities of substitution, the smaller the likelihood that each increase in X, because of improved demand for X, will be accompanied by more Y output.

Although the two goods are jointly produced, to prepare them for market may involve some separable expenses. The marginal revenue of each good must be computed net of the separable expenses, by deducting the latter from the independent market-demand schedules.

---

[2] The total-cost curve CC' is to be distinguished from the earlier isocosts in that we now measure combined output quantities rather than factors along OX and OY.

COST INTERDEPENDENCE

The analysis of joint products just elaborated assumes that the production complementarity was a resultant of natural causes, the physical impossibility of separate production. Among other causes of joint production, there is the fact that the production of commodity Y, simultaneously with X, may *lower* the cost of producing X. Let us consider the equilibrium relations under these circumstances.

Cost Complementarity

Let us postulate that 100 units of X can be produced by the application of a definite quantity of labor to a fixed volume of equipment. Suppose that, to produce commodity Y, the same equipment (essentially) can be utilized and that, as labor is hired for the production of Y, MC_x is reduced, thus lowering AC_x and enhancing profits. As more Y is produced, each increment in its output may push MC_x lower down in the chart field.

In Figure 15.3, D_y and D_x are the respective demand curves. As OM of Y is produced, the relevant marginal-cost curve for X is MC_1 in Figure 15.3(B). As Y advances to ON, the curve MC_2 is generated for commodity X. As Y mounts to the OL output level, MC_3 emerges for X.

As to the causes of the volatility in MC_x, we may assume that the productive factors hired for the Y output are complementary to those in X, lifting the marginal products of the latter and enabling any X output to be produced with fewer variable factors. As Y output expands, the joint pressure on the fixed productive facilities ought to compress the ensuing rise in the marginal productivity of the factors engaged for

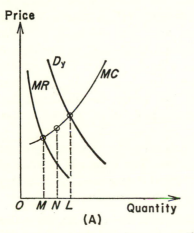

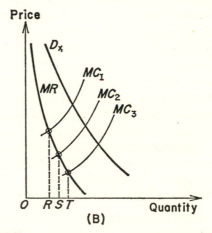

FIG. 15.3

producing X, so that the successive downward dislodgments of the MC_x curve should be smaller.

The output equilibrium conditions are now more involved, for, on producing ΔY, not only are there the additional sales proceeds in Y, but also additional profits in the X commodity ($= \Delta R_x$) due to the downward swing in the MC_x curve; hence, the condition for output equilibrium is

$$MR_y + \Delta R_x = MC_y \qquad (15.7)$$

Patently, it will be profitable to push the production of Y beyond the simple equality of $MC_y = MR_y$. In Figure 15.3(A) the ON output level for Y may prove more lucrative than that at OM.

These relations should be symmetrical; if a greater application of factors hired to increase Y output raises the marginal productivity of the factors engaged to produce X, the reverse should also be true. Figure 15.4(A) can thus be conceived as belonging to X and Figure 15.3(B) to Y. Hence, a similar equilibrium condition turns up for the production of X. But this also entails that, if ΔR_x occurs through a greater output of X, then the total cost of producing the given Y amount will be reduced by the expansion of X—in sum, say, ΔC_y. Thus, the full equilibrium condition becomes

$$MR_y + \Delta R_x = MC_y - \Delta C_y \qquad (15.8)$$

A similar relation can be written for commodity X. Hence, each separate equilibrium condition entails such mutual output adaptations that, for one commodity, $MC > MR$, and for the other commodity, $MC = MR$, while when we look at the dual adjustment it is possible that each

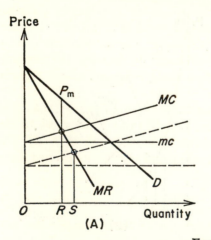

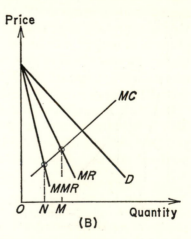

FIG. 15.4

$MC > MR$. This reciprocal influence will be missing only when one output is held rigid. Otherwise, the expansion in one sets up forces favorable for the other, which react on the first, thereby exerting a positive tremor back on the second, etc. It is probably not too unrealistic to regard these reciprocal effects as of decreasing magnitude compared to the direct rise in each MC and fall in MR. Still, for the combined output to be of maximum profitability, we need the supplementary condition that, for a joint output movement, the addition to total profits must be nil.[3] Thus,

$$\Delta TC_{x+y} = \Delta TR_{x+y} \qquad (15.9)$$

Cost Substitution

Even if the effect is to raise the MC curve of the alternate product, it may often be less expensive for a single firm to direct its equipment to the production of alternate products than for new and independent firms to be organized for the separate tasks. If the multiple products can be produced without raising the production cost of the main product too greatly, it may prove more economical than constructing specialized machinery on which capital costs, besides the special variable costs, must be recovered. Unless specialization, with its specific capital charges, promises to lower average costs below the average variable costs when the commodity is a by-product fashioned on existing equipment, then multiple-product firms will appear in even an entirely competitive world. The chief advantage enjoyed by the firm in by-product output is that the additional product varieties need only contribute, at a minimum, the separable expenses incurred in their behalf, permitting the omission of any capital charges.

A multiple-product firm may experience higher production costs than specialist firms because: (1) the equipment is not specifically designed for the conceived by-products; the amount of variable factors required, per unit of output, may be relatively excessive; (2) more products may hinder the production of the "main" products by drawing off entrepreneurial abilities, special labor skills, floor space, machinery, etc., thereby raising the latter's cost of production.

Resorting to graphics, with OM output of Y in Figure 15.3(A), the MC_3 is the relevant one for X (Figure 15.3[B]). As Y advances to the ON level, MC_2 is the appropriate curve; while, with OL of Y, MC_1 is pertinent. Hence, as an offset to the additional profits occasioned by a

[3] The price-reaction curve analysis of Figure 12.2 would be appropriate to the problem, since a rise in P_y, with less Y output, would lift MC_x and raise P_x. Similarly, for each change in P_x the maximum profit P_y can be computed. The position of maximum profitability would be the one of mutual compatibility indicated at the intersection of the price-reaction curves.

further unit of Y, there must be deducted the losses suffered through higher costs on the production of X. Under these circumstances, the equilibrium condition for commodity Y becomes

$$MR_y - \Delta R_x = MC_y \tag{15.10}$$

Production of Y will cease below the level at which $MC_y = MR_y$, or at an amount at which $MR_y > MC_y$. If the factor relations are symmetrical, a similar equality is applicable to commodity X. If the X output contracts, this will entail some reduction in the total costs of Y, in sum ΔC_y. Thus, the condition will be

$$MR_y - \Delta R_x = MC_y - \Delta C_y \tag{15.11}$$

The change ΔC_y tends to ameliorate the situation, to some degree, though normally ΔR_x ought to exceed ΔC_y. As before, if merely the Y output is permitted to expand and if MC_y is computed only after the new X adaptation, the ΔC_y component could be neglected, as subsumed in the net MC_y. The supplementary condition of nil marginal profits for a joint output variation must also be attached.

Induced By-Product Outputs

Suppose that a monopoly firm producing the $P > MC$ output volume decides to utilize its facilities in producing a differentiated by-product that competes with products of other firms, although affecting any single product insignificantly (the polypoly hypothesis). As demand curves for the main products of other firms are contracted, the latter firms may be provoked to contrive their own by-product concoctions. The process can go on interminably, each firm adopting a by-product, contracting the market demands of other firms, and thereby pressing them to diversify their own product list. A product equilibrium will be reached only when each firm doubts the feasibility of extending its list of by-product outputs. By and large, the production of more varieties and the encroachment of each firm on the market preserves of others will reduce monopoly profits all around.

Despite the disappearance of monopoly profits from this model, many of the ingredients of wasteful production would remain regardless of the display of intense competition between firms. With demand curves for each product pulled back, each particular commodity may be produced at higher average cost than for specialist firms. Thus, the by-product outputs engendered under monopoly may be costly to the economy, despite the superficial benefit of the unused facilities being diverted to alternate by-product outputs. Under competitive pricing and homogeneous entry, the degree of nonspecialization and multiple-product production, as well as product diversity, could never go so far as under monopoly pricing and heterogeneous entry.

VERTICAL INTEGRATION

In the multiple-product analysis, the firm added new products to its sales offerings. In the theory of vertical integration the relevant topic is that of the number of productive phases requisite to a finished product performed under the firm's own aegis.

In weighing the degree of integration, the firm must compare the cost of interdepartmental "purchases" as against market transactions or buying from another firm. Parenthetically, the degree of integration accomplished will affect the number of markets in which the firm appears as buyer or seller. With five stages (A, B, C, D, and E) before the output is finished for sale to consumers, if a firm at D integrates the C stage with its own D stage, it will henceforward appear as a buyer in the market for B rather than C. Integrating backward, completely through stage A, the firm will ultimately have to operate certain natural resources, as mines and farms, and be a buyer solely in the factor markets. Integrating forward from D, rather than sell to E, the firm will appear as a competitor in the sales markets of the various E-stage firms. Integration thus reduces the number of market transactions between firms prior to the final sale to consumers.

Economic Bases of Integration

In delving into the causes of integration—of why firms undertake the series of operations that they deem as falling within their province—realistically it must be confessed that the operations performed are attributable to a complex of economic and historical circumstances—the errors, the ignorance, and the caprice of the ancestral firms. And yet the degree of integration does change. Let us therefore examine some of the determining factors.

Economic and technical forces can be separated. Corresponding to the natural phenomena of fixed and variable proportions, one explanation for the full sequence of operations performed by the firm is the technical fact that certain processes must be executed (almost) simultaneously. In chemical mixtures, the preparation must be viewed as a unit; although the ingredients may come from other firms, decisions for compounding them must generally be centralized, at least when the preparation must be consummated in one operation. Besides the technical need for simultaneous processing, certain processes must be performed smoothly and successively, any disruption in the process chain being disastrous to the final result. Although it is not inconceivable for several firms to be charged with the different phases of the productive flow, there is always the chance of discord and nonfulfillment which might subject either the earlier or the later participants in the process to burdensome loss. Hence, integration is likely to be more successful than dividing responsibility at each stage among independent firms. As another aspect of continuity, a firm in possession of output contracts will have to assure itself that certain preliminary operations will be performed, that essential ingredients will be furnished to it on schedule, or that its particular specifications will be complied with. When these responsibilities are left to others, delays may occur and instructions may be slighted, making it advisable for the firm to extend its sphere of operations despite some diseconomies in so doing. In practice, these factors explain at least a minimum degree of integration within the economy.[4]

There will be an economic motive for integrating whenever the firm can lower its production costs. Intermediate factors that are purchased from other firms are, to the purchasing firm, a productive factor on a full parity with the labor, the equipment, or the natural resources it hires. When a firm can supply its own raw-material needs more economically than by purchasing materials in the markets, it can augment its profits by integration. Profitwise, it will be prudent for the firm to integrate backward whenever the marginal cost of performing an additional process is below the market price for the same intermediate factor. If extra equipment is indispensable for the new task, the full condition is that $P = MC > AC$, where P is the market price for the material, MC is the additional cost of producing it within the firm, and AC is the full average cost of producing it within the firm. The inclusion of AC in the equilibrium condition is dictated by the fact that, if MC lies below AC, it would be foolhardy for the firm to incur the separable fixed costs to widen its productive sphere.

For integrating forward, the firm must be able to execute the further operations at an MC (and AC) not higher than the difference between the market price at the new stage and the market price at its former output place. Otherwise, it will only suffer a diminution in profits for its integrating pains.

Forward integration may be countenanced because of sealed entry or institutional impediments, closing distributive facilities to the firm. Either it must build its own outlets or its entire productive endeavors will be abortive. Also, as a reminder of our discussion of joint products, integration is likely to occur if, in performing phase B, the cost of the A (or C) step is lowered. The equilibrium problem is the same problem as formerly, the difference being that the selection of the accompanying by-products entails integration. Besides MC curves being influenced, if

---

[4] Uncertainty is thus often a basic cause.

successive output stages utilize similar equipment or other productive facilities that are otherwise not fully engaged, integration can reduce the joint *AC*, as compared to the growth of independent firms for the separate tasks.

MONOPOLY AND INTEGRATION

Let us consider the special influence of monopoly on integration. Specifically, two aspects of monopoly will be investigated: (1) the effects of monopoly pricing in intermediate output stages on backward integration and (2) backward integration as a device for strategic monopoly control of later stages.

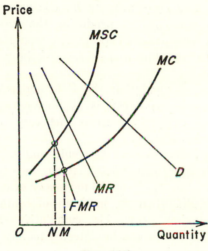

FIG. 15.5

Monopoly Pricing and Integration

A monopolist will often require materials which are themselves sold under monopoly conditions: hence, we envisage a situation in which successive stages in a nonintegrated production structure are monopolized. To simplify the exposition, we suppose that materials are bought by firm *B* from only one other firm (*A*) before being processed by *B*. Also, we assume that the *B* firm in buying materials from *A* *is only one of many buyers of A's product* and pays the market price, since its purchases are too small to influence *A*'s monopoly sales price.

In Figure 15.4, page 296, *D* is the demand curve for *B*'s finished output and *MR* is its marginal-revenue curve. Cost of materials purchased from *A* is represented by *mc*, while *MC* is the curve of full marginal costs; the difference (*MC* − *mc*) thus represents the marginal cost of factors hired directly by the B firm to process the materials acquired from A into the finished goods of the B stage. The institution of a $P = MC$ pricing policy in the A stage would lower mc, thus lowering the full MC curve of our figure. Hence, the new monopoly price adjustment for the B firm would be at a lower price than formerly. The extent of the price fall would depend on: (1) the price fall of the unfinished materials, (2) the importance of these materials in the cost curve of the B firm, and (3) the elasticity of the demand curve facing B. In the figure, the consequences of competitive pricing in the A stage are indicated by the dashed mc and MC curves. The effect of A's monopoly price on B's output is to contract production from OS to OR.

It is conceivable, therefore, that backward integration would lower B's MC curve and lead to a lower price to B's consumers despite the higher production costs involved in B's producing the materials compared to their costs to the A firm; A's monopoly price would afford an integrated nonspecialist firm an important margin for absorbing minor diseconomies of production.

Although we have assumed that the B firm purchasing from A was itself a monopolist, this hypothesis is by no means crucial. If B were one of a nucleus of competitive firms, the very same factors would motivate backward integration.

The analysis also indicates that we would underestimate the strength of monopoly pricing if we concluded that, because in any one firm the deviation between P and MC is small, monopoly pricing is unimportant; the conclusion is invalid when the final output contains materials processed by *many* monopoly firms. The cumulative effects of monopoly pricing are more potent than can be detected merely by an examination of the price policy of an individual firm.

Monopoly in Earlier and Later Stages

Let us assume that there are but two stages of production, with firms at the B stage providing the finished product and firms at the A stage providing the materials. Assume also, for simplicity, that at B's stage production costs are zero; we shall remove this restriction in a moment, but it is convenient to impose it in commencing this study.

In Figure 15.4(B), page 296, the final product demand curve is D: assuming numerous firms and competitive pricing, D is also the demand curve for the A-stage output. If, at the A stage, there is but one firm (so that A is a monopolist), then to deduce its maximum price an MR curve, as in the figure, must be drawn and its intersection with MC (or A's marginal cost) observed. Output would then be OM.

In contrast, suppose that the A product were sold under competitive conditions, so that MC now represents the supply curve of industry A, besides being the MC curve of firm B, which is now in a monopoly position. Firm B would purchase materials from the A firms in amount OM —the same quantity that would be sold if A priced monopolistically to B. Hence, *monopoly in either stage would affect the final purchaser identically;* the difference is not to the consumers but in the sharing of the monopoly profits.

Lifting the hypothesis of zero costs at the B stage, suppose that B's costs were constant and exactly those that would be experienced by A in integrating forward to the B stage; these constant amounts could be subtracted from each ordinate of the D curve. Palpably, on these hypotheses our conclusions would be unaffected. If A, on integration, were more efficient than the B firm which it supplanted, the final MC curve of A ought to be lower than that of the B monopolist, with output enhanced and price reduced; the converse would be valid when B enjoys a productive superiority. Hence, we have established that monopoly in the A stage, with competition in the B stage, will normally affect consumers in the same way as monopoly in later stages with competition in the earlier stages of the productive process.

To conclude this analysis, both A and B firms may be monopolists, with B the sole seller to consumers and A the sole seller of essential materials to B. But this problem is one of bilateral monopoly, with all of its indeterminacies.[5] If we assume that, because of the nature of the bargaining strength, B must comply with A's price terms in deciding on price policy, in effect A will derive a curve marginal to B's MR curve, as MMR in Figure 15.4(B). A's sales, and ultimately B's output, will thus be ON. Monopoly in the successive stages, therefore, will be more harmful to consumers than monopoly in but one stage. Hence, fully integrated output will be superior from the consumer's standpoint even if there is some cost disadvantage attached to this development as compared to the economies of specialization.

MONOPSONY AND INTEGRATION

Monopoly in earlier stages was shown to be a cogent influence in the backward integration of a firm; similarly, monopsony in the later stages is conducive to forward integration. If the firm at the B stage is a monopsonist buyer, the firms at the A position will weigh the prospect of undertaking the B type of productive operation. The more unfavorable the monopsony price named by B, the stronger the appeal that forward integration will carry to the A firms.

It is most realistic to discuss the case in which B is a monopolist in its sales market and a monopsonist in its purchase of the intermediate A

[5] See above, p. 284.

products—the monempory case discussed previously.[6] On these assumptions, it can be shown that consumers would fare better by forward integration of the A firms, even while monopoly pricing persisted in the final market.

In Figure 15.5, D is the market-demand curve for the end product of B's productive stage and MR is the correspondent marginal revenue curve. Deducting from MR the cost to B of associated factors at each output level, the curve FMR emerges as B's demand curve for the intermediate product of the A firms. With MC as the supply curve of the A firms, and B the monopsonist, the A output would settle at ON. Conversely, if there were but one A firm whose costs were represented by the MC curve, and if it also controlled the B stage and enjoyed the same cost experience as the B firm, output would be OM. Hence, the monempory at the B stage would be more adverse to final purchasers from the B stage than an integrated monopoly firm reaching back through both A and B operations.

The Denial of Sales Outlets

Boycotts by dealers, because of either contract commitments or a reluctance to handle the products of a new firm, provide an obvious ground for forward integration. This can be construed as a manifestation of the monopsony power of dealer purchasers who abstain from buying in the thought of impeding the entry of the new producing firm. Owning and operating its distributing outlets may be the only straw that may be grasped by the producing firm, despite higher distributing costs. Forward integration is also likely when it offers the best method of controlling selling policy at the retail stage, particularly when buyers associate price reductions with a deterioration of quality.

COST INTERDEPENDENCE IN TIME

Just as the output of product A can affect the firm's cost of producing B, its production of output in period t_1 may influence the cost of production at date t_2, t_3, . . . , etc. Inherently, the temporal interrelations are those already discussed; the difference is one of asymmetry, for the activities of t_1 influence t_2 profits, but t_2 events, which unfold after t_1 is already part of past history, are unable to exert an influence on t_1 operations.

User Costs

Normally, the typical cost interrelation will be that in which production in t_1 affects the ability of the firm to produce in t_2: mainly, it will

---

[6] See above, p. 280.

be the capacity of the equipment to render services that will be impaired. The uplift thrust upon the marginal-cost curve of t_2, and the consequent loss of t_2 profits, can be designated as the *user* cost of t_1. Using subscripts to refer to t_1 and t_2 values, we can state the condition for t_1 profit maximization as

$$P_1 \gtreqless MR_1 = MC_1 + \Delta R_2 \qquad (15.12)$$

where ΔR_2 is the current value of the decrement in profits in t_2 due to t_1 activity. This is the *user cost* of current output, which must be added to MC_1, operating to limit output in t_1.

Alternately, t_2 profits may be enhanced because t_1 production and maintenance of equipment in good order reduce t_2 costs; ΔR_2 would then have to be deducted from MC_1 volume. When costs are temporally interdependent whether ΔR_2 is positive or negative, production will fail to correspond to the $P = MC$ rule even in competitive market conditions and under perfect foresight. If costs in several future intervals are influenced by t_1 operations, the ΔR concept will have to be extended to encompass these ties.

To indicate these relations, assume for the moment that the firm's productive facilities were idle in period t_1. Supposing that the firm sells in a competitive market and the expected price is, say, OP, then the MC_1 curve in Figure 15.6(A) would describe the appropriate cost path in t_2; total output in t_2 would thus be OM and total profits would be PKR. But when 1 unit of output is produced in t_1, because of the wear and tear on equipment production costs will be higher in t_2: more labor, for example, might be necessary for each level of output so that the relevant t_2 marginal-cost curve would rise from MC_1 to MC_2. Output in

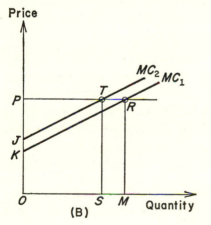

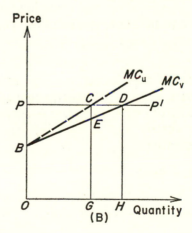

Fig. 15.6

period t_2 would consequently recede to OS and profits to PTJ, a reduction of $JKRT$.

Writing MC_v for the t_1 marginal-cost outlays, as 1 unit of current output reduces future profits by $JKRT$, this last sum, discounted to its present value, must be added to the MC_v of 1 unit of t_1 output to calculate the full marginal cost: the full t_1 cost consists of both *immediate* cash outlays and curtailed *future* profit opportunities. Ordinarily, small amounts of current outputs will not diminish future production potentialities, and might even improve them, so that the user costs for small amounts of current output will be zero or negative. As current production expands, however, the *marginal user cost*—the MC increment at each output representing future profit displacements—will become positive and more substantial. This is shown by the widening gap between MC_u and MC_v.

Observe that MC_u cuts the market price line PP' to the left of the MC_v and PP' intersection. Total t_1 sales proceeds are $OP \cdot OG$, of which total variable cash cost outlays are $OBEG$, with the difference $PCEB$ consisting of profits. In obtaining this volume of current profits, there would be the sacrifice of future profits, discounted to date and equal to BCE. Besides depressing future earnings by this amount through the advance harvest, there is the net current income of PCB. Output, however, would not surpass OG, for to do so would mean relinquishing future profits in excess of the added current earnings.

It should now be apparent that the notion of user cost refers solely to the *avoidable* depreciation, that due to use; it must not be confused with the total of depreciation allowances which, if rightly calculated, is a composite sum consisting of losses in the value of equipment attributable to both time and use.

Introducing user costs imparts a serious indeterminateness to models of equilibrium relationships even under competitive conditions, for, if all the numerous firms foresee different future prices, even if they possess identical equipments there will not be any single, uniform relation of P and MC_v.

User Costs Over Several Periods

When the economic horizon extends beyond the two periods of our model, the user cost chargeable to a unit of output can be derived as follows: First, we can find the effect of a unit of current t_1 output on t_2 profits. Next, we can suppose t_2 output to be zero and then appraise the movement in t_3 profits due to t_1 output; continuing, we can suppose zero output in t_2 and t_3 and discover the effect of t_1 output on t_4 profits; etc. The user cost attributable to a unit of output in t_1 will be *the value of the greatest of the potential profit reductions discounted to date*. In the event that producing a unit of output "today" lowers cost "tomorrow" but raises cost the "next day," then we must strike a balance among the positive and negative items in computing the net user cost, positive or negative. The factors that dominate in determining the magnitude of marginal user cost are (1) the age of the equipment—new equipment will seldom involve a (serious) positive user cost; (2) the rate of interest, which influences the rate of discounting of future profit expectations— with a high rate of interest only substantial future profit opportunities will persuade an entrepreneur to repress current output for an uncertain future gain with a low current value; and (3) expected future prices, or demand under monopoly conditions, and expected factor costs, both of which shape the magnitude of the expected future profits. With optimistic entrepreneurial profit views, user-cost phenomena will bulk larger in the economy; hence, in the emergence from depression they are likely to be extremely important influences affecting prices and production. The immediate impact would be to raise prices and curb output.

Chapter 16

〜〜〜〜〜〜〜〜〜〜〜〜〜〜〜〜〜〜〜〜〜〜〜〜〜〜〜〜〜〜〜〜〜

Interrelated Demand

Although our firm has now been endowed with control over multiple products, the reasons assigned for the phenomenon stem entirely from the cost side. In this chapter we examine several situations in which demand interrelations preponderate. The analysis generally entails a redefinition of the concept of marginal revenue.

DISCRIMINATORY PRICING

Consider, first, the problem of discriminatory pricing. In discrimination of the first degree,[1] the monopolist may charge the same buyer a different price for each unit bought in order to extract the utmost in sales proceeds. Second-degree discrimination covers those situations in which different prices are charged, not for each unit but rather for each batch of goods bought. For example, the first 10 units might carry a price of $1.00, the next 30 a price of $.75, the next 50 a price of $.40, etc. Third-degree discrimination involves the ability of the firm to segregate customers according to income, the individuality, or the use to which they will put the good or service, and to charge different prices in each purchase category despite equivalent costs incurred in serving them. As long as the demand elasticities among different buyers are unequal, it will be profitable to post separate prices whenever possible.

The Condition for Discriminatory Pricing

Secondary markets must be eliminated for successful price discrimination. Middlemen must be prevented from buying in the cheaper market and reselling in the higher-priced market, a condition usually satisfied for personal services. Doctors can exact higher fees from rich patients than from poor[2]; dentists and attorneys can act in the same way in the

[1] The classification follows the lines developed by A. C. Pigou, *Economics of Welfare,* ed. 4, Part II, Chapter XVII.

[2] Even here the policy is not uniformly successful, for in the larger cities individuals with higher incomes who can afford to pay for private treatment occasionally appear at clinics run mainly for the poor.

conviction that the lower-priced buyer cannot resell to those who pay the more exorbitant prices. In the sale of electricity, discrimination is usually practiced between household, industrial, and other users. International "dumping," wherein goods are sold for less in overseas markets than in home markets, is a recurring political grievance.

Discriminatory pricing is also occasioned, implicitly, in the practice of granting free delivery to all despite locational differences. Discounts in excess of interest savings for prompt payment, or above the cost reductions for handling large shipments, are also forms of discrimination. Similarly, the practice of granting uniform and liberal "trade-in" allowances, regardless of the value of the unit surrendered, discriminates against those who surrender superior units: when there is a conscious effort to evaluate the returned item, the trade can be looked upon as a part-cash, part-barter operation. Minimum bills submitted by public utilities also retain a flavor of discrimination against those who fail to utilize the permissible minimum service; a more baneful consequence is that it is likely to foster uneconomic use in order to utilize the minimum service. Numerous other practices with a discriminatory aspect undoubtedly can be cited.

Discrimination of the First and Second Degree

In discrimination of the first degree, we can assume either that each purchaser has an inelastic demand and will purchase at most but 1 unit, or that a continuous demand schedule can be written for each buyer. The first hypothesis provides a good introduction, inasmuch as it can be treated succinctly; it can also be characterized as a special instance of third-degree discrimination.

If the individual demand curves are perfectly inelastic at 1 unit, with an uppermost price roof for the inelasticity, and if the roofs of the curves occur at different levels for each individual, then by compounding the separate curves we can derive a fairly smooth and continuous aggregate market-demand curve. If the seller was compelled to announce but one price to all buyers, the usual $MR = MC$ pricing rules would dictate the market price. Since the seller is able to charge separate prices to each consumer, the total revenue for any volume of sales will equal the full area under the demand curve rather than (as in the normal case) the rectangular area formed by the demand price and the perpendiculars to the OX and OY axes. In this illustration of price discrimination, the demand curve itself emerges as the relevant MR curve for the discriminating monopolist.

In Figure 16.1(A), AR is the aggregate demand curve formed from individual demands for but 1 unit, while MR is the ordinary marginal-revenue curve for the nondiscriminating monopolist. Simple monopoly price would be OL ($= DP$) and output would be OD, with total sales

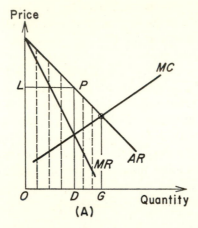

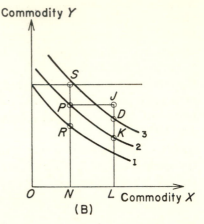

FIG. 16.1

proceeds *OLPD*. In contrast, with inelastic unit demands and price discrimination, each unit of output sells for the demand price above the
unit in question. As further units are sold, sales proceeds are increased
by the additional area included under the demand curve. The discriminating monopolist would push output to *OG*, with each unit marketed
at a different price. The total revenue would equal the full area under
the demand curve, or, alternately, *OG* multiplied by the average price
per unit sold. This result is interesting because it indicates that, despite
the objectionable features on the score of price, sales are greater than
under simple monopoly.

When the same consumer is charged a different price for each unit
purchased, an analysis similar to our monopsony scheme is then pertinent. Strictly speaking, if the discriminating monopolist extracted the
maximum outlay from a purchaser for each additional unit, the buyer
would be confined to the same satisfaction level that would be attained
if the good were removed completely from the economy. If we measured
money on *OY* and commodity on *OX*, the seller could collect the maximum purchase price for 1 unit at this indifference level. After the transaction for the first unit was completed, the seller could then extract the
maximum demand price for a second unit, etc.; in this fashion, a full
demand curve consisting of marginal-demand prices could be traced for
each consumer. Manifestly, the demand curve so constructed would be the
pecuniary expression of the diminishing marginal rate of substitution
between money and the monopolist's commodity, along the fixed indifference curve. The marginal-demand price curve of each consumer would
also be the marginal-revenue curve to the seller. In selling to each individual, the monopolist will push sales so far that the marginal revenues
secured from each buyer will be equal, and each will be equal to the firm's

marginal cost. The equilibrium marginal revenue will also be the price charged to each buyer for the final unit that the firm is prepared to sell to each. The average price paid by each buyer for the full stock purchased will, of course, exceed this marginal price.

In discrimination of the second degree, illustrated in Figure 16.1(B), the consumer may be willing to pay a total sum of SR for ON units of X or a price per unit of SR/ON. If the market price is but SP/ON, well-being will be enhanced; thereupon, the consumer would offer as much as JK/NL per unit for an additional quantity NL; any price below this, such as JD/NL, will elevate well-being. So long as the successive prices for each block of purchases are less than the maximum-demand price for the block, monopoly discrimination of the second degree is less injurious to consumer well-being than first-degree discriminatory pricing.

Price Discrimination of the Third Degree

Discrimination of the third degree, between classes of consumers, where each group buys freely at a separate price, is the most interesting and important of all the discrimination analyses. The monopolist is able to segregate classes of consumers, conceiving independent D and MR curves for each grouping; the equilibrium condition is that the marginal revenue in each market must be the same and equal to the marginal cost of production. Unless the MR's are equal, output of the firm will be transferred from markets of low marginal revenue to markets in which it is higher. It follows that it is remunerative to expand output until MC is equal to the MR obtainable in each market.

Whereas, under simple monopoly, we summate the demand quantities in each market to derive the market-demand curve, and then extract the MR curve as a prelude to the derivation of price and output policy, in discriminatory-pricing problems we summate not the demand quantities at any given price but rather *the sales quantities for any given marginal revenue*. Equating the MR curve so derived to MC, we discover first the firm's output, and, after allocating the total output among the several markets so as to secure the same MR in each, we then learn the prices in each market corresponding to the equilibrium MR.

In Figure 16.2, MR_1 is the marginal-revenue curve in market 1; MR_2 is the marginal-revenue curve in market 2. Summating these curves laterally, we establish the aggregate MR curve, MR_t. As the quantity demanded in market 1 is zero until price falls to OP_1, the MR_t curve coincides with MR_2 until this price height is reached. Drawing MC as the relevant marginal-cost curve, we observe that total output will settle at OL; the MR in each market will be OR with an output amount ON absorbed by market 1 and OM ($= NL$) absorbed by market 2. The price in each market will be the demand price of the respective quantities.

As a special case of discriminatory pricing, the demand may be perfectly elastic in one market while in the other it may assume a normal downward trend. Conceivably, the former may be a foreign market where sales are subject to local competition, while the downward-sloping curve reflects the monopoly facts in the domestic market. In this case, the aggregate marginal-revenue curve follows the MR curve of the domestic market so long as the domestic MR lies above the overseas price, after which MR_t merges with the perfectly elastic demand curve.[3]

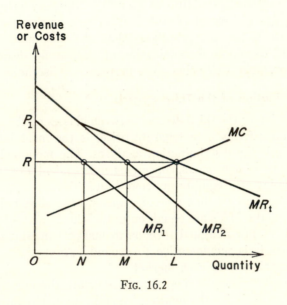

FIG. 16.2

Demand Elasticity and Price Discrimination

Discrepancies in the elasticity of demand are responsible for price discrimination; if, at each price, the demand points on the demand curves for the several market classes were isoelastic, discriminatory pricing would be unprofitable and simple monopoly pricing would prevail.

To prove this, and to deduce that price will be highest in markets in which demand is least elastic, we can invoke a variant of one of the earlier formulas, thus:

$$MR = P(1 - 1/E)^4 \tag{16.1}$$

Since MR is the same in each market, using the subscripts 1 and 2 to denote the different markets:

[3] See Mrs. Robinson, p. 184.
[4] See above, p. 19.

$$P_1(1 - 1/E_1) = P_2(1 - 1/E_2) \qquad (16.2)$$

Therefore,

$$\frac{P_1}{P_2} = \frac{E_2E_1 - E_1}{E_2E_1 - E_2} \qquad (16.3)$$

Hence, if

$$E_1 > E_2 \qquad (16.4)$$

then

$$P_1 < P_2 \qquad (16.5)$$

Simple and Discriminating Monopoly Output

One consideration alone almost suffices to establish the proposition that the discriminatory output will exceed simple monopoly output— namely, that discriminatory pricing may be effective profitwise even in circumstances where a singular price policy cannot promise profits because the AC curve lies everywhere above the simple D curve. For conclusive proof, however, it is necessary to compare the MR curves under simple and discriminating monopoly.

The demand and marginal-revenue curves under simple monopoly are clear and straightforward. Under discriminating monopoly of the third degree, at each MR the sales quantity and price in each market can be learned and hence the total sales proceeds for any given output volume can be computed. Dividing this last sum by the sales quantity, we can calculate the weighted average price for the volume of transactions; this would be the demand point on the relevant demand curve under discrimination. To supplement this average-revenue curve composed of weighted average prices, we can append the discriminatory marginal revenue curve, as MR_t in Figure 16.2. Except in the limiting case where they coincide, the AR per unit of sales for each sales quantity under discrimination exceeds the simple monopoly AR. Consequently, as total sales proceeds for any output are greater under price discrimination, and as the integral sum of the marginal revenues comprises the total revenue for any volume of sales, ordinarily the discriminatory MR curve will be above the simple MR curve, though over some ranges this may not be true. The crucial item involves the relationship of the two MR curves at the output at which $MC = MR$ under simple monopoly. There is the strong presumption that the discriminatory MR curve will be to the right of the simple MR curve, and, hence, that output under discriminatory pricing exceeds output under a singular price policy.

It can be proved that, with linear demand curves in the several markets, the simple and discriminatory MR curves coincide and total output is the same under price discrimination as under simple monopoly, although prices, profits, and the allocation of sales differ from the results achieved under a uniform price policy. In the event that total output is *reduced* under discriminatory pricing, at the simple monopoly price the ratio of the slope of the demand curve to the slope of the marginal-revenue curve in the more elastic market will be less than the value of the same ratio in the less elastic market.[5] This will mean that the less elastic demand curve will be concave, and the more elastic one, linear or convex.

Problems

1. Write a linear demand curve for markets *A* and *B*. Prove that, under price discrimination, output is equal to that of simple monopoly. (Hint: Summate the demand curves for finding the *MR* for simple monopoly. Summate the *MR* curves for discriminatory output.)
2. Using the slope ratio referred to in footnote number 5, draw the demand curves under discrimination in which output is (a) increased; (b) reduced.

Price Discrimination and Universally Lower Prices

It is intriguing to ask whether discriminating monopoly can precipitate lower prices than can simple monopoly in all markets and benefit all consumers, even though the gains are shared unevenly. If output is approximately the same despite discriminatory pricing, it is inevitable that, in some markets, price will be higher, and elsewhere lower, than with a uniform price policy. *Discriminatory pricing is likely to lower prices universally only when the MC curve is falling.* In the latter event (which also implies falling *AC*), the discriminatory *AR* at the ($MR_t =$ *MC*) output may be sufficiently below the simple monopoly price to confer upon all consumers a price lower than under a uniform price policy; with falling *MC* it may be that consumers whose demand prices are below the simple monopoly price can be served profitably.

If a firm abandons its maximum-profit objectives (perhaps being restrained by law, as are public utilities), it is easy to conjure situations where, even without falling marginal costs, price under discrimination is universally below a single monopoly price. For example, demand in a particular category of the market, as industrial demand for electric

[5] The slope ratio is thus defined as:

$$\frac{\text{Slope of demand curve at simple monopoly price}}{\text{Slope of marginal revenue curve at simple monopoly output position}}$$

This last simplification in the theory is due to Edgar O. Edwards, "The Analysis of Output Under Discrimination," *Econometrica* (1950). The original analysis simplifying the entire theory is, of course, attributable to Mrs. Robinson, *Economics of Imperfect Competition* (1933), pp. 190–195.

power, may be highly elastic, but at a price only *below* the simple monopoly price—yet above the monopoly *MR*. Some portion of this market, then, can be served profitably under price discrimination.[6] Hence, the earnings amassed on the latter group will swell the total above the legal amount, fostering a price reduction in the more lucrative and inelastic market sectors in order to restore the aggregate profit balance to the permissible sum. It is thus plausible to argue that discriminatory pricing between classes of consumers redounds beneficially even to those who pay the superficially exorbitant rates.

Price discrimination distorts both the relative economic position implicit in any income division and the real income obtainable from any given expenditure. If a wealthy man has to pay more for the same medical services, say, than a poor man, then the relative differences in money income fail to reflect the ratios of real purchasing power possessed by the two. Substitute and complementary goods will also be affected by the bounties conferred and the levies imposed through the multiple-price system.

This leads to a provocative query: does price discrimination merit a place in an optimal order, especially when cost proceeds can be recovered by discriminatory pricing tactics and market segregation, but not by a universal $(MC = P)$ policy? In those instances in which demand is too narrow to permit a $(P = MC)$ adjustment, or even a uniform $(P = AC)$ arrangement, discriminatory pricing might be advocated on the grounds that it can evoke outputs from which most consumers benefit, as revealed by their willingness to pay discriminatory prices. Nonetheless, there are elements of arbitrariness and favoritism in its practice.

SUBSTITUTE GOODS

Buyers of the firm's commodity A may also be potential purchasers of the $B, C, D, \ldots$ varieties sponsored by the multiple-product firm; the demands for the several varieties are interrelated. Compared to discrimination where the costs of preparing goods for each market were identical, we can now suppose that costs are unrelated.[7] There is an implicit element of discrimination so long as the prices of the firm's several varieties

---

[6] Suppose that the proscribed earnings of a public utility electric power company are $100,000 and that it can recover a sum of $25,000 over variable charges by selling power to a railroad only at a price below the simple monopoly figure in view of the ability of the railroad to generate its own electricity, if necessary. By selling the power to the railway, the electric power company thereupon need recover only $75,000 from household users.

[7] There may be some separable costs, but, analytically, these can be deducted from the demand curves of the particular markets, after which the solution follows directly.

are disproportionate to their marginal costs, but this is typical of all discrepancies in the degree of monopoly power among markets.

A simple illustration of the problem of pricing substitute goods is the practice of pricing theater seats according to their location; this practice has a discriminatory element in that the cost of serving all patrons is almost indistinguishable. In a sense, the propagation of substitute goods by a firm is reminiscent of discriminatory pricing in that the firm makes an effort to ferret out individuals and market sectors with different demand elasticities, and then produces goods designed to profit from the taste idiosyncrasies.

Diagrammatic Analysis

Diagrammatically, the equilibrium can be depicted by measuring the total revenue of commodity B (that is, TR_b) along the vertical axis and the price of B on the horizontal axis. If we fix a price P_a for the substitute commodity A, the TR_b curve will be bell-shaped: as P_b rises TR_b will rise, reach a maximum, and then fall as the demand for P_b enters a stretch of inelasticity. Similarly, when P_b is zero, sales in A at the given P_a will be at a minimum; A's sales will expand, by and large, as P_b mounts. Given the P_a, the total revenue in A for each P_b can thus be superimposed upon the TR_b curve, resulting in a combined TR_{a+b} curve, consisting of the total revenue obtained in both markets for the stipulated P_a linked to each possible P_b. Presumably, as P_b rises, the spread between TR_{a+b} and TR_b will widen. At some P_b, however, the composite curve will attain a maximum and then decline.

Total costs (TC) of the implicit A and B outputs can be included on the same diagram in order to compute the price combination of maximum profit. As P_b ascends, the TC_b will decrease. But, as P_b rises, the sales of A increase, so that TC_a will mount. Weighing the opposing forces, we might assume provisionally that the total TC_{a+b} sum for the relevant quantities demanded at the respective prices is fairly constant. The most profitable P_b, given the P_a, can then be extracted.[8]

A similar diagram would have to be drawn for each and every possible P_a and the true maximum (P_a,P_b) combination would have to be selected from among the various particular maxima computed in this way. With more than two substitute commodities sold by the firm, the diagrammatic technique becomes cumbersome and mathematical methods will serve best; in practice, the firm would have to form a rough estimate of the likely price arrangement for maximum profits, thereby reducing the pricing problem to manageable dimensions.

[8] It is suggested that the student draw these curves as an exercise. How can the cross-elasticity of demand be employed in this analysis?

Equilibrium Conditions

The equilibrium position can also be expressed in marginal terms; for experimental maximum-price determination this is often more informative than operating with aggregates. Positing any P_a, B output will expand until the MC_b equals MR_b minus the diminution in profits on A at the constant P_a. Symbolically,

$$MC_b = MR_b - \Delta R_a \qquad (16.6)$$

where ΔR_a represents the loss in profits on A due to its constricted sales at the fixed P_a (as P_b falls), minus the reduction in the total costs of producing A. Thus,

$$\Delta R_a = \Delta TR_a - \Delta TC_a \qquad (16.7)$$

where ΔTR_a equals the fall in sales receipts on A at the given P_a as B expands by 1 unit, and ΔTC_a represents the fall in the total cost of producing the diminished A volume. Hence, the production of B will be checked as a result of these roundabout market repercussions. Similar equations could be written for each P_a, so that the true maximum (P_a, P_b) price set could be selected. Equivalent equations can be written if P_b, instead of P_a, is regarded as the datum. Price-reaction curves can also be employed to reveal the mutually satisfactory maximum-price combination for the two-commodity case.

The equilibrium condition discloses that the output of one product will be restrained whenever the substitutes are monopolized by one firm, as compared with each being offered for sale by independent firms.

COMPLEMENTARY GOODS

Goods were generally complementary, we recall, when a fall in the price of one led to an increased demand for the other.[9] Let us examine the pricing problem when a complementary pair of goods are sold by the same firm. With separate firms there would be a tendency to keep output low and prices high, for each firm would perceive the futility of a price cut followed by a price rise of the complement.

Complementarity in Variable Proportions

Again, we posit price P_a and assume that A and B are independent in production. Demand and the total-revenue curve for B, with P_b the variable, can then be derived. Superimposing on TR_b the total revenue amassed in the A market at the given P_a and the variable P_b, we can

---

[9] This is not strictly accurate, as a review of the earlier treatment will make plain. But it will do for our purposes here. See pp. 85–86, above.

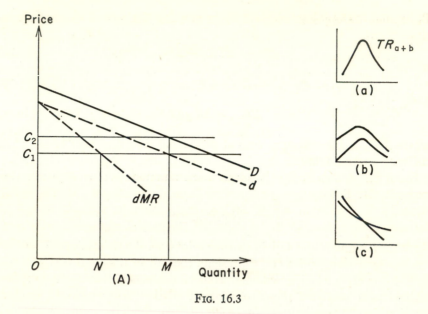

FIG. 16.3

construct a TR_{a+b} curve. This aggregate-revenue curve will taper off to the right, as shown in Figure 16.3(a), for ultimately, as P_b keeps rising, A's sales will be unaffected since the complementary bond gradually dissolves. Total revenue in A will be at its peak when P_b is zero; the likely curve relations are indicated in Figure 16.3(b). If A's only use were one complementary to B, as P_b rose sufficiently then TR_{a+b} and TR_b would fall to zero off to the right.

The combined output at the fixed P_a, clearly, will be greatest when P_b is zero. Total costs of A plus B will, therefore, reach their peak on OY and drop as P_b increases. Typically, profits will be at their highest where the spread between TR_{a+b} and TC_{a+b} is at a maximum. To find the maximal of the various maximum-price combinations, similar diagrams would have to be drawn for each P_a and the true maximum ferreted out from among all the particular maximum P_a, P_b price sets.

The marginal conditions for profit maximization necessarily resemble those adduced for substitute goods, with a change in signs. On this score we may infer that, when complementary goods are controlled by a single firm, the output volume will surpass that of independent firms.

Symbolically,

$$MC_b = MR_b + \Delta R_a \tag{16.8}$$

where ΔR_a represents the augmented profits in A at the constant P_a as P_b falls. The value ΔR_a is the compound resultant of: (1) an increase in sales revenue as more A units are sold at the fixed P_a through the fall in

P_b, minus (2) the increase in TC_a in meeting the new A demand quantity.[10] Thus,

$$\Delta R_a = \Delta TR_a - \Delta TC_a \qquad (16.9a)$$

where

$$\Delta TR_a = P_a \Delta A \qquad (16.9b)$$

and

$$\Delta TC_a = MC_a \Delta A \qquad (16.9c)$$

where MC_a is the marginal cost of producing a further unit of A, while ΔA may exceed 1 unit.[11]

Since the A commodity becomes more remunerative as B production expands, the B output will be pushed beyond the simple $(MC_b = MR_b)$ equality to a level at which $MC_b > MR_b$. As this equality would be satisfied at each possible P_a, then, of all the partial maximum-price combinations, the price combination that promised the largest profit sum of all would be announced by the multiple-commodity monopolist.[12] Using reaction curves for the equilibrium adaptation, measuring prices along the axes, the curve pair would take the path indicated in Figure 16.3(c).

Complementarity in Fixed Proportions

As a partial proof of the proposition that the output of complementary goods under unified control will surpass the combined total output when they are produced separately, we may consider the extreme illustration of complements demanded in a fixed proportion—as, for example, a pair of shoes. The demand curve for the pair is represented by the linear demand curve D in Fig. 16.3(A). The marginal-cost curve of the right shoe is constant and equal to OC_1 while the marginal-cost curve of the left shoe, also constant, is C_1C_2. If both items are processed by one firm pricing competitively, output will be OM and the sales price for the

[10] Conceivably, the firm may be unwilling to furnish the full quantity of A demanded at the fixed P_a if this would involve $MC_a > P_a$. Rationing of sales may be considered, although this will itself have repercussions on the sales of B. Ruling out rationing as inexpedient, the ensuing ΔP_a would, with the failure to produce more A, check the fall in P_b.

[11] This might be written more elegantly in formal mathematics; the expression, however, is accurate enough for our purposes.

[12] The equilibrium analysis has been couched in terms of a postulated price of one product, while the output and price of the other product vary. The results would be much the same if, instead of positing, say, P_a with A and B sales, and P_b flexible, the A output were frozen and P_a allowed to fluctuate. In some ways this procedure is simpler, for, with A's total production costs constant, ΔR_a (the profit variation) reduces itself merely to a change in total sales proceeds on the stable A output. The implications for the B output are the same: a contractionist tendency for substitutes and an expansionist force for complements.

pair, OC_2. Under monopolistic pricing, the output would be ON or $\frac{1}{2}OM$, the "competitive" total.

Suppose that each of the shoes is supplied by several independent firms and that a price equal to marginal cost, C_1C_2, is exacted for the left shoe.[13] Subtracting this sum laterally from D, we can derive a new demand curve, d, for the right shoe. If the latter were priced monopolistically, OC_1 would be equated to the marginal-revenue correspondent of d; recalling that the MR curve would fall twice as fast as curve d, and as d cuts C_1 at OM output, production would settle at ON.

Hence, when the shoes are manufactured under separate ownership, and the specialists producing the left shoe seek to equate price and MC, the output volume for the fixed complementary pair equals only that of a single monopolist producing the complementary pair of items. At separate monopoly prices, or at a price for the left shoe in excess of C_1C_2, the total output would fall short of ON, the amount for a multiple-product firm producing the complementary pair.[14] Complementary demand is thus likely to impart a strong incentive to the creation of a multiple-product firm.

Loss Leaders and Tie-in Sales

"Loss leaders" provide an illustration of the pricing of complementary goods. The term refers to the practice of retail stores of selling certain goods sharply below the customary price and publicizing this fact through advertising, intending the loss leader to arouse consumer interest in the goods and, through purchase and sampling and the cultivation of a taste for it, to swing future demand permanently to the right. Here the complementarity is between present and future demand. Alternately, retail shops will underprice well-known brand commodities in order to attract shoppers and stimulate concomitant purchases of other merchandise. If commodity A is the leader, it is quite possible for $MC_a > MR_a$ and even MC_a to be greater than P_a: the direct losses are incidental so long as they are overshadowed by the indirect gains in the accompanying complementary lines.

For a loss leader to be effective, the cross-elasticity of demand between A and B, C, D, ... will have to be strong. There is likely to be some asymmetry here; the cross-elasticity resulting from a fall in P_a may well exceed the cross-elasticity of a fall in P_b. Besides involving a high cross-elasticity, the direct elasticity of demand ought to be low, and that of supply high, for otherwise the direct losses are likely to outweigh the indirect complementary gains. A zero direct-demand elasticity and an

---

[13] To obviate the prospect of duopoly complementarity, we can assume that there are numerous suppliers of the shoes.

[14] For the original diagram and the famous illustration of knife handles and blades, see Marshall, p. 384n.

infinite but negative cross-elasticity would comprise the ideal loss-leader conditions. Frequently, purchasers of loss leaders will be rationed as to the quantity provided at the submerged price. This serves, implicitly, to cut the demand elasticity and limits the direct losses suffered by the seller while still evoking complementary buying of other commodities.

"Tie-in" sales provide another concrete example of complementarity; here the buyer is compelled to combine other purchases with the featured goods.[15] In effect, a joint good is offered the purchaser and the relevant valuations are those respecting the commodity pair; the result is to create an unnatural indivisibility. Largely, though not entirely, the practice will enable the firm to alleviate the rigors of competition in the tied-in product, extending its monopoly power over the commodity pair. Literally, there is an infinite array of tie-in arrangements: $1Y$ may be tied to $1X$, $2Y$ to $1X$, etc., with the firm choosing the combination that maximizes profits. Sometimes the tie-in proviso requires that an aggregate value sum of other goods must be bought with $1X$; in principle, this sum would be chosen in such a way as to maximize profits. Normally, "tie-ins" will be effective when it is difficult to dispense with the main commodity and, of course, when the terms of the "tie-ins" are attractive; where substitution for the presumed "lever" commodity can be readily accomplished, the policy is a notorious failure. Packaged sales, with an offer to "buy one and get one free," are a form of tie-in practice often commended to the firm as a means of introducing a new commodity to a potentially receptive audience.[16]

The "Two-Part" Tariff

The "two-part" tariff may also be treated under the general heading of the pricing of complementary goods. Here the consumer is called upon to pay two different sums: a fixed charge independent of utilization and another charge varying with use. For example, public utilities usually

---

[15] The American Shoe Machinery Co. furnishes the classic example of a "tying" agreement in intermediate products. Possessing an exclusive and essential patent in shoe-making machinery, it compelled shoemakers to buy other materials and machinery as a condition of purchase of the former. See A. R. Burns, *The Decline of Competition*, pp. 452–453. For an interesting article on related practices in the consumer market, see W. A. Lewis, "Notes on the Economics of Loyalty," *Economica* (1942).

[16] Another type of tie-in sale, "full-line forcing," compels a dealer to store and sell all the multiple products of the parent firm as a condition of purchasing one of them. When the dealer is obliged to purchase the sundry list of items, the distributive facilities may be effectively closed to a vast array of competitive producers because of the limited physical and financial resources of dealers. This tends to stifle competition at the distributive level and to narrow the list of alternatives open to consumers.

exact a minimum bill and then levy a toll contingent on extra services rendered. Or an amusement park will charge an entry fee and then charge a separate sum for each individual ride or entertainment. Economically, the two-part toll would seem to be merited if one payment referred, say, to installation costs of essential supplementary equipment, such as the telephone and wiring, or the transmission and distribution lines for gas and electric-power service, and if the other payment was levied to cover the costs involved in rendering the variable flow of services actually consumed. In this event, the facilities and the services can be conceived as complementary items in variable proportions. However, the dual toll appears to lend itself to abuse when we consider the relatively inelastic installation demand compared to the more elastic demand for the service flow.

Questions

(These involve mainly cases of interdependence on both the demand and the cost sides.)

1. A firm produces goods X, Y, Z which are substitutes on the demand side but independent on the cost side.
    a. Write the marginal-revenue condition for an expansion in X, with outputs Y and Z constant.
    b. If the marginal-cost curves for each of the products are identical, what must be the relation of MR's and MC?
    c. If the firm sells the same product in separate cities, X, Y, Z, with transport costs to X zero, and to Y amounting to T_y per unit, and T_z to Z where $T_y > T_z$, indicate the nature of the marginal-revenue relations. Assume, first, identical linear-demand curves and then, diverse demand conditions. What is the effect on output and sales allocation of a change in transport costs?

2. Write the marginal-revenue conditions for X and Y produced in fixed proportions and which are substitutes on the demand side.
    a. Assume that $\Delta P_x = \Delta P_y$ upon an output expansion, and that $\Delta X = \Delta Y \gtreqless 0$. How is the combined MR simplified in this case?
    b. What restriction must be placed on the respective MR's? What is the effect of the demand substitution on the combined output?
    c. If the goods are demand complements and the minus ΔP_x equals the positive ΔP_y, write the combined marginal revenue. What is the effect on output in this case? If $\Delta P_x \gtreqless \Delta P_y$?

3. Work out the MR relations for demand substitutes and complements produced in variable proportions, with an expansion in X with Y constant. Assume, instead, that total cost outlay is constant, while X expands and Y contracts. How do the marginal relations appear for this case? Assuming that $\Delta P_x = \Delta P_y$, how is the result simplified?

4. Suppose that X and Y are substitutes in production and consumption.
    a. Fix the X output and write the marginal revenue for Y, remembering that the cost curve for X will be dislodged. (Hint: Use the concept of average cost for X.)

b. What is the effect of each substitutionary relation on X output?

c. If the substitutionary relations are very strong, what implications can be drawn?

5. Assuming that X and Y are complements in production and consumption, proceed as in (4).

6. Assuming that they are substitutes in production, and complements in consumption, proceed as in (4). Reverse the assumptions and answer the same questions.

MONOPSONY DISCRIMINATION

After the protracted analyses of monopoly price discrimination, the exposition of monopsony price discrimination can be more modest. Instances of monopsony discrimination undoubtedly can be found; purchasers may pay different prices to various sellers of identical products or pay equally skilled workmen different wages.

It would be possible to distinguish various types of monopsony price discrimination. In discrimination of the first degree, a different price would be paid by the buyer to the seller for each *unit* purchased. To the buyer the effective supply curve (the MSC) would be the seller's ordinary market-supply curve; purchases would cease at the transaction volume at which this intersected the (marginal) demand curve. But, before proclaiming that output and price will, therefore, rest at the competitive level, we must remember that the demand curve under monopsony is drawn under different assumptions than the normal demand curve.[17] Moreover, the seller will recoup proceeds only equal to the area *under* the supply curve rather than equal to the rectangular area formed by the price and sales of the n units of output.[18]

Monopsony of the second degree, of "step" prices for different quantities, is also possible; bonuses may be paid by the buyer as part of a plan to stimulate production, just as price discounts may be given by the seller to accelerate sales.

In monopsony discrimination of the third degree—monopsony discrimination proper—the principles of discrimination follow familiar lines. When the supply and marginal-supply (MSC) curves are drawn for each seller and the quantities offered by each seller at each MSP summated, the monopsonist is pictured as equating the aggregate MSC to his demand curve, thereafter paying each seller the price implicit at the equality. Hence, the basic condition is the equality of demand price and marginal-supply price in each segment of the market. But prices paid each supplier will be different.

All this is consistent enough with our previous analyses, enabling us

[17] See above, pp. 276–277.

[18] Economic rent, in effect, would be obliterated; the monopsonist buyer would pay solely the sums necessary for compensating the desired versatile factors.

to dispense with the diagrammatics. However, it should be observed that, if the supply curve of but one selling firm is falling, the corresponding MSC will lie below the supply curve and the volume of purchases ought to surpass the competitive norm, with market price lower. Where the demand curve is one of factor hire, however, this would involve the monopsony firm in aggregate losses, for the monopsony-factor price would exceed the MVP of the factors. However, as a selling firm with decreasing supply price will capture the entire sales market, to the exclusion of the other firms, ultimately the relationship should degenerate into one of bilateral monopoly, although the presence of potential alternate suppliers will strengthen the hands of the buyer—the discriminating monopsonist—against the seller.

Monopsony and Interrelated Supply

Paralleling the discussion of demand interrelations, a monopsonist will have to exercise a keener sense of price discretion when supply curves are interrelated. For example, if X and Y are complements in production, buying fewer units and paying a lower price per unit for commodity X might lift the supply curve of commodity Y, which may also be bought by the monopsonist. Taking Y purchases as fixed in amount, the MSP_x must be reduced by $Y \Delta P_y$, for this decrease in expenditure on the fixed amount of Y occurs as more X is bought and a higher P_x is paid. In view of these ramifications, the monopsonist would be disposed to buy more and pay a higher price for X than indicated at the simple $D_x = MSC$ equality. Conversely, when X and Y are production substitutes, buying but a few units and paying a lower P_x might lower the supply curve for Y, forcing it to the right and lowering P_y. This would impel the monopsonist to buy fewer X and pay a lower P_x than in those situations in which these ramifications could be overlooked.

DEMAND INTERDEPENDENCE OVER TIME

Just as a multiple-product firm may produce substitute and complementary goods, when we view the time dimensions of the production problem future demand may be influenced by current price. Essentially, the same physical product available at different dates is a different good so that the firm producing one physical item for different time intervals is regarded as producing different goods.

Price Policy and Future Demand

Just as current output will influence future production costs and profits, a monopolist will also perceive a relationship between the t_1 price and the $t_2, t_3, t_4, \ldots, t_n$ demand. There are at least three discrete cases to be distinguished: (1) Firms frequently conclude that consumers can be encouraged by a low current price to purchase their product and thereby become permanent purchase adherents. This might be termed the "introductory offer" case, essentially an evidence of complementary demand. (2) Firms will predict the extent to which consumers will accelerate their purchases and advance them to t_1 from t_2, t_3, ... dates by lower current prices below the expected (perhaps publicized) future levels. This can be called a case of "accelerated selling" wherein current and future purchases are substitutes. (3) Firms will weigh the consequences of low current prices on future demand, fearing the possibility of "spoiling the market." That is to say, a low current price may engender a reluctance of the buyers to pay more in the future in the belief that the commodity "is not worth more," or because of the revulsion toward the ethics of a seller whose price is unduly raised. Although there are elements common to each, to delineate their distinctive features each case is accorded a brief and independent exposition.

In introducing new goods or to enlarge the market for known goods, a monopolist will often reason that a lower current price will encourage some consumers to experiment and purchase the good in lieu of substitute commodities, with the result that he builds some lasting attachments and future demand is permanently shifted to the right. Alternately, just as low prices stimulate experimentation, relatively high prices will deter even customary demand and encourage the trial of substitute commodities. Hence, monopolists will be willing to charge prices below the immediate maximization figures, foregoing present profits in the expectation that these will be recouped in the future. The action pattern, however, can pertain only to monopoly markets, for the thoroughly competitive firm would be unable to exert more than an imperceptible influence over future demand and price.

In terms of the cross-elasticities of demand, where the relative current price change constitutes the denominator and future purchases the numerator, the cross-elasticity would be negative—the usual complementarity relation. The principle determining the extent to which it will pay to forego current profits (or accept current losses) may be stated tersely: it will be worth while to lower the current price and suffer a diminution in current profits so long as the immediate sacrifice is outweighed by a future gain in profits, with the latter discounted to date. In the continuous case, where the future gains in profit stemming from a current fall of price successively diminish, equilibrium will emerge at the equality of the two. Equationally, we have:

$$MR_1 + \Delta R_2 = MC_1 \qquad (16.10)$$

where ΔR_2 is the increment in profits in t_2 caused by the rightward movement in the t_2 demand curve emanating from the decrement ΔP_1 in P_1.

Hence, when account is taken of the temporal relationships, output and sales will be greater and price lower than if the firm were blind to this interdependence.[19]

In contrast to the preceding analysis, where a lower t_1 price increased demand and profit opportunities in t_2, a firm will often conclude that, as price falls in t_1, demand in t_2 will be depressed, with the t_2 demand curve shifting to the left, as with all substitute goods. The cross-elasticity of demand between the goods is thus positive; from each current MR there must now be deducted (or to each current MC there must now be added) this additional cost of the expected loss in future revenue: ΔR_2 in the preceding equation is a negative quantity. User costs become unduly repressive, with future-cost curves raised and future-demand curves contracted. Needless to say, this bodes ill for output and price in t_1: production will be restrained and price will be higher than with an uncorrected $MR = MC$ policy in t_1. Any suggestion of reducing t_1 prices will arouse misgivings; firms will shy away from advancing customer purchase dates and destroying future profit opportunities.[20]

The notion of a price policy "spoiling the market" (historically associated with the name of Alfred Marshall) is, unfortunately, unduly vague in many respects. To Marshall it appeared to mean an unwillingness to sell at lower prices because of the depressing influences on future demand; consumers in the future would be unwilling to pay higher prices.[21] In a period of low current demand and costs, as in the midst of a business depression, in contemplating current price below "normal" past levels a firm will apprehend that, in a future business upsweep, consumers may rebel at higher prices, forestalling their purchases from t_2 to t_3, t_4, ..., etc., in the belief that the t_2 price rise is but temporary. This effect must

[19] Diagrammatically, a construction similar to the user-cost construction of Figure 15.6 could show the equilibrium position; rather than add on "user costs" to MC_v, we could deduct sums in amount equal to the discounted value of the greater future profits occasioned by each t_1 price fall and output advance. If there are user costs of equipment, however, these could neutralize the future demand and profit rise. If a lower t_1 price favored profits through a longer future extending beyond t_2, the full current value of these sums would constitute the ΔR component.

[20] As a possible exception, however, if the firm plans to go out of business or convert its facilities to another commodity variety, this negative future effect will be disregarded, for the firm will literally want to advance consumer purchase dates.

[21] This appears to be the usual impression, although Marshall was not very specific (*Principles*, pp. 377, 849). Professor Pigou in one place interpreted it as "selling a thing in bad times at such a price, and, therefore, in such quantities, that in subsequent good times the market is already stocked." We have already included this relationship under the heading of temporal substitutability and accelerated selling (*Industrial Fluctuations*, ed. 2, p. 186).

be weighed before proclaiming a low current price; it has its analogy, in principle, in the version of accelerated selling.

But, more than this, the firm will reason that the subsequent "necessary" price rise in t_2, because of changed cost circumstances, say, will incur the wrath of consumers and dissipate their "good will," transferring their custom to more "ethical" competitors. The suspicion that the firm is "unfair" will grow—that it charges low prices until an advantage can be gained. Rather than inflame some very human sentiments, a firm might hold prices in t_1 *above* the immediate minimum that would be counseled by a more rigid application of the current maximum-profit rule.

Low Price and Poor Quality

As an alternative interpretation of "market spoiling" through a current price fall, in the partly irrational real world a lowering of price may cast an aura of cheapness about the commodity so that not only is the demand quantity at lower prices immediately reduced in t_1—rather than enlarged—but also forever after there will lurk in the minds of uninformed consumers an aversion to the commodity and a belief that it is essentially an inferior variety. Future demand may never recover from this hapless price move—a phenomenon that has its roots in consumer ignorance of quality and the "conspicuous-consumption" attitudes of buyers of some goods. Hence, a firm will be wary of temporary "low-price" innovations: the higher current income may auger substantial losses through time.

Price Policy and Potential Competition

There are a few more cases akin to the intertemporal demand relations that deserve some scrutiny; they can be joined in this section for expository convenience. Briefly, the subjects are (1) the influence of potential competition on current price policy, (2) the effect on monopsony price policy of the interdependence of current price and future supply, and (3) advertising outlays and future demand.

Potential competition is often declared to be a potent force checking maximum monopoly pricing on the grounds that the resulting swell of profits will hasten the entry of producers of substitutes; this will, it is averred, enforce a less avaricious price policy in order to forestall future competition and enable the firm to enjoy a lower but more permanent level of profits. In a similar vein, it is alleged that a nonmaximum monopoly price policy will be instituted to banish the specter of government regulation. But there is a subtle difference in the two cases: to block entry of new sellers, price will have to be depressed to levels *below* the monopoly level; however, to still the clamor for regulation it is only essential that profits do not appear exorbitant. The latter result can be achieved, and the issue obscured just as effectively, as much by an inordinately high price as by a low one, for net income is reduced on both sides of the monopoly price.

The main principle covering these cases is scarcely novel. It will be prudent, where new entry is threatened, to lower current prices and maintain them low, so long as the expected discounted future additions to revenue in forestalling entry exceed the current revenue sacrifices through lowering price. Each further lowering of current price that succeeds in deterring entry will work to sustain the future demand curves for the firm. A higher t_1 price, say, which invites entry in t_2, would reduce the t_2 and later demand curves of the firm. Price policy, thus, is transformed into a persuasive instrument that enables the firm to live a quieter, more secure, but less spectacular profit life. As the lower current price is correlated with greater future demand, so that the cross-elasticity of demand is negative, we witness another case of complementarity.

Despite frequent protestations and professions of its validity, the weight to be assigned to such phenomena in the real world is rather dubious. When entry is easy because fixed and specialized equipment is unimportant to a new firm, it is hardly likely that a firm will forego the bird in hand for the hypothetical and very uncertain future bird in the bush. If entry is difficult, requiring expensive equipment, only if the existing firm scents plans for encroachments by a new and huge transgressor need it commence a low-price policy. In brief, it is most likely that the bludgeon of price reductions will be exhibited only when the rumblings of entry are audible, for, until they crystallize, the firm will perceive the advantage in a maximum current price policy designed to enrich it immediately and gird it for a lasting conflict.[22] In the same way, the view that the fear of government regulation invariably restrains monopoly-price exactions seems altogether too sanguine. Everything will depend on the political climate and the shrewdness, the deliberateness, and the callousness of the monopolist. If the atmosphere is ominous and charged with the threat of government regulation, the monopolist will have to assess the degree to which this can be mitigated by judicious price manipulations. In times when regulatory control is unlikely, caution and price restraint can be discarded.

Temporal Aspects of Monopsony and Sales-Outlay Policies

Under monopoly, it was demonstrated that the firm might well maneuver its price policy to sway future demand or supply. A monopsonist

---

[22] Rightly, this aspect of the case falls in the realm of strategy and tactics of economic warfare. See Chapter 11.

may likewise ponder the influence of its current price policy on future profits. For example, a low wage may dissuade labor from moving to the area, may prejudice the acquisition and the development of skills, etc. A calculating monopsonist, therefore, will weigh the future perturbations evoked by the present market-price policy. As future profits will be affected, the discounted value of these sums, positive or negative, must be set off against t_1 profits at each t_1 price. Thus, at each point on the *MSC* curve of Figure 14.1, we must add or deduct the discounted incremental future profits or losses through paying the associated supply-curve price. Injecting "user" costs in this way, the effect ordinarily will be to drive current monopsony price closer to the $(P = S)$ alignment. Writing ΔR_2 for the future gains attributable to a *higher* current price, the maximum condition becomes

$$MDP + \Delta R_2 = MSP \qquad (16.11)$$

Time Dimensions of Sales Outlays

In a similar vein, it was presumed in the earlier analysis of sales outlays that the augmented demand that was attracted accrued in precisely the same time period as that in which the promotional disbursements were incurred. Although this assumption is, of course, false, for the demand rise is maintained through successive time intervals, the corrections to be made are quite minor. Whatever the sales outlays, the firm must be conceived as weighing its effect on demand in $t_1, t_2, t_3, \ldots, t_n$. The estimated surge in profits through the future must be discounted to date, and balanced against sales outlays, prior to embarking upon the selling program. Insisting on the time dimensions of the problem, it seems unlikely that a firm will, in t_1, recoup the full amount of t_1 sales outlay, especially if the product is a new one, struggling for a place on the consumer's purchase scale and requiring heavy educational expenditures. Immediate losses, rather than profits, may be the conspicuous element.

INVENTORY AND PROFIT EXPECTATIONS

More so than most phenomena, inventory accumulations cannot be poured into the stationary mold, however ingenious the effort: they belong only to the dynamic and uncertain world. Holding stocks of goods is costly; business men must expect to reap some gain from the idle stockpile. If prices never changed, and if future demand and cost were invariant, inventories would be practically nil, arising mainly from physical discontinuities in production and consumption, such as seasonal harvests and recurring daily consumption. In principle, however, the analysis resembles that of price discrimination among several markets. Briefly, the following motives might be distilled to explain the vast majority of inventory accumulations, where these include the salable goods that the firm, at its discretion, chooses to carry over to a future period:

1. The prospect of financial gain through a price rise or, under monopoly, a future lift of demand and/or cost—it is a notorious fact that, when price optimism pervades, stockpiles increase sharply.

2. The firm's desire to guarantee its ability to accommodate an abnormally high volume of sales so that unforeseen custom is not refused; here inventory is a buffer—an uncertainty allowance whose additional cost may be small and whose potential lucrativeness may be large. In recent years this has been analyzed in probability terms, as a case involving random variations in demand.

3. The desire to save on transportation charges by making "block" purchases rather than piecemeal purchases—dealers are likely to hold abnormal stocks that fluctuate discontinuously between the high point at moment of delivery to the low point just prior to replenishment.

4. The desire to ensure stability of operations when dislocations are foreseen, such as strikes, physical factors, etc.

5. The observance of customary business practices that call for window displays and well-stocked shelves as sales-promotion measures (in this instance, the inventories are a form of selling cost).

6. A final reason (though not a motive) for inventory accumulations is found in the unexpected and unplanned accumulations due to a rate of sales below that expected. This last case will be analyzed later in discussing the reaction of the system to change, for these stocks, which are utterly unplanned, are not the result of conscious entrepreneurial calculations.

On a general plane, these are probably the major reasons for holding goods that are already complete and ready for resale. For goods in process, in various states of completion, there would have to be added the rate of input and the time length of production. In the list enumerated above, we can ignore the third, the fifth, and the sixth reasons as irrelevant at this stage, while the fourth reason itself involves an expectation of future demand and costs, for dislocations ultimately involve costs. Hence, the prospect of price rises and a rate of sales greater than estimated (the first and second reasons above) command our attention; the buffer motive, however, may be disposed of rather summarily.

If a firm holds on hand quantities in excess of those required for current sales or expected future price rises, the cause will mainly be the lack of complete confidence in its sales forecasts.[23] The cost of holding inventory may be small, whereas the prospects may be good that prices

---

[23] See p. 343.

or sales will currently or in the near future vastly exceed estimates. On the balance of considerations, the firm will be led to hold stocks. The firm may rule out as highly improbable those prices and sales that are lower than estimated, with better prospects possible even if not likely; inventory holdings will impart to the firm the flexibility to profit by a favorable turn in fortunes. Virtually we are led to argue that, after the firm's forecasts are completed, it engages in another series of estimates to allow for undue pessimism in its projected estimates.[24] The maximum inventory total will then be selected after an appraisal of inventory-holding costs compared with the possible augmentation of price proceeds over and above the most probable levels.

Before elaborating the effects that potential demand and supply changes have upon decisions to produce for inventory, we might enumerate the costs associated with inventory carry-over. They are: (1) interest costs on the current money value of the inventory; (2) storage and maintenance cost on the stockpile; (3) physical depreciation and possible obsolescence of the inventory components; (4) insurance charges, to guard against fire, theft, malfeasance, etc.; and (5) a risk allowance for loss through erroneous predictions. These elements will appear as instrumental in the ensuing analysis.

Production for Inventory: Competitive Markets

Figure 16.4 facilitates the analysis of the degree of production for inventory by competitive firms when their forecast for prices for t_2 differs from the opinion held for t_1. The horizontal P_2P_2 line represents the expected t_2 price and P_1P_1, the current price; MC is the current marginal-cost curve. Drawing $P_2P_1'P_2'$, the ordinate amounts $P_2 - P_2'$ at each output summarize the additional carrying costs for the corresponding unit of output when held over in reserve for sales in t_2. Consequently, the curve $P_2P_1'P_2'$ embodies the *net* t_2 price expectation on each unit of current output.

Considering these relations, until an output OM has been reached it will be profitable to assign t_1 output to inventory rather than to sell it currently, for this will enlarge aggregate income in amount $P_2P_1'P_1$. But beyond OM, current sales will be more lucrative than withholding for future disposal. Clearly, if the current price P_1 rose relative to P_2, the inventory carryover would be cut; in the limit if $P_1 \geqq P_2$, inventory holdings will be nil. In the event that the horizontal P_1P_1 line cuts MC

---

[24] Calculations of this nature lend credence to A. G. Hart's insistence that, in an uncertain world, the uncertainty allowances cannot be discounted and equated to a simple indifference equivalent. See his *Anticipations, Uncertainty and Dynamic Planning* (1940).

at or below the intersection of MC and $P_2P_1'P_2'$, all of t_1 output would be destined for inventory and t_2 sale. If we posit the t_2 price expectations of each competitive firm, then so long as the general view is that $P_2 > P_1$, there will be production for inventory. If the spread in expected prices is at all large, then current output may vastly exceed the current rate of sales. Even if there are discrepant views on the future, with a scatter of individual ideas involving $P_1 \gtrless P_2$, some inventory production will appear.[25]

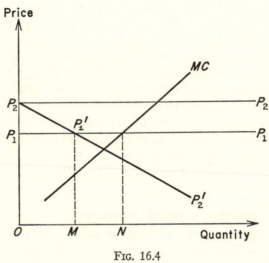

Fig. 16.4

Production for Inventory: Monopoly

The usual monopoly $P > MC = MR$ output principle may also be suspended when provision is made for production for inventory; the current output may surpass the simple, single-period output foreshadowed at the $MR = MC$ adjustment.

In general terms, the equilibrium condition of monopoly production for inventory can be stated concisely. Glossing over the complication due to the discounting of future MR's and the carrying costs on holding

[25] By a like analysis, we can determine whether it will be remunerative for the firm to consign to future sale inventory that has been built up in the past, or to unload it immediately; if the carryover amounts to OM or less, all of it will be reserved for t_2; if it exceeds OM, the excess will be disposed of currently.

When the time horizon is enlarged to include t_3, t_4, . . . , etc., the principle governing the time dimensions of sales is obvious enough: the firm will plan to sell quantities of current output until the marginal net revenue expected in each period is equal to current market price and marginal cost. This plan will entail that the future price expectations exceed the t_1 price, by some positive balance even after deducting carrying costs.

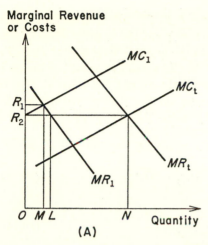

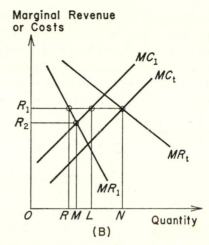

FIG. 16.5

current output until the future, in the final equilibrium there must be the full equality of

$$MR_1 = MR_2 = MC_1 = MC_2 \qquad (16.12)$$

where the subscripts refer to t_1 and t_2, respectively. Otherwise, if $MR_2 > MR_1$, it would be profitable to carry over some units of stock, while, if $MC_2 > MC_1$, current production would be a profitable substitute for future output.

A supplementary note must be appended: if in t_1 the equation $MR_1 = MC_1$ exceeds the direct equation $MR_2 = MC_2$, then inventory carryovers will vanish, for in this case (if it were physically possible) the firm would transfer t_2 output to t_1 in order to enhance its profits. Thus, production for inventory is dependent on an antecedent condition; namely, that

$$MR_1 = MC_1 < MR_2 = MC_2 \qquad (16.13)$$

If this relation holds, then inventory opportunities are open and the full condition will hold.[26]

The theory lends itself to exposition by means of the diagrammatic apparatus of Figure 16.5. Initially, as a simplification it is supposed that the later MR's are not discounted so that $1 forthcoming in t_2 is regarded as equivalent to $1 in t_1; likewise, carryover costs are nil so that an MC of $1 incurred for t_1 output to be held until t_2 imposes the same expense as an MC outlay of $1 in t_2.

Curves MR_1 and MC_1 in each diagram of Figure 16.5 are the curves

[26] Thus, the problem is one in which it is possible to ship products from market A to B, but impossible to ship them the other way.

belonging to t_1, prior to any appraisal of the profitability of inventory accumulations for t_2. MR_t represents merely a lateral summation of the MR curves for the two periods, computed by adding to MR_1 the quantity that can be sold in t_2 at equivalent MR's. Similarly, MC_t requires the lateral addition to MC_1 of the quantities that can be produced in t_2 at equivalent marginal costs.

According to Figure 16.5(A), simple single-period analysis would evoke the production of OM in t_1, and sold to yield an MR of R_1. In these circumstances, production for inventory would be distinctly unprofitable, for to equalize

$$MR_1 = MR_2 = MC_1 = MC_2 \qquad (16.14a)$$

or

$$MR_t = MC_t \qquad (16.14b)$$

it would be necessary to produce and sell the quantity ON over the two periods at an MR of R_2, requiring that OL be produced and sold in t_1, a quantity at which $MR_1 < MC_1$. In doing so, the firm will sustain some avoidable losses in period 1; hence, the aggregate profit realized over both periods cannot be a true maximum. Thus, with the inequality of (16.13) reversed, the monopolist will secure maximum profits by producing in each period the normal single-period quantities for immediate sale.

Figure 16.5(B) offers a marked contrast, for now the equation of $MC_t = MR_t$ occurs at a higher MR level than does $MR_1 = MC_1$. Simple single-period analysis would lead the monopolist to equate $MR_1 = MC_1$ and produce OM for immediate sale. But, because future events are propitious, a deeper vision would order a t_1 production of OL, corresponding to the MC at which $MR_t = MC_t$, of which OR would be disgorged in t_1 while RL would be withheld for inventory, comprising part of the RN sales of t_2. Thus, an MR in each period equal to R_1 would ensure maximum profits over the full time interval.

A perusal of the MR_2 and MC_2 curves of Figure 16.5 will show that, under monopoly, it is a rise in either the future MR or MC curve, or a concerted movement, which is responsible for inventory. *Under competition it was solely the movement in future prices*, not costs, that favored production for inventory, although palpably an expected cost movement might be taken as an omen of a higher t_2 price. A monopolist who expected the MC_2 curve to rise relative to MC_1, even if the MR_1 and MR_2 curves were identical replicas of one another, would still profit from inventory carryover and t_2 sale.

We need to erase the assumption that a future MR is viewed as equally valuable with a current MR. The correction is evident: MR_2 must be discounted, in the light of the effective interest rate and subjective uncertainty, to a current value. Thereafter, the sales that yield a present MR, and the sales in t_2 that yield an equally valued current MR, need be summed laterally to comprise the MR_t curve of our diagram. Likewise, when the carrying costs per unit of t_1 output are acknowledged, each MC_2 is equivalent to a smaller MC_1, so that our lateral addition of MC curves consists of the output at each MC_1 level, plus the corrected MC_2 level. Hence, the reduction of future MR values to a current value, and the intrusion of carryover charges on t_1 output, will operate to restrain production for inventory.

Inventory Holdings and Expected Sales

Aside from expected price fluctuations, the amount of inventory held will depend on cost factors. It has been demonstrated that the most economic purchase quantity or volume of goods to be ordered (resulting in an immediate inventory of this amount) can be given by the following formula[27]:

$$Q = \sqrt{\frac{2YS}{IC}} \qquad (16.15)$$

where Q refers to the purchase quantity (in physical units), $C =$ unit purchase cost of the good, $Y =$ annual expected sales, S denotes procurement expense for each ordering of goods, and I involves the interest, risk, depreciation—carrying charges—lumped into a percentage figure per dollar of inventory.

Clearly, from (16.15) it follows that, say, an expected doubling of sales will not lead a firm to double its purchase order and, thus, its average inventory holding.

Questions

1. By how much will purchases increase, according to (16.15) if sales are expected to double? What will this mean for the average inventory holding?
2. What connection do you see between (16.15) and the Quantity Theory of Money, which alleges that a doubling of prices will lead to a doubling in the demand for money balances? (Hint: Treat the demand for money as a demand for the inventory, cash.)

[27] This results from the equation for total variable costs:

$$TVC = \frac{QC}{2}I + \frac{Y}{Q}S \qquad (16.16)$$

Differentiating this with respect to Q, and setting it equal to zero to find the minimum, yields (16.15). See Thomson M. Whitin, *The Theory of Inventory Management* (1953), pp. 32–33.

Chapter 17

રુઝ

Path Analysis and Imperfect Adaptations

It remains to analyze the manner in which markets react to dynamic change; constancy in the data, we can surmise, will culminate in equilibrium; it is change and the dynamic shifts in the data that arouse our misgivings over the equilibrium configuration. The analytic boldness of this procedure can be excused only if we are convinced that new obstacles do not obtrude along the path to impede the equilibrium development; the theory is suspect until this proof is forthcoming. Finally, we shall also want to consider the possibility of less than complete equilibrium adaptations.

THE COBWEB THEOREM

Let us envisage a model in which the market is in competitive balance with $D_x = S_x$. If we superimpose an increase in demand onto our mental scheme, equilibrium analysis will immediately conclude that, if supply is a rising function of price, price will be higher and output greater.

Pondering the process by which this equilibrium is reached, we conclude that either of two hypotheses is available: (1) All producers estimate the new equilibrium price correctly, and implement their estimates by correct production-schedule variations; the old equilibrium is thereby transformed into a new equilibrium immediately and mechanistically, in one smooth stage. This hypothesis might provide the sustenance for the method of comparative statics. (2) Producers may be individually ignorant of the spontaneous change in demand. One assumption—one of many —is that they continue to produce the former equilibrium output despite the demand rise. Price may immediately be elevated to the new demand price for the former equilibrium output quantity, and an equilibrating process may be touched off whose content, duration, and amplitude are contingent upon their revised anticipations of the price course over the subsequent "days."

Incremental Adaptations

In Figure 17.1(A), D_1 and S_1 are the demand and supply curves for date t_1 in a competitive market, with the equilibrium price P_1 and output OM. Demand—on t_2, say—rises to D_2. Assuming that producers had expected P_1 to persist to t_2, an output of only OM would be forthcoming. The impact effect of the demand shift would be to elevate price to P_2.

Suppose that entrepreneurs expect P_2 to prevail on t_3 and strive to equate MC to P_2. If this could be accomplished immediately, output would advance to OR, well beyond the equilibrium quantity ON. However, it may be impossible in the short period to advance output by more than finite incremental amounts, equal to the horizontal lengths of the small steps engrafted upon S_1 and D_2 in Figure 17.1(A). Thus, if the ultimate equilibrium output (ON) exceeds OM by 1,000 units, and the daily output can be increased by but 100 units, it will be 10 "days" before the new equilibrium is achieved. Each "day," output will expand until a daily production rate of ON and the equilibrium price P_3 have

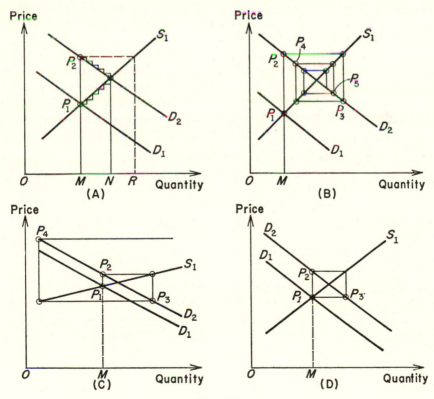

FIG. 17.1

been established. The transition to equilibrium is in orderly stages rather than in one heroic plunge.

Hence, when only incremental output variations are possible, and sellers' actions are predicated on the ruling price,[1] the equilibrium is determinate: the theory of the path in this case buttresses conventional analysis.

If producers act on misguided beliefs of the direction of price change, until the erroneous price expectations have been corrected market determinateness cannot be posited: the theory of the path would then become a proper vehicle for study while equilibrium analysis would distort market events.

Output Fluidity

We now examine the possible consequences of more fluid output adaptations in which substantial daily variations in the productive flow are possible: here, rather than $\Delta X/X$ approaching zero, it is possible for it to exceed even unity. The argument probably fits discontinuous temporal sequences better than continuous daily output sequences; for example, in agriculture substantial additions to the output volume are possible from one harvest season to another.

In Figures 17.1(B), (C), and (D), we presume that OM is initially produced, for this is the equilibrium volume prior to the upward tilt in demand. After the demand rise, price immediately goes to P_2, after which all firms expand output to a total indicated by the relevant S_1 point at the price P_2. But this output can be sold only at the demand price shown on D_2. Output will subsequently contract, to the supply point at price P_3; price will thereupon rise to P_4, etc.

Working through the adaptive process in Figure 17.1(B), each successive $\Delta P/\Delta t$ movement ensures a closer approximation to the $D_2 = S_1$ equilibrium price. Equilibrium will be the ultimate outcome whenever, for linear curves, the gradient of the supply curve exceeds that of the demand curve (neglecting its negative sign). Figure 17.1(C) depicts a thoroughly unstable configuration, with each successive adaptation bringing a more serious departure from the $D_2 = S_1$ equilibrium intersection: this explosive development results from a linear supply curve of lesser slope than that of a linear demand curve. Equilibrium will be indeterminate unless expectations and adjustments are recast.

Figure 17.1(D) illustrates a range of neutral oscillations, with the price and output amplitude fluctuating regularly about equilibrium at the same level. Here the slopes of the linear S and D curves are equal. Price alternates between P_1 ($= P_3$) and P_2. Surveying the skein sketched in Figure (B) makes the etymology of the "cobweb" term apparent.

---

[1] Or predict the *direction* of price change correctly.

Other than the assumption that firms expect market price to continue constant, a major presupposition of the cobweb theorem is that, during the full course of the adaptative process, it is assumed that the D and S curves are rigidly fixed despite the passage of time. Once this assumption is relaxed, the diagrammatic presentation of the cobweb skein becomes hopelessly intricate, for there are many alternate types of propagation to unravel.

Question

1. Suppose, after two periods, that the supply curve shifts markedly to the right. Draw and explain the resulting cobweb.

Repercussions in Other Markets

Substitutes and complements will, of course, experience some shocks and tremors as the price in market A oscillates along the adaptative path. With each new P_a, the demand curve in the various B markets will be dislodged. Along the course of the cobweb, therefore, other markets will be upset, echoing the perturbations in P_a, with the degree and amplitude of the reverberations determined by the degree of commodity inter-dependence.[2]

CHANGE AND EQUILIBRIUM PROCESSES

Next, consider a shift in either or both the D and the S functions while the market is in the throes of adaptation to a previous D or S displacement; here new data erupt along the equilibrium path.

Continuous-Demand Changes

Suppose that the supply curve is rigid while the market-demand curve grows continuously.

Everything rests on the degree and the frequency of demand shifts, the price forecasts, and the degree of output fluidity. If output is fluid, as in the cobweb analysis, and if price expectations are accurate, then equilibrium may evolve. Likewise, when demand advances in the course of the cobweb adaptation, an otherwise unwarranted expansion in output may be absorbed by the demand rise. Situations could be concocted in which price swings are wide and explosive, and other situations in which,

---

[2] This very interdependence constitutes a new threat to stability and equilibrium in the market for A, for it was observed earlier that, when P_b remains constant while P_a fluctuates, the demand curve for A is rendered flatter and more elastic than when P_b follows P_a upward and downward. This very steepness of D_a might, given the supply curve, provoke an explosive cobweb. Hence, markets that promise equilibrium when other prices are presumed constant during the equilibrium course may be rendered unstable by roundabout price interrelations.

in alternate periods, price is close to and farther from the equilibrium levels. But it is unavailing to dwell on these points unless we care to outline precise, but probably uncommon, sequences. In sum, incessant demand changes are inimical to equilibrium concepts unless the changes are foreseen and output is fluid.

"Supply Catching Up with Demand"

In part, the popular phrase, "supply catching up with demand" (so commonly employed in describing postwar market phenomena) can be

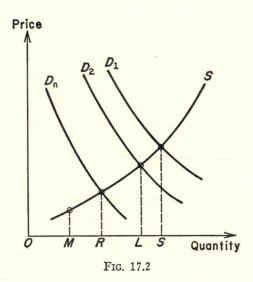

FIG. 17.2

construed as signifying sustained changes in demand. Unfortunately, the phrase is ambiguous, for at least two distinct ideas can be distilled: (1) that the demand curve is rigid while the rate of output is well below equilibrium levels and (2) that current demand is unduly high and, as output is produced and sold, the demand curve will recede. The former might describe commodities of daily recurrent demand, such as bread, milk, newspapers, etc. The latter might fit items of nonrecurring demand, such as automobiles and refrigerators, where current purchasers drop out of the market for several "tomorrows."

For goods of recurring demand, the analysis is simple. In Figure 17.1(A), perhaps *OM* is produced while *ON* is consistent with equilibrium. If output can be expanded only incrementally, equilibrium is eventually determinate, although it may be several time periods before it is realized. If output is volatile, is immediately expansible, and if equilibrium price forecasts are accurate, the time-lag characteristic of supply "catching up with demand" vanishes. The cobweb theorem comes into its own, however, if prevision is wrong and the output expansion fluid.

With nonrecurrent (daily) demand phenomena, as with automobiles, the "current" demand level is conceived as abnormally high while output is abnormally low. There are two dynamic properties here that should be distinguished: (1) the Δt growth in demand from new sources superimposed upon the unfilled demands of those waiting to purchase from the past; (2) the daily Δt diminution of demand as new output is produced and sold and former purchasers are removed from the market. Let us disregard (1) and concentrate on the second element.

In Figure 17.2, for t_1 we commence with D_1 and S; output in t_1 is OM while the t_1 equilibrium output is OS. As OM is marketed, the demand curve for t_2 will recede—reduced, say, by OM in the upper reaches; since the t_1 buyers may desire additional units at very low prices, the t_2 demand curve (D_2) approaches D_1 in the lower regions. Each week, while the rate of output advances, the demand curve is pulled back; perhaps a temporary equilibrium is secured at output OL; thereafter, with demand continuing to fade, there must also be a retrenchment in output. If the demand curve ultimately settles at D_n, the ultimate equilibrium output is at OR; supply can be described as having "caught up with demand" in the range between OR and OS.

Simultaneous Demand and Supply Changes

Simultaneous movements in both D and S need to be covered briefly. Conceivably, at the same time that demand has swung to the right, longer-run forces might dislodge the supply curve and push it to the right. The equilibrium solution is obvious: the market mechanism by which the equilibrium is attained is far more obscure.

As a first principle, the new supply curve is the one relevant for the market analysis. Complexities that troubled us in the cobweb theorem also disconcert us now, for, whatever the stage from which the equilibrium adaptation commences, the ultimate equilibrium is given by the demand curve that prevails on the market date and the supply curve that is real at the date output is prepared. If sellers delude themselves into thinking that the last price will persist, equilibrium demonstrations will be futile when both D and S are subject to simultaneous variation and intersect at other than the preceding period's price. Most damaging to the equilibrium concept would be the combination of continuous-demand increases and supply decreases, or, conversely, demand decreases and supply increases. Equilibrium models that proclaim eternal determinateness in such an atmosphere undoubtedly are misleading.

Oscillating movements in demand and supply are entitled to some mention; undoubtedly, interesting specimens can be envisaged, but without knowledge of market facts it becomes but a mental pastime to proceed to unravel them. It is, of course, the unforeseen oscillations that matter; ordinarily, merely seasonal switches in demand can be prognosticated with a fair degree of certitude without gravely upsetting markets.

Speculation and Change

A notable omission in the discussion of change has been the failure to advert to the role of speculation. In its simplest form, speculation evolves whenever buyers or sellers predict future prices as a guide to their current actions: any belief that these will diverge from current prices will foster "speculative" operations. Added to this, whenever prices are expected to change there will be scope for the proclivities of a professional and specialist group interested in buying and selling solely to profit from the price movement.

Manifestly, whenever important price swings are expected, the field is rife for speculation, at least where commodities are standardized. *A priori*, we cannot argue that the price swings will be tempered by the practice unless we have in mind some particular types of expectations, recognizing that, in each period, the activities of speculators must be added to either or both the demand and the supply sides. Their activities may sometimes accentuate, rather than dampen, the price swings. For example, given underlying future data as but a replica of the present, and assuming the market to be already in equilibrium, prices will fluctuate so long as speculators *expect* them to change; in this chain of events, speculators can hardly be described as restraining price movements. In other sequences, however, when their views on the future are more accurate than those of producers, they can render a stabilizing influence.

MONOPOLY PRICE MOVEMENTS

So far, the discussion of dynamic phenomena has been conducted wholly within a competitive framework. This assumption needs to be lifted and some attention devoted to the response of monopoly markets to economic change. We shall find that, although the theory of the path is simpler, the effects of change are more indeterminate than in competitive analysis. In the latter, when the theory of the path was disregarded and the method of comparative statics applied, we could be sure that, when the demand curve moved to the right, price and output would rise so long as the supply curve sloped upward. But even this elementary proposition cannot be vouchsafed when monopoly prevails.

Equilibrium Theory and an Increase in Demand

Since it is not the demand curve but rather the MR curve that is instrumental in monopoly-equilibrium analysis, it requires but a modicum of perspicacity to apprehend that, even if the full-demand curve moves rightward, its slope may change so that price or output may be *lower*

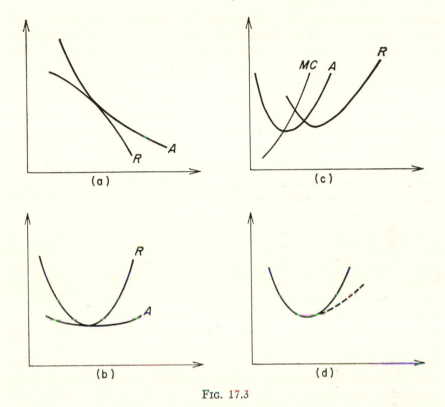

(a)

(c)

(b)

(d)

FIG. 17.3

after the demand lift than before. Let us prove this statement, for it offers a strange contrast to competitive theory.

In monopoly equilibrium, $MC = MR$ and $P/MR = E_d/(E_d - 1)$.[3] Invoking the assumption that MC is constant, thereby fixing the MR in the new equilibrium despite the demand shift, we see that all that is required for price to be reduced despite a growth in demand is that the elasticity of demand should be so increased as to overshadow even an MC rise. Considering that the demand shift need not be a uniform lateral movement, we are divested of any analytical warrant for concluding that price will rise. In competitive analysis, where MC curves had to be rising, price had to go higher. In monopoly, as falling MC phenomena are not precluded, there is further reason for suspecting a possible price fall.

To make matters worse, there is the possibility that, after the demand curve shifts, the new MR curve may be steeper than the old. Conceivably, it may intersect the MC curve to the left of the old intersection so that price will be higher than prior to the demand change, *but output will be lower.*

Fortunately, movements in the cost curve under monopoly do not imply

---

[3] See above, p. 19.

the same indeterminateness: a rise or a fall in the MC curve operates in the usual way. Still, we are left with the uncomfortable thought that, with monopoly, we are without a simple theory of comparative statics as a guide to the final effects of a change in demand on price and output; not even the directional tendencies of change are assured to us.

Changes and Incomplete Adaptation

If further changes in the data occur while the monopolist is adjusting to previous developments, the determinacy of the results centers on the direction of the new change and the accuracy of the prognostication of the seller: if the new changes are small, a wide departure from equilibrium should not be imminent. In general, we are left with the conclusion reached in competitive analysis; namely, that stationary equilibrium requires that the demand and cost curves possess sufficient durability to enable producers to know them. Otherwise, the stationary strictures are devoid of descriptive significance and are indicative only of the equilibrium relations, and not of the actual market results.

Situations similar to those discussed under the heading of "supply catching up with demand" also have a place in monopoly theory; as no new subtleties are involved, it is superfluous to repeat the analysis.

Duopoly, Change, and Equilibrium Analysis

Nothing has been said of the response of duopoly and oligopoly markets to change. Little need be done here, for we already know that, even when demand and cost phenomena are stationary, these markets might display some strange aberrations. Analytically, not much can be said as to the transition process or the final equilibrium in the event of change; we can surmise that a general "market" rise in demand or costs should raise prices and a fall should lower them. But, when we reflect on the diverse reaction patterns and the importance of the psychology of the participants, the security of even this conventional conclusion is denied us.

Incomplete Equilibrium Adaptations

Equilibrium analyses of the firm are predicated on the supposition that either initially, or through trial and error, the pertinent facts on costs and demand (or price) are known. Costs and price are treated as objective phenomena known sooner or later to the acting subjects.

Once we realize that it is not the actual objective facts on demand and costs that provide the well-spring to action, but rather the subjective estimates of them, a whole new range of possibilities is opened. We must now consider the demand and cost curve as *subjective* facts, residing in the minds of the sellers, rather than being a fully accurate portrayal of market phenomena. The two (the imagined and the actual) curves must be put into juxtaposition with one another.

Ignoring for the moment the cost curves, and postulating that a subjective demand curve is fixed in the entrepreneurial mind, let us consider the equilibrium possibilities. Firstly, if the subjective demand curve is an accurate projection of the real market curve, the problem dissolves: this possibility deserves mention solely for expositional completeness.

Secondly, we can envisage the real market-demand curve as intersecting or being tangential to the subjective-demand curve at the point of prospective maximum monopoly revenue. Here, to the undiscerning eye of the monopolist seller, the actual sales at the planned equilibrium price will coincide with the expected sales; this equilibrium position can be maintained through time despite the erroneous image of the full course of the market-demand curve.[4] However, propositions derived from an uncorrected comparison of monopoly and competitive output, where both are presumed to rest on the real objective manifestations, would have to be amended.

Provision must now be made for the influence of the *estimated* and the *actual* costs on the equilibrium adaptation; the prices announced, the outputs prepared, and the sales planned will result from the subjective views of demand and cost: the output level will be pushed to the point where the expected *MR* equals the *expected MC*.

Let us examine the situations in which the expected cost situation will be compatible with the actual cost results. Briefly, for the equilibrium the subjective *MC* curve must cut the subjective *MR* curve at an output not only where the actual and imagined demand (or total revenue) curves intersect, but also where the *estimated average-* (or total-) cost curve cuts the *actual average-* (or total-) cost curve.[5] This is the full condition of subjective and objective compatibility and continuing equilibrium in stationary real conditions; unless it is fulfilled, a revision in price and output will be in order. Examining his total-cost outlay for the completed output, the entrepreneur would observe that it differed from what he expected, indicating that marginal costs were wrongly computed *ex ante*. The belief that plans were correct could be confirmed only when the subjective and actual average-cost curves coincided at the planned output, simultaneously with the equality of estimated and actual demand points; the facts would then corroborate the entrepreneur's advance calculations

---

[4] For costless output, the intersection would have to occur at the output volume where the expected marginal revenue is zero.

[5] Symbolically, with subscripts r denoting the real market curve and a the subjective, imagined curve, we must have:

$$\frac{D_r}{D_a} = \frac{AC_r}{AC_a} = 1, \text{ with } D_r > AC_r$$

and delude him into thinking that it would be unnecessary to reconsider costs or to rearrange price and output policy.

If the estimated and actual AC equality is satisfied through time at the planned output, the cost-curve pair could diverge only through the rest of their length by virtue of miscalculations of input-output relations, for cost curves are a resultant of the dual forces of factor prices and factor productivity. A disparity between the estimated and the actual factor prices would soon be detected and inspire its own corrective; an inaccurate assessment of factor productivity could be concealed for a long time. Hence, any discrepancy between the cost curves must originate in this source.

Although erroneous demand anticipations may be compatible with equilibrium in monopoly markets, under competition the anticipated price must be the ultimate market price; for, in shaping his output decision, the individual producer will equate estimates of MC and P and, if the actual events disclose the falsity of the original forecast, a review of output policy is inevitable. As the competitive firm, just as the monopoly firm, must prejudge the full course of its cost curve, opportunities for miscalculation abound here: if the actual AC is equal to the expected AC at the output at which expected MC equals both actual *and* expected P, then any suspicion of error in the forecast will be dispelled. Confused ideas on the full course of the TC or AC curves may persist for a long time and yet be consistent with equilibrium in competitive markets, so long as actual and expected AC coincide at the output chosen for the *ex ante* maximum adaptation.[6]

Stable Equilibria with Incomplete Information

Apparently, a determinate equilibrium may evolve despite erroneous ideas on the full course of the demand or cost curves. Pushing this inquiry a step farther, it is instructive to outline the conditions under which this balance will be stable. Stability, it will be remembered, refers to the question of whether or not a slight departure from the equilibrium adjustment evokes forces to restore the original balance.[7]

---

[6] The analysis can be extended to encompass monopsony markets. The monopsonist's offer price will be contingent on the subjective demand-curve image which, in consumer markets, is itself a function of the estimated supply curve. If, at the output at which the subjective $D_x = MSP_x$, the actual and estimated S curves merge, are tangent, or intersect, then the monopsonist's offer price will be fully compatible with equilibrium, in the sense that the amount of the product or factor forthcoming for sale at the monopsony price will be exactly the quantity anticipated. This situation can endure until either the actual supply phenomena change or estimates, income, or tastes of the monopsonist change.

[7] See Chapter 8.

The problem may be envisaged in the following way. Suppose that the monopolist produces, by accident or design, a little more or a little less than the *ex ante* amount which, by virtue of the subjective and objective curve relations, and as revealed by experience, is known to be compatible with equilibrium. In order for the seller to revert back to the compatible adjustment, and to discourage further experiments with price and output, the anticipated revenue for the greater (or smaller) quantity must exceed the actual receipts; the disappointment presumably will hasten a retreat to the safety of the known equilibrium position. The compatible adjustment could then be described as a stable one. From the standpoint of costs, the contrary must be true for stability; realized costs must exceed those contemplated prospectively. In terms of the full curves, whether output accidentally falls below or progresses beyond the adjustment compatible with equilibrium, for complete stability the realized demand curve must lie underneath the anticipated one; similarly, the realized cost curve must stand above the estimated curve. Consequently, for objective and subjective linear demand curves that intersect one another at the output where the imaginary *MR* and *MC* are equal, stability is to be found on only one side, *not on both sides,* of the demand-curve intersection. Full stability would require a convex anticipated, and concave realized, demand-curve combination tangent at the *ex ante* equilibrium demand price, as in Figure 17.3(a), where *A* refers to the anticipated demand curve and *R* to the realized or market curve.

Normally, if the real and imaginary cost curves intersect at the subjective equilibrium output, one average-cost curve will lie above the other at one side of the initial equilibrium position, but not at the other. For U-shaped curves, however, if the realized curve is more tightly constricted than the anticipated cost curve, as in Figure 17.3(b), with the two curves tangent at the *ex ante* equilibrium adjustment, then the equilibrium will be stable for output movements in both directions.

Incomplete stability will predominate when only cost curves or demand curves, but not both, satisfy the stability criteria. Even though an initial price-output position may be temporarily stable because of the losses occasioned by an accidental expansory adaptation, once the monopolist apprehends that his original views on either cost or revenue are erroneous, then demand and cost recalculation and price experimentation at a later date are likely. In stationary circumstances, this should yield correct information and ultimate consistency of subjective estimates and objective facts.

Question

1. State symbolically—and draw diagrams—for cases of complete and partial stability when the subjective and objective demand and cost curves are recognized. Interpret Figures 17.3(a, d) in terms of the stability of equilibrium.

RIGID PRICES

Price inflexibility may be the response to change. Rigid prices, for our purposes, can be defined analytically as prices that are constant in the historical time-sweep even when market forces are conducive to price change: the price mechanism becomes effectively suspended although output and sales quantities may disclose some substantial fluctuations. Rigid prices are characteristic of many markets; some writers have gone so far as to ascribe most of the economic ills of the system to the "stickiness" of prices in many sectors of the economy.

Price rigidity, patently, is wholly a matter of degree. A price that fluctuated daily could be labeled "rigid" in the sense of being inflexible over the one day in which it prevailed. On this interpretation, unless all prices manifested the hypersensitivity of prices on the commodity and stock exchanges, they could be characterized as rigid. Palpably, it would be absurd to construe price rigidity so severely: an economic system in which prices fluctuated continually would contain irrationalities of its own, rendering, for one thing, the use of the price system a chore rather than a help, and reducing the economic process to a huge price-guessing contest. What is largely intended by price rigidity is fixity despite strong upheavals in demand or supply conditions.

Rigid Equilibrium Prices Through Time

Let us eliminate some causes of rigidity that are beyond reproach. In competitive markets, as one example, if marginal costs are constant, however exaggerated the swings in demand, price will be stable. Or, if demand was always perfectly elastic at the same level—implying usually rigid prices of perfect substitutes—then price will not yield despite the passage of time. Analogously, demand and supply may move simultaneously and in such wise as to maintain price constant even though the changes may evoke some wide output gyrations. Finally, unchanging supply-and-demand data would be the simplest cause of price rigidity. In all these circumstances, price rigidity through time would be perfectly compatible with the equilibrium postulates, while price flexibility would itself denote a market imbalance.

Under monopoly a price variation is unnecessary if cost and demand forces are rigid. Similarly, movements in D, MR, and MC may so neutralize one another that, for profit maximization, remedial price action is unnecessary, although output will fluctuate. Hence, monopoly price rigidity is sometimes quite explicable by the course of the shifts in MR and MC. All too frequently, these perfectly comprehensible causes of price rigidity are disregarded in observations on real markets.

Let us cite some of the more substantial reasons for price rigidity that can be detected even when the underlying demand and cost facts appear to warrant a price change: (1) the practice of market planning of price and output for a definite period of time; (2) costs of administering price changes; (3) estimates of the effects of price changes on future demand; (4) duopoly and oligopoly price interdependence; (5) full-cost pricing ideas. The list undoubtedly could be extended.

Monopoly Price Policy for a Rigid Clock Length

Empirically, in monopoly markets the prime cause of price rigidity (in the short period, at least) seems to be that firms plan their price and output policy for a finite time length—say, a quarter-year—and, in general, refuse to reconsider their judgment until this time has elapsed. One reason for this adamancy may be the cost of administering price change; let us now see how a rational decision on a maximum price would be formed if it were stipulated that this price was to be effective for the full time interval.

Immediately, we might inquire into the factors determining the length of the pricing period. Frequently this will be fixed by custom, by directorate interest, by ideas and persuasions of what is "sound management practice"—a set of rule-of-thumb precepts. Logically, a firm would plan output and price only for that period forward for which it could gauge demand and costs.

In forming its price decision to cover a quarter-year, say, the sum of daily sales at each possible price would have to be estimated in order to mold the daily demands into the period composite. Likewise, the daily MC curves would be summated into a quarterly aggregate. Thereupon, the price that maximizes profits, at which $MR = MC$, would be learned. Although by now this appears elementary, there are some complications: if sales do not proceed at an even daily rate, but are higher in the later stages, there will be need for some early production for inventory, which will entail some added costs. Or, the other way, output may initially have to be pushed beyond the ultimate ($MC = MR$) equality, or sales will have to be rationed, either consciously or haphazardly.

So far, it is presumed that the firm's estimates on the sales volume at the stipulated price are correct. But this may not be so. If the firm had been too optimistic, inventories would accumulate toward the end of the period, perhaps uncomfortably; the firm could, of course, reconsider and retrench in its output scale. If sales are outrunning the production rate, a decision will have to be made on whether or not output is to be accelerated. Perhaps the management is so obdurate as to refrain from any alteration in its plans until the next quarter-year. Generally, however, even if the fixed price pronouncement is maintained, there will be some latitude granted management to adjust the output flow to sales rates. Still, unless rates of sale and output are uniform, the maximum profit implicit in the daily equality of MC and MR will not be attained. Hence, a rigid price policy imposed for a length of time will not maximize profits; a truly maximum price policy will oscillate with daily flurries in demand and costs. Even if total sales at the period price equal the sum of sales at each *daily* maximum price, profits from the latter will be greater—unless each day's D and MC curves are identical replicas. Because of the time distribution of output and price differences, the total sales receipts will be different.

That periodic price announcements fail to secure maximum monopoly profits is a significant proposition. And yet firms persist in the practice. When a proposition flagrantly violates actual operating principles, there is need to inquire whether there are some ameliorating forces at work tending to soften the theoretical strictures.

Cost of Administering Price Changes

Daily fluctuations in D and MC may be so small that the profit discrepancy accruing from a daily maximum compared to a periodic rigid price may be minute. In items of recurring demand, it may be surmised that a price fixed for a fairly short period ahead is likely to be tantamount to a daily maximum-price announcement. For items of nonrecurring demand, however, where sales are bunched rather than flowing at a uniform daily rate, a more flexible price policy would probably repay itself. Yet, this is just the paradox: it is in these fields—the "durable goods" outputs—that price rigidity is most rampant. Holding in abeyance the matter of the cost of administering a price change, one explanation of the anomaly is the opportunities for speculation when prices of durable goods are subject to frequent fluctuation: dealers, for example, would become speculators in inventory. Rather than incur their wrath and rancor through a fluctuating price policy, and perhaps lose custom to rigidly priced substitute wares, a measure of rigidity is inevitable if other firms adhere to a rigid price policy. Thus, in items of recurring demand, there is usually little to be gained by daily price fluctuation; in items of nonrecurring demand, both speculative buying and the reluctance of dealers to participate in a speculative venture will militate against the practice. We are committed, then, to a substantial degree of price rigidity in the economy over at least short periods of time.

To surmount the objections of middlemen who intervene between the early stages of production and final consumers, the practice of compensating them for their losses introduces a new cause of price rigidity; namely, the *cost* of administering price changes.[8] Retailers, for example, must

---

[8] If output, besides prices, fluctuated markedly from day to day, productive resources would alternate between employment and unemployment, involving wastages on this score. See the argument of E. F. M. Durbin on the consequences of excessive fluidity in *The Problem of Credit Policy*, p. 49.

carry an inventory as part of the cost of doing business because of the vagaries of sales and conventional modes of shop-keeping—that is, of stocking goods for display purposes. Even when the climate is favorable for a price change, the sums that will have to be allotted for their inventory protection will be a persuasive deterrent to frequent price reductions. For price rises, on the other hand (especially in duopoly or oligopoly circumstances), unless rivals are ready to follow suit, an upward price adjustment may not be feasible.

Other expenses are involved for the firm in varying the price. Large merchandising outlets will incur at least nuisance expenses in changing price placards, in changing the nature of the sales appeal, and in disseminating information on price movements, besides reaping the bad harvest of greater price consciousness on the part of shoppers. For the manufacturer, there will be the need to recompute and arrange for credits on purchases on which price reduction allowances are granted, to reconsider price, sales, and production schedules on their product (in practice, many products), to notify salesmen by printed matter or otherwise of the impending price change, and in general to publicize the price trend. All this will involve cost and will militate against minor price fluctuations that do not vastly enhance the net revenues of the firm.

Writing R_1 as the total profits ensuing from perpetuating the historical P_1 price, R_2 as the profits from a new price P_2 that would maximize the firm's profits, and C as the cost of changing the historical price, then we must have, *for whatever time length the price change is planned,*

$$R_2 - C > R_1 \tag{17.1}$$

This is the condition of price change in a dynamic world where prices are named by individuals in response to changing circumstances. The point has been sorely neglected in the peremptory application of the mechanistic methods of comparative statics which argue as if prices are changed automatically without cost or human intervention.

Oligopoly and Price Rigidity

Although the analysis has dealt chiefly with competitive and monopoly price rigidity, frequently it was declared that rigid prices could be attributed to the loss in custom to a constant price rival. However pernicious it is to economic analysis, consumers *do* gauge quality by price: very frequently, quality can be appraised only by qualified technicians. Consumers are thus likely to be wary of the quality of commodities whose prices fall relative to those of other firms. Likewise, in the field of durable consumer goods, they, too, are prone to rebel against the speculative flavor of purchasing items subject to chronic price fluctuations, preferring to direct their expenditure to the presumed safety of a constant price rival. We need not dwell on any of the several reasons why rivals maintain their price; we need merely note that, when the tendency exists, it will limit the upward price freedom of firms competing in an oligopoly market of close substitutes. Oligopoly relations must be viewed as a major factor in price rigidity.

If price rises are largely stifled, and if price falls are unattractive because of competitors following suit in a "market" of demand inelasticity, change in the demand for the product of any one firm will spend itself largely in narrowing or expanding sales at the fixed price. Depending on the initial relationship of P and MC, if $P > MC$, a rise in demand will establish a closer rapprochement of the two, perhaps lifting MC even above P unless the firm chooses to ration sales. A fall in demand would widen the gap and raise the index of monopoly power even further.

Full cost pricing concepts—with constant MC—should also be mentioned as another possible reason for price rigidity. If firms are motivated by thoughts of a fair profit per unit of sales, this is likely to result in constant prices despite big swings in demand. Cost movements alone, but not demand changes, will drive prices up or down.

Chapter 18

Time and Uncertainty

The reality of the passage of time in both production and consumption processes has been touched upon only slightly in preceding pages. This chapter attempts to remedy shortcomings in this respect.

Once we recognize the time dimensions of the economic process and the forward-looking nature of economic actions, then we immediately become cognizant of the fact of uncertainty, of the reality that decisions are taken in an atmosphere of incomplete and imperfect knowledge. We shall want to understand how consumers and producers attempt to cope with the complexities raised and the implications posed for optimal adaptations. Uncertainty colors all human events; how well or how badly economic systems operate is substantially dependent on the accuracy with which current decisions predict future circumstances.

The most important time relations are those involving the sequences of production and sales. We shall find it convenient to refer to each time date, whether an hour, a day, a week, or a month, etc., as a point in time; when the intervals follow upon one another we shall regard the time sequences as continuous. The meaning of point-time and continuous-time concepts should be clear from the following illustrations.

Point-Output and Point-Sales Phenomena

The adjustment of rates of output to rates of sale is typically the key problem of the firm and the one that our theoretical superstructure ought to illuminate.

Point-output, point-sales phenomena may be illustrated by the example of the concert artist who has a recital only once a year (or at irregular intervals). The illustration also has an additional attribute, a point-input, point-output conjunction. The analysis of this phenomenon comprises the unperishable material of the elementary textbooks; it fits the single-period analyses conventionally elaborated in the theory of price determination. If the producer maintains a monopoly foothold, the price that maximizes the total revenue for the output actually produced can be announced. When production is still in the planning stages, the endeavor is to balance MC against the expected MR; excluding errors, the expected and the actual MR will coincide. In competitive markets, the output is sold at the ruling price, and, if errors are not committed, the market price will evoke that output at which $P = MC$.

Point-Output, Continuous Sales

Agriculture furnishes some rough approximations of point-output, continuous-sales phenomena. Once output is produced, the farmer has the option of selecting the most advantageous selling dates. But, after the crop is harvested, the analysis parallels that of costless output[1] and continuous sales. If expectations are fulfilled then, for the competitive seller disposing of output in each period, $P_1 = DP_2 = DP_3, \ldots$, etc., where the DP's are the future unit price receipts reduced to a current value because of holding costs—this is the competitive inventory problem expounded earlier. For a monopolist, assuming that the demand curves between the different dates are independent, $MR_1 = DMR_2 = DMR_3, \ldots$, etc. Inventory depends not only on demand and cost-curve movements between the several dates, but also on carrying costs.

Continuous-Output, Point Sales: Competitive Selling

Let us consider now what appears to be a quixotical case: that of continuous-output and point sales. Essentially, the analysis devolves into the theory of inventory; on reflection, we can detect many applications of this conjunction. For example, with certain qualifications it encompasses most of the seasonal selling problems. Products turned out continuously during the year might realize a selling outlet, say, only during the Christmas holidays.[2] Perfume and toys—not to mention Christmas cards—come readily to mind; turkeys produced (mainly) for Thanksgiving provide another appropriate illustration.

The competitive case can be handled quickly. If we restrict the concept of the MC curve to a "day," the expected future price must first be reduced to a current value, and from this reduced price there must be deducted the marginal storage costs attached to each unit currently produced that must be consigned to inventory. It will be to the latter—the daily price residue—that the daily MC curve will be equated. Hence, production farthest in time from the date of sale will tend to be depressed for two reasons: (1) the current value of the expected future price will be at its lowest daily ebb and (2) storage costs, because of the time and risks involved, will be high. Therefore, for commodities sold only at the

---

[1] That is, the sale of a fixed stock.

[2] Generally, sales will recur throughout the year, but their volume may be so small as to be dismissed from the calculations of the business man.

Christmas season, say, production should literally collapse the week after Christmas. Later, the daily outputs are likely to expand with the approach of the sales date.[3]

As the day of ultimate sales approaches, price expectations may change. If they are revised upward, this will give a lift to all future output: the firm would even regret its failure to produce in greater volume in the past. But if views suddenly take a more pessimistic tone, then production will thereafter be contracted. Although past output may now appear excessive in the light of the newly forecast market facts, only if the future price is not expected to cover the storage costs over the remaining time length will the present holdings be abandoned, being either destroyed or allowed to deteriorate. When unduly pessimistic expectations loom larger only as the final output date approaches, they are likely to be far less serious for the total output volume than similar views entertained in the beginning of the continuous-output sequence.

Autonomous changes in factor prices can also occur during the production sequence. Rises in costs, while future price or demand expectations are unchanged, work in the usual way, to contract output; cost declines will augment the production volume. There seems to be much scope for some curious types of production anomalies not visualized in the conventional price analysis. As one example, firms with point-sales dates, perhaps because of seasonal unemployment in neighboring industries, can reap the benefit of this temporary phenomenon, hiring more labor in their "off" period and accelerating the production tempo on these dates. The portion of the labor force ordinarily subject to seasonal unemployment could, in theory, secure continuous employment if the discontinuous production programs of different seasonal trades were effectively synchronized.

Continuous-Output, Point Sales: Monopoly Markets

Continuous-output, point-sales analysis under monopoly is more complex than the competitive juxtaposition: under competition, in each day the MC curve was equated to expected price. Under monopoly, a daily D and MR curve to suspend against the daily MC curve is lacking.

To solve the problem of production over the full time interval until the point-sales date, the lateral sum of each day's MC curves must be combined in a composite "annual" MC curve, which is then balanced

---

[3] Some interdependence between the amount produced on t_1 and consigned to inventory, and the cost of storing output of t_2, t_3, ... to the date t_n (the sales date) is a likely contingency. When this interrelation is significant, the solution can be sought on these lines: to each MC point of t_1 there can be added the highest *addition* to storage costs engendered in either t_2, t_3, ..., etc., by the utilization of storage space in t_1. It will be the latter MC curve, inclusive of "user" storage cost, that is equated to the daily "reduced" price expectation.

against the "annual" D and MR curves, to decide each day's contribution to the annual output. The subtlety lies in defining equal MC's, for the ultimate equilibrium principle is clear: the MC on the composite of the daily cost curves must equal the MR of the point-demand curve. Manifestly, to the daily MC curves we must add the carrying costs associated with each unit of output until the final sales date. As these costs diminish when output is produced later on (assuming factor prices as constant), the later MC curves will lie farther to the right than the earlier ones, so that production will be enlarged toward the end of the

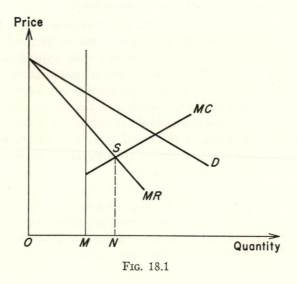

FIG. 18.1

time cycle. In equilibrium, the "annual" MR will equal the composite "annual" MC, and both will equal $MC_1 = MC_2 = MC_3, \ldots$, etc., where the latter are the daily cost phenomena inclusive of carrying costs. For it would always be remunerative to produce later on if current MC exceeded future MC, or produce earlier if the relations were reversed.

For a revision in anticipations as the sales date approaches, the major point lies in the recognition that, once production has been completed, nothing very much can be done but plan to dispose of the output at the best price obtainable and adjust subsequent output in the light of the new estimates. If, by chance, the volume of output already completed exceeds the quantity at which MR is zero, further production will cease. As an interesting conjecture, if both demand and production costs fall while storage costs increase, it may prove profitable to destroy existing stocks and produce fresh output for the approaching sales date.

Figure 18.1 contains a diagrammatic analysis of the problem. Suppose that, at the date when anticipations of future point-demand are revised,

OM quantity has already been produced. *D* is the newly estimated demand curve and *MR* is its correspondent, while *MC* is compounded out of the daily *MC* curves remaining until the sales date. Over the remaining period, then, *MN* output will be produced, being distributed among each remaining day in such wise that the sum of the daily output levels is *MN* and the daily *MC* level is *NS*, equal to the composite *MC*. If *OM* were so large that the composite *MC* lay everywhere above *MR*, further output would cease.[4]

Continuous-Output, Continuous-Sales Sequences

The continuous-output, continuous-sales sequence is undoubtedly the most important of the temporal categories and is the model most commonly envisaged when temporal processes are described. Approximating this continuous-output and continuous-demand sequence are many items in which output is continuous but in which the regularly recurring demand is confined mainly to one or two days a week: these are hybrid cases susceptible to attack by the methods to be outlined. Bread, newspapers, weekly periodicals, and milk are prize illustrations of output-sales continuity. With each of them, too, the analysis of inventory accumulation can generally be dispensed with.

Impounding any temporal interdependence, the result appears as the traditional price theory, with conscious stress on the multiple-period equilibrium continuum, and with firms in each daily interval foreseeing their market correctly and equating *MC* and *MR*.[5] A revision in estimates will have its effect on output almost immediately—the "next day"—unless this is technically impossible.

Multiple Products and Excess Capacity

As another interesting ramification of these ideas, discontinuous demand—either point or intermittent demand through the year—may be conducive to the growth of multiple products. For example, where the cost of storing goods for inventory is excessive, or where all the output that can be most profitably produced can be most economically concentrated into a time sequence shortly preceding sales, then for the rest of the annual period the firm will seek out by-products, being anxious to devote its facilities to any profitable pursuit. A simple illustration of this principle can be drawn from the ice wagon that is converted into a coal delivery cart in winter. Seasonal demand and highly perishable (and

---

[4] Under competition, whatever the dimensions of inventory, as long as the downward estimates of future price enabled current production to promise profits, output would continue.

[5] Realistically, we might often take a time lag between production and sales of one "day."

therefore costly) storage products, or products that are subject to the vicissitudes of taste, can foster a series of supplementary commodity variations to occupy the firm in the interim periods.

As a major implication of this analysis, a firm with continuous sales may perceive the greater profitability of discontinuous production over continuous production. For example, say that the *AC* curve is U-shaped, and that the demand curve intersects *AC* at the minimum point on the latter. Also, suppose that, in view of the shape of the demand and cost curves, the monopoly output is exactly one half the competitive total. It may well be profitable in these circumstances for the firm to produce the minimum *AC* quantity, the volume indicated at the $P = MC$ position, and sell one half currently while storing the remainder until the next sales date, when it can be disgorged. The procedure might prove more profitable than equating *MC* and *MR* in each period and producing continuously. The critical elements are the carrying costs and the minimum *AC*, compared to the *AC* at the daily $MC = MR$ output. By and large, the analysis applies to those nonperishables that are subject to decreasing *AC* and can be stored without excessive cost. When the firm is producing the large quantity, its equipment will be idle in every alternate time period. This fact should exert a strong incentive for the propagation of suitable by-products.

The important point is that firms will not, when the continuous time dimensions of the equilibrium adaptations are discerned, produce the output that is disclosed at the point at which the single-period MR = MC. Future time intervals of sale and production are an integral part of the problems.[6]

Input-Output Intervals

The assumption of the simultaneity of input and output (where inputs consist of the application of productive factors in order to obtain output results) must also be relaxed, if not generally dropped. The alternate hypotheses are: (1) input, applied continuously or not, ripens into output on one date; in farming this approximates the facts; (2) input, however applied, yields output over a series of dates; (3) input can create output on several possible *alternate* dates; if the input is directed to output on one date the output that might be secured on other days is

---

[6] Not infrequently, the *AC* at the single-period $MR = MC$ output volume is drawn as about double the level of the minimal *AC*. Unless inventory costs are prohibitive, this solution indubitably conveys a wrong impression; temporal sequences are far more appropriate for the problem. Yet, such mischievous "analyses" tend to be perpetuated in the expositions of the theory of monopolistic competition.

foregone. As a fourth hypothesis there is a simultaneity, or negligible time lag, between input and output, ultimately a special case of (1) above.

When there is simultaneity, or an inappreciable time lag between input and output, as in bread baking or newspaper publishing, the earlier analyses can stand firm. Likewise, when output emerges at but one date, even when the time lag is not negligible, the earlier analyses are unaffected: part of the production costs, however, are interest charges associated with the application of variable factors. A homely illustration of a continuous input that culminates in a continuous output sequence is the sausage machine where, after an initial time lag, the rate of output is synchronized to the rate of input.

When output from current input accrues on not one but several ultimate dates, the factor's marginal-revenue product is the current value of its full series of future outputs. So long as the marginal-revenue product so computed exceeds the factor's price, the factor will be hired: the equilibrium condition is the equality of the two, as observed earlier. For point sales, however, all outputs that accrue *after* the selling date must be written off as valueless. If the selling is discontinuous, costs of storage until the sales dates must be included in computing the marginal-revenue products. Either way, these considerations combine to reduce productivity.[7]

Questions

1. For each of the several sequences, list about 10 products. Which sequence, or sequences, do you regard as most important? Which of lesser importance?
2. What is your judgment of the validity of the assumption of simultaneity of input and output sequences?
3. In (1) above, list the multiple-product firms that you think owe their existence to production or selling discontinuities.

[7] It is well to consider the validity of the isoquant apparatus when input and output belong to different dates. When the two are simultaneous, the isoquant field is an enlightening tool, of geometrical eloquence. Even if output is not strictly coterminous with input, so long as the services of the two factors are addressed to the same output date, the structure is not demolished: part of the factor costs consists of an inherent interest charge because of payment in advance of production. But when the output attributable to different factors ripens at different dates, the isoquant approach is futile, for the product curves are deprived of any straightforward interpretation.

Further, it was argued earlier that an entrepreneur might be badly deceived in his estimates of the actual shape of the cost curve by an incomplete appraisal of input-output relations. When outputs recur on several dates from a given input dose, the chances of obscure and muddled ideas are multiplied.

UNCERTAINTY AND OPTIMAL OUTPUT

Uncertainty colors all economic behavior. Seldom does an economic subject have full and accurate information of all the data relevant for his purchase, production, or sale decision. Some idea of the dimensions of the new problems can be detected when we ponder the fact that consumers make purchases in advance of consumption; at the time of buying they must predict what their tastes will be when they are actually using the goods. Producers must estimate not only consumer wants (and hence market prices—or, under monopoly—demand) but also factor prices and productivity. Capital goods must be erected years ahead of their actual use; their productivity and complementarity with other resources must be predicted. Individuals must acquire special skills and prepare to enter definite occupations well in advance of the application of their knowledge. All of these decisions and preparations are made in an atmosphere enshrouded in uncertainty, by individuals cognizant that the future is but dimly foreseeable. Any study pretending to relevance cannot ignore these facts.

Consumer Estimation and Error

Consider first the possibility of divergence in the consumer's subjective estimates of prices and the objective price facts. For one thing, in buying commodity A in market A, the buyer's prescience must extend to the ultimate prices in markets $B, C, \ldots$, for otherwise errors in buying would occur. If, in shopping in market A, the prices $P_b, P_c, \ldots$ are predicted as being, by and large, lower than they in fact come to be, they will buy too little of A. This error normally can be rectified without too much time lost in reshopping. Conversely, if they expect higher prices in markets other than those ultimately forthcoming, they will overstock on good A. With perfect markets, they would be able to dispose of their excess purchases without loss: in actual markets, excess purchases would entail both financial and psychic loss through the irksomeness of having to return the goods or behave as temporary sellers, or stock the goods as an inventory at home. Ultimately, the possible errors due to price uncertainty of this sort are attributable to the brute fact of the spatial separation of markets.

An even greater source of uncertainty and loss is inherent in the fact that the consumer, at the time of purchase, must foretell what his tastes— and the tastes of the household for which the purchases are made—will be at the time when consumption actually takes place. Perforce, these anticipations will be imperfect. Knowledge of the physiological, environmental, psychological, and social circumstances—as we may term the tastes and proclivities of the dinner guest, for example—cannot be complete. Everything must be predicted. The plaint that preparations would have been different "if I had only known" is a familiar refrain.

The chief way in which consumers can reduce the uncertainty of future tastes and climb closer to the maximum-consumption summit is through narrowing the time dates between purchase and consumption, or by increasing the frequency of purchases; if the cost of shopping were nil (and selling outlets were always open) purchases could be made almost simultaneously with use. In the real world, there are of course definite elements of irksomeness involved in frequent trips to the store; moreover, most retail outlets are not open for business at all hours so that purchase must, to some extent, antedate consumption. If purchases had to precede consumption by a longer time length, the best way of limiting purchase losses would be to buy varieties of goods appealing to a diversity of palates and with manifold alternate uses.[8]

Uncertainty and Optimal Output

We have seen earlier that there are manifold possibilities of error in the calculations of the firm and that these can have important economic consequences. The sources of error can be traced to predicting: (1) prices at the time output is ready for sale, or market demand under monopoly; (2) the productivity of factors of production; and (3) the size of firms and the economic productivity of long-lived plant and equipment over the years it will be used. We shall consider some aspects of the problems that arise; we noted earlier the possibility of the continuance of imperfect adaptation.[9]

Consider, first, errors in anticipations, with all firms overoptimistic and producing in excess of the output flow that would prevail under better foresight. As disappointment will be the common lot, the output and employment position will not be maintained through time. If all views have been unduly pessimistic, a later expansion will be the upshot despite the immanently stationary real conditions. Normally, the views of individual producers will not lean preponderantly in the one direction or the other, but if there is an "average" tendency that can be isolated, these conclusions will be substantially correct. If equilibrium is to exist in the

[8] Other than in prices and tastes, there is just the chance that income prognoses may go awry, particularly for those purchases, such as installment commitments that are made in anticipation of a definite income stream in the (near) future. Perhaps it is not too inaccurate to surmise that errors here are less likely than errors with respect to the other data.

[9] See pp. 344–346. For a discussion of the methods of estimating future prices, the nature of uncertainty-allowances made, and the effects on output, see *Price Theory*, Chapter 19.

stationary economy, the expected and actual facts on prices, sales, and costs *must* synchronize. Harmony should in time be accomplished as clearer ideas on the market are uncovered, unless, in the very process of equilibrating, the shift of income to or from producers because of price miscalculations, and the demands of entrepreneurs for capital equipment engendered by the errors, push the equilibrium inherent in the initial data beyond recall; by modifying the income and equipment data a new and different equilibrium becomes implicit.

Coincidence of Estimates and Facts

We have seen that a stationary equilibrium may perpetuate itself even without fully correct ideas on demand or costs; this implies that the actual price and output adjustment, though compatible with the real facts, may diverge from the maximum position that would obtain under perfect foresight. Let us consider the implications of this proposition.

To begin with competitive firms, while price anticipations had to be correct to prevent output revision, the adjustment could continue through time so long as $AC_a = AC_r$ despite muddled ideas on the full course of the AC_r curve. Suppose that the two curves resemble those in Figure 17.3(c), with the actual output confined to their intersection. Assuming that the AC_a curve is the one to the left, indicating some innate caution and conservatism at the bottom of the mistaken cost calculations, more enlightened views would promote an output expansion. If the same attitude permeated all the firms in the competitive field, output would be repressed much below the real maximum, while price would be higher than necessary. Contrariwise, the overoptimism and the misinformation on cost data would foster greater output and lower prices than with fuller knowledge.

Under monopoly, the equalities $D_a = D_r$ and $AC_a = AC_r$ may be on either side of the real monopoly maximum position so that the actual output is indeterminate relative to the *real* maximum $MC_r = MR_r$ position: *a priori* there is no reason why the errors should fall one way or the other. Wherever the actual output falls, the effects of monopoly on the economic system will depend on a comparison of the *actual* output and the real competitive output, and not on a comparison of the real monopoly maximum under perfect foresight.[10]

---

[10] Part of the answer on the likely direction of error will be contingent upon the monopolist's attitude toward production. If, despite the monopoly power, he is disposed to be a large producer, with an urge to lead a "big" producing firm, the actual output is likely to advance toward the competitive optimal. Where the monopolist prefers to live a small and peaceful business life, the output level ought to be relatively compressed. If both types of monopoly personalities enjoy decision-making authority in the real world, so that some surpass the real monopoly maxi-

Ex Ante Plans and Economic Well-Being

The conclusion that miscalculations compatible with equilibrium may push monopoly output closer to the competitive $MC_r = P_r$ output than heretofore suspected is hardly to be construed as a defense of monopoly. Nor should it foster complacency on the ground that little damage is wrought upon the structure by monopoly domination: such a conclusion does not follow. So long as man is committed to *ex ante* judgments and decisions, and fallibility and imperfect foresight mark the human lot, the crucial issue is one of *intent*—the output planned and executed as compared to the policy that an optimal adaptation would condone. Measured by this standard, monopoly-price practices restrain outputs as compared to a competitive motivation in the sense of a conscious effort to equate P_a and MC_a. If the firm sought to equate $P_a = MC_a$, then, with the same anticipatory bases, particular outputs undoubtedly would be greater. In the light of the respective *ex ante* urges and objectives, the usual criticisms of monopoly behavior thus retain their force even though, fortuitously, the monopoly decision may actually correspond more closely with the real competitive facts. But the reverse may also be true: the actual monopoly output curtailment may drive the adaptation farther from the real competitive level. It would be irrational to advocate actions that on a forward-looking view are deprecated just because occasionally and accidentally they may achieve the desired ends.

UNCERTAINTY AND PLANT LAYOUT

Let us consider the influence of uncertainty on the scale of plant chosen. In an earlier passage it was suggested that, if economic changes were expected in either market price or demand, then the entrepreneur would erect a plant that, while not least costly at any one output level, was flexible enough to involve lowest average costs over a wider output range than more specialized layouts.[11] But this analysis presumed that the entrepreneur merely anticipated the change and then acted with full certitude, as if the very fact of expectations of market change did not create some uneasiness and disquietude over the question of the right plant to erect. Contemplating that the new firm will require financing, normally neither entrepreneurial borrowers nor lenders will display such calmness

---

mum output and others fail to approach it, then the level of employment, if not the composition of output, ought to correspond approximately to the monopoly level so that employment propositions that derive their support from monopoly and full-knowledge hypotheses for the full system may be largely unimpaired. With the mistakes falling in one direction or the other, then the usual conclusions on the actual effects of monopoly have to be corrected upon the recognition of imperfect foresight.

[11] See pp. 61–63.

and confidence in an uncertain future; the uncertainty will color the choice of layout in devious ways.

Lenders' Risk

Whatever the prospects of a business, the very fact of uncertainty will compel lenders to exact a higher rate of interest on loans for the *same* expectation than they would require if the future were an open book, transparent to all, with the expectation elevated to the status of a certainty. In itself this interest-rate factor will elevate the full average-planning-cost (ACP) curve. If all AC curves subsumed in the ACP curve were lifted proportionately, it probably would not affect the choice of the particular layout installed.[12] However, the vagaries of the capital markets are such that, for relatively small sums, interest charges are severe, declining somewhat as borrowings grow and then rising as sums requested exceed conventional levels (and the variety of securities offered lenders multiplies). If this is the typical capital market situation, it should work to pinch the ACP curve somewhat, to push both extremities closer together while lifting the course of the entire curve. Because of lenders' risk, therefore, the plant layout is likely to assume dimensions different from those it would take in a more certain world.

Moreover, some firms may learn that the sums open to them are "rationed"; although we could draw the usual array of U-curves corresponding to the diverse technical installations, the maximum sum at the firm's command will limit the layouts that might be chosen, leaving the extreme right-hand portion of the planning-curve chart field blank.

The aversion of lenders to unlimited commitments is a less extreme illustration of the consequences when firms and individuals are unable to borrow even when they envisage an investment opportunity. Even though lenders' profit prognostications may be more accurate than borrowers', nevertheless the unwholesome fact is that entry can be throttled as successfully by the refusal of finance funds to production aspirants as it can be by bleak entrepreneurial estimates of potential ACP and P relationships.[13]

Borrowers' Risk

Besides lenders' risk we have to allow for the borrowers' restraint and unwillingness to borrow because of the fear of default and the stigma of bankruptcy, unless it is expected that the borrowed sums can be recovered through sales revenues with some margin to spare. The entrepre-

[12] This is precluded because larger plants involve more equipment per unit of output.

[13] These very real elements have been virtually ignored despite their importance even in the most rarefied accounts of the theory of entry.

neurial group may refrain from implementing their entry plans unless a "risk allowance," over and above average costs, can be earned at each output level. Hence, entry may be retarded through entrepreneurial abstention from the capital markets until there is the mental assurance that the venture will cover potential costs with a surplus to spare. Although the relation of P and ACP may warrant the installation, the equilibrium unit excess $(P - ACP)$ may be too narrow to overcome the entrepreneurial misgivings of a minimum "safety margin." The effect of including these sums in the ACP curve is to lift the full envelope upward; if the borrowers' risk allowance varies with the output, the MCP curve will also be affected, tending to modify the ultimate layout chosen.

As another aspect of the same class of phenomena, entrepreneurs may forecast an excessive annual rate of depreciation as part of their capital charges that are included in the ACP curve. This too will have the effect of elevating the entire ACP curve, perhaps relatively more so in the rightward portions of the curve. Allowances of this nature, attributable ultimately to uncertainty, will dislodge the stationary ACP curves elucidated earlier. The ACP curve is thus a highly subjective phenomenon, in large measure a creature of the mentality of the entrepreneur.

The Size of Firms

Once we acknowledge the fact of uncertainty and the borrower's and lender's risk which it engenders, we can understand some of the forces limiting the size of the firm. For, in stationary conditions of clear foresight, there are literally no bounds to the growth of the firm. One suggestion is that "personality and historical accident rather than intelligible general principles"[14] account for the size of firms. Unfortunately, "personality" is as suitable a rationalization for giant one-firm industries as for industries with a multiplicity of firms. Moreover, if the firm is a result of historical accident and chance, *it is a creature of imperfect foresight,* otherwise the "accident" would not have occurred. Emphasizing accidental factors is but a circumlocution for stressing uncertainty.

Another view, unequivocally premised upon uncertainty, contends that, with the limited personal capitals of entrepreneurs, they will be increasingly reluctant to borrow the sums required for expansion and personal domination of the particular industry. For they will not wish, through selling stock, to let new equity stockholders share their current rate of profits; funded debt, on the other hand, is regarded as unsatisfactory because additional borrowing reduces the margin of safety between earnings and fixed charges, and hence any miscalculation invites bank-

---

[14] Knight, *Risk, Uncertainty, and Profit,* Preface to the reissue edition, London School of Economics series of reprints, Scarce Tracts in Economic and Political Science (1933), p. xxi.

ruptcy and financial loss to present owners.[15] This explanation, predicated upon uncertainty, provides scant relief to the theorist intent upon fitting the firm into the competitive stationary framework of perfect foresight; ultimately, this explanation can be reduced to the inability to borrow unlimited funds at a fixed rate of interest and the uncertainties that create the fears of default.

Another suggestion holds that capital rationing is the factor limiting the size of firms.[16] Either lenders will proffer to the firm certain definite sums and no more, or they will offer larger sums only at graduated rates. Competing firms could thus enter the field, for they could procure at least a limited quantity of capital funds at lower costs than those charged to expanding firms borrowing additional capital amounts. Again, the firm comes to be the product of an uncertain world: capital rationing would vanish in a world of certainty and assurance.

Either of the last two reasons, the increasing cost of funds because of borrowers' risk and the increasing cost of funds because of lenders' risk, should in most instances explain the size of firms. To these can be added actual technical diseconomies when scope is allowed for the exercise of the entrepreneurial functions of judgment and decision-taking. To illustrate: in small enterprises a frequent limitation is distrust in the ability of the available administrative personnel; there can thus be diseconomies of scale long before the firm has exhausted its borrowing facilities. In large-scale duopoly and oligopoly enterprise the stress on an alleged financial limitation is likely to miss the mark entirely; more formidable is the aversion to the economic warfare and the struggle for power that would accompany further growth. The inevitable conflict after expansion will be cause for sober reflection and will temper any rash move for growth that will provoke a costly internecine struggle. Lastly, in a régime of private property, public policy on size cannot be ignored: statutory laws may obstruct growth or the public hostility to combination may foster new legislation, impelling firms to forego the profits of combination and to abstain from tempting the legislative fates.

Change and Profit Calculations

It is now time to exhibit some of the implicit assumptions that all but demolish the planning-curve apparatus in handling all but stationary

---

[15] M. Kalecki, "The Principle of Increasing Risk," in his *Theory of Economic Fluctuations,* pp. 95–106.

[16] A. G. Hart, *Anticipations, Uncertainty and Dynamic Planning,* Chapter III, p. 39, especially. If the firm, under perfect foresight and certainty, can borrow more, but only at higher rates, it is the imperfect lending market that limits the firm's size. In determining its borrowing volume, the firm is in the position of a monopsonist.

problems; it offers a precise version of the process of equipment selection only in highly rarefied stationary circumstances where the following conditions are met: (1) the sales price or demand curve is expected to be constant through time; (2) the service life of all the equipment implicit in the planning curve is of the same duration; (3) prices of the complementary variable factors engaged for each layout remain constant through time or their alterations leave the relative position of the individual cost-curve components unaffected.[17]

As the planning curve offers an outline of some basic relations only with stationary phenomena, we are driven inexorably to perform separate profit calculations for each layout and, thereafter, to compare the ultimate profit prospects of each.

Drawing our time periods to encompass periods of constant demand, factor costs, and productivity phenomena, and including in each period's cost calculations both variable and fixed costs, it is possible to compute the current value of each period's surplus (S) of receipts over the current value of its costs, and summate these differences. Thus, for layout 1, the current value of these surpluses will be

$$S_c = S_1 + S_2 \cdots + S_n{}^{18}$$

Performing these calculations for layout 2 and then for each alternative layout, and in each time interval planning to equate $MC = MR$, we find that generally there will be one plant that promises most profits. With complete subjective certainty, and with ready access to the requisite funds for its installation, the entrepreneur would order this layout to be constructed—provided that the person of the entrepreneur could be located and imbued with a profit-maximization conviction. With uncertainty present, especially when the "entrepreneur" consists of a promotional group sponsoring the firm and anxious to demonstrate the profitability of the business prior to the sale of their investment holdings, if the most profitable layout amasses most of its earnings toward the close of the period (instead of the plant being extremely profitable in the early years) this is likely to be a force militating against the layout's adoption.

The shape of the prospective profit stream may thus be highly important, whereas with complete certitude and access to loan markets one time-stream of income can always be converted into another by appro-

---

[17] The explanation of why a breach in these stipulations defeats the apparatus is not pursued, but is left to the student as an analytic exercise. See my *Price Theory,* Chapter 19.

[18] The final surplus S_n, rather than representing a sales-receipt, production-outlay difference, may represent the ultimate scrap value of the equipment.

priate borrowing and lending operations.[19] Recognizing all these contingencies, we find that one plant will appear best—perhaps because of its flexibility in being diverted to an alternative use if planning errors are disclosed; perhaps because of the greater certitude of its cost elements; perhaps because of limitations of finance; or perhaps because financing groups entertain views on the correct scale of layout through their ability to sell one volume of securities more readily than another. The plant that satisfies these many requirements will ultimately be ordered.

Question

1. Consider the planning curve of average costs.
   a. To what time period does it refer?
   b. Suppose that price-or-demand conditions change over time, and shift irregularly: how can the optimal equipment be selected, according to this apparatus?
   c. Suppose that wages rise and capital costs fall over time: what is the effect on the planning curve?
   d. Suppose that the large plants (and their equipment)—those to the right—are very durable, while those on the left wear out quickly: how can this matter be dealt with by the *ACP* apparatus?

UNCERTAINTY AND ECONOMIC DEVELOPMENT

Digressing from the investigation of the effects of uncertainty on prices and output and on the demand- and cost-curve apparatus of the economist, let us consider some of the more general influences of uncertainty on the nature and content of economic life. Uncertainty allowances will, in all real situations, undoubtedly distort the structure of production and consumption as compared to a perfectly sure world. But there are even deeper implications; to combat the uncertainty, operations, and institutions that would not exist in an economy where the future was perfectly foreseeable becomes commonplace when the unfolding events are obscure and unforeseeable. To enumerate, there is the use of money, the parallel existence of numerous independent firms, the place for entrepreneurial talent, speculators, Stock Exchanges, forward markets, and the like. With complete awareness of the future by all participants in the economic process, neither the functions implied nor the institutions intimated could subsist. Let us consider a few of this partial list.[20]

[19] I. Fisher, *The Theory of Interest*, Chapter V.

[20] It is fascinating to contemplate political or social institutions in a perfectly certain world. Policemen would be needed only at the moment of crime, firemen only at the time of fire; laws could be more pointed to cover precisely the specific objectionable future occurrence, etc. The mere knowledge of future developments would not always be sufficient to prevent antisocial outbreaks, for some of them may not be amenable to advance control.

If the future expenditure plans were known with certainty, no one would want to hold money, for it is an unprofitable cash balance; interest-yielding investments would always be sought. Money to use for discontinuous purchases out of income could also be dispensed with; goods could be shipped directly to consumers in sum exactly equivalent to their projected expenditure plan, and claims could be recognized for their temporary or permanent savings. The circulation of money would be superfluous under this idyllic scheme.

The entrepreneur has traditionally been associated with the function of risk bearing. But risk arises only in a world of uncertainty. Likewise, the separate and independent existence of firms can be explained only by reference to the world of change whose future dimensions are vague and conjectural; giant amalgamations would be more pervasive and probably would be unobjectionable because of their susceptibility to regulatory control under full foresight of the future. Speculative markets are indubitably linked with the reality of change and risk, the by-product of uncertainty; speculation would disappear, for it would be without purpose if the future were known—speculation and certainty being mutually contradictory terms. Contracts that transfer future claims could be entered into at the full future price, discounted only at the going interest rate in a known environment; there would be no uncertainty as to the probability of fulfillment of the contract, and no need for hedging or shifting the risk to others.[21]

Certainty Seeking and Disproportionate Development

Turning from institutions to individuals, the proposition that uncertainty will color choice is irrefutable. Well-being might be permanently constrained by the reluctance of consumers to experiment and purchase new-fangled substitutes that, if tried, might improve their real-income position. Like consequences ensue when individuals decide to postpone consumption on the grounds of an uncertain future—and yet the future continues uncertain. Limitation in the span of human life may make consumption and enjoyment ultimately impossible, while, by a subsequent fortuitous twist, future events may make a mockery of all the years of denial; hindsight would have told us that these events were inevitable. Production plans must be flexible in the face of unforeseeable contingencies. Economy in a certain world, or on an *ex post* view, would require that they be rigid and precise, directed to definite events. Whereas capital equipment would probably be more widely adopted under known conditions, labor will be substituted for machinery when uncertainty preponderates, when price and output fluctuations are expected down-

[21] See Keynes, Chapter VIII.

ward as well as upward. Exceptions would be found among those individuals who, blinded by optimism and heedless of cost, go on building monuments to themselves in the way of capital projects; some over-expansion thus supplies a compensating tendency despite the pessimism that uncertainty usually breeds. The fact of uncertainty thus affects the exact content of consumption, prices, and production in the unfolding equilibria.

Unproductive Labor

An incidental effect of uncertainty, as remarked, is the creation of a professional body of speculators and a retinue of clerks and legal aides, whose functions would dissolve in the certain economy; on these grounds, they can be labeled unproductive in a way that agents contributing to form, time, and place utility cannot be. Their services are wanted and they perform a valuable function only in the uncertain (the real) world; so long as uncertainty is the fact it is idle to deny their usefulness or to talk of dispensing with their services.[22]

Incomes will, as a rule, be lower to the extent that certainty prevails in particular trades. Choosing occupations, learning trades, considering shifts—all involve future estimates. The greater the uncertainties of the future in one line, with a wide dispersion of the earning probabilities, the more attractive will be the acceptance of lower incomes in other more certain fields, all in the pursuit of security. Removal of uncertainty—to indulge for the moment in a pipe dream—would thus modify rather substantially the allocation of economic resources and the distribution of incomes. Everyday institutions and a good portion of the normal run of occupations would display a sharply altered status if knowledge of the future were increased or predictions were rendered more accurate.

Economic Insurance

Insurance plans are the usual response of our society to risk. Consequently, we may well ask why insurance against uncertainty and losses cannot succeed in the economic world. There is copious evidence that it cannot, and that economic uncertainties are uninsurable; there is the brute fact that insurance companies have disdained to underwrite such policies—or will write them only at impossible and prohibitive cost.

Ostensibly, we are devoid of any actuarial basis on which to write premiums and reduce the risks to insurable certainties; the movements in the data are too irregular and incalculable. Under properly executed insurance plans, the amounts collected would have to be just large enough

[22] H. J. Davenport, *Economics of Enterprise*, Chapter IX, is recommended reading for some unusually pithy remarks on productivity in our economic world.

to absorb the losses sustained. In the economic process the actuarial imponderables are too numerous and the movements too haphazard to be intelligently charted or foreshadowed.[23] Laws governing changes of taste or changes of inventive, legislative, and productive resources have yet to be discovered and reduced to precise mathematical formulas. Furthermore, an insurance scheme would be utterly impracticable in a world of recurring boom and depression. During the boom, profits are general and premiums ought to exceed any insurance payments. Depression, however, cannot be accurately predicted in amplitude and duration. It is fantastic to expect that a balanced collection of premiums to cover the general losses could be made; if accurate forecasts of aggregate depression losses were possible, we could take more intelligent action to avert these social catastrophes, obviating the very need for the insurance.

Ultimately, it is well that such insurance is impossible. Compensating firms for losses would lead to uneconomical output; entrepreneurs would have less incentive to keep costs down and to predict the future accurately; the entrepreneur would have scant reason to prepare output in the quantities and types wanted by consumers for the insurance would (largely) protect him from losses, while larger profits would tend to be partly dissipated in paying premiums. A system of resource organization that succeeded in freezing output or relieving the pressure on entrepreneurs to make correct decisions on output types and quantities would be indefensible; the very backbone of the private-enterprise economy is the element of risk and the social advantages when risk is borne by the more venturesome spirits in the community who are willing and able to assume it in conditions of change in tastes and productivity.

PRICING AND ECONOMIC WELFARE

With few exceptions, we have refrained from drawing the welfare implications of the different modes of price determination. And yet we cannot help but raise questions on their significance for well-being. We want to know whether we ought to prohibit monopoly pricing, whether competitive pricing is socially superior, whether there is not another alternative better entitled to be designated as "optimal." We want answers on whether nonprice competition is a wholesome development, whether multiple-product firms born of profit motivation rather than of natural causes are in the public interest. Similarly, we want to know whether commodity diversification has gone too far or, alternately, whether greater commodity standardization would confer greater benefits. Should

---

[23] This is not to be construed as a rejection of health, old age, or unemployment insurance. In great part, no thorough actuarial base is ascribed to these plans and their problems are not comparable to those that would be encountered in insuring entrepreneurs against losses.

prohibitions on entry be removed or, in some cases, should barriers be erected? Should pricing, in industries where demand is too small to permit profitable operations with a $P = MC$ adjustment, be subject to $P = MC$ precepts, with a government subsidy redressing the balance, or should the price be based on average costs? Is discriminatory pricing preferable to a uniform price policy? Should monopsony price practices be corrected? Should the volume and nature of sales outlays be circumscribed? Should firms, through current price policy, be free to influence future demand? These, and a host of other questions, immediately suggest themselves.

These questions must be answered. They cannot be evaded by the economist, especially when recognition of the phenomena emanates from his investigations. Ultimately, if economics (or any science) has any social pretensions, it is because it aims to improve the lot of mankind. Nonetheless, the positive portion of the study—the diagnosis of the precise causes and nature of the practice—must be mastered as an essential preliminary to prescription and policy making. This volume has been devoted to this first phase of the matter.

Acknowledging that price theory can provide us with some answers to these queries, it is by itself incomplete and inadequate to the task. For any change in prices, through altered modes of price conduct, involves not only a reapportionment of relative outputs and a reallocation of productive factors, but may also have implications for the normal *level* of productive activity—the level of aggregate income and the aggregate employment in the economy. Even if it is postulated that full employment is always maintained, either through the natural recuperative forces of the private enterprise economy or by interventionist measures on the part of government, there is the further complication that any change in the modes of price making will alter the incomes of owners of productive factors. Usually, when examining the implications of a change in the mode of pricing, it is assumed that tastes, income, and productivity conditions remain constant. Plainly this will not do when, as a result of the price change, incomes *are* modified. Hence, the study of optimal modes of price conduct should come after, and not before, a comprehensive study embracing not only the theory of price determination but also the theory of aggregate income and the theory of income division.

There are other difficulties connected with welfare applications of price theory. The one proposition around which its constructions have revolved is that, as economists, we can sanction only those changes that confer benefit on some (or all) without simultaneously working injury upon others. Normally, any new policy will affect some individuals adversely. In most cases, therefore, it is suggested that a system of bounties be arranged whereby those hurt by the change are compensated out of the gains obtained by others. But here is the rub: there is the need to prescribe techniques and, usually, administrative agencies of government, by which this can be accomplished. Hence, the study of economic analysis alone falls short; political mechanisms must also be provided, requiring that we invade the normal preserves of the political theorist. There has been an unbecoming reticence about these matters; the bare statement of the principle of economic sanction, the justification for compensation without details on the means of doing so and its *cost,* and other economic implications of its implementation, impart a vagueness and an unreality to most of these discussions.

Much of the comment on the superiority of competitive modes of price making is barren for similar reasons. Often it is taken for granted that competitive modes are optimal, without inquiring whether there are other adjustments that approach the ideal even more closely, satisfying it in more respects: the optimal may have more than one facet.[24] From the scanty remarks the student is led to believe that we ought precipitately, and universally, to institute $P = MC$ pricing modes. Yet, what do we mean by "cost"—is user cost to be included? If so, cost is partly a subjective phenomenon dependent on entrepreneurial estimates.

All this must leave the economist open to the charge of reasoning in a vacuum. If we are to be frank about the matter, we must confess that we do not possess any simple device for restoring competitive price making, even if we are convinced of its manifest superiority. Exhortation to business men to change their pricing tactics would surely not suffice, so long as stronger reasons, profitwise, counsel their current behavior. Every plan of government supervision contains its share of disadvantages: these ought be made explicit, so long as we are meddling in policy, so that the best of the alternatives is secured. Even when these disadvantages are held to a minimum, *we are not entitled to assume, once we recognize that price making must be an ex ante phenomenon, that it will, ex post, surpass the results obtained under an unregulated, partially monopolized, mechanism.* Further, it is a spurious, and perhaps dangerous, pastime to suggest price changes as a means of improving the resource-allocating efficiency of the price mechanism without first probing the effects of price changes on such dynamic phenomena as commodity innovation and commodity progress, and the impact of controls upon the spirit of business enterprise. So much of the analysis presumes that we have an original choice of instituting one mode of price making rather than another, while realistically we must always remember that the economy is a "going" one; any change will work hardships and will be resisted by those ad-

[24] For example, should entry be completely open? But industries with ease of entry (as agriculture and retail trade) have not been models of efficiency.

versely affected. Policy cannot assume this problem away by presupposing that the damages are unimportant, that the hostility is misguided, or that the ill effects fall only upon powerful "vested interests" whose welfare can be disregarded. Animated by a bitter political philosophy, the policy will be self-defeating, inimical as it is to our institutions, ethics, and concepts of freedom.

Perhaps this accounts for the signal failure of modern price theory to influence legislative patterns. Undoubtedly, the greater explicitness of aggregate income theory on the instruments necessary to implement its welfare implications accounts in good measure for the success of thinking in this sphere on economic policy, in contrast to the practical impotence of price theory.[25] Yet, the understanding of tools, concepts, and implications, as brought together in the previous pages, is undoubtedly indispensable for understanding and improving the fabric of economic life.

[25] See A. Radomysler, review article, "Welfare Economics and Economic Policy," *Economica* (1946).

Index

Absenteeism, 149n
Active reactions, 228
Administering price changes, 350–351
Advertising, and costs, 243
  and entry, 245
  and product variation, 234
  as a productive agent, 234
  cross-advertising, 242
  cross-elasticities and, 240
  diminishing returns to, 235
  price interdependence and, 240
Affluent Society, 4
Allen, R. G. D., 54, 64n, 73n, 89, 249n
Alternative use-value, 4
Analysis and theory, 5
Arc elasticity, 20–22
Average, and marginal costs, 46–47
  and marginal revenue, 16
  revenue and demand curve, 12

Backward-bending, supply, demand, 151
Bankruptcy, and duopoly, 214
Baumol, W. J., 100n, 114n, 117n, 190n, 194n
Bishop, R. L., 124n
Boulding, K., 171n, 237n
Bowley, A. L., 60n, 190n
Box diagram, 102
Buchanan, N. S., 237n, 246
Budget line, 77
Burns, A. R., 321n

Cassel, Gustav, 156n
Certainty-seeking, 369
Chamberlin, E. H., 121, 124n, 262n, 263n, 266n, 267n
Change, and profit calculation, 366
Chenery, H. B., 164n
Clark, J. B., 67n
Clark, P. G., 164n
Coalitions, 220
Cobb-Douglas function, 89
Coefficient of price interdependence, 23
Commodity innovation, 255

Communal demand, 131
Competition and monopoly, comparisons, 175
Complementarity, 70
  and monopolistic competition, 231
  fixed proportions, 319–320
  variable proportions, 317–318
Conjectural variations, 206
Consistency relation, 94
Constant marginal utility, 105
Consumer, commodity determination, 91
  equations, 158
  errors in estimates, 360
Contesting leadership, 211
Continuous output and sales, 354
Contract curve, 103
  and bilateral monopoly, 285
Corporate consolidation, 221
Correspondence, of estimates and facts, 362
  principle, 151
Cost, complementarity, 295–296
  curves and expansion path, 48
  in administering price changes, 350–351
  interdependence, 218
  substitution, 297–298
Cournot, Augustin, 199
Cross, advertising, 242
  elasticity of demand, 22–23

Davenport, H. J., 131n, 370n
Dealer boycotts, 304
Demand, and price consumption curve, 80
  and utility theory, 69
  backward-falling, 17, 18n
  premises, 10–11
  short and long run, 12
Demand elasticity, and marginal revenue, 19
  and total revenue, 18
  comparisons of, 19

Demand elasticity (*continued*)
  geometrical measure, 19
Denial of sales outlets, 304
Diminishing returns, 48–50, 53–54
Discriminatory pricing, 308–315
Displacement costs, 4
Disproportionate development, 369
Divisible factors, 28
Dorfman, R., 162n, 168, 169n, 171n
Douglas, Paul H., 89n
Dunlop, J., 282n

Economic change, 63
  and insurance, 370
Economic factor utilization, 53
Economic principle, the, 3
Edwards, Edgar O., 314n
Elasticity, of costs, 64–65
  of demand, 19
  of productivity, 55–57
  of substitution and demand, 87–89
  of supply, 65
Emulation demand, 93
Endogenous variables, 157
Entry equilibrium, 140
Equilibrium concepts, reality, 125
Equimarginal utilities, 68–69
Equivalent income variations, 117
Ex ante plans and well-being, 363
Excess capacity, 262
  and multiple products, 357
  and nonprice competition, 262
Excess profits and advertising, 239n
Excessive product differentiation, 254
Exit from industry, 141–142
Expansion of existing firms, 140
Expansion path, and cost curves, 48
External economies and diseconomies,
  143–144

Factor cost line, 34
Factor heterogeneity, 60
  and rising factor prices, 60
Factor redundancy, 32, 40, 51
Factor services, as inputs, 27
"Fair" price laws, 264
  and nonprice competition, 264
"Fair" profits, 192
Fellner, William, 124, 207n
Finance, availability of, 153
Financial strength, 212, 217
Fisher, Irving, 67, 131n, 368n
Fixed factors, 28
  proportions, 291–292
  stocks, 128–129
Forecasting, and economic theory, 6
Fowler, R. F., 65n

Full-cost pricing, 193
Full employment, 4

Games, and indeterminacy, 206
General equilibrium, reality of, 153
Giffen-case, 84
Guns versus butter, 4

Hart, A. G., 115n, 366n
Hayek, F. von, 27n
Henderson, A., 118n
Henderson, John S., 19n
Heterogeneous, entry, 254
  factors, 42
Hicks, J. R., 40n, 73n, 74n, 85, 95n,
  118n, 171n
Higgins, B., 282n
High-wage policies, 282
Homogeneous production function, 52n,
  55n
Houthakker, H. S., 95n

Income-consumption curve, 79–80
Income-effect, 81
Income-factors, 26
Incomplete equilibrium adaptations,
  344–347
Indifference boundary, 248
Indivisible factors, 28, 41–42
Induced by-products, 298
Input-output, relations, 30
  and isoquants, 30
  intervals, 358–359
Insurance, and economic change, 370
Integration, economic bases, 299–300
  monopoly pricing and, 301
  monopsony and, 303–304
Interdependence of demand and sup-
  ply, 186
Inventories, and economic warfare, 212
Inventory, production, 331–335
  and expected sales, 335
  and supply, 137
Irreversibility of supply, 142
Isoclines, 32
Isocosts, 35
Isoquants, 30

Jevons, W. S., 67
Johnson, W. E., 73n

Kalecki, M., 366n
Keynes, J. M., 369n
  and borrowers' risk, 365
  and lenders' risk, 364
  and user cost, 305–307

Kinked demand curves, 212
Knight, F. H., 72n, 365n

Laboratory tests, 6
Lancaster, K., 107n
Lange, O., 85n
Leader-follower patterns, 226
Leadership indeterminateness, 205–206
Lenders' risk, 364
Leontief, W. W., 164, 166
Lerner, A. P., 19n, 183, 185
Lewis, H. Gregg, 207n
Lewis, W. A., 321n
Limitational factors, 40–41
Linear and homogeneous equations, 166
Linear transformations, 98
Little, I. M., 95n
Long run equilibrium, 145
Loss leaders, 320–321
Low prices and poor quality, 327
Lump sum sales outlays, 239

Majumdar, T., 97n
Marginal costs, 46
  and average costs, 46–47
  one variable factor, 58
  several variable factors, 59
Marginal demand price, 275
Marginal product, 30
  and marginal rate of transformation, 110
  private product, 113
  social product, 113
Marginal productivity ratios, 36
Marginal revenue products, 176
Marginal supply curve, 272
Marginal value product, 136
Market borderland, 247
Marshall, Alfred, 19n, 67n, 70n, 84n, 101n, 117, 125, 150, 247n, 254n, 320n, 326n
Mathematics, an incomplete language, 7n
Maximization psychology, 191
Maximum maximorum, 238
Maximum sales revenue, 194
Menger, Carl, 67
Minimum cost, condition of, 35–36
Money, constant marginal utility of, 105
Monopoly, and competition, comparisons, 175
  and employment, 180–181
  and planning curve, 265
  earlier and later stages, 303
  foundations of, 269–270
  impact of, 182–183
Monopsony, advertising, 282

Monopsony (*continued*)
  and interrelated supply, 324
  demand curve, 276
  power, 273n
  temporal aspects of, 328–329
Morgan, J. N., 118n
Morgenstern, O., 97, 198n
Mosak, J., 82n
Multiple equilibria, 151, 188
Multiple plant firms, 289
Multiple products and excess capacity, 357
Mutual interdependence, 229

Negative marginal product, 51
New products, and conflict of interest, 257
Neumann, J. von, 97, 198n
Neutral equilibria, 149
Nichol, A. J., 280n
No-gain locus, 207
Nonhomogeneous production function, 54
Nonminimum costs, 38
Norris, Ruby Turner, 84
Numerical utility, 97–99

Offer curve, 104
Opportunity costs, 4, 109
Optimal plant layout, 139
  resource use, 110–112
Output, agreements, 219
  equations, 160
  equilibrium of firm, 133
  factors, 26
  flexibility, 63
  restriction, measure of, 185

Pareto, Vilfredo, 71n, 72n, 103, 131n
Passive reactions, 226
Patent sealing, 256
Patinkin, Don, 162n
Phelps Brown, E. H., 156n
Phillips, Almarin, 164n
Pigou, A. C., 113n, 125, 308n, 326n
Planning curve, 62–63
Point output and sales, 353
Potential competition, and price policy, 327
Predictions, and theory, 6
Price, agreements, 220
  and marginal revenue, 15
  and potential competition, 327
  cutting and economic warfare, 210
  follower, 209–210
  line, 76–77

Price (*continued*)
  policy and future demand, 324–325
  reaction curves, 230
Price consumption curve, 80
  and demand curve, 81
  and supply curve, 128
Production function, 25
Productivity, elasticity of, 55–57
Profit curve, 135, 201–202
Profitless monopoly, 266
Proportionality and returns to scale, 57

Quality, judged by price, 327
Quantity equivalent variation, 117

Radomysler, Asik, 374n
Reaction curves, 200–201
Reder, Melvin, 112n
Redundant equation, 161
Redundant factors, 32, 40, 51
Regulated industries, pricing in, 192
Relative marginal utility, 74
Returns to scale, 55
Revealed preference theory, 94–96
Ridge lines, 32–33
Rigid equilibrium prices, 348
Rising demand curves, 187
Robinson, E. A. G., 221n
Robinson, Joan, 16n, 19n, 90, 121, 182n,
  312n, 314n
Rothschild, K., 282n

Sales, curve, 12
  function, 259
  outlay policies, 329
  outlays and plant selection, 265
  rationing, 216
Samuelson, Paul A., 94n, 113n, 151,
  162n, 171n
Scale, returns to, and factor propor-
  tions, 57
Schumpeter, J., 125n
Science, economics as a, 5–6
Scitovsky, Tibor, 110n, 188n
Sellers' demand, 131
Selling-costs, equilibrium of, 236–237
Shubik, Martin, 198n, 215n
Size, law of, 57
  of firms, 365–366
Slopes, proposition on, 31
Snob demand, 93–94

Solow, R. M., 162n, 171n
Specific factors, 27
Speculation and change, 342
Spivey, W. Allen, 171n
Stable equilibrium, 147
Strotz, Robert, 100n
Subjective valuation, 73
Substitutes, 70
  and multiple products, 315–316
Substitution effect, 81
  and instability, 86
Supply, and inventory, 137
  and price consumption curve, 128
  "catching up with demand," 340–341
  irreversibility of, 142

Taxes, subsidies, and monopoly, 181
Theory and analysis, 5
Tie-in sales, 320–321
Total product curves, 49
Transformation curve, 109
Transitivity relation, 94
Transport costs, nonuniform, 249
  changes in, 250
Triffin, Robert, 122
Two-part tariff, 321–322

Uncertainty estimates, 361
Unique factor combinations, 34
Unproductive labor, 370
Unstable equilibria, 147–148
User costs, 305–307

Vajda, S., 171n
Variable, factors, 28
  proportions, 292–294
Veblen, Thorstein, 93
Versatile factors, 27
Viner, Jacob, 62n
Vying leaders, 228

Wagner, Harvey, 94
Walras, Leon, 67, 150, 156, 160, 163
Warfare, and differentiated products,
  229
Wasteful resource use, 38
Wheat, grown in flower pot, 54
Whitin, Thomson, 335n
Wicksteed, P. H., 131n
Wieser, F. von, 27n